INTERNATIONAL MONETARY FUND

D1917181

WORLD ECONOMIC OUTLOOK

Global Manufacturing Downturn, Rising Trade Barriers

2019
OCT

©2019 International Monetary Fund

Cover and Design: IMF CSF Creative Solutions Division
Composition: AGS, An RR Donnelley Company

Cataloging-in-Publication Data

Joint Bank-Fund Library

Names: International Monetary Fund.
Title: World economic outlook (International Monetary Fund)
Other titles: WEO | Occasional paper (International Monetary Fund) | World economic and financial surveys.
Description: Washington, DC : International Monetary Fund, 1980- | Semiannual | Some issues also have thematic titles. | Began with issue for May 1980. | 1981-1984: Occasional paper / International Monetary Fund, 0251-6365 | 1986-: World economic and financial surveys, 0256-6877.
Identifiers: ISSN 0256-6877 (print) | ISSN 1564-5215 (online)
Subjects: LCSH: Economic development—Periodicals. | International economic relations—Periodicals. | Debts, External—Periodicals. | Balance of payments—Periodicals. | International finance—Periodicals. | Economic forecasting—Periodicals.
Classification: LCC HC10.W79

HC10.80

ISBN 978-1-51350-821-4 (English Paper)
978-1-51351-617-2 (English ePub)
978-1-51351-616-5 (English PDF)

The *World Economic Outlook* (WEO) is a survey by the IMF staff published twice a year, in the spring and fall. The WEO is prepared by the IMF staff and has benefited from comments and suggestions by Executive Directors following their discussion of the report on October 3, 2019. The views expressed in this publication are those of the IMF staff and do not necessarily represent the views of the IMF's Executive Directors or their national authorities.

Recommended citation: International Monetary Fund. 2019. *World Economic Outlook: Global Manufacturing Downturn, Rising Trade Barriers.* Washington, DC, October.

Publication orders may be placed online, by fax, or through the mail:
International Monetary Fund, Publication Services
P.O. Box 92780, Washington, DC 20090, USA
Tel.: (202) 623-7430 Fax: (202) 623-7201
E-mail: publications@imf.org
www.imfbookstore.org
www.elibrary.imf.org

BIBLIOTHEK
der Industrie- und Handelskammer
für München und Oberbayern
NZ. 1340/92 (2019, OCT)

CONTENTS

Tables

Online Tables—Statistical Appendix

Figures

ASSUMPTIONS AND CONVENTIONS

A number of assumptions have been adopted for the projections presented in the *World Economic Outlook* (WEO). It has been assumed that real effective exchange rates remained constant at their average levels during July 26 to August 23, 2019, except for those for the currencies participating in the European exchange rate mechanism II (ERM II), which are assumed to have remained constant in nominal terms relative to the euro; that established policies of national authorities will be maintained (for specific assumptions about fiscal and monetary policies for selected economies, see Box A1 in the Statistical Appendix); that the average price of oil will be $61.78 a barrel in 2019 and $57.94 a barrel in 2020 and will remain unchanged in real terms over the medium term; that the six-month London interbank offered rate (LIBOR) on US dollar deposits will average 2.3 percent in 2019 and 2.0 percent in 2020; that the three-month euro deposit rate will average –0.4 percent in 2019 and –0.6 in 2020; and that the six-month Japanese yen deposit rate will yield, on average, 0.0 percent in 2019 and –0.1 percent in 2020. These are, of course, working hypotheses rather than forecasts, and the uncertainties surrounding them add to the margin of error that would, in any event, be involved in the projections. The estimates and projections are based on statistical information available through September 30, 2019.

The following conventions are used throughout the WEO:

. . . to indicate that data are not available or not applicable;

– between years or months (for example, 2018–19 or January–June) to indicate the years or months covered, including the beginning and ending years or months; and

/ between years or months (for example, 2018/19) to indicate a fiscal or financial year.

"Billion" means a thousand million; "trillion" means a thousand billion.

"Basis points" refers to hundredths of 1 percentage point (for example, 25 basis points are equivalent to ¼ of 1 percentage point).

Data refer to calendar years, except in the case of a few countries that use fiscal years. Please refer to Table F in the Statistical Appendix, which lists the economies with exceptional reporting periods for national accounts and government finance data for each country.

For some countries, the figures for 2018 and earlier are based on estimates rather than actual outturns. Please refer to Table G in the Statistical Appendix, which lists the latest actual outturns for the indicators in the national accounts, prices, government finance, and balance of payments indicators for each country.

What is new in this publication:

- Mauritania redenominated its currency in January 2018 by replacing 10 old Mauritanian ouguiya (MRO) with 1 new Mauritanian ouguiya (MRU). Local currency data for Mauritania are expressed in the new currency beginning with the October 2019 WEO database.
- São Tomé and Príncipe redenominated its currency in January 2018 by replacing 1,000 old São Tomé and Príncipe dobra (STD) with 1 new São Tomé and Príncipe dobra (STN). Local currency data for São Tomé and Príncipe are expressed in the new currency beginning with the October 2019 WEO database.
- Beginning with the October 2019 WEO, the regional group Commonwealth of Independent States (CIS) is discontinued. Four of the CIS economies (Belarus, Moldova, Russia, and Ukraine) are added to the regional group Emerging and Developing Europe. The remaining eight economies—Armenia, Azerbaijan, Georgia, Kazakhstan, Kyrgyz Republic, Tajikistan, Turkmenistan, and Uzbekistan, which comprise the regional subgroup Caucasus and Central Asia (CCA)—are combined with Middle East, North Africa, Afghanistan, and Pakistan (MENAP) to form the new regional group Middle East and Central Asia (MECA).

In the tables and figures, the following conventions apply:

- If no source is listed on tables and figures, data are drawn from the WEO database.
- When countries are not listed alphabetically, they are ordered on the basis of economic size.
- Minor discrepancies between sums of constituent figures and totals shown reflect rounding.

As used in this report, the terms "country" and "economy" do not in all cases refer to a territorial entity that is a state as understood by international law and practice. As used here, the term also covers some territorial entities that are not states but for which statistical data are maintained on a separate and independent basis.

Composite data are provided for various groups of countries organized according to economic characteristics or region. Unless noted otherwise, country group composites represent calculations based on 90 percent or more of the weighted group data.

The boundaries, colors, denominations, and any other information shown on the maps do not imply, on the part of the IMF, any judgment on the legal status of any territory or any endorsement or acceptance of such boundaries.

FURTHER INFORMATION

Corrections and Revisions

The data and analysis appearing in the *World Economic Outlook* (WEO) are compiled by the IMF staff at the time of publication. Every effort is made to ensure their timeliness, accuracy, and completeness. When errors are discovered, corrections and revisions are incorporated into the digital editions available from the IMF website and on the IMF eLibrary (see below). All substantive changes are listed in the online table of contents.

Print and Digital Editions

Print

Print copies of this WEO can be ordered from the IMF bookstore at imfbk.st/28248.

Digital

Multiple digital editions of the WEO, including ePub, enhanced PDF, and HTML, are available on the IMF eLibrary at www.elibrary.imf.org/OCT19WEO.

Download a free PDF of the report and data sets for each of the charts therein from the IMF website at www.imf.org/publications/weo or scan the QR code below to access the *World Economic Outlook* web page directly:

Copyright and Reuse

Information on the terms and conditions for reusing the contents of this publication are at www.imf.org/external/terms.htm.

DATA

This version of the *World Economic Outlook* (WEO) is available in full through the IMF eLibrary (www.elibrary.imf.org) and the IMF website (www.imf.org). Accompanying the publication on the IMF website is a larger compilation of data from the WEO database than is included in the report itself, including files containing the series most frequently requested by readers. These files may be downloaded for use in a variety of software packages.

The data appearing in the WEO are compiled by the IMF staff at the time of the WEO exercises. The historical data and projections are based on the information gathered by the IMF country desk officers in the context of their missions to IMF member countries and through their ongoing analysis of the evolving situation in each country. Historical data are updated on a continual basis as more information becomes available, and structural breaks in data are often adjusted to produce smooth series with the use of splicing and other techniques. IMF staff estimates continue to serve as proxies for historical series when complete information is unavailable. As a result, WEO data can differ from those in other sources with official data, including the IMF's International Financial Statistics.

The WEO data and metadata provided are "as is" and "as available," and every effort is made to ensure their timeliness, accuracy, and completeness, but these cannot be guaranteed. When errors are discovered, there is a concerted effort to correct them as appropriate and feasible. Corrections and revisions made after publication are incorporated into the electronic editions available from the IMF eLibrary (www.elibrary.imf.org) and on the IMF website (www.imf.org). All substantive changes are listed in detail in the online tables of contents.

For details on the terms and conditions for usage of the WEO database, please refer to the IMF Copyright and Usage website (www.imf.org/external/terms.htm).

Inquiries about the content of the WEO and the WEO database should be sent by mail, fax, or online forum (telephone inquiries cannot be accepted):

World Economic Studies Division
Research Department
International Monetary Fund
700 19th Street, NW
Washington, DC 20431, USA
Fax: (202) 623-6343
Online Forum: www.imf.org/weoforum

PREFACE

The analysis and projections contained in the *World Economic Outlook* are integral elements of the IMF's surveillance of economic developments and policies in its member countries, of developments in international financial markets, and of the global economic system. The survey of prospects and policies is the product of a comprehensive interdepartmental review of world economic developments, which draws primarily on information the IMF staff gathers through its consultations with member countries. These consultations are carried out in particular by the IMF's area departments—namely, the African Department, Asia and Pacific Department, European Department, Middle East and Central Asia Department, and Western Hemisphere Department—together with the Strategy, Policy, and Review Department; the Monetary and Capital Markets Department; and the Fiscal Affairs Department.

The analysis in this report was coordinated in the Research Department under the general direction of Gita Gopinath, Economic Counsellor and Director of Research. The project was directed by Gian Maria Milesi-Ferretti, Deputy Director, Research Department, and Oya Celasun, Division Chief, Research Department.

The primary contributors to this report were John Bluedorn, Christian Bogmans, Gabriele Ciminelli, Romain Duval, Davide Furceri, Guzman Gonzales-Torres Fernandez, Joao Jalles, Zsóka Kóczán, Toh Kuan, Weicheng Lian, Akito Matsumoto, Giovanni Melina, Malhar Nabar, Natalija Novta, Andrea Pescatori, Cian Ruane, and Yannick Timmer.

Other contributors include Zidong An, Hites Ahir, Gavin Asdorian, Srijoni Banerjee, Carlos Caceres, Luisa Calixto, Benjamin Carton, Diego Cerdeiro, Luisa Charry, Allan Dizioli, Angela Espiritu, William Gbohoui, Jun Ge, Mandy Hemmati, Ava Yeabin Hong, Youyou Huang, Benjamin Hunt, Sarma Jayanthi, Yi Ji, Christopher Johns, Lama Kiyasseh, W. Raphael Lam, Jungjin Lee, Claire Mengyi Li, Victor Lledo, Rui Mano, Susana Mursula, Savannah Newman, Cynthia Nyanchama Nyakeri, Emory Oakes, Rafael Portillo, Evgenia Pugacheva, Aneta Radzikowski, Grey Ramos, Adrian Robles Villamil, Damiano Sandri, Susie Xiaohui Sun, Ariana Tayebi, Nicholas Tong, Julia Xueliang Wang, Shan Wang, Yarou Xu, Yuan Zeng, Qiaoqiao Zhang, Huiyuan Zhao, and Jillian Zirnhelt.

Joseph Procopio from the Communications Department led the editorial team for the report, with production and editorial support from Christine Ebrahimzadeh, and editorial assistance from James Unwin, Lucy Scott Morales, and Vector Talent Resources.

The analysis has benefited from comments and suggestions by staff members from other IMF departments, as well as by Executive Directors following their discussion of the report on October 3, 2019. However, both projections and policy considerations are those of the IMF staff and should not be attributed to Executive Directors or to their national authorities.

FOREWORD

The global economy is in a synchronized slowdown, with growth for 2019 downgraded again—to 3 percent—its slowest pace since the global financial crisis. This is a serious climbdown from 3.8 percent in 2017, when the world was in a synchronized upswing. This subdued growth is a consequence of rising trade barriers; elevated uncertainty surrounding trade and geopolitics; idiosyncratic factors causing macroeconomic strain in several emerging market economies; and structural factors, such as low productivity growth and aging demographics in advanced economies.

Global growth in 2020 is projected to improve modestly to 3.4 percent, a downward revision of 0.2 percent from our April projections. However, unlike the synchronized slowdown, this recovery is not broad based and is precarious. Growth for advanced economies is projected to slow to 1.7 percent in 2019 and 2020, while emerging market and developing economies are projected to experience a growth pickup from 3.9 percent in 2019 to 4.6 percent in 2020. About half of this is driven by recoveries or shallower recessions in stressed emerging markets, such as Turkey, Argentina, and Iran, and the rest by recoveries in countries where growth slowed significantly in 2019 relative to 2018, such as Brazil, Mexico, India, Russia, and Saudi Arabia.

A notable feature of the sluggish growth in 2019 is the sharp and geographically broad-based slowdown in manufacturing and global trade. A few factors are driving this. Higher tariffs and prolonged uncertainty surrounding trade policy have dented investment and demand for capital goods, which are heavily traded. The automobile industry is contracting owing also to idiosyncratic shocks, such as disruptions from new emission standards in the euro area and China that have had durable effects. Consequently, trade volume growth in the first half of 2019 is at 1 percent, the weakest level since 2012.

In contrast to weak manufacturing and trade, the services sector across much of the globe continues to hold up; this has kept labor markets buoyant and wage growth healthy in advanced economies. The divergence between manufacturing and services has persisted for an atypically long duration, which raises concerns of whether and when weakness in manufacturing may spill over into the services sector. Some leading indicators, such as new services orders, have softened in the United States, Germany, and Japan, while remaining robust in China.

It is important to keep in mind that the subdued world growth of 3 percent is occurring at a time when monetary policy has significantly eased almost simultaneously across advanced and emerging markets. The absence of inflationary pressures has led major central banks to move preemptively to reduce downside risks to growth and to prevent de-anchoring of inflation expectations, in turn supporting buoyant financial conditions. In our assessment, in the absence of such monetary stimulus, global growth would be lower by 0.5 percentage points in both 2019 and 2020. This stimulus has therefore helped offset the negative impact of US–China trade tensions, which is estimated to cumulatively reduce the level of global GDP in 2020 by 0.8 percent. With central banks having to spend limited ammunition to offset policy mistakes, they may have little left when the economy is in a tougher spot. Fiscal stimulus in China and the United States have also helped counter the negative impact of the tariffs.

Advanced economies continue to slow toward their long-term potential. For the United States, trade-related uncertainty has had negative effects on investment, but employment and consumption continue to be robust, buoyed also by policy stimulus. In the euro area, growth has been downgraded due to weak exports, while Brexit-related uncertainty continues to weaken growth in the United Kingdom. Some of the biggest downward revisions for growth are for advanced economies in Asia, including Hong Kong Special Administrative Region, Korea, and Singapore, a common factor being their exposure to slowing growth in China and spillovers from US–China trade tensions.

Growth in 2019 has been revised down across all large emerging market and developing economies, linked in part to trade and domestic policy uncertainties. In China, the growth downgrade reflects not only escalating tariffs but also slowing domestic demand following needed measures to rein in debt. In a few major economies, including India, Brazil, Mexico, Russia, and South Africa, growth in 2019 is sharply lower than in 2018, also for idiosyncratic reasons, but is expected to recover in 2020.

Growth in low-income developing countries remains robust, though growth performance is more heterogenous within this group. Robust growth is expected for noncommodity exporters, such as Vietnam and Bangladesh, while the performance of commodity exporters, such as Nigeria, is projected to remain lackluster.

Downside risks to the outlook are elevated. Trade barriers and heightened geopolitical tensions, including Brexit-related risks, could further disrupt supply chains and hamper confidence, investment, and growth. Such tensions, as well as other domestic policy uncertainties, could negatively affect the projected growth pickup in emerging market economies and the euro area. A realization of these risks could lead to an abrupt shift in risk sentiment and expose financial vulnerabilities built up over years of low interest rates. Low inflation in advanced economies could become entrenched and constrain monetary policy space further into the future, limiting its effectiveness. The risks from climate change are playing out now and will dramatically escalate in the future, if not urgently addressed.

As policy priorities go, undoing the trade barriers put in place with durable agreements and reining in geopolitical tensions top the list. Such actions can significantly boost confidence, rejuvenate investment, halt the slide in trade and manufacturing, and raise world growth. In its absence, and to fend off other risks to growth and raise potential output, economic activity should be supported in a more balanced manner. Monetary policy cannot be the only game in town and should be coupled with fiscal support where fiscal space is available and where policy is not already too expansionary. A country like Germany should take advantage of negative borrowing rates to invest in social and infrastructure capital, even from a pure cost-benefit perspective. If growth were to further deteriorate, an internationally coordinated fiscal response, tailored to country circumstances, may be required.

While monetary easing has supported growth, it is important to ensure that financial risks do not build up. As discussed in the October 2019 *Global Financial Stability Report*, with interest rates expected to be "low for long," there is a significant risk of financial vulnerabilities growing, which makes effective macroprudential regulation imperative.

Countries should simultaneously undertake structural reforms to raise productivity, resilience, and equity. As Chapter 2 of this *World Economic Outlook* demonstrates, reforms that raise human capital and improve labor and product market flexibility can help reverse a trend of growing divergence across regions within advanced economies that started in the late 1980s. The evidence points to automation—not trade shocks—as being behind the divergence in labor market performance across regions for the average advanced economy, which requires preparing the workforce for the future through appropriate skills training.

Chapter 3 makes a strong case for a renewed structural reform push in emerging market and developing economies and low-income developing countries. Structural reforms have slowed since the 2000s. The chapter shows that the appropriate sequencing and timing of reforms matters, as reforms deliver larger results during good times and when good governance is already in place.

With a synchronized slowdown and uncertain recovery, the global outlook remains precarious. At 3 percent growth, there is no room for policy mistakes and an urgent need for policymakers to cooperatively deescalate trade and geopolitical tensions. Besides supporting growth, such actions can also help catalyze needed cooperative solutions to improve the global trading system. Moreover, it is essential that countries continue to work together to address major issues, such as climate change (the October 2019 *Fiscal Monitor* provides concrete solutions), international taxation, corruption, and cybersecurity.

Gita Gopinath
Economic Counsellor

EXECUTIVE SUMMARY

After slowing sharply in the last three quarters of 2018, the pace of global economic activity remains weak. Momentum in manufacturing activity, in particular, has weakened substantially, to levels not seen since the global financial crisis. Rising trade and geopolitical tensions have increased uncertainty about the future of the global trading system and international cooperation more generally, taking a toll on business confidence, investment decisions, and global trade. A notable shift toward increased monetary policy accommodation—through both action and communication—has cushioned the impact of these tensions on financial market sentiment and activity, while a generally resilient service sector has supported employment growth. That said, the outlook remains precarious.

Global growth is forecast at 3.0 percent for 2019, its lowest level since 2008–09 and a 0.3 percentage point downgrade from the April 2019 World Economic Outlook. *Growth is projected to pick up to 3.4 percent in 2020 (a 0.2 percentage point downward revision compared with April), reflecting primarily a projected improvement in economic performance in a number of emerging markets in Latin America, the Middle East, and emerging and developing Europe that are under macroeconomic strain. Yet, with uncertainty about prospects for several of these countries, a projected slowdown in China and the United States, and prominent downside risks, a much more subdued pace of global activity could well materialize. To forestall such an outcome, policies should decisively aim at defusing trade tensions, reinvigorating multilateral cooperation, and providing timely support to economic activity where needed. To strengthen resilience, policymakers should address financial vulnerabilities that pose risks to growth in the medium term. Making growth more inclusive, which is essential for securing better economic prospects for all, should remain an overarching goal.*

After a sharp slowdown during the last three quarters of 2018, global growth stabilized at a weak pace in the first half of 2019. Trade tensions, which had abated earlier in the year, have risen again sharply, resulting in significant tariff increases between the United States and China and hurting business sentiment and confidence globally. While financial market sentiment has been undermined by these developments, a shift toward increased monetary policy accommodation in the United States and many other advanced and emerging market economies has been a counterbalancing force. As a result, financial conditions remain generally accommodative and, in the case of advanced economies, more so than in the spring.

The world economy is projected to grow at 3.0 percent in 2019—a significant drop from 2017–18 for emerging market and developing economies as well as advanced economies—before recovering to 3.4 percent in 2020. A slightly higher growth rate is projected for 2021–24. This global growth pattern reflects a major downturn and projected recovery in a group of emerging market economies. By contrast, growth is expected to moderate into 2020 and beyond for a group of systemic economies comprising the United States, euro area, China, and Japan—which together account for close to half of global GDP (Figure 1).

The groups of emerging market economies that have driven part of the projected decline in growth in 2019 and account for the bulk of the projected recovery in 2020 include those that have either been under severe strain or have underperformed relative to past averages. In particular, Argentina, Iran, Turkey, Venezuela, and smaller countries affected by conflict, such as Libya and Yemen, have been or continue to be experiencing very severe macroeconomic distress. Other large emerging market economies—Brazil, Mexico, Russia, and Saudi Arabia, among others—are projected to grow in 2019 about 1 percent or less, considerably below their historical averages. In India, growth softened in 2019 as corporate and environmental regulatory uncertainty, together with concerns about the health of the nonbank financial sector, weighed on demand. The strengthening of growth in 2020 and beyond in India as well as for these two groups (which in some cases entails continued contraction, but at a less severe pace) is the driving factor behind the forecast of an eventual global pickup.

Figure 1. GDP Growth: World and Group of Four
(Percent)

The global growth pattern reflects a major downturn and projected recovery in a group of emerging market economies. By contrast, growth is expected to moderate into 2020 and beyond for a group of systemic economies.

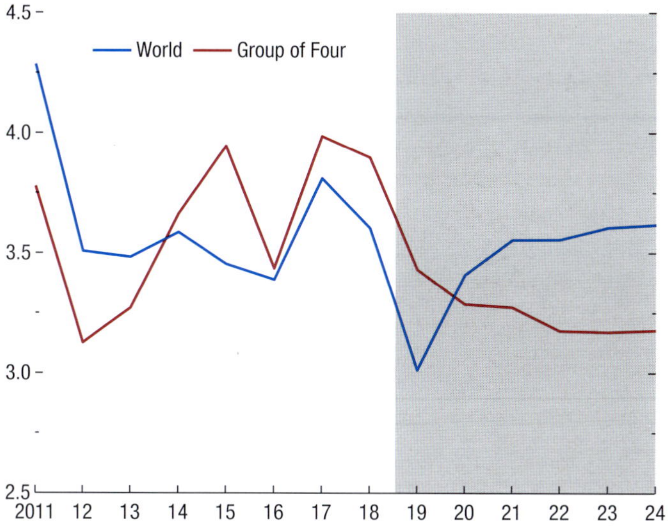

Source: IMF staff estimates.
Note: Group of Four = China, euro area, Japan, United States.

Growth has also weakened in China, where the regulatory efforts needed to rein in debt and the macroeconomic consequences of increased trade tensions have taken a toll on aggregate demand. Growth is projected to continue to slow gradually in coming years, reflecting a decline in the growth of the working-age population and gradual convergence in per capita incomes.

Among advanced economies, growth in 2019 is forecast to be considerably weaker than in 2017–18 in the euro area, North America, and smaller advanced Asian economies. This lower growth reflects to an important extent a broad-based slowdown in industrial output resulting from weaker external demand (including from China); the widening global repercussions of trade tensions and increased uncertainty on confidence and investment; and a notable slowdown in global car production, which has been particularly significant for Germany. Growth is forecast to remain broadly stable for the advanced economy group at 1¾ percent in 2020, with a modest pickup in the euro area offsetting a gradual decline in US growth. Over the medium term, growth in advanced economies is projected to remain subdued, reflecting a moderate pace of productivity growth and slow labor force growth as populations age.

The risks to this baseline outlook are significant. As elaborated in the chapter, should stress fail to dissipate in a few key emerging market and developing economies that are currently underperforming or experiencing severe strains, global growth in 2020 would fall short of the baseline. Further escalation of trade tensions and associated increases in policy uncertainty could weaken growth relative to the baseline projection. Financial market sentiment could deteriorate, giving rise to a generalized risk-off episode that would imply tighter financial conditions, especially for vulnerable economies. Possible triggers for such an episode include worsening trade and geopolitical tensions, a no-deal Brexit withdrawal of the United Kingdom from the European Union, and persistently weak economic data pointing to a protracted slowdown in global growth. Over the medium term, increased trade barriers and higher trade and geopolitical tensions could take a toll on productivity growth, including through the disruption of supply chains, and the buildup in financial vulnerabilities could amplify the next downturn. Finally, unmitigated climate change could weaken prospects, especially in vulnerable countries.

At the multilateral level, countries need to resolve trade disagreements cooperatively and roll back the recently imposed distortionary barriers. Curbing greenhouse gas emissions and containing the associated consequences of rising global temperatures and devastating climate events are urgent global imperatives. As Chapter 2 of the *Fiscal Monitor* argues, higher carbon pricing should be the centerpiece of that effort, complemented by efforts to foster the supply of low-carbon energy and the development and adoption of green technologies. At the national level, macroeconomic policies should seek to stabilize activity and strengthen the foundations for a recovery or continued growth. Accommodative monetary policy remains appropriate to support demand and employment and guard against a downshift in inflation expectations. As the resulting easier financial conditions could also contribute to a further buildup of financial vulnerabilities, stronger macroprudential policies and a proactive supervisory approach will be critical to secure the strength of balance sheets and limit systemic risks.

Considering the precarious outlook and large downside risks, fiscal policy can play a more active role, especially where the room to ease monetary policy is limited. In countries where activity has weakened or could decelerate sharply, fiscal stimulus can be provided if fiscal space exists and fiscal policy is not already overly expansionary. In countries where fiscal consolidation is necessary, its pace could be adjusted if market conditions permit to avoid prolonged economic weakness and disinflationary dynamics. Low policy rates in many countries and the decline in long-term interest rates to historically very low or negative levels reduce the cost of debt service while these conditions persist. Where debt sustainability is not a problem, the freed-up resources could be used to support activity as needed and to adopt measures to raise potential output, such as infrastructure investment to address climate change.

Across all economies, the priority is to take actions that boost potential output growth, improve inclusiveness, and strengthen resilience. As the analysis presented in Chapters 2 and 3 suggests, structural policies for more open and flexible markets and improvements in governance can ease adjustment to shocks and boost output over the medium term, helping to narrow within-country differences and encourage faster convergence across countries.

CHAPTER 1

GLOBAL PROSPECTS AND POLICIES

Subdued Momentum, Weak Trade and Industrial Production

Over the past year, global growth has fallen sharply. Among advanced economies, the weakening has been broad based, affecting major economies (the United States and especially the euro area) and smaller Asian advanced economies. The slowdown in activity has been even more pronounced across emerging market and developing economies, including Brazil, China, India, Mexico, and Russia, as well as a few economies suffering macroeconomic and financial stress.

One common feature of the weakening in growth momentum over the past 12 months has been a geographically broad-based, notable slowdown in industrial output driven by multiple and interrelated factors (Figure 1.1, panel 1):

- *A sharp downturn in car production and sales, which saw global vehicle purchases decline by 3 percent in 2018 (Box 1.1).* The automobile industry slump reflects both supply disruptions and demand influences—a drop in demand after the expiration of tax incentives in China; production lines adjusting to comply with new emission standards in the euro area (especially Germany) and China; and possible preference shifts as consumers adopt a wait-and-see attitude with technology and emission standards changing rapidly in many countries, as well as evolving car transportation and sharing options.
- *Weak business confidence amid growing tensions between the United States and China on trade and technology.* As the reach of US tariffs and retaliation by trading partners has steadily broadened since January 2018, the cost of some intermediate inputs has risen, and uncertainty about future trade relationships has ratcheted up. Manufacturing firms have become more cautious about long-range spending and have held back on equipment and machinery purchases. This trend is most evident in the trade- and global-value-chain-exposed economies of east Asia. In Germany and Japan, industrial production was recently lower than one year ago, while its growth slowed considerably in China and the United Kingdom and, to some extent, in the United States (Figure 1.1, panel 2). The weakness appeared particularly pronounced in the production of capital goods.[1]
- *A slowdown in demand in China, driven by needed regulatory efforts to rein in debt and exacerbated by the macroeconomic consequences of increased trade tensions.*

With the slowdown in industrial production, trade growth has come to a near standstill. In the first half of 2019, the volume of global trade stood just 1 percent above its value one year ago—the slowest pace of growth for any six-month period since 2012. From a geographical standpoint, major contributors to the weakening in global imports were China and east Asia (both advanced and emerging) and emerging market economies under stress (Figure 1.2). Downturns in global trade are related to reduced investment spending—as was the case, for instance, in 2015–16. Investment is intensive in intermediate and capital goods that are heavily traded. Global investment did indeed slow (Figure 1.3), in line with reduced import growth, reflecting cyclical factors, the steep downturn in investment in stressed economies, and the impact of increased trade tensions on business sentiment in the manufacturing sector. Another contributor to the slowdown in global trade has been the downturn in car production and sales, which is reflected in a slowdown in purchases of consumer durables (Figure 1.4).

In China—the country with the highest investment spending in the world—the slowdown in investment in 2019 has been much more limited than the slowdown in imports, similar to what happened in 2015–16. Factors contributing to import weakness (beyond domestic capital spending) include reduced export growth, which is intensive in imports, and a decline in demand for cars (Box 1.1) and technology products, such as smartphones. The front-loading of exports, before tariffs were imposed in late 2018, likely also played a role by bringing forward demand for import components.

[1]Global semiconductor sales declined in 2018, in part related to seeming market saturation in smartphones and fewer launches of new tech products more broadly (ECB 2019).

Figure 1.1. Global Activity Indicators
(Three-month moving average; year-over-year percent change, unless noted otherwise)

Over the past 12 months there has been a geographically broad-based, notable slowdown in industrial output.

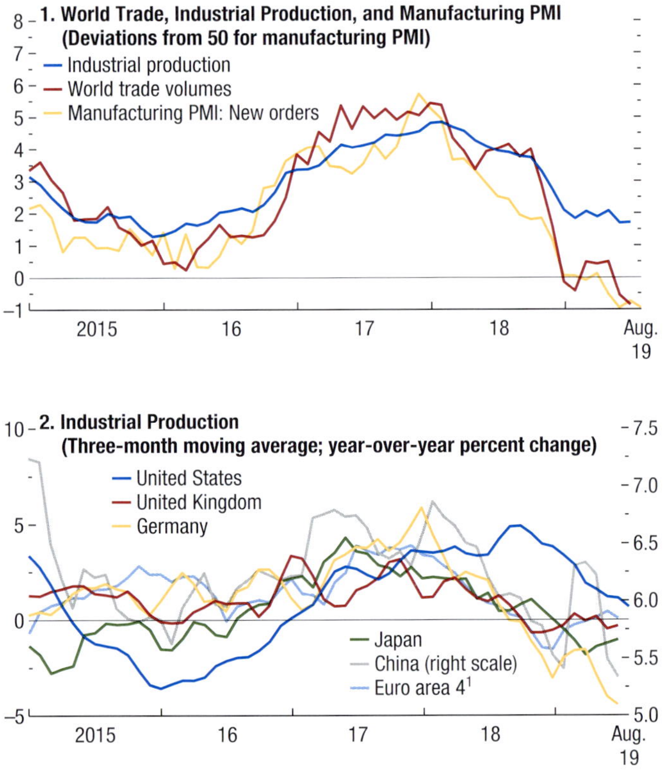

Sources: CPB Netherlands Bureau for Economic Policy Analysis; Haver Analytics; Markit Economics; and IMF staff calculations.
Note: PMI = purchasing managers' index.
[1]Euro area 4 comprises France, Italy, the Netherlands, and Spain.

Figure 1.2. Contribution to Global Imports
(Percentage points, three-month moving average)

In the first half of 2019, the volume of global trade stood just 1 percent above its value one year ago—the slowest pace of growth for any six-month period since 2012.

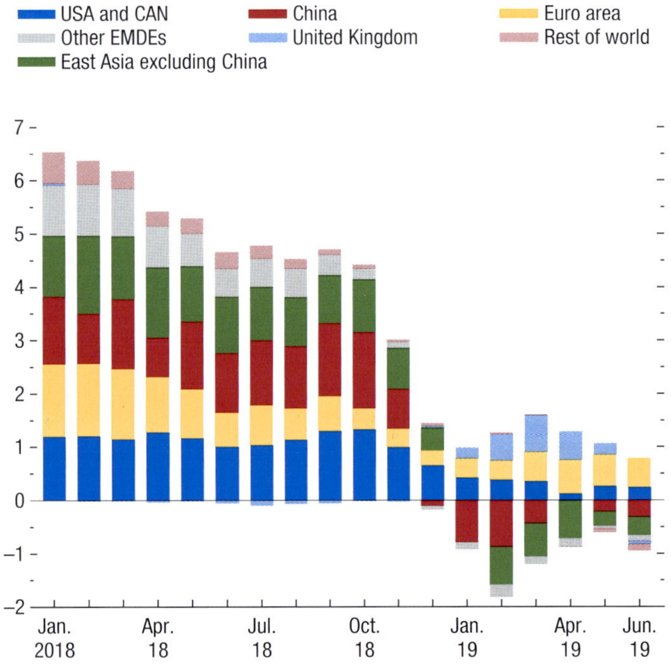

Source: IMF staff calculations.
Note: CAN = Canada; EMDEs = emerging market and developing economies; USA = United States.

While manufacturing lost steam, services (a larger share of the economy) broadly held firm (Figure 1.5, panel 1). Resilient services activity has meant steady aggregate employment creation, which supported consumer confidence (Figure 1.5, panel 2) and, in turn, household spending on services. This favorable feedback cycle between service sector output, employment, and consumer confidence has supported domestic demand in several advanced economies.

Weakening Growth

Growth in the advanced economy group stabilized in the first half of 2019, after a sharp decline in the second half of 2018. The US economy shifted to a somewhat slower pace of expansion (about 2 percent on an annualized basis) in the past few quarters as the boost from the tax cuts of early 2018 faded, and the UK economy slowed, with investment held back by Brexit-related uncertainty. The euro area economy registered stronger growth in the first half of this year than in the second half of 2018, but the German economy contracted in the second quarter as industrial activity slumped. In general, weak exports have been a drag on activity in the euro area since early 2018, while domestic demand has, so far, stayed firm. Japan posted strong growth in the first half of this year, driven by robust private and public consumption.

Preliminary data suggest a modest pickup in growth in the first half of 2019 for the emerging market and developing economy group, but well below its pace in 2017 and early 2018. China's growth was lifted by fiscal stimulus and some easing

Figure 1.3. Global Investment and Trade
(Percent change)

Global investment slowed in 2019, in line with reduced import growth.

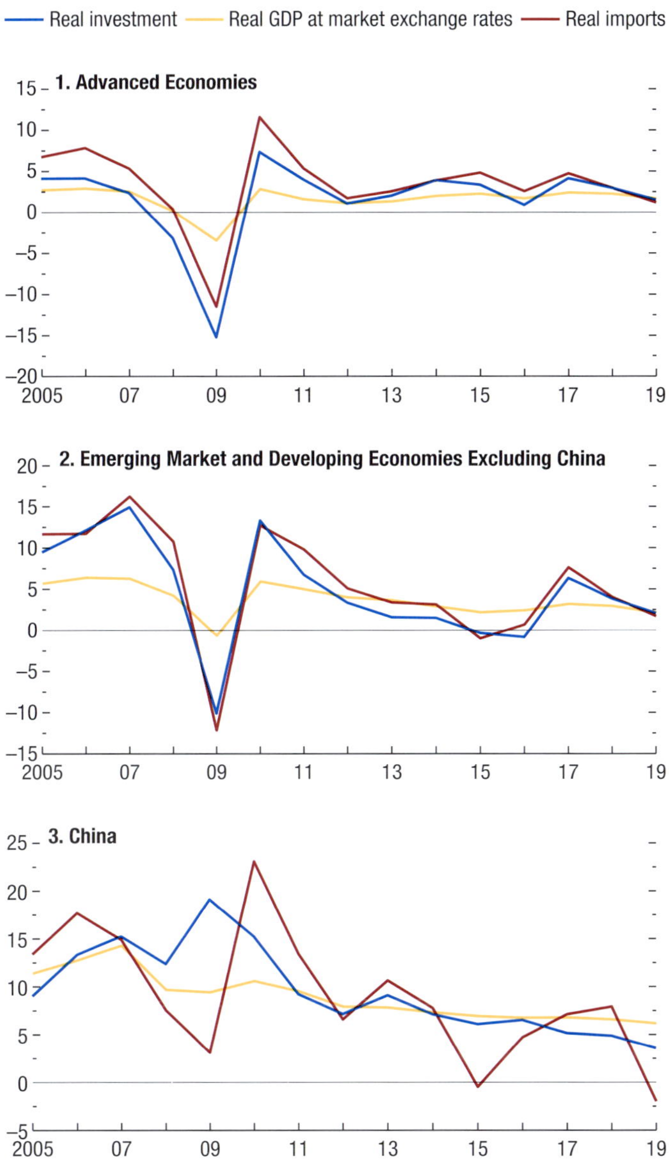

Source: IMF staff estimates.

Figure 1.4. Spending on Durable Goods
(Percent change from a year ago)

Weaker spending on machinery, equipment, and consumer durables has been an important contributor to the slowdown in global trade.

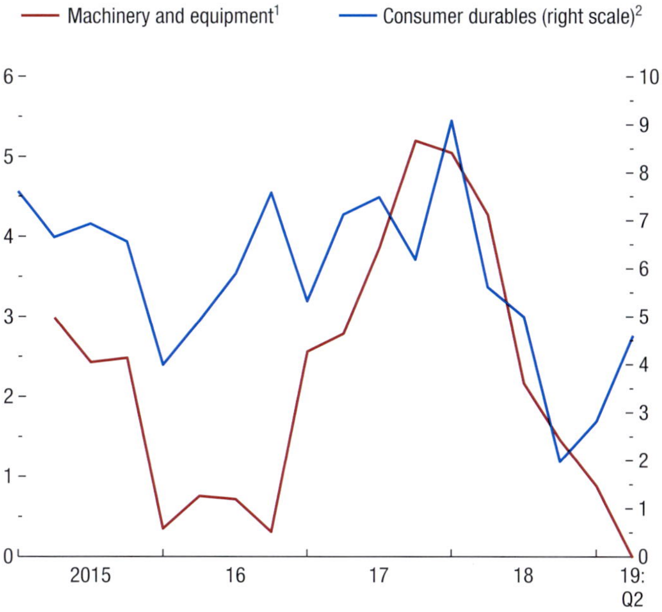

Sources: Haver Analytics; Markit Economics; and IMF staff calculations.
[1]Australia, Brazil, Canada, Chile, China, euro area, India, Indonesia, Japan, Korea, Malaysia, Mexico, Russia, South Africa, Turkey, United Kingdom, United States.
[2]Australia, Brazil, Canada, Chile, China, euro area, Indonesia, Japan, Korea, Malaysia, Mexico, South Africa, Turkey, United Kingdom, United States.

of the pace of financial regulatory strengthening initiated in the second half of 2018. India's economy decelerated further in the second quarter, held back by sector-specific weaknesses in the automobile sector and real estate as well as lingering uncertainty about the health of nonbank financial companies. In Mexico, growth slowed sharply during the first half of the year owing to elevated policy uncertainty, budget under-execution, and some transitory factors. On the other hand, growth resumed in the second quarter in Brazil after a first-quarter contraction driven in part by a mining disaster. Likewise, growth recovered modestly in the second quarter in South Africa, helped by improved electricity supply. Growth recovered in Turkey in the first half of the year following a deep contraction in the second half of 2018, benefiting from more favorable global financial conditions and fiscal and credit support. In contrast, the contraction in Argentina continued through the first half of the year, albeit at a slower pace, and risks going forward are clearly to the downside due to the sharp deterioration in market conditions.

Muted Inflation

The broad synchronized global expansion from mid-2016 through mid-2018 helped narrow output gaps, particularly in advanced economies, but did not

Figure 1.5. Global Purchasing Managers' Index and Consumer Confidence

While manufacturing lost steam, services broadly held firm.

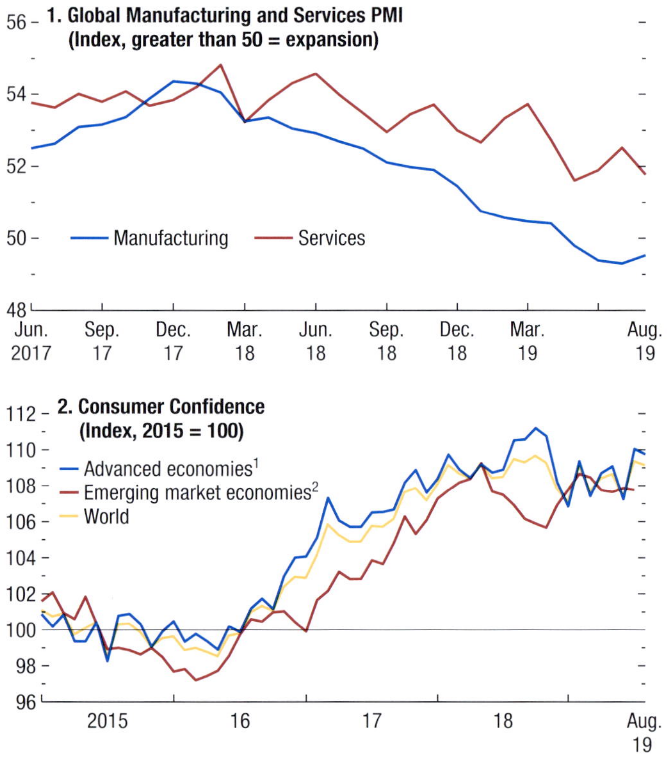

Sources: Haver Analytics; Markit Economics; and IMF staff calculations.
[1]Australia, Czech Republic, Denmark, euro area, Hong Kong SAR, Israel, Japan, Korea, Norway, Sweden, Switzerland, Taiwan Province of China, United Kingdom, United States.
[2]Argentina, Brazil, Chile, China, Colombia, Hungary, Indonesia, Malaysia, Mexico, Philippines, Poland, Russia, South Africa, Thailand, Turkey, Ukraine.

Figure 1.6. Global Inflation

(Three-month moving average; annualized percent change, unless noted otherwise)

Since mid-2018, core inflation has slid further below target across advanced economies and below historical averages in many emerging market and developing economies.

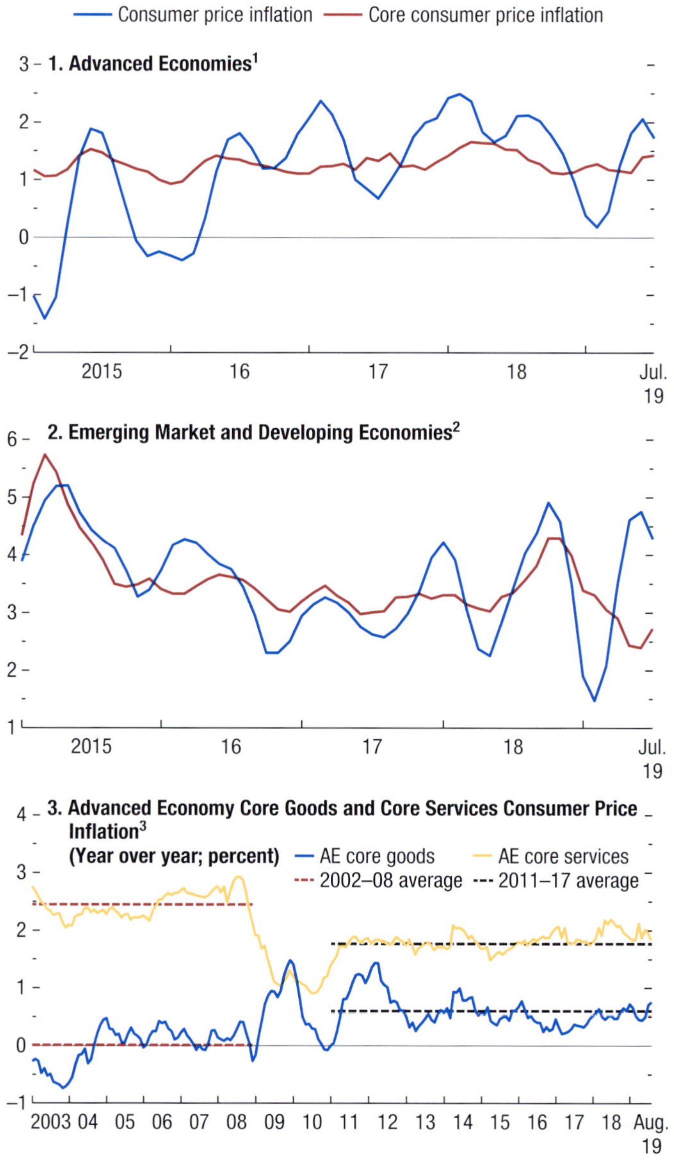

Sources: Consensus Economics; Haver Analytics; and IMF staff calculations.
Note: Country lists use International Organization for Standardization (ISO) country codes.
[1]Advanced economies are AUT, BEL, CAN, CHE, CZE, DEU, DNK, ESP, EST, FIN, FRA, GBR, GRC, HKG, IRL, ISR, ITA, JPN, KOR, LTU, LUX, LVA, NLD, NOR, PRT, SGP, SVK, SVN, SWE, TWN, USA.
[2]Emerging market and developing economies are BGR, BRA, CHL, CHN, COL, HUN, IDN, IND, MEX, MYS, PER, PHL, POL, ROU, RUS, THA, TUR, ZAF.
[3]Sample comprises 16 advanced economies (AE): Australia, Austria, Canada, Denmark, Finland, France, Germany, Italy, Japan, Netherlands, Norway, Portugal, Spain, Sweden, United Kingdom, and United States.

generate sustained increases in core consumer price inflation. Not surprisingly, as the global expansion has weakened, core inflation has slid further below target across advanced economies and below historical averages in many emerging market and developing economies (Figure 1.6). The few exceptions to this broad pattern of softening are economies where large currency depreciations have fed through to higher domestic price pressure (such as in Argentina) or where there are acute shortages of essential goods (Venezuela).

Despite higher import tariffs in some countries, cost pressures have generally remained subdued. Wage growth has inched up from modest levels as unemployment rates have dropped further (close to record lows, for example, in the United States and the United Kingdom) (Figure 1.7, panel 1). The labor share of

Figure 1.7. Wages, Unit Labor Costs, and Labor Shares

Wage growth and the labor share of income have increased recently in some advanced economies.

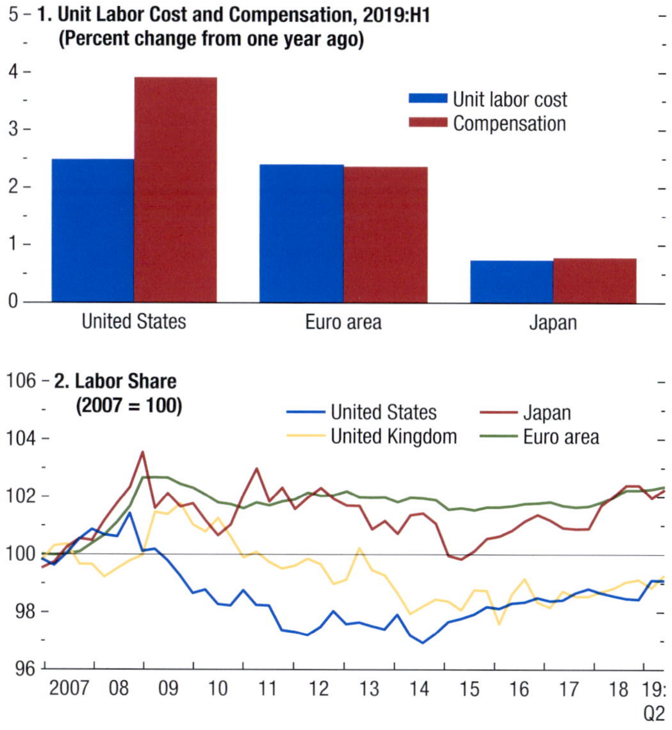

Sources: Haver Analytics; and IMF staff calculations.

Figure 1.8. Commodity Prices
(Deflated using US consumer price index; 2014 = 100)

Commodity price indices have generally softened since the spring.

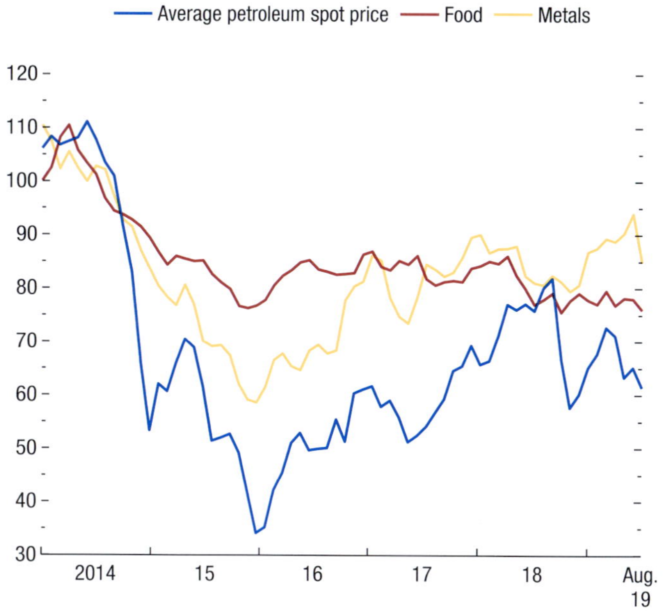

Sources: IMF, Primary Commodity Price System; and IMF staff calculations.

income has been on a gentle upward trend since around 2014 in Japan, the United Kingdom, and the United States, and has increased in the euro area since early 2018 (Figure 1.7, panel 2). These developments appear not to have passed through to core consumer price inflation, suggesting some modest compression of firms' profit margins. In the emerging and developing Europe region, labor shortages have contributed to robust wage growth in many economies. Nonetheless, as discussed in Chapter 2 of the *Regional Economic Outlook* for Europe, wage growth has not transmitted to rising final goods price inflation across the region (Turkey's relatively high inflation can be attributed to other drivers, including past currency depreciation).

Energy prices declined by 13 percent between the reference periods for the April 2019 and current *World Economic Outlook* (WEO) as record-high US crude oil production, together with soft demand, outweighed the influence of supply shortfalls related to US sanctions on Iran, producer cuts by the Organization for the Petroleum Exporting Countries, and strife in Venezuela and Libya (Figure 1.8). The September 14 attack on key oil refining facilities in Saudi Arabia threatened severe supply disruptions, causing crude oil prices to spike by more than 10 percent in the immediate aftermath. Prices subsequently retreated somewhat on reports of less damage than initially feared. Coal and natural gas prices also declined between the reference periods as a result of weak demand prospects. Metal prices remained broadly flat, with declines in copper and aluminum prices offsetting increases in those for nickel and iron ore between the two reference periods (see the Commodities Special Feature).

Overall, low core inflation readings and subdued impulses from commodity prices to headline inflation have led to declines in market pricing of expected inflation, especially in the United States and the euro area.

Volatile Market Sentiment, Monetary Policy Easing

Market sentiment has been volatile since April, reflecting multiple influences that include additional US tariffs on Chinese imports and retaliation by

China, fears of disruptions to technology supply chains, prolonged uncertainty on Brexit, geopolitical strains, and policy rate cuts and dovish communication by several central banks. The net effect of these forces is that financial conditions across advanced economies are now generally easier than at the time of the April 2019 WEO, but they are broadly unchanged across most emerging market and developing economies (see the October 2019 *Global Financial Stability Report* (GFSR)).

Among *advanced economies*, major central banks have turned more accommodative, with a dovish shift in communications earlier in the year followed by easing actions during the summer. The US Federal Reserve cut the Federal Funds rate in July and September and ended its balance sheet reduction. In September, the European Central Bank reduced its deposit rate and announced a resumption of quantitative easing. These policy shifts, together with rising market concerns of slower growth momentum, contributed to sizable declines in sovereign bond yields—in some cases, deep into negative territory (Figure 1.9). Yields on 10-year US Treasury notes, UK gilts, German bunds, and French securities, for example, dropped between 60 and 100 basis points from March to late September, while yields on Italian 10-year bonds declined by 175 basis points on the formation of a new government. Prices of riskier securities have been volatile. Credit spreads on US and euro area high-yield corporate securities have widened marginally since April but remain below their levels in late 2018. Equity markets in the United States and Europe have lost some ground since April but are still well above the lows during the sell-off at the end of 2018.

Currency movements for advanced economies have been notable in some cases. In real effective terms, the yen appreciated by more than 5 percent and the Swiss franc by 3 percent between March and late September as market volatility spiked. In contrast, the British pound has depreciated by 4 percent on increased concern about a no-deal Brexit. The US dollar has strengthened by about 2½ percent, whereas the euro has depreciated by about 1½ percent. Financial flows to and from advanced economies have remained generally subdued, especially since early 2018. One factor explaining these developments is the notable decline in foreign direct investment flows, which have been affected by financial operations of multinational corporations following tax reform in the United States (Box 1.2).

Figure 1.9. Advanced Economies: Monetary and Financial Market Conditions

(Percent, unless noted otherwise)

Sovereign bond yields have declined notably in recent months, in some cases, deep into negative territory.

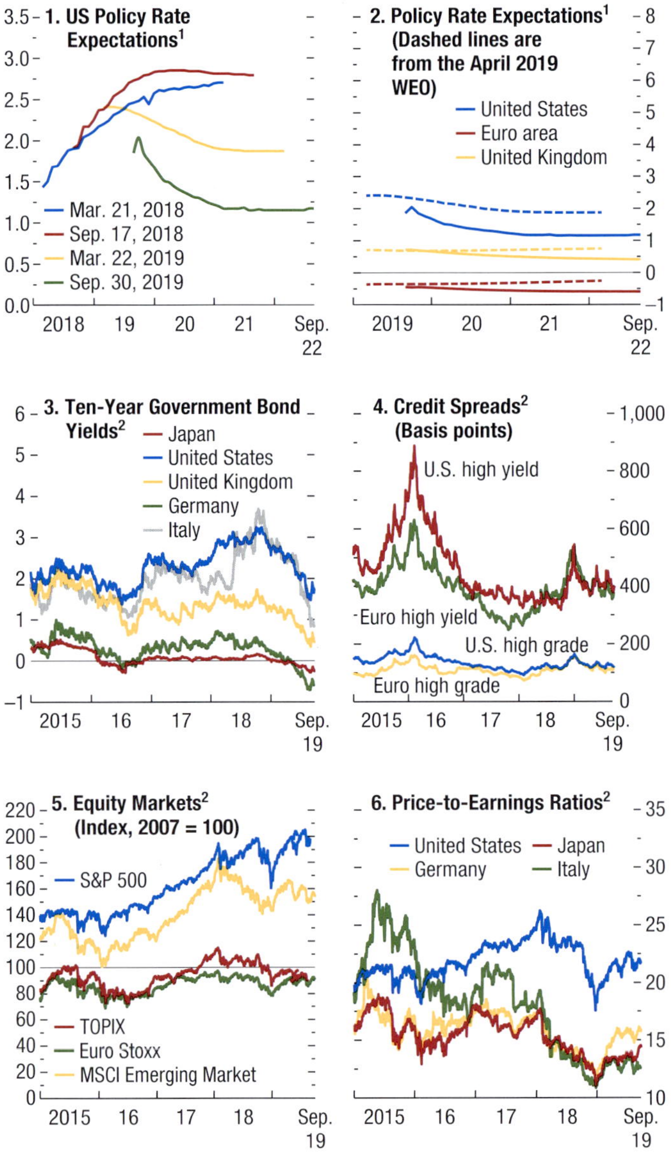

Sources: Bloomberg Finance L.P.; Haver Analytics; Thomson Reuters Datastream; and IMF staff calculations.
Note: MSCI = Morgan Stanley Capital International; S&P = Standard & Poor's; TOPIX = Tokyo Stock Price Index; WEO = *World Economic Outlook.*
[1]Expectations are based on the federal funds rate futures for the United States, the sterling overnight interbank average rate for the United Kingdom, and the euro interbank offered forward rate for the euro area; updated September 30, 2019.
[2]Data are through September 27, 2019.

Among *emerging market and developing economies*, central banks in several countries (for example, Brazil, Chile, India, Indonesia, Mexico, Peru, Philippines, Russia, South Africa, Thailand, and Turkey) have cut policy rates since April. Sovereign spreads have been broadly stable over this period, with a few exceptions (Figure 1.10). Spreads narrowed in Brazil on growing optimism that the long-awaited pension reform would be enacted. Mexico's sovereign spreads widened temporarily following a credit rating downgrade in June. Meanwhile, in Argentina, the primary elections in August triggered a sharp increase in government bond yields amid a wider sell-off in Argentine assets. In Turkey, spreads decompressed significantly following municipal elections in June and are still wider than in April. Emerging market equity indices are broadly trading at April levels, which reflects offsetting influences on earnings prospects from increased domestic and external monetary policy support and intensifying trade tensions (Figure 1.11).

Capital flows to emerging market economies have reflected the broader shifts in risk sentiment since April, with investors lowering their exposure to equities and rotating toward hard currency bonds (Figure 1.12). Portfolio flows into the emerging market asset class remain stronger overall than during the retrenchment of late 2018; investors continue to differentiate across individual economies based on economic and political fundamentals. Most currencies appreciated between March and July, helped by the US Federal Reserve's dovish communications and move toward a more accommodative stance. But several currencies lost ground in August with the deterioration in risk sentiment, particularly the Argentine peso. The Chinese renminbi has depreciated by about 3½ percent since March (Figure 1.13).

Global Growth Outlook: Modest Pickup amid Difficult Headwinds

Projected growth for 2019, at 3.0 percent, is the weakest since 2009. Except in sub-Saharan Africa, more than half of countries are expected to register per capita growth lower than their median rate during the past 25 years. The marked deceleration reflects carryover from broad-based weakness in the second half of 2018, followed by a mild growth uptick in the first half of 2019 and supported, in some cases, by more accommodative policy stances (such as in China and, to some extent, the United States). With growth estimates for both the second half of 2018 and the

Figure 1.10. Emerging Market Economies: Interest Rates and Spreads

Barring a few cases, emerging market sovereign spreads have been broadly stable since April.

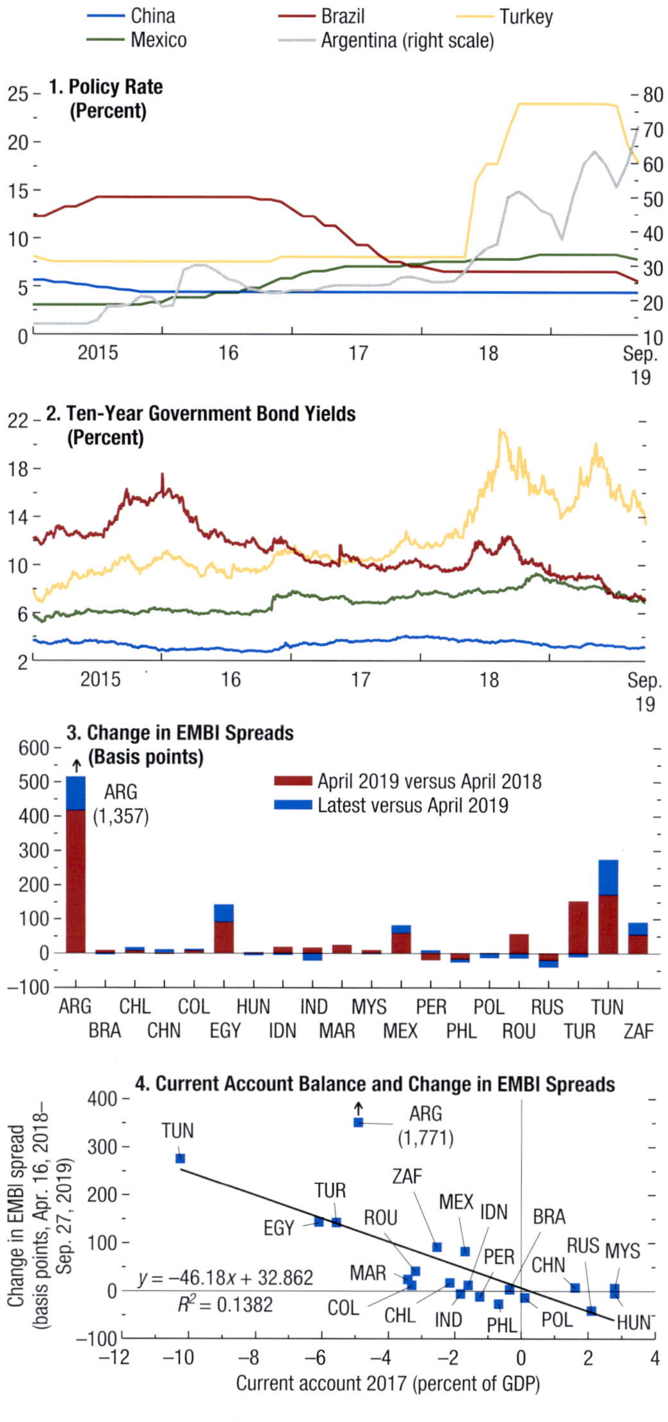

Sources: Haver Analytics; IMF, *International Financial Statistics*; Thomson Reuters Datastream; and IMF staff calculations.
Note: EMBI = J.P. Morgan Emerging Markets Bond Index. All financial market data are through September 27, 2019. Data labels use International Organization for Standardization (ISO) country codes.

Figure 1.11. Emerging Market Economies: Equity Markets and Credit

Emerging market equity indices are broadly trading at April levels, which reflects offsetting influences on earnings prospects from increased domestic and external monetary policy support and intensifying trade tensions.

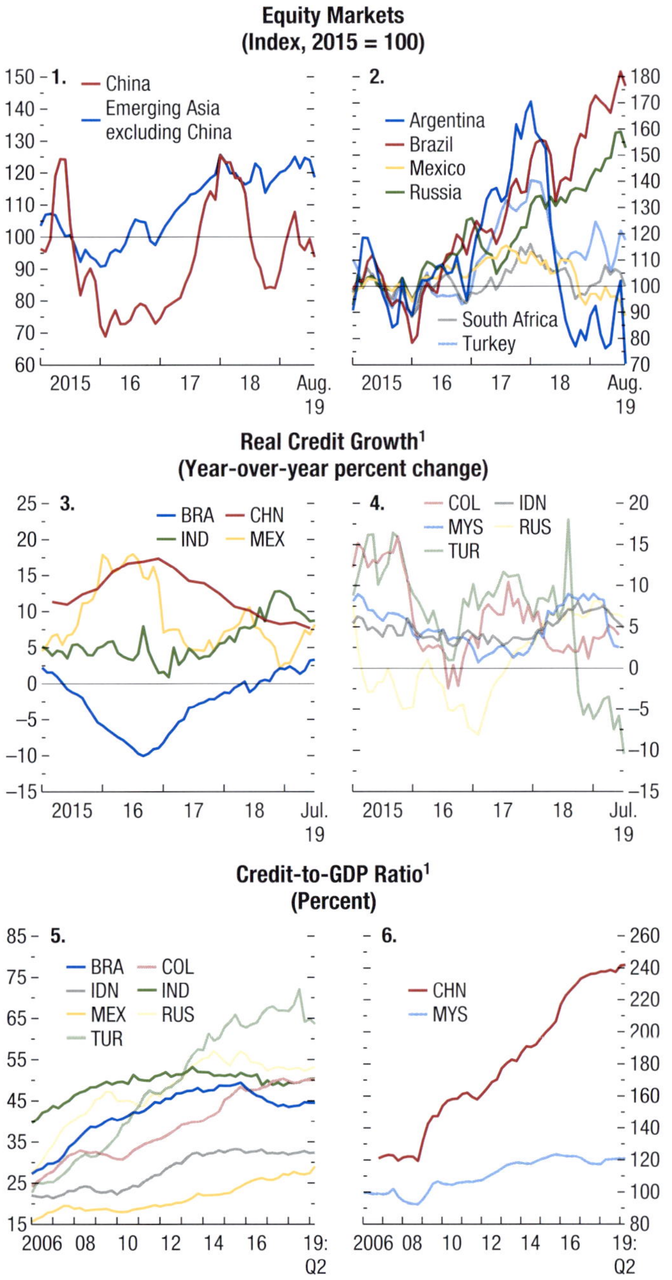

Sources: Bloomberg Finance L.P.; Haver Analytics; IMF, *International Financial Statistics* (IFS); Thomson Reuters Datastream; and IMF staff calculations.
Note: Data labels use International Organization for Standardization (ISO) country codes.
[1]Credit is other depository corporations' claims on the private sector (from IFS), except in the case of Brazil, for which private sector credit is from the Monetary Policy and Financial System Credit Operations published by Banco Central do Brasil, and China, for which credit is total social financing after adjusting for local government debt swaps.

Figure 1.12. Emerging Market Economies: Capital Flows

Capital flows to emerging market economies have reflected the broader shifts in risk sentiment since April, with investors lowering their exposure to equities and rotating toward hard currency bonds.

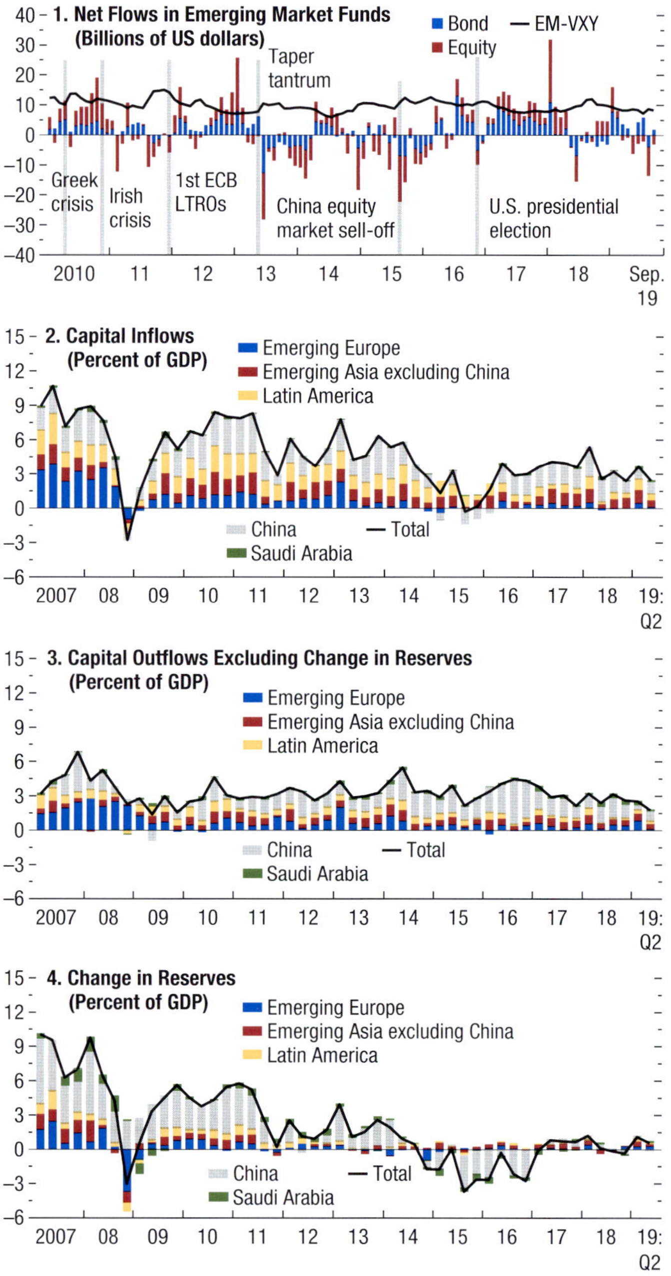

Sources: EPFR Global; Haver Analytics; IMF, *International Financial Statistics*; Thomson Reuters Datastream; and IMF staff calculations.
Note: Capital inflows are net purchases of domestic assets by nonresidents. Capital outflows are net purchases of foreign assets by domestic residents. Emerging Asia excluding China comprises India, Indonesia, Malaysia, the Philippines, and Thailand; emerging Europe comprises Poland, Romania, Russia, and Turkey; Latin America comprises Brazil, Chile, Colombia, Mexico, and Peru. ECB = European Central Bank; EM-VXY = J.P. Morgan Emerging Market Volatility Index; LTROs = long-term refinancing operations.

Figure 1.13. Real Effective Exchange Rate Changes, March 2019–September 2019
(Percent)

Most emerging market currencies appreciated between March and July, helped by the US Federal Reserve's dovish communications and move toward a more accommodative stance. But several currencies lost ground in August with the deterioration in risk sentiment.

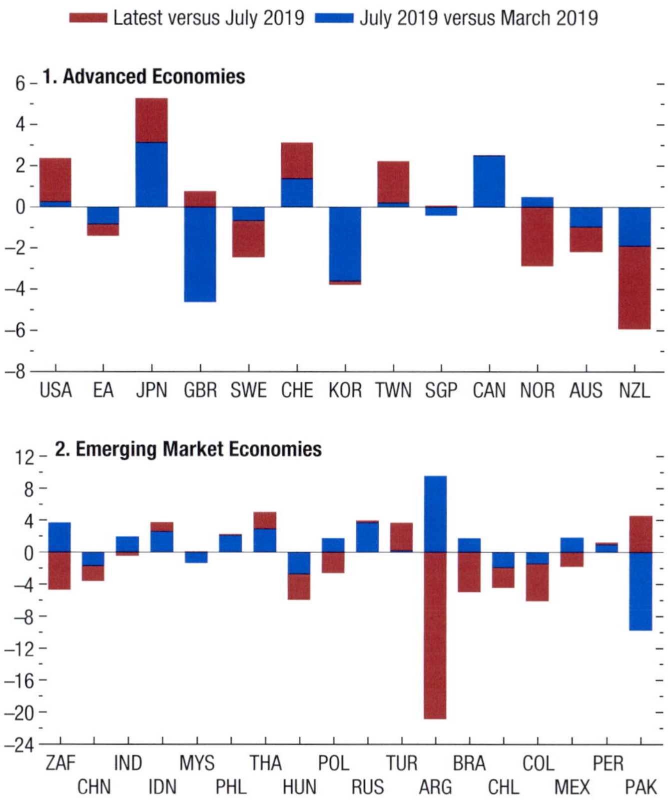

Source: IMF staff calculations.
Note: EA = euro area. Data labels use International Organization for Standardization (ISO) country codes. Latest data available are for September 27, 2019.

first half of this year marked down, the 2019 growth projection is 0.3 percentage point weaker than in the April 2019 WEO.

The forces behind the slowdown in global growth during 2018–19—apart from the direct effect of very weak growth or contractions in stressed economies—include a return to a more normal pace of expansion in the US economy; softer external demand and disruptions associated with the rollout of new car emission standards in Europe, especially Germany; weaker macroeconomic conditions, largely because of idiosyncratic factors, in a group of key emerging market economies such as Brazil, Mexico, and Russia; a softening in China's growth because of necessary financial regulatory strengthening and drag from trade tensions with the United States; slowing demand from China and broader global trade policy uncertainty weighing on east Asian economies; a slowdown in domestic demand in India; and the shadow cast by the possibility of a no-deal Brexit on the United Kingdom and the European Union more broadly.

Continued macroeconomic policy support in major economies and projected stabilization in some stressed emerging market economies are expected to lift global growth modestly over the remainder of 2019 and into 2020, bringing projected global growth to 3.4 percent for 2020 (Table 1.1). The forecast markdown of 0.2 percentage point for 2020 relative to the April 2019 WEO largely reflects the fact that tariffs have risen and are costing the global economy: following tariff announcements in May and August 2019, the average US tariff on imports from China will rise to just over 24 percent by December 2019 (compared with about 12¼ percent assumed in the April 2019 WEO), while the average China tariff on imports from the United States will increase to about 26 percent (compared with about 16½ percent assumed in the April 2019 WEO). Scenario Box 1.2 provides simulations of the direct impact of the tariffs included in the baseline on global economic activity as well as their potential repercussions for financial market sentiment, business confidence, and productivity. As Scenario Box 1.2 illustrates, trade diversion spillovers for some economies, while positive, are temporary and are likely outweighed by business confidence and financial market sentiment effects. Box 1.3 provides more details on the key policy and commodity price assumptions behind the global growth forecast.

Figure 1.14 illustrates the countries and regions where growth fluctuations have affected changes in world growth since its peak in 2017. The dramatic worsening of macroeconomic conditions between 2017 and 2019 in a small number of economies under severe distress (in particular Argentina, Iran, Turkey, and Venezuela) accounts for about half of the decline in world growth from 3.8 percent in 2017 to 3.0 percent in 2019. These same economies—together with Brazil, Mexico, and Russia, all three of which are expected to grow by about 1 percent or less in 2019—account for over 70 percent of the pickup in growth for 2020. Argentina's economy is projected to contract again in 2020, but by less than this year; and in Venezuela, the multiyear collapse in output is projected to continue,

Table 1.1. Overview of the *World Economic Outlook* Projections
(Percent change, unless noted otherwise)

		Projections		Difference from July 2019 WEO Update[1]		Difference from April 2019 WEO[1]	
	2018	2019	2020	2019	2020	2019	2020
World Output	**3.6**	**3.0**	**3.4**	**–0.2**	**–0.1**	**–0.3**	**–0.2**
Advanced Economies	**2.3**	**1.7**	**1.7**	**–0.2**	**0.0**	**–0.1**	**0.0**
United States	2.9	2.4	2.1	–0.2	0.2	0.1	0.2
Euro Area	1.9	1.2	1.4	–0.1	–0.2	–0.1	–0.1
Germany[2]	1.5	0.5	1.2	–0.2	–0.5	–0.3	–0.2
France	1.7	1.2	1.3	–0.1	–0.1	–0.1	–0.1
Italy	0.9	0.0	0.5	–0.1	–0.3	–0.1	–0.4
Spain	2.6	2.2	1.8	–0.1	–0.1	0.1	–0.1
Japan	0.8	0.9	0.5	0.0	0.1	–0.1	0.0
United Kingdom	1.4	1.2	1.4	–0.1	0.0	0.0	0.0
Canada	1.9	1.5	1.8	0.0	–0.1	0.0	–0.1
Other Advanced Economies[3]	2.6	1.6	2.0	–0.5	–0.4	–0.6	–0.5
Emerging Market and Developing Economies	**4.5**	**3.9**	**4.6**	**–0.2**	**–0.1**	**–0.5**	**–0.2**
Emerging and Developing Asia	6.4	5.9	6.0	–0.3	–0.2	–0.4	–0.3
China	6.6	6.1	5.8	–0.1	–0.2	–0.2	–0.3
India[4]	6.8	6.1	7.0	–0.9	–0.2	–1.2	–0.5
ASEAN-5[5]	5.2	4.8	4.9	–0.2	–0.2	–0.3	–0.3
Emerging and Developing Europe	3.1	1.8	2.5	0.6	0.4	0.6	0.2
Russia	2.3	1.1	1.9	–0.1	0.0	–0.5	0.2
Latin America and the Caribbean	1.0	0.2	1.8	–0.4	–0.5	–1.2	–0.6
Brazil	1.1	0.9	2.0	0.1	–0.4	–1.2	–0.5
Mexico	2.0	0.4	1.3	–0.5	–0.6	–1.2	–0.6
Middle East and Central Asia	1.9	0.9	2.9	–0.5	–0.3	–0.9	–0.4
Saudi Arabia	2.4	0.2	2.2	–1.7	–0.8	–1.6	0.1
Sub-Saharan Africa	3.2	3.2	3.6	–0.2	0.0	–0.3	–0.1
Nigeria	1.9	2.3	2.5	0.0	–0.1	0.2	0.0
South Africa	0.8	0.7	1.1	0.0	0.0	–0.5	–0.4
Memorandum							
European Union	2.2	1.5	1.6	–0.1	–0.2	–0.1	–0.1
Low-Income Developing Countries	5.0	5.0	5.1	0.1	0.0	0.0	0.0
Middle East and North Africa	1.1	0.1	2.7	–0.6	–0.4	–1.2	–0.5
World Growth Based on Market Exchange Rates	3.1	2.5	2.7	–0.2	–0.2	–0.2	–0.2
World Trade Volume (goods and services)	**3.6**	**1.1**	**3.2**	**–1.4**	**–0.5**	**–2.3**	**–0.7**
Imports							
Advanced Economies	3.0	1.2	2.7	–1.0	–0.6	–1.8	–0.5
Emerging Market and Developing Economies	5.1	0.7	4.3	–2.2	–0.8	–3.9	–1.0
Exports							
Advanced Economies	3.1	0.9	2.5	–1.3	–0.4	–1.8	–0.6
Emerging Market and Developing Economies	3.9	1.9	4.1	–1.0	–0.5	–2.1	–0.7
Commodity Prices (US dollars)							
Oil[6]	29.4	–9.6	–6.2	–5.5	–3.7	3.8	–6.0
Nonfuel (average based on world commodity import weights)	1.6	0.9	1.7	1.5	1.2	1.1	0.6
Consumer Prices							
Advanced Economies	2.0	1.5	1.8	–0.1	–0.2	–0.1	–0.3
Emerging Market and Developing Economies[7]	4.8	4.7	4.8	–0.1	0.1	–0.2	0.1
London Interbank Offered Rate (percent)							
On US Dollar Deposits (six month)	2.5	2.3	2.0	–0.1	–0.3	–0.9	–1.8
On Euro Deposits (three month)	–0.3	–0.4	–0.6	–0.1	–0.3	–0.1	–0.4
On Japanese Yen Deposits (six month)	0.0	0.0	–0.1	0.0	–0.1	0.0	–0.1

Note: Real effective exchange rates are assumed to remain constant at the levels prevailing during July 26–August 23, 2019. Economies are listed on the basis of economic size. The aggregated quarterly data are seasonally adjusted. WEO = *World Economic Outlook*. Beginning with the October 2019 WEO, the regional group Commonwealth of Independent States (CIS) is discontinued. Four of the CIS economies (Belarus, Moldova, Russia, and Ukraine) are added to the regional group Emerging and Developing Europe. The remaining eight economies—Armenia, Azerbaijan, Georgia, Kazakhstan, Kyrgyz Republic, Tajikistan, Turkmenistan, and Uzbekistan, which comprise the regional subgroup Caucasus and Central Asia (CCA)—are combined with Middle East, North Africa, Afghanistan, and Pakistan (MENAP) to form the new regional group Middle East and Central Asia (MECA).

[1]Difference based on rounded figures for the current (July 2019) WEO Update and April 2019 WEO forecasts and on revised and new groups.

[2]For Germany, the definition of GDP has been changed from a working-day-adjusted basis (through the April 2019 WEO) to an unadjusted basis from the July 2019 WEO Update onward. The change in definition implies a higher level of GDP for 2020, which is a leap year.

[3]Excludes the Group of Seven (Canada, France, Germany, Italy, Japan, United Kingdom, United States) and euro area countries.

Table 1.1 *(continued)*

	Year over Year				Q4 over Q4[8]			
			Projections				Projections	
	2017	2018	2019	2020	2017	2018	2019	2020
World Output	**3.8**	**3.6**	**3.0**	**3.4**	**4.1**	**3.2**	**3.2**	**3.4**
Advanced Economies	**2.5**	**2.3**	**1.7**	**1.7**	**2.8**	**1.8**	**1.6**	**1.8**
United States	2.4	2.9	2.4	2.1	2.8	2.5	2.4	2.0
Euro Area	2.5	1.9	1.2	1.4	3.0	1.2	1.0	1.8
Germany[2]	2.5	1.5	0.5	1.2	3.4	0.6	0.4	1.3
France	2.3	1.7	1.2	1.3	3.0	1.2	1.0	1.3
Italy	1.7	0.9	0.0	0.5	1.7	0.0	0.2	1.0
Spain	3.0	2.6	2.2	1.8	3.1	2.3	2.0	1.8
Japan	1.9	0.8	0.9	0.5	2.4	0.3	0.3	1.2
United Kingdom	1.8	1.4	1.2	1.4	1.6	1.4	1.0	1.6
Canada	3.0	1.9	1.5	1.8	2.9	1.6	1.8	1.7
Other Advanced Economies[3]	2.9	2.6	1.6	2.0	3.0	2.2	1.7	2.1
Emerging Market and Developing Economies	**4.8**	**4.5**	**3.9**	**4.6**	**5.2**	**4.5**	**4.5**	**4.7**
Emerging and Developing Asia	6.6	6.4	5.9	6.0	6.8	6.0	6.0	5.9
China	6.8	6.6	6.1	5.8	6.7	6.4	6.0	5.7
India[4]	7.2	6.8	6.1	7.0	8.1	5.8	6.7	7.2
ASEAN-5[5]	5.3	5.2	4.8	4.9	5.4	5.2	4.8	4.9
Emerging and Developing Europe	3.9	3.1	1.8	2.5	...	...	...	...
Russia	1.6	2.3	1.1	1.9	0.5	2.9	1.8	1.2
Latin America and the Caribbean	1.2	1.0	0.2	1.8	1.3	0.3	0.4	1.8
Brazil	1.1	1.1	0.9	2.0	2.2	1.1	1.2	2.3
Mexico	2.1	2.0	0.4	1.3	1.5	1.6	1.0	0.7
Middle East and Central Asia	2.3	1.9	0.9	2.9	...	...	...	...
Saudi Arabia	–0.7	2.4	0.2	2.2	–1.3	4.3	–0.9	3.0
Sub-Saharan Africa	3.0	3.2	3.2	3.6	...	...	...	...
Nigeria	0.8	1.9	2.3	2.5	...	...	...	...
South Africa	1.4	0.8	0.7	1.1	2.2	0.2	0.8	0.6
Memorandum								
European Union	2.8	2.2	1.5	1.6	3.0	1.7	1.3	1.8
Low-Income Developing Countries	4.7	5.0	5.0	5.1	...	...	...	...
Middle East and North Africa	1.8	1.1	0.1	2.7	...	...	...	...
World Growth Based on Market Exchange Rates	3.2	3.1	2.5	2.7	3.5	2.6	2.5	2.8
World Trade Volume (goods and services)	**5.7**	**3.6**	**1.1**	**3.2**	**...**	**...**	**...**	**...**
Imports								
Advanced Economies	4.7	3.0	1.2	2.7	...	...	...	...
Emerging Market and Developing Economies	7.5	5.1	0.7	4.3	...	...	...	...
Exports								
Advanced Economies	4.7	3.1	0.9	2.5	...	...	...	...
Emerging Market and Developing Economies	7.3	3.9	1.9	4.1	...	...	...	...
Commodity Prices (US dollars)								
Oil[6]	23.3	29.4	–9.6	–6.2	19.6	9.5	–3.8	–8.8
Nonfuel (average based on world commodity export weights)	6.4	1.6	0.9	1.7	3.5	–1.8	4.9	–1.0
Consumer Prices								
Advanced Economies	1.7	2.0	1.5	1.8	1.7	1.9	1.7	1.6
Emerging Market and Developing Economies[7]	4.3	4.8	4.7	4.8	3.7	4.2	4.1	4.0
London Interbank Offered Rate (percent)								
On US Dollar Deposits (six month)	1.5	2.5	2.3	2.0	...	...	...	...
On Euro Deposits (three month)	–0.3	–0.3	–0.4	–0.6	...	...	...	...
On Japanese Yen Deposits (six month)	0.0	0.0	0.0	–0.1	...	...	...	...

[4]For India, data and forecasts are presented on a fiscal year basis, and GDP from 2011 onward is based on GDP at market prices with fiscal year 2011/12 as a base year.
[5]Indonesia, Malaysia, Philippines, Thailand, Vietnam.
[6]Simple average of prices of UK Brent, Dubai Fateh, and West Texas Intermediate crude oil. The average price of oil in US dollars a barrel was $68.33 in 2018; the assumed price, based on futures markets, is $61.78 in 2019 and $57.94 in 2020.
[7]Excludes Venezuela. See country-specific note for Venezuela in the "Country Notes" section of the Statistical Appendix.
[8]For World Output, the quarterly estimates and projections account for approximately 90 percent of annual world output at purchasing-power-parity weights. For Emerging Market and Developing Economies, the quarterly estimates and projections account for approximately 80 percent of annual emerging market and developing economies' output at purchasing-power-parity weights.

Figure 1.14. Global Growth

The slowdown in global growth since 2017 and the projected pick up in 2020 reflects a major downturn and projected recovery in a group of emerging market economies under severe distress.

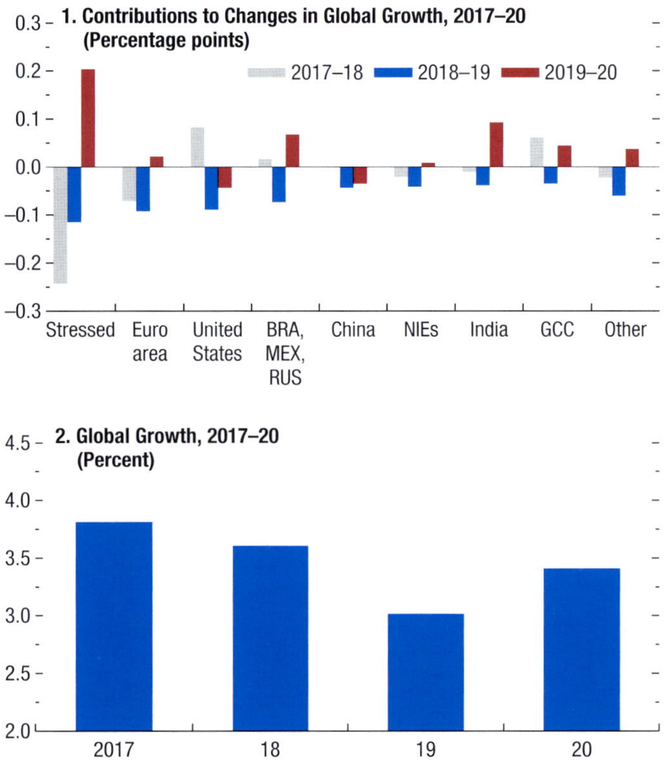

Source: IMF staff estimates.
Note: NIEs = newly industrialized Asian economies (Hong Kong SAR, Korea, Macao SAR, Singapore, Taiwan Province of China); stressed = Argentina, Iran, Libya, Sudan, Turkey, Venezuela; GCC = Gulf Cooperation Council (Bahrain, Kuwait, Oman, Qatar, Saudi Arabia, United Arab Emirates). Data labels use International Organization for Standardization (ISO) country codes.

albeit at a less dramatic pace than in 2019. In Iran, modest growth is expected to resume after recession. Activity should pick up in Brazil, Mexico, Russia, Saudi Arabia, and Turkey. The projected uptick in global growth also relies importantly on financial market sentiment staying supportive and continued fading of temporary drags, notably in the euro area, where industrial output is expected to improve gradually after protracted weakness. In turn, these factors rely on a conducive global policy backdrop that ensures that the dovish tilt of central banks and the buildup of policy stimulus in China are not blunted by escalating trade tensions or a disorderly Brexit.

The world economy faces difficult headwinds over the forecast horizon. Despite the recent decline in long-term interest rates creating more fiscal room, the global environment is expected to be characterized by relatively limited macroeconomic policy space to combat downturns and weaker trade flows, in part reflecting the increase in trade barriers and anticipated protracted trade policy uncertainty (global export and import volume projections have been cumulatively marked down by about 3½ percent over the forecast horizon relative to the April 2019 WEO). Weighed down by aging populations and tepid productivity growth, advanced economies are expected to return to their modest potential rate of expansion. Moreover, China is projected to slow gradually to a more sustainable rate of growth.

Against this backdrop, beyond 2020 global growth is projected at about 3.6 percent. The forecast relies, to a large extent, on durable normalization in emerging market and developing economies currently in macroeconomic distress and on continued healthy performance of relatively faster-growing emerging market and developing economies. The resultant shifting weights in the global economy toward faster-growing emerging market and developing economies help support the projected stable medium-term growth profile, contributing ¼ percentage point to global growth by the end of the forecast horizon, compared with a global growth projection with country weights held constant at their 2018 level.

Growth Forecast for Advanced Economies

For advanced economies, growth is projected to soften to 1.7 percent in 2019 and 2020. The forecast is 0.1 percentage point lower for 2019 than in the April 2019 WEO.

- In the *United States*, the economy maintained momentum in the first half of the year. Although investment remained sluggish, employment and consumption were buoyant. Growth in 2019 is expected to be 2.4 percent, moderating to 2.1 percent in 2020. The projected moderation reflects an assumed shift in the fiscal stance from expansionary in 2019 to broadly neutral in 2020 as stimulus from the recently adopted two-year budget deal offsets the fading effects of the 2017 Tax Cuts and Jobs Act. Overall, the growth forecast is revised up from the April 2019 WEO (0.1 percentage point higher for 2019 and 0.2 for 2020). Revisions to past GDP data imply weaker carryover into 2019, and trade-related policy uncertainty imparts further negative effects, but the two-year budget deal and the Federal Reserve's policy rate cuts yield net upward revisions.

- In the *euro area*, weaker growth in foreign demand and a drawdown of inventories (reflecting weak industrial production) have kept a lid on growth since mid-2018. Activity is expected to pick up only modestly over the remainder of this year, and into 2020, as external demand is projected to regain some momentum and temporary factors (including new emission standards that hit German car production) continue to fade. Growth is projected at 1.2 percent in 2019 (0.1 percentage point lower than in April) and 1.4 percent in 2020. The 2019 forecast is revised down slightly for *France* and *Germany* (due to weaker-than-expected external demand in the first half of the year). Both the 2019 and 2020 forecasts were marked down for *Italy*, owing to softening private consumption, a smaller fiscal impulse, and a weaker external environment. The outlook is also slightly weaker for *Spain*, with growth projected to slow gradually from 2.6 percent in 2018 to 2.2 percent in 2019 and 1.8 percent in 2020 (0.1 percentage point lower than in April).
- The *United Kingdom* is set to expand at 1.2 percent in 2019 and 1.4 percent in 2020. The unchanged projection for both years (relative to the April 2019 WEO) reflects the combination of a negative impact from weaker global growth and ongoing Brexit uncertainty and a positive impact from higher public spending announced in the recent Spending Review. The economy contracted in the second quarter, and recent indicators point to weak growth in the third quarter. The forecast assumes an orderly exit from the European Union followed by a gradual transition to the new regime. However, as of early September, the ultimate form of Brexit remains highly uncertain.
- *Japan*'s economy is projected to grow by 0.9 percent in 2019 (0.1 percentage point lower than anticipated in the April 2019 WEO). Strong private consumption and public spending in the first half of 2019 outweighed continued weakness in the external sector. Growth is projected at 0.5 percent in 2020 (unchanged from the April 2019 WEO), with temporary fiscal measures expected to cushion part of the anticipated decline in private consumption following the October 2019 increase in the consumption tax rate.

Beyond 2020, growth in the advanced economy group is projected to stabilize at about 1.6 percent, similar to the April 2019 WEO forecast. A modest uptick expected in productivity is projected to counteract the drag on potential output growth from slower labor force growth as populations continue to age.

Growth Forecast for Emerging Market and Developing Economies

Growth in the emerging market and developing economy group is expected to bottom out at 3.9 percent in 2019, rising to 4.6 percent in 2020. The forecasts for 2019 and 2020 are 0.5 percentage point and 0.2 percentage point lower, respectively, than in April, reflecting downward revisions in all major regions except emerging and developing Europe.[2]

- *Emerging and Developing Asia* remains the main engine of the world economy, but growth is softening gradually with the structural slowdown in China. Output in the region is expected to grow at 5.9 percent this year and at 6.0 percent in 2020 (0.4 and 0.3 percentage point lower, respectively, than in the April 2019 WEO forecast). In *China*, the effects of escalating tariffs and weakening external demand have exacerbated the slowdown associated with needed regulatory strengthening to rein in the accumulation of debt. With policy stimulus expected to continue supporting activity in the face of the adverse external shock, growth is forecast at 6.1 percent in 2019 and 5.8 percent in 2020—0.2 and 0.3 percentage point lower than in the April 2019 WEO projection. *India*'s economy is set to grow at 6.1 percent in 2019, picking up to 7 percent in 2020. The downward revision relative to the April 2019 WEO of 1.2 percentage points for 2019 and 0.5 percentage point for 2020 reflects a weaker-than-expected outlook for domestic demand. Growth will be supported by the lagged effects of monetary policy easing, a reduction in corporate income tax rates, recent measures to address corporate and environmental regulatory

[2]Beginning with the October 2019 WEO, the regional group Commonwealth of Independent States (CIS) is discontinued. Four of the CIS economies (Belarus, Moldova, Russia, and Ukraine) are added to the regional group Emerging and Developing Europe. The remaining eight economies—Armenia, Azerbaijan, Georgia, Kazakhstan, Kyrgyz Republic, Tajikistan, Turkmenistan, and Uzbekistan, which comprise the regional subgroup Caucasus and Central Asia (CCA)—are combined with Middle East, North Africa, Afghanistan, and Pakistan (MENAP) to form the new regional group Middle East and Central Asia (MECA).

uncertainty, and government programs to support rural consumption.

- Subdued growth in *emerging and developing Europe* in 2019 largely reflects a slowdown in Russia and flat activity in Turkey. The region is expected to grow at 1.8 percent in 2019 and 2.5 percent in 2020. The upward revision to 2019 growth relative to the April 2019 forecast reflects a shallower-than-expected downturn in *Turkey* in the first half of the year as a result of fiscal support. In *Russia*, by contrast, growth has been weaker this year than forecast in April, but is projected to recover next year, contributing to the upward revision to projected 2020 growth for the region. Several countries in central and eastern Europe, including *Hungary* and *Poland*, are experiencing solid growth on the back of resilient domestic demand and rising wages.
- In *Latin America*, activity slowed notably at the start of the year across the larger economies, mostly reflecting idiosyncratic factors. Growth in the region is now expected at 0.2 percent this year (1.2 percentage point lower than in the April 2019 WEO). The sizable downward revision for 2019 reflects downgrades to *Brazil* (where mining supply disruptions have hurt activity) and *Mexico* (where investment remains weak and private consumption has slowed, reflecting policy uncertainty, weakening confidence, and higher borrowing costs). *Argentina*'s economy is expected to contract further in 2019 on lower confidence and tighter external financing conditions. *Chile*'s growth projection is revised down, following weaker-than-expected performance at the start of the year. The deep humanitarian crisis and economic implosion in *Venezuela* continue to have a devastating impact, with the economy expected to shrink by about one-third in 2019. For the region as a whole, growth is expected to firm up to 1.8 percent in 2020 (0.6 percentage point lower than in the April forecast). The projected strengthening reflects expected recovery in Brazil (on the back of accommodative monetary policy) and in Mexico (as uncertainty gradually subsides), together with less severe contractions for 2020 compared to this year in Argentina and Venezuela.
- Growth in the *Middle East and Central Asia* region is expected to be 0.9 percent in 2019, rising to 2.9 percent in 2020. The forecast is 0.9 and 0.4 percentage point lower, respectively, than in the April 2019 WEO, largely due to the downward forecast revision for *Iran* (owing to the effect of tighter US sanctions) and *Saudi Arabia*. While non-oil growth is expected to strengthen in 2019 on higher government spending and confidence, oil GDP in Saudi Arabia is projected to decline against the backdrop of the extension of the OPEC+ agreement and a generally weak global oil market. The impact on growth of the recent attacks on Saudi Arabia's oil facilities is difficult to gauge at this stage but adds uncertainty to the near-term outlook. Growth is projected to pick up in 2020 as oil GDP stabilizes and solid momentum in the non-oil sector continues. Civil strife in some other economies, including *Libya*, *Syria*, and *Yemen*, weigh on the region's outlook.
- In *sub-Saharan Africa*, growth is expected at 3.2 percent in 2019 and 3.6 percent in 2020, slightly lower for both years than in the April 2019 WEO. Higher, albeit volatile, oil prices earlier in the year have supported the subdued outlook for *Nigeria* and some other oil-exporting countries in the region, but *Angola*'s economy—because of a decline in oil production—is expected to contract this year and recover only mildly next year. In *South Africa*, despite a moderate rebound in the second quarter, growth is expected to be weaker in 2019 than projected in the April 2019 WEO following a very weak first quarter, reflecting a larger-than-anticipated impact of labor strikes and energy supply issues in mining, together with weak agricultural production. While the three largest economies of the region are projected to continue their lackluster performance, many other economies—typically more diversified ones—are experiencing solid growth. About 20 economies in the region, accounting for about 45 percent of the sub-Saharan African population and 34 percent of the region's GDP (1 percent of global GDP), are estimated to be growing faster than 5 percent this year while growth in a somewhat larger set of countries, in per capita terms, is faster than in advanced economies.

Over the medium term, growth for the emerging market and developing economies group is projected to stabilize at about 4.8 percent, but with important differences across regions. In emerging and developing Asia, it is expected to remain at about 6 percent through the forecast horizon. This smooth growth profile rests on a gradual slowdown in China to 5.5 percent by 2024 and firming and stabilization of growth in India at about 7.3 percent over the medium term, based on continued implementation of structural reforms. In Latin America, growth is projected to increase from the 1.8 percent projected for 2020, but remain below 3 percent over the medium term as structural rigidities, subdued terms of trade, and fiscal imbalances (particularly for Brazil) weigh on the outlook. Activity in emerging and developing Europe is projected to pick up from its current post-global-financial-crisis low, with the region expected to grow at about 2½ percent over the medium term. Prospects vary across sub-Saharan Africa, but growth for the region as a whole is projected to increase from 3.6 percent in 2020 to 4.2 percent in 2024 (although for close to two-fifths of economies, the average growth rate over the medium term is projected to exceed 5 percent). The medium-term outlook for the Middle East and Central Asia region is largely shaped by the outlook for fuel prices, needed adjustment to correct macroeconomic imbalances in certain economies, and geopolitical tensions.

Forty emerging market and developing economies (about a quarter of the total) are projected to grow in per capita terms above the 3.3 percent weighted average of the group, which is more than 2 percentage points above the average for advanced economies (Figure 1.15). For these economies—which include China, India, and Indonesia—the challenge is to ensure that these growth rates materialize and that the benefits of growth are shared widely. Convergence prospects are instead bleak for some emerging market and developing economies. Across sub-Saharan Africa and in the Middle East and Central Asia region, 47 economies, accounting for about 10 percent of global GDP in purchasing-power-parity terms and close to 1 billion in population, are projected to grow by less than advanced economies in per capita terms

Figure 1.15. Emerging Market and Developing Economies: Per Capita GDP Growth
(2019–24 average)

Forty emerging market and developing economies are projected to grow in per capita terms above the 3.3 percent weighted average of the group, which is more than 2 percentage points above the average for advanced economies.

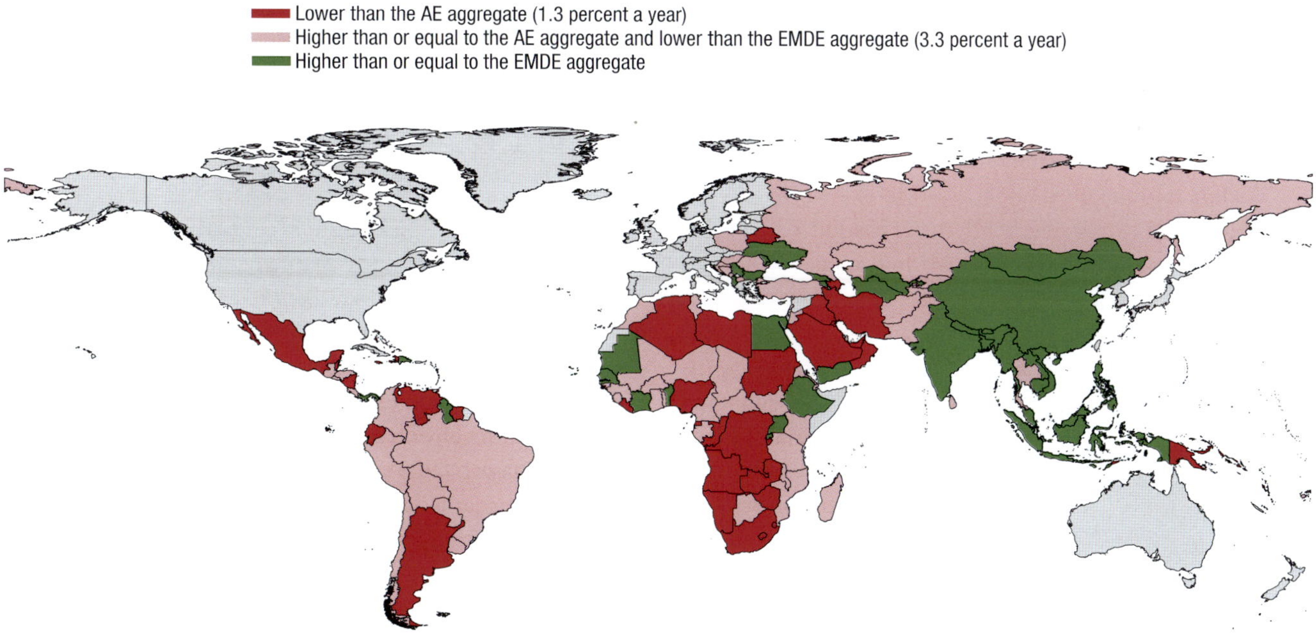

Source: IMF staff estimates.
Note: The AE (EMDE) aggregate per capita growth rate refers to the growth rate of per capita real GDP in the advanced economy (emerging market and developing economy) group, calculated as the sum of real GDP at purchasing-power-parity rates divided by total population in the group. See also Annex Table 1.1.6.
AE = advanced economy; EMDE = emerging market and developing economy. Country borders shown on this map do not imply official endorsement or acceptance by the IMF.

Figure 1.16. Sub-Saharan Africa: Population in 2018 and Projected Growth Rates in GDP per Capita, 2019–24

In sub-Saharan Africa, most countries are projected to grow at rates well above the weighted average for the region.

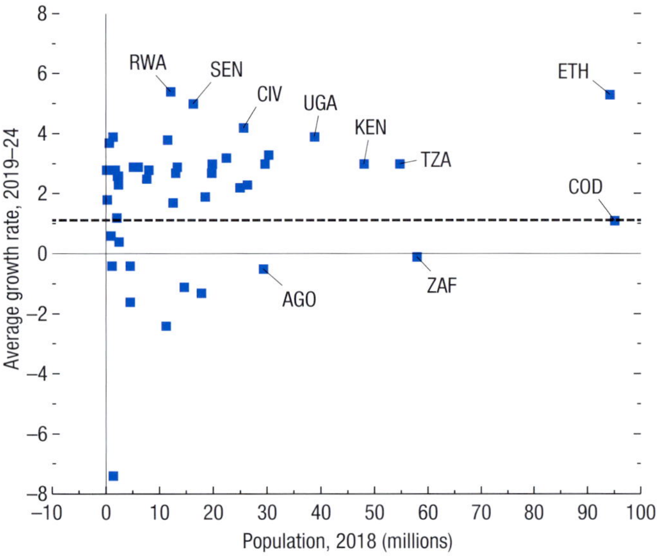

Sources: National statistical agencies; United Nations; and IMF staff estimates.
Note: The dashed line shows the weighted average per capita growth rate in sub-Saharan Africa during 2019–24. Nigeria is not shown on the chart as its population, estimated by the United Nations at about 196 million in 2018, is outside the *x*-axis range. Its average projected per capita growth rate in 2019–24 is about zero. Data labels use International Organization for Standardization (ISO) country codes.

over the next five years, implying that their income levels are set to fall further behind those economies. Figure 1.16 documents the heterogeneity in per capita growth rates in sub-Saharan Africa, where most countries are projected to grow at rates well above the weighted average for the region.

Inflation Outlook

Consistent with the softening of energy prices and the moderation in growth, consumer price inflation is expected to average 1.5 percent this year in advanced economies, down from 2.0 percent in 2018. With the US economy operating above potential, core consumer price inflation is projected at about 2.6 percent in 2020–21, above its medium-term value of 2.2 percent (the level consistent with the medium-term target of 2.0 percent for personal consumption expenditure inflation). Japan's core inflation rate (excluding fresh food and energy) is projected to rise to about 1 percent in 2019–20 due to the October consumption tax rate increase, inching up further to 1.2 percent in the medium term. Headline inflation is expected to rise gradually in the euro area, from 1.2 percent in 2019 to 1.4 percent in 2020.

Inflation in emerging market and developing economies excluding Venezuela is expected to inch down to 4.7 percent this year. Exceptions include Argentina, where inflation has increased on the back of the peso depreciation; Russia, where an increase in the value-added tax rate early in the year boosted inflation; and, to a lesser degree, China, in part due to rising pork prices. As inflation expectations become better anchored around targets in some economies and the pass-through from previous depreciations wanes further, inflation in the emerging market economy group is set to moderate to about 4.4 percent over the medium term.

External Sector Outlook

Trade Growth

After peaking in 2017 global trade growth slowed considerably in 2018 and the first half of 2019 and is projected at 1¼ percent in 2019. The slowdown reflects a confluence of factors, including a slowdown in investment, the impact of increased trade tensions on spending on capital goods (which are heavily traded), a tech cycle, and a sizable decline in trade in cars and car parts. Global trade growth is projected to recover to 3.2 percent in 2020 and 3.75 percent in subsequent years. The waning of some temporary factors, together with some recovery in global economic activity in 2020, buttressed by a gradual pickup in investment demand in emerging market and developing economies, should support the pickup in trade growth, offsetting the slowdown in capital spending in advanced economies that is projected for 2020 and beyond. However, there is sizable uncertainty concerning the future structure of value chains and the repercussions of tensions related to technology, and these could weigh on trade growth.

Current Account Positions

After widening marginally in 2018, primarily reflecting higher oil prices, global current account deficits and surpluses are projected to gradually narrow in 2019 and subsequent years (Figure 1.17). Among surplus countries, current account balances are projected to gradually decline in oil exporters, advanced European creditors, and advanced Asian economies in 2019 and into the medium term.

Figure 1.17. Global Current Account Balance
(Percent of world GDP)

Global current account deficits and surpluses are projected to gradually narrow in 2019 and subsequent years.

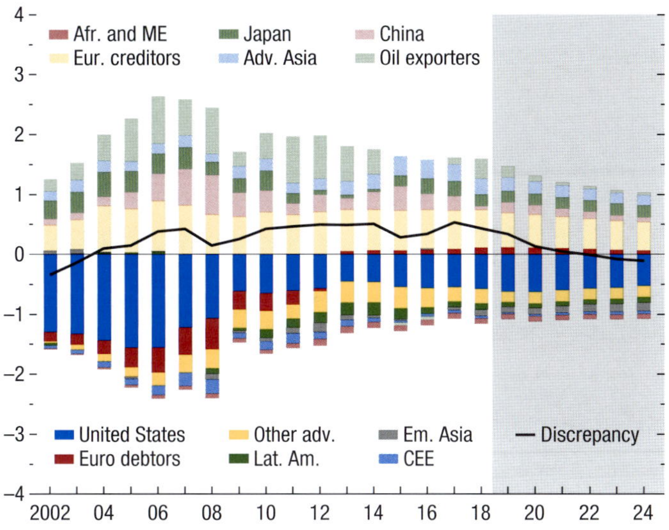

Source: IMF staff estimates.
Note: Adv. Asia = advanced Asia (Hong Kong SAR, Korea, Singapore, Taiwan Province of China); Afr. and ME = Africa and the Middle East (Democratic Republic of the Congo, Egypt, Ethiopia, Ghana, Jordan, Kenya, Lebanon, Morocco, South Africa, Sudan, Tanzania, Tunisia); CEE = central and eastern Europe (Belarus, Bulgaria, Croatia, Czech Republic, Hungary, Poland, Romania, Slovak Republic, Turkey, Ukraine); Em. Asia = emerging Asia (India, Indonesia, Pakistan, Philippines, Thailand, Vietnam); Eur. creditors = European creditors (Austria, Belgium, Denmark, Finland, Germany, Luxembourg, Netherlands, Norway, Sweden, Switzerland); Euro debtors = euro area debtors (Cyprus, Greece, Ireland, Italy, Portugal, Spain, Slovenia); Lat. Am. = Latin America (Argentina, Brazil, Chile, Colombia, Mexico, Peru, Uruguay); Oil exporters = Algeria, Azerbaijan, Iran, Kazakhstan, Kuwait, Nigeria, Oman, Qatar, Russia, Saudi Arabia, United Arab Emirates, Venezuela; Other adv. = other advanced economies (Australia, Canada, France, Iceland, New Zealand, United Kingdom).

The modest widening of China's current account surplus in 2019 is projected to be reversed in subsequent years as the rebalancing process continues. Current account deficits are projected to shrink in central and eastern Europe in 2019, reflecting the balancing of the current account in Turkey following a sharp reduction in domestic demand. After widening in 2019–20, driven by expansionary fiscal policy and a strengthening dollar, the US current account deficit is projected to shrink over the medium term as the growth rate of domestic demand declines.[3]

The recently imposed trade measures by the United States and retaliatory actions by trading partners are expected to have a limited impact on overall external imbalances (see the IMF's 2018 *External Sector Report* and Chapter 4 of the April 2019 WEO for a discussion of the relationship between trade costs and external imbalances).

As highlighted in the 2019 *External Sector Report*, many countries' current account imbalances in 2018 were too large in relation to country-specific norms consistent with underlying fundamentals and desirable policies. As shown in panel 1 of Figure 1.18, excess current account balances in 2019 are projected to decline modestly, with medium-term projections suggesting, on average, further movement in the same direction (Figure 1.18, panel 2).[4] At the same time, given that changes in macroeconomic fundamentals relative to 2018 affect not only current account balances but also their equilibrium values, the path of future excess imbalances cannot be precisely inferred from this exercise.[5]

International Investment Positions

Changes in international investment positions reflect both net financial flows and valuation changes arising from fluctuations in exchange rates and asset prices. Given that WEO projections assume broadly stable real effective exchange rates and limited variation in asset prices, changes in international investment positions are driven by projections for net external borrowing and lending (in line with the current account balance), with their ratios to domestic and world GDP affected by projected growth rates for individual countries and for the global economy as a whole.[6,7]

[3]Balance of payments data show a notable positive world current account discrepancy in recent years. This discrepancy is assumed to decline gradually during the forecast period, with projected global current account surpluses compressing more than global current account deficits.

[4]The change in the current account balance during 2019 is estimated to have offset, on average, about one-fifth of the 2018 current account gap; the change between 2018 and 2024 would offset less than half of the 2018 gap.

[5]For instance, an improvement in the terms of trade is typically associated with a more appreciated equilibrium exchange rate.

[6]WEO forecasts include projections of 10-year government bond yields, which would affect bond prices, but the impact of those changes in bond prices on the valuation of external assets and liabilities is typically not included in international investment position forecasts.

[7]In addition to changes in exchange rates, the decline in global equity prices in late 2018 (compared with levels at the end of 2017) implies deterioration of international investment positions at the end of 2018 in countries with significant net holdings of equity and foreign direct investment abroad, and a corresponding improvement in positions for countries with net equity liabilities.

Figure 1.18. Current Account Balances in Relation to Economic Fundamentals

Excess current account balances in 2019 are projected to decline modestly, with medium-term projections suggesting, on average, further movement in the same direction.

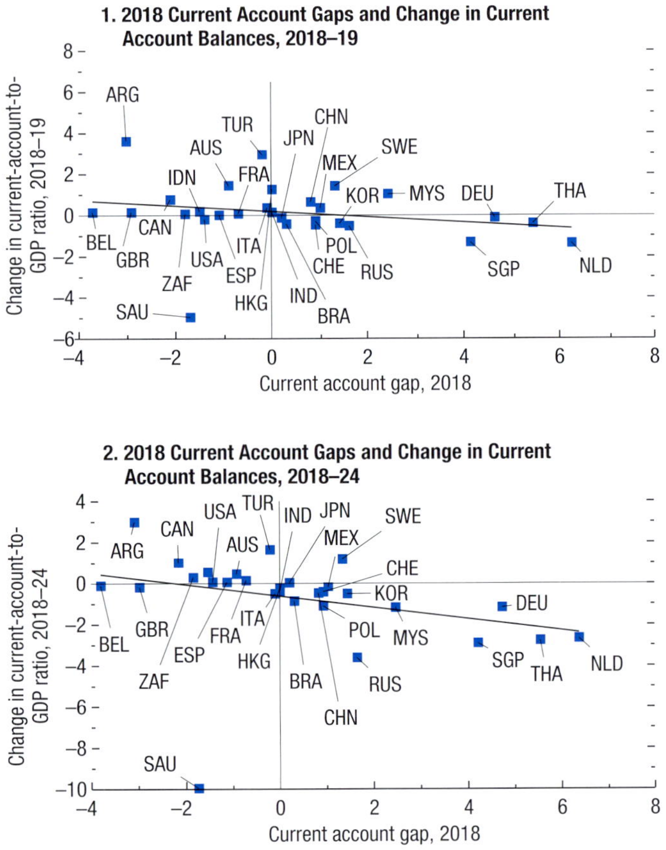

Source: IMF staff calculations.
Note: Data labels use International Organization for Standardization (ISO) country codes.

Figure 1.19. Net International Investment Position

Creditor and debtor positions as a share of world GDP are projected to widen slightly this year and then stabilize over the forecast horizon.

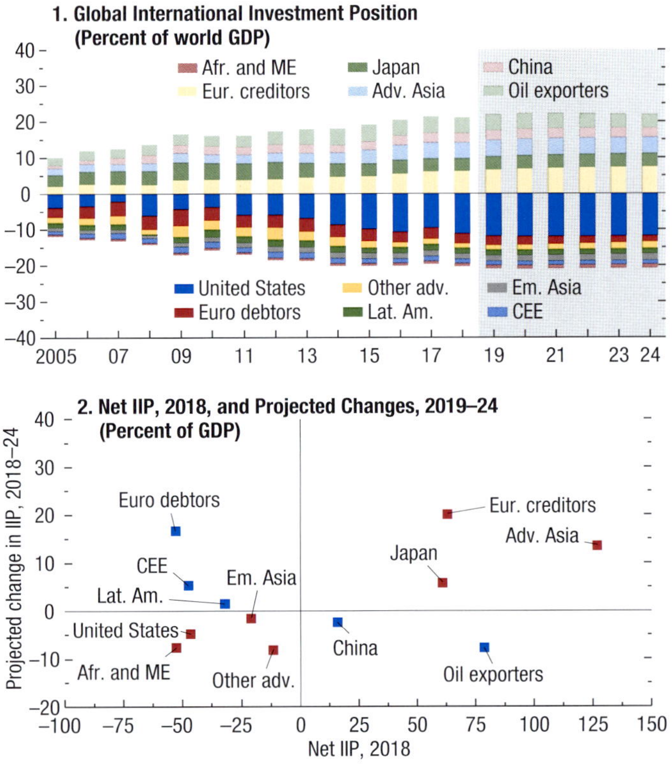

Source: IMF staff estimates.
Note: Adv. Asia = advanced Asia (Hong Kong SAR, Korea, Singapore, Taiwan Province of China); Afr. and ME = Africa and the Middle East (Democratic Republic of the Congo, Egypt, Ethiopia, Ghana, Jordan, Kenya, Lebanon, Morocco, South Africa, Sudan, Tanzania, Tunisia); CEE = central and eastern Europe (Belarus, Bulgaria, Croatia, Czech Republic, Hungary, Poland, Romania, Slovak Republic, Turkey, Ukraine); Em. Asia = emerging Asia (India, Indonesia, Pakistan, Philippines, Thailand, Vietnam); Eur. creditors = European creditors (Austria, Belgium, Denmark, Finland, Germany, Luxembourg, Netherlands, Norway, Sweden, Switzerland); Euro debtors = euro area debtors (Cyprus, Greece, Ireland, Italy, Portugal, Spain, Slovenia); IIP = international investment position; Lat. Am. = Latin America (Argentina, Brazil, Chile, Colombia, Mexico, Peru, Uruguay); Oil exporters = Algeria, Azerbaijan, Iran, Kazakhstan, Kuwait, Nigeria, Oman, Qatar, Russia, Saudi Arabia, United Arab Emirates, Venezuela; Other adv. = other advanced economies (Australia, Canada, France, Iceland, New Zealand, United Kingdom).

As panel 1 of Figure 1.19 shows, creditor and debtor positions as a share of world GDP are projected to widen slightly this year, and then to stabilize as a share of world GDP over the forecast horizon. On the creditor side, the growing creditor positions of a group of European advanced economies and—to a lesser extent—of advanced economies in Asia is partly offset by some reduction in the creditor position of China and oil exporters. On the debtor side, the net liability position of the United States increases initially and then stabilizes with the forecast reduction in its current account deficit as fiscal stimulus is withdrawn, while the position of euro area debtor countries improves further.

Similar trends are highlighted in panel 2 of Figure 1.19, which shows projected changes in net international investment positions as a percentage of domestic GDP across countries and regions between 2018 and 2024, the last year of the WEO projection horizon. The net creditor position is projected to be more than 80 percent GDP for European advanced economies, more than 65 percent for Japan, and more than 140 percent of GDP for smaller advanced economies in Asia, while the net creditor position of China would decline to about 12 percent. The debtor position of the United States is projected to rise to about 50 percent of GDP, some 5 percentage points above the 2018 estimate, while the net international investment position of a group of euro area debtor countries, including Italy and Spain, is expected to improve by more than 16 percentage points of their collective GDP.

Implications of Imbalances

Sustained excess external imbalances in key economies and policy actions that threaten to widen such imbalances pose risks to global stability. Expansionary fiscal policy in the United States is projected to increase the current account deficit over 2019–20, which could further aggravate trade tensions. Over the medium term, widening debtor positions in key economies could constrain global growth and possibly result in sharp and disruptive currency and asset price adjustments (see also the 2019 *External Sector Report*).

As discussed in the "Policy Priorities" section, the US economy—which is already operating beyond full employment—should implement a medium-term plan to reverse the rising ratio of public debt, accompanied by fiscal measures to gradually boost domestic supply potential. This would help ensure more sustainable growth dynamics and contain external imbalances. Stronger reliance on demand growth in some creditor countries, especially those such as Germany with the policy space to support it and facing a weakening of demand, would help facilitate domestic and global rebalancing while sustaining global growth over the medium term.

Risks: Skewed to the Downside

Risks around the baseline forecasts remain skewed to the downside. Though the recent easing of monetary policy in many countries could lift demand more than projected, especially if trade tensions between the United States and China ease and a no-deal Brexit is averted, downside risks seem to dominate the outlook. As discussed in the section on the Global Growth Outlook, about 70 percent of the projected 2020 pickup in global growth is accounted for by a small group of emerging market and developing economies in severe distress or currently underperforming relative to past averages. Moreover, the global forecast is predicated on continued steady growth in a number of emerging market economies that are expected to maintain relatively healthy performance, even as growth is projected to moderate in the United States and China. Global growth will fall short of the projected baseline if strains fail to dissipate in the stressed and underperforming economies, or if activity disappoints among the group of economies expected to maintain healthy rates of expansion.

Further disruptions to trade and supply chains: Tensions in trade and technology linkages have continued to ratchet up in recent months. Since the spring, financial markets have been buffeted by the broadening of US tariffs to all imports from China, restrictions placed by the United States on commerce with Chinese technology companies, and a greater perceived risk of a no-deal Brexit (see Scenario Box 1 of the April 2019 WEO for a discussion of the macroeconomic implications of the United Kingdom withdrawing from the European Union without a free trade deal). These developments have followed a sequence of tariff hikes and threats since early 2018 between the United States and China that have contributed to the generalized retreat in business confidence and investment and the marked slowdown in global trade, leading fiscal and monetary policymakers, in some cases, to deploy policy space to counter drags on confidence and demand. If tensions in these areas were to intensify, the harm to investment would deepen and could lead to dislocation of global supply chains as well as reduced technology spillovers, harming productivity and output growth into the medium term (see Scenario Box 1.1 for an analysis of the impact of advanced economy firms reshoring production in response to growing uncertainty on trade policies). The latest data on input-output linkages point to ever-more-interrelated technology, including the US technology sector's increasing dependence on imports of value added from Chinese producers (Figure 1.20). Trade policy uncertainty and barriers have risen more broadly, including with Japan and Korea imposing strengthened procedures for exports to one another. While these restrictions have had limited effects so far, an escalation of tensions could affect both economies significantly, with regional repercussions through technology sector supply chains.

As discussed above, still-resilient service sector activity is a relative bright spot in the global economy, particularly

Figure 1.20. Tech Hardware Supply Chains
(Percent)

Input-output linkages point to ever-more-interrelated technology, including the US technology sector's increasing dependence on imports of value added from Chinese producers.

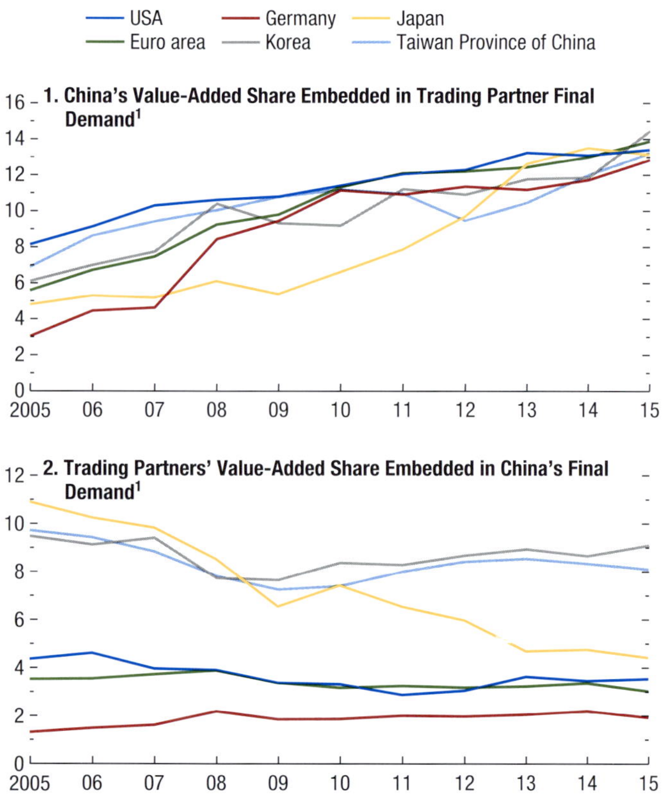

Source: Organisation for Economic Co-operation and Development, Trade in Value Added database.
[1]Computers, electronics, and electrical equipment.

among advanced economies. With protracted weakness in global manufacturing, business-facing services, such as logistics, finance, legal, and wholesale trading, are vulnerable to a softening in demand. Depending on the severity, firms in these services categories could cut back on hiring and weaken the feedback cycle between employment growth, consumer confidence, and consumer spending. Resultant lower demand for consumer-facing services, such as retail and hospitality, would dampen business sentiment among these categories and amplify the feedback to the labor market.

Abrupt declines in risk appetite: Amid easy monetary policy and supportive financial conditions in many economies, financial markets are susceptible to abrupt drops in sentiment. In recent months, rising tensions between the United States and China surrounding trade and technology companies triggered rapid declines in global risk appetite and flight to safe assets. Scenario Box 1.2—which updates the scenarios first presented in the October 2018 WEO to incorporate recent tariff measures—highlights the large effects of trade tensions on global growth via worsening financial market sentiment as well as productivity. Potential triggers for risk-off episodes remain plentiful. These include further increases in trade tensions; protracted fiscal policy uncertainty and worsening debt dynamics in some high-debt countries; an intensification of stress in large emerging markets currently undergoing difficult macroeconomic adjustment processes; a no-deal Brexit; or a sharper-than-expected slowdown in China, which is dealing with multiple drags on growth from trade tensions and needed domestic regulatory strengthening. An abrupt risk-off episode could expose financial vulnerabilities accumulated during years of low interest rates and depress global growth as highly leveraged borrowers find it difficult to roll over debt and as capital flows retrench from emerging market and frontier economies (see the October 2019 GFSR for further discussion on financial vulnerabilities).

Continued buildup of financial vulnerabilities: Muted inflation pressures have allowed central banks to ease policy in response to mounting downside risks to growth. These actions, together with shifts in market expectations regarding future policy moves, have helped ease financial conditions (possibly more than warranted by central bank communications, notably in the case of the market-implied path of the federal funds rate, which remains well below the Federal Open Market Committee's "dot plot" projection). While easier financial conditions have supported demand and employment, they could also lead to an underpricing of risk in some financial market segments. Insufficient regulatory and supervisory responses to risk underpricing in this context could allow for a further buildup of financial vulnerabilities, potentially amplifying the next downturn.

Threat of cyberattacks: Cyberattacks on financial infrastructure pose a threat to the outlook because they can severely disrupt cross-border payment systems and the flow of goods and services.

Disinflationary pressures: Concerns about disinflationary spirals eased during the cyclical upswing of mid-2016 to mid-2018. Slower global growth and a softening of core inflation across advanced and emerging market economies have revived this risk. Lower inflation and entrenched lower inflation expectations can increase the real costs of debt service for borrowers and weigh on corporate investment spending. By keeping nominal interest rates low, softer inflation would also constrain the monetary policy space that central banks have to counter downturns, meaning that growth could be persistently lower for any given adverse shock.

Geopolitical tensions, domestic political uncertainty, and conflict: Perceived changes in the direction of policies in some countries and elevated uncertainty regarding reforms have been weighing on investment and growth. At the same time, some geopolitical risk factors discussed in previous WEOs have become more salient—notably rising tensions in the Persian Gulf following attacks on major oil refining facilities in Saudi Arabia, which have added to broader conflict in the Middle East—and tensions in east Asia (Figures 1.21 and 1.22). These factors in isolation may not have a strong impact on growth beyond the countries directly affected, but an accumulation of such events—combined with trade tensions and tighter global financial conditions—could have outsized effects on sentiment that are felt on a broader scale. At the same time, ongoing civil strife in many countries raises the risks of horrific humanitarian costs, migration strains in neighboring countries, and—together with geopolitical tensions—higher volatility in commodity markets.

Climate change: Mitigating the serious threats posed by climate change to health and livelihoods in many countries requires a rapid transition to a low-carbon economy on an ambitious scale (Chapter 2 of the *Fiscal Monitor*). However, domestic mitigation policy strategies are failing to muster wide societal support in some countries, while international cooperation is diluted by large emitters declining to participate (see Commodities Special Feature Box 1.SF.1 for more discussion on emissions). The Intergovernmental Panel on Climate Change warned in October 2018 that, at current rates of increase, global warming could reach 1.5°C above preindustrial levels between 2030

Figure 1.21. Policy Uncertainty and Trade Tensions
(Index)

Global economic policy uncertainty remains elevated.

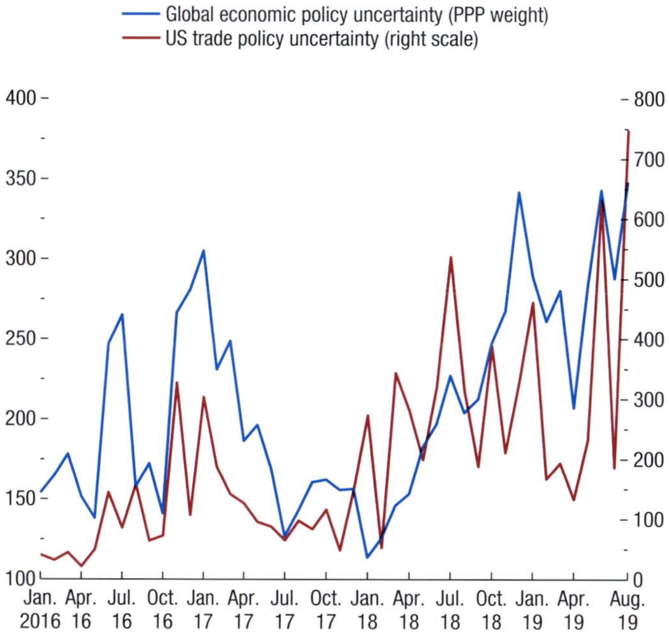

Source: Baker, Bloom, and Davis (2016).
Note: Baker Bloom Davis Index of Global Economic Policy Uncertainty (GEPU) is a GDP-weighted average of national EPU indices for 20 countries: Australia, Brazil, Canada, Chile, China, France, Germany, Greece, India, Ireland, Italy, Japan, Korea, Mexico, the Netherlands, Russia, Spain, Sweden, the United Kingdom, and the United States. Mean of global economic policy uncertainty index from 1997 to 2015 = 100; mean of US trade policy uncertainty index from 1985 to 2010 = 100. PPP = purchasing power parity.

Figure 1.22. Geopolitical Risk Index
(Index)

High geopolitical tension raises the risk of severe humanitarian costs and intensifying economic strains in some regions.

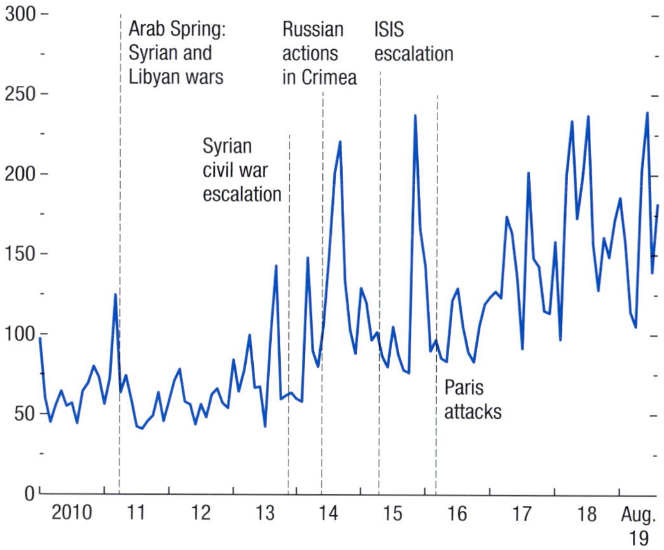

Source: Caldara and Iacoviello (2018).
Note: The Caldara and Iacoviello Geopolitical Risk (GPR) index reflects automated text-search results of the electronic archives of 11 national and international newspapers. The index is calculated by counting the number of articles related to geopolitical risk in each newspaper for each month (as a share of the total number of news articles) and normalized to average a value of 100 in the 2000–09 decade. ISIS = Islamic State.

and 2052, accompanied by extremes of temperature, precipitation, and drought. Given the uncertainties, the climate could warm faster, engendering more catastrophic outcomes, which would have devastating humanitarian effects and inflict severe, persistent output losses across many economies. Climate change may also exacerbate inequality within countries, even in advanced economies, which are expected to be more adaptable (see Chapter 2, Box 2.2).

Globally consistent risk assessment of the WEO forecast: Confidence bands for the WEO forecast are obtained using the G20MOD module of the IMF's Flexible System of Global Models.[8] The confidence bands for the WEO forecast for most regions are asymmetric, skewed toward lower growth than in the baseline. This reflects both the preponderance of negative growth surprises in the past and limited monetary policy space available to offset negative growth shocks as interest rates in most advanced economies are at or close to their effective lower bounds.[9] The resulting risk assessment can also be used to calculate the probability of a global economic downturn. The estimated probability of one-year-ahead global growth below 2.5 percent—the 10th percentile of global growth outturns in the past 25 years—has increased since the spring and now stands at close to 9 percent (Figure 1.23).

Figure 1.23. Probability of One-Year-Ahead Global Growth of Less than 2.5 Percent
(Percent)

The estimated probability of one-year-ahead global growth below 2.5 percent—the 10th percentile of global growth outturns in the past 25 years—has increased since the spring.

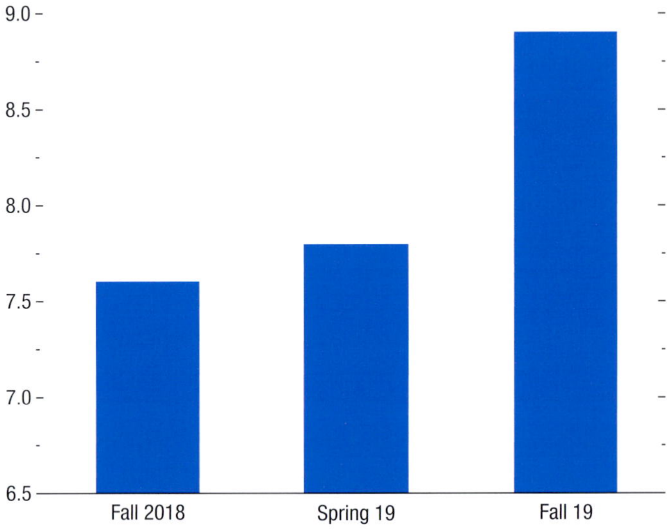

Source: IMF staff estimates.
Note: Probabilities are calculated using the G20MOD module of the IMF's Flexible System of Global Models. G20MOD is a global, structural model of the world economy, capturing international spillovers and key economic relationships among the household, corporate, and government sectors, including monetary policy.

Policy Priorities

The global economy remains at a delicate juncture. Even if the threats discussed in the previous section are thwarted, as assumed in the baseline, per capita growth is projected to stay below past norms across most groups, except in sub-Saharan Africa, over the medium term. Moreover, conditions are very challenging for a number of emerging market economies that need to adjust their macroeconomic policies sharply.

As discussed in the section on the Global Growth Outlook, the world economy is confronting a diverse set of headwinds. These headwinds affect countries differently, adding to idiosyncratic factors and varied cyclical positions, meaning that policy objectives and priorities vary widely across countries. A common thread and the foremost priority, in many cases, is to remove policy-induced uncertainty or threats to growth. Policy missteps at this juncture, such as a no-deal Brexit or a further deepening of trade disputes, could severely undermine sentiment, growth, and job creation and may exhaust policy space for avoidable reasons.

Multilateral Policies

Multilateral cooperation is indispensable for tackling some of the short- and long-term issues that threaten the sustainability and inclusiveness of

[8]G20MOD is a global, structural model of the world economy, capturing international spillovers and key economic relationships among the household, corporate, and government sectors, including monetary policy.

[9]Using the model to provide a risk assessment of the forecast is done in two steps. First, the model is used to solve for economic shocks that drove the world economy in the past. Historically, the key drivers of the cyclical dynamics of output, inflation, and interest rates were domestic demand and oil price shocks. Second, these estimated shocks are then used to generate a large number of counter-factual scenarios for the world economy by sampling five-year histories from their empirical joint distribution function. The resulting joint predictive distribution for a rich set of economic variables is internally and globally consistent and is suitable for risk assessment both at the global and individual-country level.

global growth. The most pressing needs for greater cooperation are in the areas of trade and technology. Likewise, closer multilateral cooperation on international taxation, global financial regulatory reform, climate change, and corruption would help address vulnerabilities and broaden the gains from economic integration.

Trade and technology: Policymakers should work together to reduce trade tensions, which have weakened global activity and hurt confidence. They should also expeditiously resolve uncertainty around changes to long-standing trade arrangements (including those between the United Kingdom and the European Union as well as between Canada, Mexico, and the United States). Countries should not use tariffs to target bilateral trade balances. More fundamentally, trade conflicts signal deeper frustrations with gaps in the rules-based multilateral trading system. Policymakers should cooperatively address the roots of dissatisfaction with the system and improve the governance of trade. This requires resolving the deadlock over the World Trade Organization (WTO) dispute settlement system's appellate body to ensure the continued enforcement of existing WTO rules; modernizing WTO rules to encompass areas such as e-commerce, subsidies, and technology transfer; and advancing negotiations in new areas, such as digital trade. The idea that all countries need to participate in all negotiations could be reconsidered, potentially allowing countries that wish to move further and faster to do so, while keeping new agreements inside the WTO and open to all its members. At the least, calling a truce on further escalation of trade barriers would avoid injecting more destabilizing forces into a slowing global economy. Policymakers should also cooperate more closely to curb cross-border cyberattacks on national security and commercial entities, as well as limit distortionary practices, such as requiring companies to hand over their intellectual property in return for market access. Without definite progress in these areas, technology tensions are likely to intensify, impeding the free flow of ideas across countries and potentially impairing long-term productivity growth.

International taxation: With the rise of multinational enterprises, international tax competition has made it increasingly difficult for governments to tackle tax evasion and collect revenue needed to finance their budgets. Efforts to minimize cross-border opportunities for tax evasion and avoidance, such as the Organisation for Economic Co-operation and Development–G20 Base Erosion and Profit Shifting initiative (see Box 1.3 of the April 2019 *Fiscal Monitor*), should be reinforced. As discussed in IMF (2019), this initiative has made significant progress in international tax cooperation, but vulnerabilities remain. Limitations of the arm's-length principle—under which transactions between related parties are to be priced as if they were between independent entities—and reliance on notions of physical presence of the taxpayer to establish a legal basis to impose income tax have allowed apparently profitable firms to pay little tax. Some improvements can be achieved unilaterally or regionally, but more fundamental solutions require stronger institutions for global cooperation.

Financial regulatory reforms and global financial safety net: The reform agenda begun after the global financial crisis is still unfinished. Some areas of progress—such as greater supervisory intensity for globally important financial institutions and more effective resolution regimes—are under pressure or being reversed. Policymakers should ensure the reform agenda is completed, including through enhanced international resolution frameworks and further improvements to macroprudential policy frameworks (which may entail simplification of complex rules in some areas, as discussed in Adrian and Obstfeld 2017). Emerging risks to cybersecurity in the financial system, and combating money laundering and the financing of terrorism, also require coordinated and collective action. Complementing these moves, policymakers should ensure that the global financial safety net is adequately resourced to help counteract disruptive portfolio adjustments in a world economy heavily laden with debt and reduce the need for countries to self-insure against external shocks.

Climate change and migration: Curbing greenhouse gas emissions and containing the associated consequences of rising global temperatures and devastating climate events are urgent global imperatives.[10] In that respect, the ongoing political polarization and discord in many economies does not bode well for reaching agreement on domestic and international strategies in time to contain climate change to manageable levels. A redoubling of efforts is urgently needed, which will require a distribution of the costs and benefits in a

[10]See Chapter 3 of the October 2017 WEO on the macroeconomic impacts of weather shocks and IMF (2019) and Chapter 2 of the October 2019 *Fiscal Monitor* for a discussion of fiscal policy options for implementing climate change mitigation and adaptation strategies.

manner than can muster sufficient domestic and international political support. By adding to migrant flows, climate-related events also compound an already-complex situation of refugee flight from conflict areas. International migration will become increasingly important, too, as many advanced economies confront issues related to aging populations. International cooperation would facilitate the integration of migrants—and, so, help to maximize the labor supply and productivity benefits they bring to destination countries—and to support remittance flows that lessen the burden on source countries.

Corruption and governance: A global effort is also needed to curb corruption, which is undermining faith in government and institutions in many countries (see the April 2019 *Fiscal Monitor*). Left unchecked, pervasive corruption can lead to distorted policies, lower revenue, declining quality of public services, and deteriorating infrastructure.

Country-Level Policies

In response to continued weakness and downside risks, macroeconomic policies—particularly monetary policy—have already turned more supportive in many countries. Looking ahead, macroeconomic policies in most economies should seek to stabilize activity and strengthen the foundations for a recovery or continued growth. Where fiscal space is available and growth has decelerated sharply, more active fiscal policy support—including through greater public investment in workforce skills and infrastructure to raise growth potential—may be warranted. Making growth more inclusive and avoiding protracted downturns that disproportionately affect the most vulnerable segments of population are essential for securing better economic prospects for all. Strengthening resilience to adverse shifts in financial market sentiment and alleviating structural constraints on potential output growth also remain overarching needs.

Advanced Economies

For advanced economies, where growth in final demand is generally subdued, inflation pressure is muted, and market-pricing-implied measures of inflation expectations have softened in recent months, accommodative monetary policy remains appropriate to guard against a further deceleration in activity and a downshift in inflation expectations. This is especially important in economies with inflation persistently below target and output that already is, or may fall below, potential. As discussed in Box 1.4, the sluggishness in inflation suggests that potential output could be higher and output gaps could be more negative than currently estimated. However, given that continued monetary accommodation can foster a buildup of financial vulnerabilities, stronger macroprudential policies and a proactive supervisory approach will be critical. As discussed in the October 2019 GFSR, financial sector policies should aim to secure the strength of balance sheets and limit systemic risks by deploying such tools as liquidity buffers, countercyclical capital buffers, or targeted sectoral capital buffers; developing borrower-based tools to mitigate debt vulnerabilities where needed; and enhancing macroprudential oversight of nonbank financial institutions. In some countries, bank balance sheets need further repair to mitigate the risk of sovereign-bank feedback loops. Avoiding a rollback of postcrisis regulatory reforms is of essence in the context of continued monetary policy accommodation and high debt levels.

Considering the precarious outlook and large downside risks, fiscal policy can play a more active role, especially where room to ease monetary policy is limited. The low level of policy rates in many countries and the decline in long-term interest rates to historically very low or negative levels, while reducing the likely impact of further monetary policy easing, expands fiscal room as long as these conditions last. In this context, in countries where activity has weakened or could decelerate sharply, fiscal stimulus can be provided if fiscal space exists and fiscal policy is not already overly expansionary. In countries where demand is weak, yet fiscal consolidation is necessary, its pace could be slowed if market conditions permit, to avoid prolonged economic weakness and disinflationary dynamics. Policymakers would need to prepare for a contingent fiscal policy response, in advance, to be able to act quickly and plan ahead for the appropriate composition of fiscal easing. Infrastructure spending or investment incentives (including for clean energy sources) would be ideal as they would boost output not only in the near term but also in the medium term, helping to improve debt sustainability. More generally, modest medium-term potential output in most advanced economies calls for the composition of fiscal spending and taxes to be calibrated carefully, with a view to raising labor force participation rates and productivity growth through public investment in workforce skills, physical infrastructure, and research and development.

National structural policies that encourage more open and flexible markets in advanced economies would not only boost economic resilience and potential output, but could also help reduce within-country disparities in performance and improve the labor market adjustment to shocks by lagging regions within countries (see Chapter 2). There is also a pressing need to reduce carbon emissions to avert the severe economic and social risks associated with climate change. Moving toward less-carbon-intensive production structures—including through carbon taxation, boosting low-carbon infrastructure, and encouraging innovation in green technologies (see Chapter 2 of the October 2019 *Fiscal Monitor*)—are therefore necessary. Beyond fiscal measures to boost potential output, protecting opportunities and dynamism—by ensuring that competition policies facilitate new-firm entry and curb incumbents' abuse of market power—remains vital when a minority of big firms are capturing increasingly larger market shares in advanced economies (Chapter 2 of the April 2019 WEO).

In the *United States*, where the unemployment rate is historically low and inflation is close to target, a combination of accommodative monetary policy, vigilant financial regulation and supervision, and a gradual fiscal consolidation path would help maintain the expansion and limit downside risks. The absence of strong wage and inflation pressures (inflation has averaged just below target over the past year, and expectations have recently softened) has allowed the Federal Reserve to reduce the federal funds rate to guard against downside risks from the global economy. The path of the policy interest rate going forward should depend on the economic outlook and risks, as informed by incoming data. Supportive financial conditions require maintaining the current risk-based approach to regulation, supervision, and resolution (and strengthening it in the case of nonbank financial institutions) to limit vulnerabilities from rising corporate leverage and emerging cybersecurity threats. Public debt remains on a clear upward trajectory, calling for consolidation. There is a need to raise the revenue-to-GDP ratio by putting in place a broad-based carbon tax, a federal consumption tax, and a higher federal gas tax. Doing so would create the fiscal space to provide support to low- and middle-income families (including through help with childcare expenses and smoothing out the existing "cliffs" in social benefits) and to pursue policies that raise potential growth—infrastructure investment (including to facilitate the supply of green energy alternatives), support for lifelong learning and workforce skills, and steps to raise labor force participation. Counteracting the anticipated rise in aging-related spending requires indexing social security benefits to chained inflation and raising the retirement age.

In the *United Kingdom*, desired policy settings in the near term will depend on the ultimate form of the country's departure from the European Union. The extra public spending envisaged by the government should mitigate the cost of Brexit for the economy, but continued efforts to bring down the debt ratio remain important to build buffers against future shocks. In case of a disorderly Brexit accompanied by a sharp rise in barriers to goods and services trade with the European Union, the policy response will need to take into account the extent of the adverse financial market reaction and its likely impact on macroeconomic stability. Structural reforms should focus on improving infrastructure quality and boosting labor skills as well as ensuring smooth reallocation of workers to expanding sectors from those adversely affected by Brexit.

In the *euro area*, monetary policy has become appropriately more accommodative in response to stubbornly weak core inflation and a significant loss of momentum since mid-2018. The fiscal stance, though ideally more supportive than envisaged before the slowdown, needs to vary across countries depending on the extent of fiscal space. In *Germany*, where there is room to ease fiscal policy and growth has been weak, raising public investment in physical and human capital or reducing the labor tax wedge would boost demand, help reduce the excess current account surplus, and strengthen potential output. In countries with high debt, including *France, Italy*, and *Spain*, fiscal buffers should be rebuilt gradually while protecting investment. Credibly committing to a downward-sloping debt path over the medium term is particularly critical in Italy, where debt and gross financing needs are large. If growth were to weaken significantly, countries with fiscal space would need to use it more actively to complement monetary easing to guard against disinflationary dynamics and a prolonged period of weak growth. In parallel, the path of fiscal consolidation could be adjusted temporarily in countries where fiscal space is at risk, provided their financing conditions remain amenable and debt sustainability is not jeopardized. A synchronized fiscal response, albeit differentiated appropriately across member countries, can amplify the area-wide impact. Completing the banking union and continuing the cleanup of bank balance sheets remain vital for raising resilience and strengthening credit intermediation in some economies. Amid prolonged monetary accommodation and disparate cyclical positions, regulators need to calibrate macroprudential instruments to address any emergent financial stability risks. Reforms are urgently needed in many economies to lift productivity and competitiveness. Further deepening the single market for services would boost efficiency across the European Union. EU-level instruments can be used to foster reform efforts at the national level. Raising labor market flexibility, removing barriers to entry in product markets, upgrading the functioning of corporate insolvency regimes, and cutting administrative burdens are cross-cutting needs.

In *Japan*, demand is expected to slow from its recent strong pace following the October consumption tax rate increase, while government mitigating measures will moderate the decline. Inflation remains well below the central bank's target. Sustained monetary accommodation will be necessary over a long period to durably lift inflation expectations. Fiscal policy should be geared toward long-term fiscal sustainability amid a rapidly aging and shrinking population while protecting demand and the reflation effort. Averting fiscal risks over the long term requires additional increases in the consumption tax rate and reforms to curb pension, health, and long-term-care spending. Some progress has been made on structural reforms with the adoption of the Work Style Reform that aims at improving working conditions, a new residency status for foreign workers with professional and technical skills, and further trade integration with the European Union and the economies comprising the Comprehensive and Progressive Agreement for Trans-Pacific Partnership. More effort is needed on labor market reform—including to improve workers' skills and career opportunities for nonregular workers, reduce duality, and raise mobility—and in product market and corporate reforms to lift productivity and investment.

Emerging Market and Developing Economies

The circumstances of emerging market and developing economies are diverse. Some economies are experiencing extremely challenging conditions because of political discord or cross-border conflict; others are experiencing tight external financing conditions, given their macroeconomic imbalances and needed policy adjustments. Among countries facing more stable conditions, the recent softening of inflation has given central banks the option of easing monetary policy to support activity. Against a volatile external backdrop and possible adverse turns in market sentiment, ensuring financial resilience is a key objective for many emerging market and developing economies. Regulation and supervision should ensure adequate capital and liquidity buffers to guard against disruptive shifts in global portfolios and a possible deterioration in growth and credit quality. Efforts to monitor and minimize currency and maturity mismatches on balance sheets are also vital to preserve financial stability and will help exchange rates to cushion against shocks. In the many economies with high public debt, fiscal policy should generally aim for consolidation to contain borrowing costs and create space to counter future downturns as well as to address development needs, while adjusting its pace and timing to avoid prolonged weakness. Improving the targeting of subsidies, rationalizing recurrent expenditure, and broadening the revenue base can help preserve investments needed to boost potential growth and social spending—on education, health care, and safety net policies. Revenue mobilization is particularly important in low-income developing countries that need to advance toward the United Nations Sustainable Development Goals.

Beyond getting the mix of macroeconomic and financial policies right, many emerging market and developing economies can strengthen their institutions, governance, and policy frameworks through structural reforms to bolster their growth prospects and resilience. Indeed, the key findings of Chapter 3 make a strong case for a renewed structural reform push in emerging market and developing economies. The chapter documents that much scope remains for further reforms in domestic and external finance, trade, labor and product market regulations, and governance in these countries, especially in low-income developing countries. The chapter finds that, for a typical economy, major simultaneous reforms across these areas could add 1 percentage point to growth over 5–10 years, roughly doubling the speed of convergence.

In *China*, the overarching policy objective is to raise the sustainability and quality of growth while navigating headwinds from trade tensions and weaker global demand. Meeting this goal calls for short-term action to support the economy while making progress with shifting the underlying sources of growth from credit-fueled investment toward private consumption, and improving the allocation of resources and efficiency in the economy. In addition to some monetary easing, fiscal support (financed mainly on-budget) has prevented trade tensions from exerting a sharp drag on confidence and activity. Any further stimulus should emphasize targeted transfers to low-income households, rather than large-scale infrastructure spending. In support of the transition to sustainable growth, regulatory efforts to restrain shadow banking have helped lessen reliance on debt, but corporate leverage remains high and household debt is growing rapidly. Further progress with reining in debt requires continued scaling back of widespread implicit guarantees and enhancing the macroprudential toolkit. Meanwhile, continuing with reducing the role of state-owned enterprises and lowering barriers to entry in such sectors as telecommunications and banking would help raise productivity while improving labor mobility. Moving toward a more progressive tax code and higher spending on health care, education, and social transfers would help lower precautionary saving and support consumption.

In *India*, monetary policy and broad-based structural reforms should be used to address cyclical weakness and strengthen confidence. A credible fiscal consolidation path is needed to bring down India's elevated public debt over the medium term. This should be supported by subsidy-spending rationalization and tax-base enhancing measures. Governance of public sector banks and the efficiency of their credit allocation needs strengthening, and the public sector's role in the financial system needs to be reduced. Reforms to hiring and dismissal regulations would help incentivize job creation and absorb the country's large demographic dividend. Land reforms should also be enhanced to encourage and expedite infrastructure development.

In *Brazil*, pension reform is an essential step toward ensuring the viability of the social security system and the sustainability of public debt. Further gradual fiscal consolidation will be needed to comply with the constitutional expenditure ceiling over the next few years. Monetary policy should remain accommodative to support economic growth, provided that inflation expectations remain anchored. To lift potential growth, the government will need to pursue an ambitious reform agenda, including tax reforms, trade openness, and infrastructure investment.

In *Mexico*, adherence to the government's medium-term fiscal consolidation plan is essential to preserve market confidence and stabilize public debt. More ambitious medium-term fiscal targets would create larger buffers to respond to negative shocks and better deal with long-term spending pressure from demographic trends. If inflation remains on a downward path toward the target and inflation expectations are anchored, monetary policy could become more accommodative in the coming months. The exchange rate should remain flexible, with foreign-exchange intervention being used only if market conditions are disorderly.

In *Russia*, the authorities should move toward a more growth-friendly composition of taxes and public spending while refraining from using the National Welfare Fund for quasi-fiscal activities. Monetary policy can be eased toward a neutral stance if inflationary pressures continue to abate. To enhance the efficiency of credit intermediation, the authorities should continue to consolidate the banking sector while reducing the state's footprint. Further structural reforms are needed to boost potential growth, including measures to enhance competition, improve public procurement, and reform the labor market.

In *Turkey*, a comprehensive and clearly communicated policy plan is needed to repair private balance sheets; increase public balance sheet transparency; and ultimately restore the credibility, independence, and rules-based functioning of economic institutions. To achieve these goals, the policy agenda should include (1) keeping monetary policy rates on hold until there is a durable downturn in inflation and inflation expectations, which would also help underpin the lira and rebuild reserves; (2) steps to bolster medium-term fiscal strength; (3) restoring confidence in banks through thorough assessment (third-party asset quality reviews, rigorous stress tests), credible bank recapitalization plans, and reining in state bank credit; (4) further improving the insolvency regime and the out-of-court restructuring framework to promote meaningful restructuring solutions and free up lending capacity to healthy and productive firms; and (5) focusing structural reforms to support more sustainable, total-factor-productivity-led growth.

In *South Africa*, gradual but meaningful and growth-friendly fiscal consolidation is needed to stabilize public debt. Measures should include reducing the public wage bill, downsizing and eliminating wasteful spending by public entities, expanding the tax base, and strengthening tax administration. Monetary policy should continue to be data-dependent and carefully monitor inflation risks. Structural reforms are needed to regain investors' trust, lift growth potential, and foster job creation. Priorities include revamping the business models of state-owned enterprises, improving competition in the product market by reducing entry barriers and streamlining regulations, and increasing labor market flexibility.

Low-income countries share many of the policy priorities of the emerging market economy group, especially in enhancing resilience to volatile external conditions. Several "frontier" low-income countries have seen external financing conditions fluctuate sharply in the past year. Strengthening monetary and macroprudential policy frameworks while preserving exchange rate flexibility will help them withstand this environment. During the recent period of low interest rates, public debt stocks in this group have increased rapidly. When financial conditions turn less accommodative, rollover risks may rise, and wider sovereign spreads may lead to higher borrowing costs for firms and households. Fiscal policy should be geared toward ensuring debt sustainability while protecting measures that help the vulnerable and support progress toward the United Nations Sustainable Development Goals. This requires broadening the revenue base; improving tax administration; eliminating wasteful subsidies; and prioritizing spending on infrastructure, health care, education, and poverty reduction. Low-income countries also bear the brunt of natural disasters and increasing climate change. Lowering the fallout from these events will require adaptation strategies that invest in disaster readiness and climate-smart infrastructure, incorporate appropriate technologies and zoning regulations, and deploy well-targeted social safety nets to help reduce vulnerability and improve countries' ability to respond.

Commodity-exporting developing economies have similar policy priorities, but face additional pressure on their public finances from the subdued outlook for commodity prices. Beyond placing public finances on a sustainable footing, economies in this group also need to diversify away from dependence on resource extraction and refining. Although country circumstances differ, policies to help achieve this broad goal include sound macroeconomic management; lifting of education quality and worker skills to encourage more broad-based labor force participation; investment to reduce infrastructure shortfalls; boosting of financial development and inclusion; strengthening of property rights, contract enforcement; and reduction of trade barriers to incentivize the entry of firms and private investment.

Scenario Box 1.1. Implications of Advanced Economies Reshoring Some Production

Activity would suffer in advanced and emerging market economies if production were reshored to advanced economies that could not match the efficiency and lower labor costs of the abandoned foreign value chains. If multinational firms absorb some of the implications by allowing margins to be squeezed, it could soften the implications. However, a possibly more likely outcome is that a less open global economy could constrain technology diffusion, causing activity to fall further.

The IMF's Global Integrated Monetary and Fiscal Model is used here to examine the implications of multinational firms reshoring production to advanced economies. This reshoring could be motivated by a desire to keep some production closer to final consumers to avoid potential supply chain disruptions from developments in distant countries or by policy actions closer to home. A very stylized experiment is considered, designed to illustrate the implications and highlight the possible channels through which they could play out.

The assumption is that, over a three-year horizon, multinational firms in the United States, the euro area, and Japan reshore enough production that their nominal imports decline by 10 percent (blue line in Scenario Figure 1.1.1). Given the relative costs of production, reshoring leads to higher-priced consumption and investment goods in advanced economies. Domestic demand declines, as does output, despite the decline in imports.[1] In emerging market economies, lower production and exports reduce incomes, households and firms cut expenditure, and output declines more modestly than in advanced economies. However, households in both advanced and emerging market economies suffer equally, owing to the deterioration in emerging market economies' terms of trade. Advanced economy exchange rates appreciate, raising the real cost of emerging market economies' imports. More emerging market production must be exported to pay for their import bundle, leaving less for domestic consumption.

[1]It is worth noting that, in sectors where domestic production expands, employment could increase; here, however, the aggregate net impact is shown, which is negative.

Scenario Figure 1.1.1. Advanced Economies Reshoring
(Percent deviation from control)

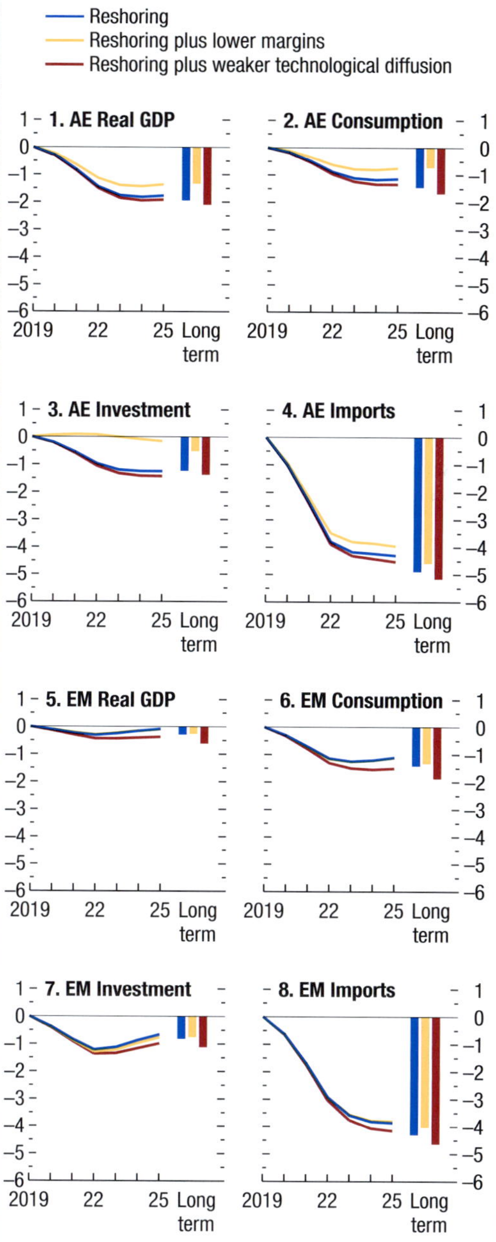

Source: IMF staff estimates.
Note: AE = advanced economy; EM = emerging market.

Scenario Box 1.1 *(continued)*

One possible response of multinational firms might be to not pass on the higher production costs fully and, so, allow their profit margins to be squeezed (yellow line). Moderating the resulting price increase helps maintain household consumption and supports investment as firms need more capital to produce the additional goods. The extent to which firms would compress margins is highly uncertain, and the modest reduction considered here is for illustrative purposes only. The more margins are squeezed, the less harmful is the impact of reshoring on advanced economies. However, lower margins do little to ameliorate the impact on emerging markets.

Although reductions in profit margins could offset some of the negative implications of reshoring, a less favorable implication of a more closed global economy could be less technological diffusion. Empirical evidence points to trade openness as a key driver of technological diffusion.[2] If multinational firms shorten supply chains by producing more goods closer to final consumers in advanced economies, emerging markets could have much less access to the latest technological developments. This box considers modest temporary reductions in productivity growth in tradable goods sectors (red line) that are a function of a country's or region's distance from the productivity frontier and relative openness (0.1 percentage point for advanced economies, 0.25 percentage point for emerging markets).[3] Weaker technological diffusion would notably amplify the negative implications for emerging markets and modestly exacerbate the impact on advanced economies.

[2]See "Is Productivity Growth Shared in a Globalized Economy?" in Chapter 4 of the April 2018 *World Economic Outlook*.

[3]A temporary decline in productivity growth is assumed. However, it is possible that a more closed global economy could lead to some lasting damage to productivity growth. If that were the case, the longer-term implications would be much worse than those estimated here.

Scenario Box 1.2. Trade Tensions: Updated Scenario

Updates of the estimated impact of ongoing global trade tensions on economies are generated here using the IMF's Global Integrated Monetary and Fiscal Model (GIMF). Inputs to the model's simulations include explicit tariff measures and off-model analysis of the possible impact of confidence effects on investment, financial conditions for firms, and productivity developments that result when resources are reallocated across economies. Given that all of the tariff measures considered in these simulations are incorporated in the baseline projections of this *World Economic Outlook* (WEO), their impact on global GDP should be interpreted as relative to a no-tariff baseline (such as the one in the October 2017 WEO).[1]

The first three layers (out of six) of the analysis estimate the direct trade impacts of tariff measures, both implemented and announced. All of the measures are assumed to be permanent. The first layer contains the impact of implemented tariff measures included in the April 2019 WEO baseline. Among them are tariffs that the United States imposed on aluminum and steel, 25 percentage points in tariffs on $50 billion in imports from China, and 10 percentage points in tariffs on an additional $200 billion in imports from China. All retaliatory measures by US trading partners are included in this layer. The second layer adds the impact of the May 2019 US tariff increase of $200 billion on Chinese imports and China's retaliation. The third layer adds the US imposition of 15 percentage points in tariffs on all goods from China (roughly $300 billion) that had not yet incurred tariffs, starting in September 2019, and a 5 percentage-point increase on the already-tariffed $250 billion in imports from China. China's retaliation is included in this layer.

The remaining three layers are based on off-model analysis. The fourth layer adds the potential impact on investment of declining confidence. This is the same temporary effect that is included in the October 2018 WEO analysis of the impact of trade tensions on investment via confidence effects.[2] However, the timing has been altered to more closely match changes in timing of implementation of tariff measures from that assumed in 2018. The peak impact on activity is delayed, given that the tariff measures were imposed later than had been assumed. The fifth layer adds the impact on corporate spreads of the potential market reaction to the trade tensions. The size of the impact is identical to that used in the October 2018 WEO, but the timing is adjusted to match the delayed implementation of the tariff measures. The peak in the increase in corporate bond spreads now occurs in 2020, one year later than assumed in the October 2018 WEO analysis.[3] The final layer adds the potential impact on productivity resulting from the reallocation of resources across sectors within economies. This layer is new and is not included in the analysis in the October 2018 WEO. The impact of tariff measures in GIMF captures the macroeconomic distortions that tariffs induce in the utilization of productive factors, capital, and labor, as well as income effects. However, tariffs also lead to sectoral distortions from the reallocation of factors across sectors within economies, which highly aggregated models, such as GIMF, cannot capture. Computable general equilibrium (CGE) trade models, in contrast, capture the impact on output of the shift of resources across sectors,

[1]The analysis in the October 2018 WEO also includes a layer of US-imposed tariffs on all imported cars and car parts. This layer is not included in this analysis.

[2]The magnitude of this effect was calibrated based on the Baker, Bloom, and Davis (BBD) overall "economic policy uncertainty" measure and its estimated impact on investment in the United States. (For details on the BBD Uncertainty Index, see http://www.policyuncertainty.com.) A one-standard-deviation increase in the BBD uncertainty measure (which is roughly one-sixth of the change during the global financial crisis) leads to an estimated 1 percent drop in investment in the United States in one year. Here, this 1 percent decline in investment is spread over three years, with the peak effect in 2020. The impact of the decline in investment in other countries is then scaled by their trade openness relative to the United States—countries more dependent on trade than the United States experience greater declines in investment than does the United States. Note that, since fall 2018, some of this impact would already be factored into WEO forecasts, given that the tariff measures were imposed.

[3]The magnitude of this tightening is based on several financial market participants' estimates of the impact on US corporate earnings of a worst-case United States–China trade war. (In the worst-case scenario, the United States imposes tariffs of 25 percent on all Chinese imports and China does the same in response.) Based on historical relationships, this estimated 15 percent decline in earnings is then mapped into an increase in US corporate bond spreads. The rise in US spreads is then mapped into corporate bond spreads in other countries based on their credit rating relative to US corporate debt. This increase in spreads is assumed to start in 2019 and peak in 2020, with half of the peak increase remaining in corporate spreads in 2021.

Scenario Box 1.2 *(continued)*

under the assumption that total utilization of resources remains unchanged. Implicitly, this is an estimate of the impact on productivity of the movement of factors between sectors with different underlying productivity. To estimate the possible magnitude of this productivity effect, the tariff increases in the first three layers are run on a new global CGE model detailed in Caliendo and others (2017). The resulting impact on activity is an estimate of the medium-term effect and embodies an implicit change in labor productivity. The final layer adds this change in labor productivity, phased in over five years beginning in 2020.

Consistent with past scenarios, all layers assume that the euro area and Japan are unable to ease (conventional) monetary policy further in response to macroeconomic developments, given the lower bound on nominal interest rates. If other unconventional monetary policy measures are implemented, the decline in GDP in Japan and the euro area would be smaller in the near term than estimated here. In all other countries and regions, conventional monetary policy responds according to a Taylor-type reaction function. It is important to note the considerable uncertainty surrounding the magnitude and persistence of the confidence effects on investment and the tightening in corporate spreads. These effects could be either milder or more severe than assumed here. Regarding the layer that contains the tightening in corporate spreads, one aspect not included in the analysis is the potential for safe-haven flows to mitigate the impact of financial tightening in such countries as Germany, Japan, and the United States.

The estimated impact on activity (shown in Scenario Figure 1.2.1) indicates that tariffs included in the April 2019 WEO baseline (dark blue line) are estimated to have a fairly mild direct effect: the United States and China are most affected and China bears the greatest burden. The largest effect falling on the United States and China also holds true for the direct effect of tariff measures implemented in May 2019 (gray line) and those announced in August 2019 (yellow line). However, the magnitude of the impact becomes much more material. The short-term spillovers on other countries from these measures are estimated to be positive as some countries—notably the North American trading partners of the United States—benefit from trade diversion. These benefits, however, disappear in the medium term, and the spillovers become negative as households and firms in China and the United States are able to source more goods domestically that

Scenario Figure 1.2.1. Real GDP
(Percent deviation from control)

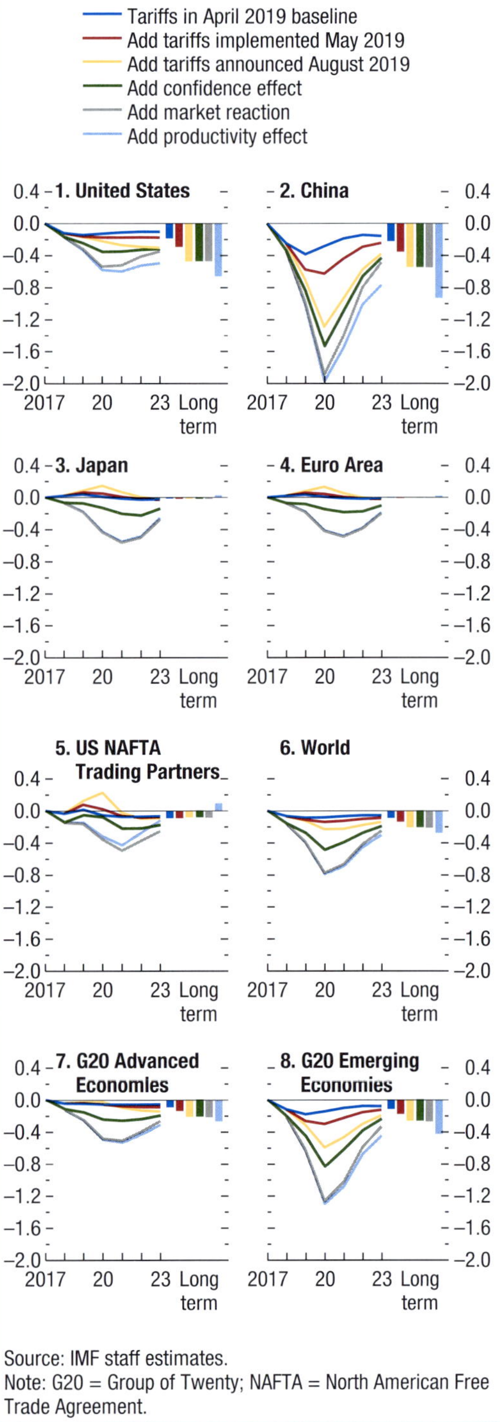

Source: IMF staff estimates.
Note: G20 = Group of Twenty; NAFTA = North American Free Trade Agreement.

Scenario Box 1.2 *(continued)*

were previously imported. Adding the confidence effects on investment (green line) and the increase in corporate spreads (red line) results in a negative result for all countries. For the United States and China, adding the estimated productivity effects (light blue line) amplifies the economic damage, but because they are phased in over five years, that negative impact grows over time and is substantial in both the medium and the long term. For some other countries, the productivity impact is positive, but small. Changes in global demand reallocate resources in these countries from less to more productive sectors.[4]

Overall, China suffers the most, as output falls by 2 percent in the short term and 1 percent in the long term (light blue bar). The United States runs a close second, with output falling by 0.6 percent in both time spans. The trough in global activity is estimated to take place in 2020, with output about 0.8 percent below baseline. The trough in activity across advanced economies is very similar to the trough in the United States, at roughly –½ percent. Unlike in the United States, the long-term direct trade effects are small and negative in advanced economies, although they are more than offset by positive productivity effects in some countries.

[4]As noted earlier, the productivity effect arises from resources shifting between sectors with different productivity. The countries with the closest trading ties to Canada, Mexico, and the United States benefit the most. In the trade model analysis, resources shifting from agriculture and mining to manufacturing in these two countries drives the improvement in aggregate productivity.

Box 1.1. The Global Automobile Industry: Recent Developments and Implications for the Global Outlook

The automobile industry contracted in 2018 for the first time since the global financial crisis, contributing to the global slowdown since last year. Two main factors explain the downturn: the removal of tax breaks in China and the rollout of new carbon emission tests in Europe. Near-term prospects for the industry remain sluggish, and efforts to decarbonize pose a fundamental challenge in the medium term.

The automobile sector is a globally interconnected industry with a large economic footprint. The size of the sector's gross output (that is, the sum of its value added and intermediate consumption) is about 5.7 percent of global output, according to the World Input-Output Database (Timmer and others 2015). Vehicles and related parts are the world's fifth largest export product, accounting for about 8 percent of global goods exports in 2018 (Figure 1.1.1). The sector is also a major consumer of commodities, other manufactured products, and services: the vehicle industry is the second largest consumer of steel and aluminum and demands significant amounts of copper, rubber, plastic, and electronics (Figure 1.1.2).

During the 2018 contraction (measured in units; Figure 1.1.3, panel 1) global automobile production declined by about 1.7 percent, or about –2.4 percent after correcting for differences in unit values (for example, German cars, on average, are more expensive than Indian cars). Global car sales fell by about 3 percent. China (the largest vehicle market in the world) experienced a 4 percent contraction in units produced, its first decline in more than two decades. Large declines were registered in Germany, Italy, and the United Kingdom, while production in the United States and large emerging markets expanded marginally (Figure 1.1.3, panel 2). The downturn has continued into 2019, as indicated by declining global light vehicle sales through June 2019 (Figure 1.1.4, panel 1) on continued subdued momentum in China and Europe. Consistent with performance, stock prices of the largest 14 car manufacturers have declined by 28 percent, on average, since March 2018 (compared with about a 1 percent increase in the MSCI World index during that time).

The industry's downturn contributed to the slowdown in global growth beginning in the second half of 2018. National income account data by sector are not yet available for 2018 in many countries. However, assuming a proportional decline in value added, IMF estimates suggest that the contraction in car production directly subtracted 0.04 percentage point from global output growth last year (following a positive contribution of 0.02 percentage point in 2017). Considering that global growth slowed by 0.2 percentage point last year—from 3.8 percent in 2017 to 3.6 percent—these estimates suggest that automobile production has been an important factor in the global slowdown.

Developments in the automobile industry also played a role in global trade dynamics. Automobile exports from the 14 biggest car-producing countries fell by 3.1 percent in 2018 when measured in units. Controlling for differences in unit values across exporters, IMF estimates suggest that the contraction in car exports directly subtracted 0.12 percentage point from global trade volumes

The author of this box is Luisa Charry, with research assistance from Aneta Radzikowski.

Figure 1.1.1. Global Vehicle Industry: Share of Total, 2018
(Percent)

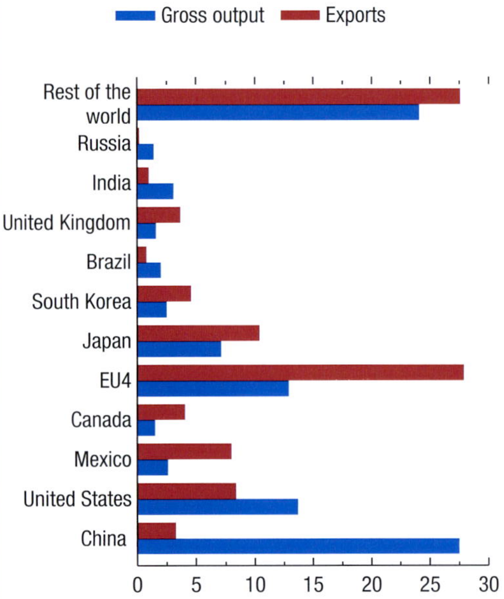

Sources: CEIC; Haver Analytics; Japan Automobile Manufacturers Association; National statistics offices; Spanish Association of Automobile and Truck Manufacturers (ANFAC); Statista; Society of Motor Manufacturers and Traders; United Nations Conference on Trade and Development; World Input-Output Database; and IMF staff calculations.
Note: EU4 = France, Germany, Italy, Spain.

Box 1.1 *(continued)*

Figure 1.1.2. Global Vehicle Industry: Structure of Production, 2014

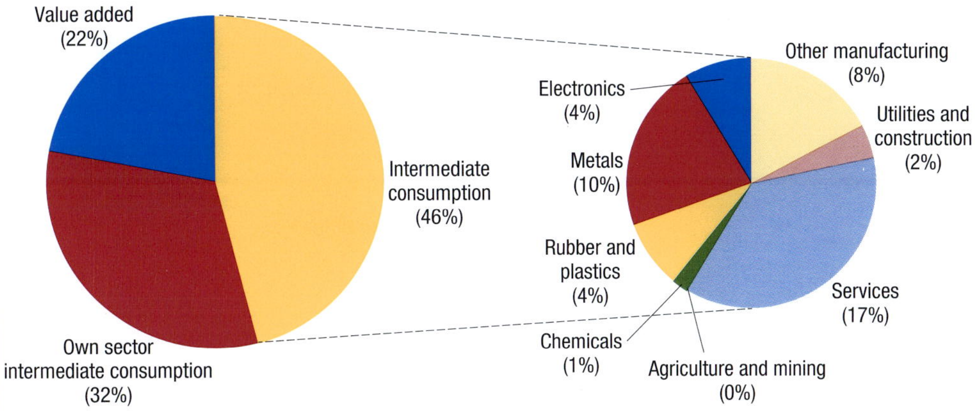

Sources: World Input-Output Database; and IMF staff calculations.

in 2018 (following a positive contribution of 0.03 percent in 2017). In addition, the sector's extensive value-chain linkages imply that the overall effects may be larger once the impact on trade in car parts—for which volume data are not yet available for a sufficiently large number of countries—and other intermediate goods used in car production is considered. A global input-output framework based on Bems, Johnson, and Yi (2011) suggests that the sector may have subtracted as much as 0.5 percentage point from global trade in 2018, once these spillover effects are factored in. For reference, the growth of all global exports of goods and services was 3.8 percent points in 2018 (down from 5.4 percent growth in 2017).

Several factors help explain the sector's performance:

- Vehicle demand in China was weighed down by higher taxes and tighter financial conditions. Tax breaks have been used in China to encourage vehicle ownership. In late 2015, the purchase tax on small and medium vehicles was lowered to 5 percent from 10 percent and subsequently increased to 7.5 percent in 2017 and to 10 percent in 2018 (Figure 1.1.4, panel 2). According to industry analysts, the lower tax rates in 2016–17 brought sales forward by 2–7 million units (about 20 percent of total production), which then reduced sales in 2018–19.[1] Tighter regulations on peer-to-peer lending also weighed on demand, while tariff increases on US car imports and decreases on car imports from other countries may have led consumers to take a precautionary stance.
- The rollout of new emission tests in Europe disrupted car production and trade. In September 2018, a new euro-area-wide emission test (known as WLTP) went into effect. The large number of models requiring certification led to bottlenecks at testing agencies, and several automakers had to adjust production schedules to avoid unwanted inventory accumulation. Other developments weighing on activity included falling demand from emerging markets (most notably Turkey) and the United Kingdom and acceleration of the shift out of diesel into gasoline and alternative-fuel vehicles.
- Car demand in the United States held up in 2018 despite tighter financial conditions (and the higher steel and aluminum tariffs). Although higher interest rates on car financing throughout 2017–18, and tighter lending standards, weighed on demand, provisions for vehicle depreciation in the Tax Cuts and Jobs Act provided support. In addition, although higher tariffs on steel and aluminum added an estimated $240 to the production cost of an average car in the United States in 2018 (Schultz and others 2019), it is unclear how much of that was passed on to final consumers.

[1]Mian and Sufi (2012) document similar intertemporal reallocation in the United States during the "Cash for Clunkers" program of 2009.

Box 1.1 *(continued)*

Figure 1.1.3. Global Vehicle Production

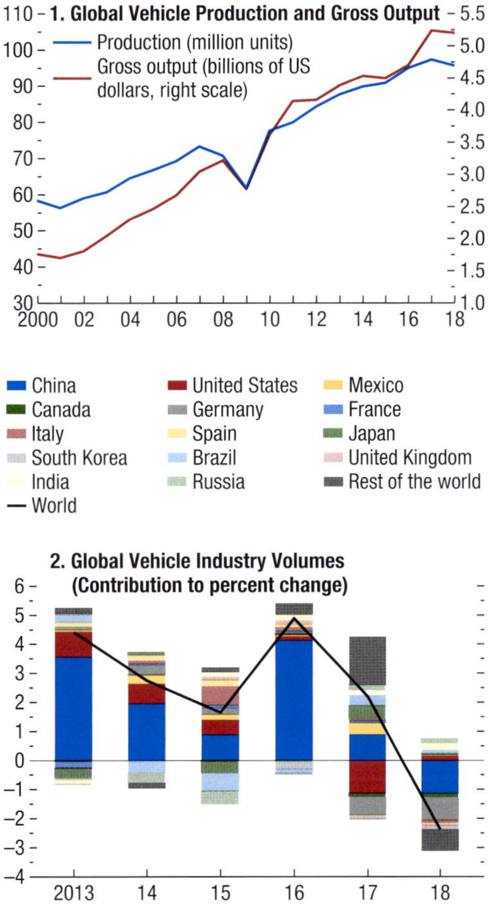

Sources: International Organization of Motor Vehicle Manufacturers; national statistics offices; World Input-Output Database; and IMF staff calculations.

Figure 1.1.4. World Passenger Vehicle Sales and Usage

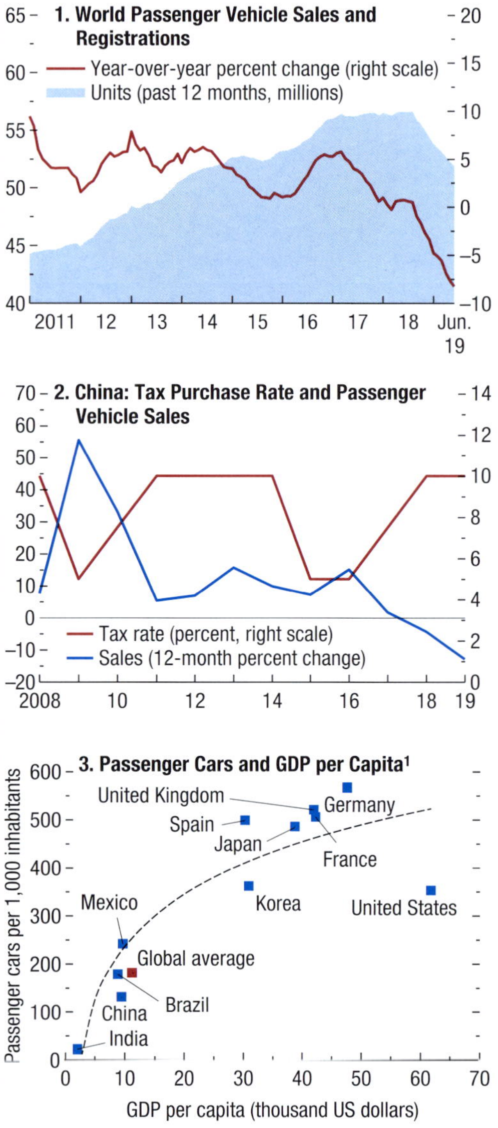

Sources: Economist Intelligence Unit; Haver Analytics; International Organization of Motor Vehicle Manufacturers; and IMF staff calculations.
[1]Dashed line indicates logarithmic trend.

The outlook for the industry remains conservative. Some analysts (such as IHS Markit) anticipate a 4 percent contraction in light vehicle production in 2019 and flat growth in 2020 (0.1 percent). In China, higher tariffs on light vehicle imports from the United States (set to take effect in December 2019), increasing market

Box 1.1 *(continued)*

saturation (Figure 1.1.4, panel 3), a young vehicle fleet, and lower subsidies on purchases of electric vehicles are likely to continue to hold back demand; the introduction of a new emission standard in mid-2019 could also disrupt production. The outlook for Europe is affected by falling demand for diesel-powered vehicles, continued Brexit-related uncertainty, and emission tests set for late 2019. Elsewhere, easier financial conditions should provide support, especially in the United States and large emerging markets, but ongoing discussions around Section 232 tariffs on US imports from the European Union and Japan could weigh on activity in the near term.

More fundamentally, efforts to decarbonize are set to shape the medium-term outlook. A significant ramp-up of investment in the production of electric and other alternative-fuel vehicles is expected in the medium term, particularly in Europe. However, the supply chains for electric vehicles are several orders of magnitude shorter than those for fuel-powered vehicles. Furthermore, entry-level prices remain higher than for fuel-powered cars, which could limit demand uptake. Accordingly, automakers are facing challenges that mean they will have to make changes to business models above and beyond those required by technological reconfiguration.

Box 1.2. The Decline in World Foreign Direct Investment in 2018

Financial flows to and from advanced economies have been much weaker since the global financial crisis (Figure 1.2.1). In particular, portfolio debt flows have weakened, reflecting a combination of factors: large government debt asset purchases by central banks, increased fragmentation in euro area debt markets, and much-reduced accumulation of reserves by emerging market and developing economies. Other investment flows have also fallen sharply as global banks reduced the size of their balance sheets after dramatic expansion of their cross-border activities during the precrisis boom. But, until the end of 2017, foreign direct investment (FDI) flows had actually increased slightly relative to the precrisis period, averaging more than 3 percent of GDP annually (more than $1.8 trillion).

The data for 2018 show a different picture: FDI abroad by advanced economies, as well as inward FDI, came to a virtual standstill. This box looks at the factors behind this large decline as well as the implications for emerging market and developing economies. Does this decline in FDI point to increased fragmentation? This box argues that it does not and that most of the decline in FDI reflects purely financial operations by large multinational corporations, including in response to changes in US tax law.

Specifically, a significant policy development affecting FDI in 2018 was the 2017 US Tax Cuts and Jobs Act, which generally eliminated taxes on repatriated earnings by US multinationals.[1] In response to the law, US multinational corporations repatriated accumulated prior earnings of their foreign affiliates. During 2011–17 these multinationals, on average, reinvested in their overseas affiliates about $300 billion a year in earnings on FDI (about two-thirds of their total overseas earnings), but in 2018 they repatriated $230 billion. In other words, the dividends paid to parent companies by overseas affiliates exceeded these affiliates' earnings by $230 billion (Figure 1.2.2, panel 1, blue bars). This repatriated amount exceeded new FDI abroad and, hence, total FDI abroad by US corporations was negative in 2018 (Figure 1.2.2, panel 1, black line).

Where did this repatriation of earnings originate? As documented by the US Bureau of Economic Analysis and as discussed in Setser (2019), it originated primarily in a few financial centers, with dividends paid out of Bermuda, the Netherlands, and Ireland accounting for about $500 billion—almost three times more than the income reported by US affiliates in these locations. The evidence also suggests that the repatriated assets were invested primarily from overseas in US financial instruments (Smolyansky, Suarez, and Tabova 2019). Hence, the repatriation of earnings would reduce FDI abroad and, correspondingly, reduce claims of nonresidents

Figure 1.2.1. Advanced Economies: Financial Flows
(Percent of GDP)

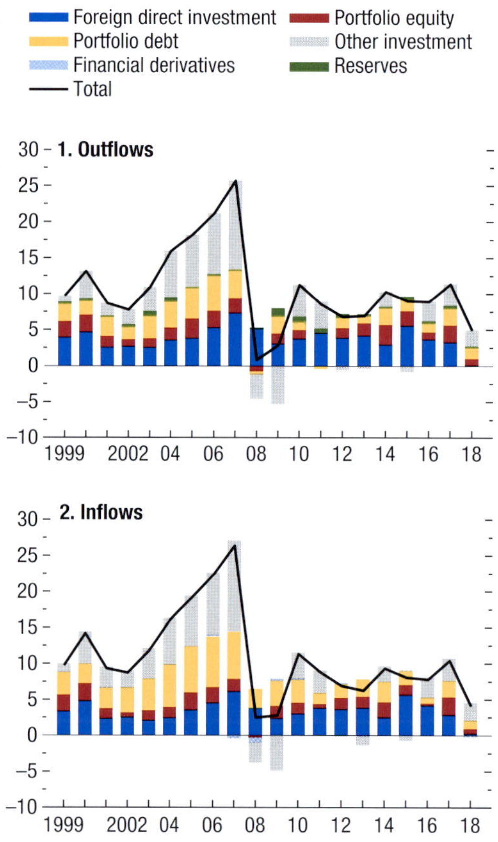

Source: IMF staff calculations.

The author of this box is Gian Maria Milesi-Ferretti.

[1]Earnings by foreign affiliates can be repatriated to the parent company in the form of dividends or reinvested in the foreign affiliate. Both types of earnings are reflected as primary income in the current account, and reinvested earnings are counted as new FDI abroad (a financial outflow). Under the previous tax system, US companies would typically retain most of their earnings abroad.

Box 1.2 *(continued)*

Figure 1.2.2. Foreign Direct Investment Flows
(Percent of GDP)

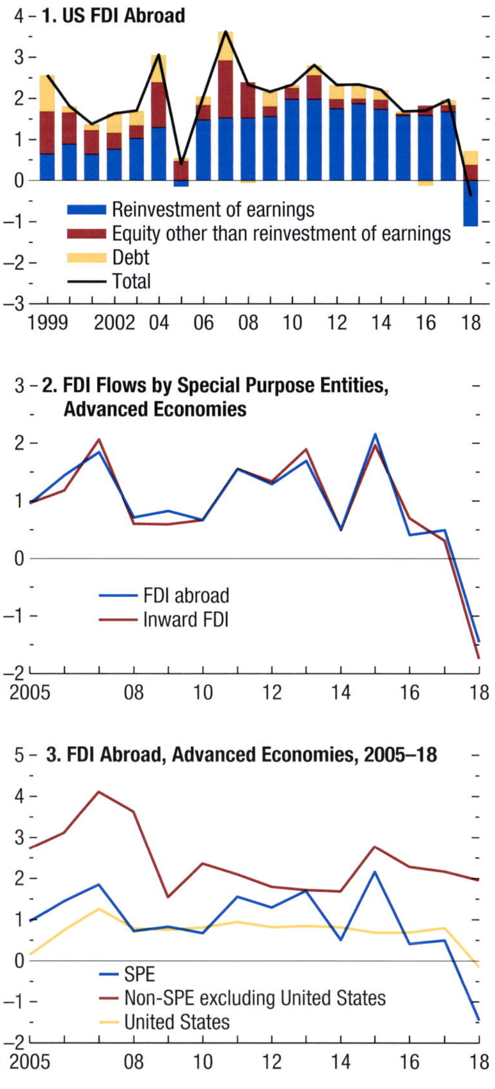

Sources: Organisation for Economic Co-operation and Development; US Bureau of Economic Analysis; and IMF staff calculations.
Note: FDI = foreign direct investment; SPE = special purpose entity.

on the US economy (for instance, in the form of portfolio investment in debt securities), given that overseas affiliates of US multinational corporations are residents of the country where they are established.

But the decline in US FDI abroad by itself explains only part of the $1.5 trillion reduction in advanced economies' FDI abroad between 2017 and 2018. The remainder comes mostly from the euro area, in particular from Luxembourg and the Netherlands, where FDI abroad fell from $340 billion in 2017 to –$730 billion in 2018. In these countries, the lion's share of FDI reflects financial operations of special purpose entities. These multinational corporation affiliates are pass-through entities with little or no employment or value added, whose financial balance sheets are composed primarily of cross-border assets and liabilities. They are established to (1) access capital markets or sophisticated financial services, (2) isolate owner(s) from financial risk, (3) reduce regulatory and tax burdens, or (4) safeguard the confidentiality of their transactions and owner(s).[2]

Statistics published by the Organisation for Economic Co-operation and Development suggest that FDI abroad by advanced economy special purpose entities—mostly domiciled in Luxembourg and the Netherlands—declined from $240 billion in 2017 to –$740 billion in 2018 and hence accounts for more than 90 percent of the decline in FDI flows. Panel 2 of Figure 1.2.2 shows the pattern of special purpose entities' investment in advanced economies since 2005, highlighting the large decline in 2018 as well as the symmetry between the behavior of assets and liabilities.[3] The decline in FDI positions by special purpose entities is also the main factor explaining the sharp reduction in inward FDI for advanced economies highlighted in panel 2 of Figure 1.2.1. Panel 3 of Figure 1.2.2 highlights the contributions of the United States and of special purpose entities to the decline in advanced economies' FDI abroad.

[2]See IMF (2018) for a discussion of the nature of special purpose entities and the recording of their activities in the balance of payments.

[3]Not all countries report FDI transactions and holdings by special purpose entities separately; hence, the estimates in the figure understate to some extent their role.

Box 1.2 *(continued)*

As noted in DNB (2019) and BCL (2019), these transactions reflect mostly operations by US-based multinationals seeking to simplify their international group structure by liquidating intermediate holdings, also in relation to the US tax reform of 2017. Similarly, SNB (2019) notes that the US tax reform led foreign-controlled finance and holding companies domiciled in Switzerland to reduce their balance sheets. On the liability side, inward FDI was negative: nonresident parent companies withdrew equity capital from companies in Switzerland. Other factors are also likely to have been at play, including ongoing broader tax reform initiatives, such as the Base Erosion and Profit Shifting initiative and the European Union's Anti-Tax Avoidance Directives 1 and 2.

Figure 1.2.3 depicts the pattern of capital flows to and from the largest emerging market economies. Inflows in 2018 were weaker than in 2017, but FDI inflows fell only slightly in relation to GDP, and this decline is entirely accounted for by another large reduction in FDI positions by special purpose entities in Hungary. The picture for financial outflows also shows some decline in 2018, including in FDI. The largest component of this decline is, again, the reduction in FDI by special purpose entities in Hungary, coupled with some reduction in FDI abroad by China, which is the largest overseas investor among emerging market economies. On net, emerging market economies remain FDI destinations, and their FDI liabilities exceed their assets.

In sum, the sharp decline in global FDI flows in 2018 seems to be explained almost entirely by multinational corporations' financial operations, with no meaningful aggregate impact on emerging market economies. These developments further underscore how FDI transactions and positions recorded in the balance of payments are often unrelated to greenfield investment or mergers and acquisitions, but rather reflect tax and regulatory optimization strategies by large multinational corporations (see, for instance, Lane and Milesi-Ferretti 2018 and Damgaard and Elkjaer 2017). Efforts under way to enhance data collection on the activity of special purpose entities should help clarify the nature of FDI flows and positions.

Figure 1.2.3. Emerging Markets: Financial Flows
(Percent of GDP)

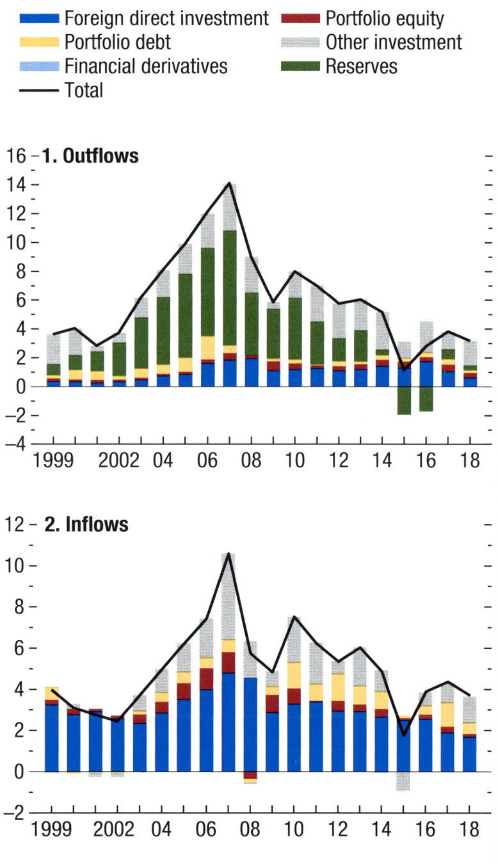

Source: IMF staff calculations.

Box 1.3. Global Growth Forecast: Assumptions on Policies, Financial Conditions, and Commodity Prices

The global forecast rests on the following key assumptions on policies, financial conditions, and commodity prices:

- *Tariffs*: The tariffs imposed and announced by the United States as of August 2019 and retaliatory measures by trading partners are factored into the baseline forecast. For US actions, besides tariffs on solar panels, washing machines, aluminum, and steel announced in the first half of 2018, these include a 25 percent tariff on $50 billion in imports from China (July and August 2018), rising to 30 percent in October 2019; tariffs on an additional $200 billion in imports from China (September 2018, at 10 percent until May 2019, 25 percent from May through September 2019, and 30 percent thereafter); and the August 2019 announcement of a further 10 percent tariff on the remaining $325 billion of imports from China (subsequently increased to 15 percent for a subset of the list beginning in September 2019 and the remainder beginning in December 2019). China's retaliation included a 25 percent tariff on $50 billion of imports from the United States (July and August 2018); tariffs of 5–10 percent on $60 billion of imports from the United States (September 2018); and additional tariffs of 5–10 percent on $75 billion of imports from the United States (effective September and December 2019). Following the May and August 2019 announcements, the average US tariff on imports from China will rise to just over 24 percent by December 2019 (compared with about 12¼ percent assumed in the April 2019 *World Economic Outlook* (WEO)), while the average Chinese tariff on imports from the United States will increase to about 26 percent (compared with about 16½ percent assumed in the April 2019 WEO).
- *Fiscal policy*: Fiscal policy in 2019 is projected to be expansionary both in advanced economies (Canada, Germany, Hong Kong SAR, Korea, Spain, United States) and emerging market economies (China, Turkey). It is assumed to be neutral across advanced economies in 2020—as opposed to contractionary as assumed in the April 2019 WEO—given that the unwinding of the US tax stimulus will be more than offset by spending increases in a new budget deal. It is expected to be contractionary in emerging market economies, given that stimulus in China is assumed to unwind to some extent (Figure 1.3.1).
- *Monetary policy*: Compared with the April 2019 WEO, monetary policy of major central banks is assumed to be more accommodative over the forecast horizon. The US federal funds rate is expected to be in the 1.75–2 percent range through 2023, rising to 2–2.25 percent in 2024. Policy rates are assumed to remain below zero in the euro area and Japan through 2024.
- *Commodity prices*: Based on oil futures contracts, average oil prices are projected at $61.8 in 2019, declining to $57.9 in 2020 (compared with $59.16 and $59.02, respectively, in the April 2019 WEO). Oil prices are expected to decline to about $55 a barrel by 2023 (lower than in the April 2019 WEO forecast), consistent with subdued medium-term demand prospects (Figure 1.3.2). Metal prices are expected to increase by 4.3 percent year over year in 2019, before declining by 6.2 percent in 2020 (compared with a decrease of 6 percent and a further decline of 0.8 percent in the April 2019 WEO assumptions). Price forecasts of most major agricultural commodities have been revised down for 2019. Food prices are projected to decline by 3.4 percent year over year in 2019 before increasing by 2.8 percent in 2020 (compared with the projected decrease of 2.6 percent and increase of 1.7 percent in the April 2019 WEO).

Box 1.3 *(continued)*

Figure 1.3.1. Forecast Assumptions: Fiscal Indicators

(Percent of GDP)

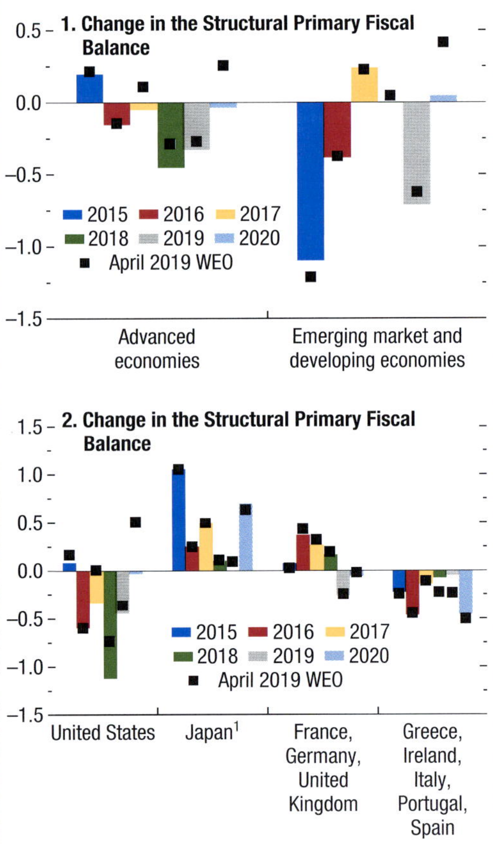

Source: IMF staff estimates.
Note: WEO = *World Economic Outlook.*
[1]Japan's latest figures reflect comprehensive methodological revisions adopted in December 2016.

Figure 1.3.2. Commodity Price Assumptions and Terms-of-Trade Windfall Gains and Losses

(Percent of GDP, unless noted otherwise)

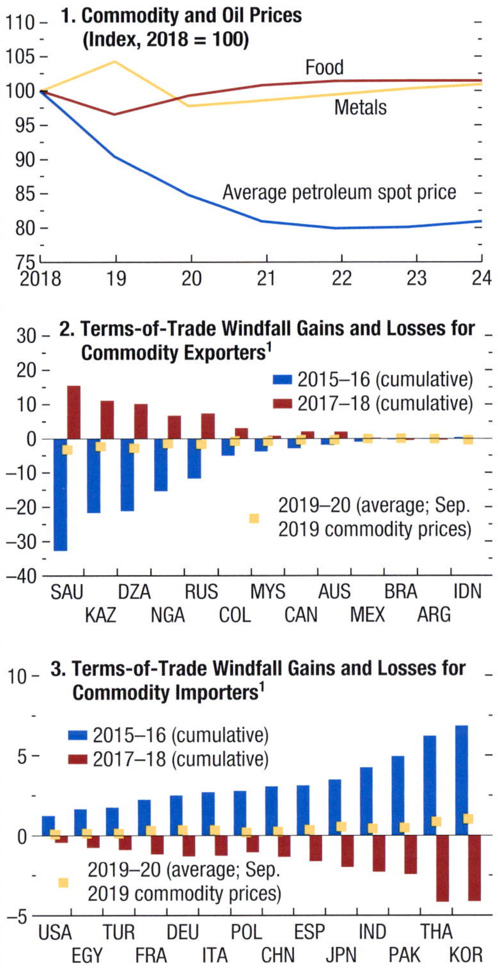

Sources: IMF, Primary Commodity Price System; and IMF staff estimates.
Note: Data labels use International Organization for Standardization (ISO) country codes.
[1]Gains (losses) for 2019–20 are simple averages of annual incremental gains (losses) for 2019 and 2020. The windfall is an estimate of the change in disposable income arising from commodity price changes. The windfall gain in year t for a country exporting x US dollars of commodity A and importing m US dollars of commodity B in year $t-1$ is defined as $(\Delta p_t^A x_{t-1} - \Delta p_t^B m_{t-1}) / Y_{t-1}$, in which Δp_t^A and Δp_t^B are the percentage changes in the prices of A and B between year $t-1$ and year t, and Y is GDP in year $t-1$ in US dollars. See also Gruss (2014).

Box 1.4. The Plucking Theory of the Business Cycle

According to conventional business cycle theory, the economy fluctuates symmetrically around a certain level of potential output. Consistent with this view, estimates of potential output are generally obtained by fitting a smooth trend through output, removing business cycle fluctuations. These techniques imply that several advanced economies are now operating close to or above potential, facing inflation risks. Nonetheless, inflation has been remarkably subdued in recent years, raising questions about the state of the business cycle and suggesting that potential output could be higher than currently estimated.

The sluggish behavior of inflation has renewed interest in alternative interpretations of the business cycle. One prominent hypothesis is that economic fluctuations may behave in line with the "plucking theory" originally proposed by Friedman (1964, 1993). According to this view, the economy suffers occasional contractions that reduce the level of output below potential, as illustrated in Figure 1.4.1. In Friedman's words, "output is viewed as bumping along the ceiling of maximum feasible output except that every now and then it is plucked down by a cyclical contraction."

Dupraz, Nakamura, and Steinsson (2019) shows that business cycle dynamics consistent with the plucking theory can occur when wages are sticky downward but can freely adjust upward. In this case, negative shocks pluck the economy below potential, while positive shocks are absorbed through higher prices. Accordingly, potential output should be estimated not by smoothing out economic fluctuations, but by interpolating historical peaks of the business cycle. Therefore, current estimation techniques may significantly underestimate potential output and provide premature alarms about the risk of overheating.

Conventional estimates of potential output can be too conservative, even if wages are also sticky upward, provided downward nominal rigidities are more severe. Building on this idea, Abbritti and Fahr (2013) provides a model in which asymmetric wage rigidities generate economic contractions below potential that are more severe than economic expansions above it. Aiyar and Voigts (2019) points out that this leads, on average, to negative output gaps and that, when conventional filtering techniques are applied to the model-generated data, they underestimate potential output by generating output gaps centered around zero.

The author of this box is Damiano Sandri.

Figure 1.4.1. An Illustration of the Plucking Theory

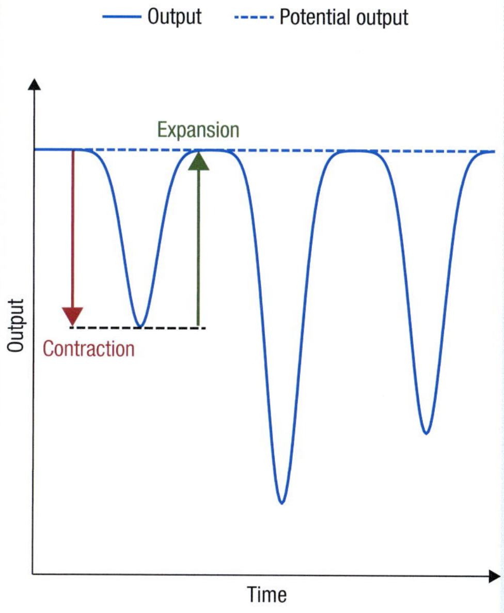

Source: IMF staff.

To test the validity of the plucking theory, the business cycle can be analyzed for particular asymmetries. As shown in Figure 1.4.1, if output is temporarily plucked down by occasional contractions, the severity of an economic downturn should predict the strength of the subsequent economic expansion. By contrast, the amplitude of economic expansions should have no bearing on the depth of subsequent contractions.

Dupraz, Nakamura, and Steinsson (2019) performs a similar test looking at the behavior of the unemployment rate in the United States.[1] Consistent with the plucking theory, the study finds that increases in the unemployment rate during economic downturns tend to be followed by reductions of a similar size (Figure 1.4.2, panel 1). Declines in unemployment during economic expansions are, however, not

[1]The method requires identifying peaks and troughs in seasonally adjusted monthly unemployment rates. A point in the unemployment series, $\underline{u}_t$, qualifies as a trough if it satisfies the following criterion. Take the first month in which the unemployment rate increases by 1.5 percent above $\underline{u}_t$. If up to that month the unemployment rate never falls below $\underline{u}_t$, then $\underline{u}_t$ is an unemployment trough. A symmetric procedure is used to identify unemployment peaks.

Box 1.4 *(continued)*

correlated with subsequent unemployment increases (Figure 1.4.2, panel 2).

How well does the plucking theory fit the data for other economies? Unemployment dynamics in other Group of Twenty advanced economies reveal similar behavior. Panel 3 of Figure 1.4.2 displays the pooled data.[2] It shows that increases in unemployment during economic contractions are followed by proportional unemployment declines during subsequent recoveries. However, the relationship is marginally weaker than in the United States, and the regression coefficient, equal to 0.52, indicates that increases in the unemployment rate are only partially reversed during subsequent economic expansions, reflecting a trend increase in structural unemployment. Consistent with the plucking theory, there is no significant relationship between unemployment declines and subsequent increases (Figure 1.4.2, panel 4).

In sum, unemployment dynamics in major advanced economies display patterns that appear consistent with theories that generate asymmetric business cycle fluctuations; while increases in unemployment are at least partially reversed, declines in unemployment are not. More research on the robustness of these asymmetric dynamics and the mechanisms behind them is warranted.

The implications of the plucking theory for macroeconomic policy are not trivial. For example, the insight that conventional filtering techniques underestimate potential output could be used to argue that countries have a stronger structurally adjusted fiscal position (and a smaller fiscal consolidation need) than generally assessed. However, the plucking theory also implies that economies operate below potential, on average. Therefore, a proper assessment of fiscal sustainability should not be based on a measure of potential output consistent with the plucking theory, but on the lower expected output path. Regarding monetary policy, the plucking theory implies a non-linear Philips curve, with prices being slow to decline in a downturn because of downward nominal rigidities. Monetary policy may therefore want to rely more on measures of economic slack to calibrate the appropriate level of stimulus, withdrawing accommodation only when inflationary pressures are clearly materializing.

[2]Data is pooled across the other advanced economies, given that they display much fewer observations for the analysis than in the case of the United States. This is for two reasons. First, the unemployment rate series in the United States starts in the late 1940s, while data for the other countries tend to be available beginning in the 1970s. Second, the US unemployment rate involves much more regular swings, while it follows more slow-moving trends in other countries.

Figure 1.4.2. Unemployment Dynamics in Advanced Economies
(Percentage points)

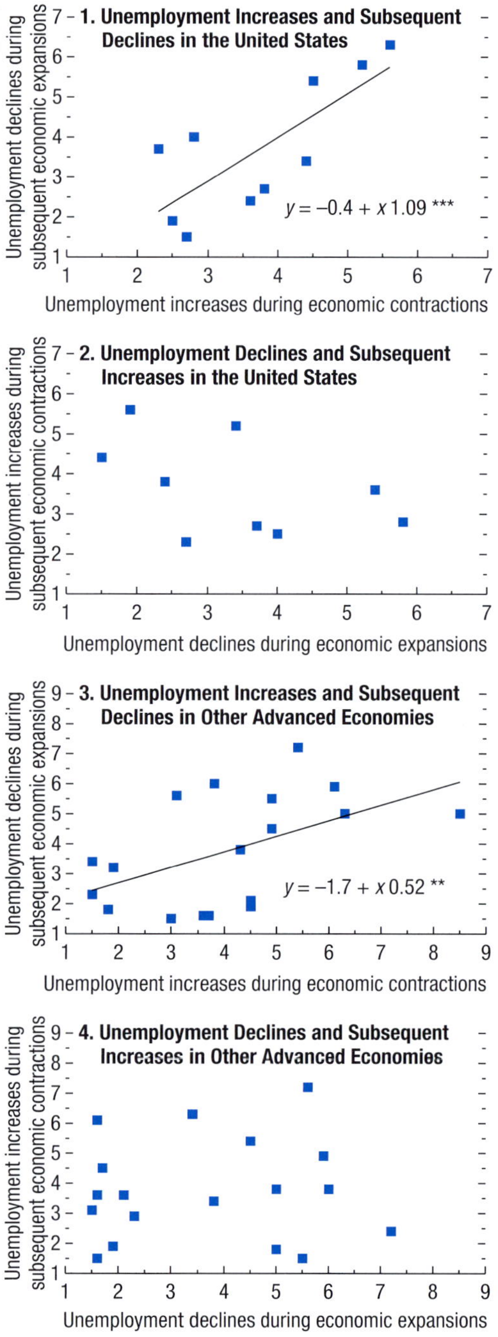

Sources: Haver Analytics; and IMF staff calculations.
Note: *** $p < 0.01$, ** $p < 0.05$.

Special Feature: Commodity Market Developments and Forecasts

Energy prices—especially for coal and natural gas—have seen a broad-based decline since the release of the April 2019 World Economic Outlook *(WEO). After a temporary rebound in April led by positive market momentum and supply cuts, oil prices have retrenched following record-high US production growth and weaker economic growth prospects, especially in emerging markets. In response to declining oil prices, Organization for the Petroleum Exporting Countries (OPEC) and non-OPEC oil exporters (including Russia) agreed to extend their production cuts until March 2020. While supply concerns caused iron ore and nickel prices to rally, most base metal prices declined following continued trade tensions and fears of a global economic slowdown. Agricultural prices decreased slightly as an increase in meat prices caused by disease outbreaks was more than offset by price declines of other foods. This special feature includes an in-depth analysis of precious metals.*

The IMF's primary commodity price index declined by 5.5 percent between February 2019 and August 2019, the reference periods for the April 2019 and current WEO, respectively (Figure 1.SF.1, panel 1). Energy prices drove that decline, falling by 13.1 percent; food prices decreased by 1.2 percent, and base metal prices decreased by 0.9 percent, driven by continued trade tensions and fears of a global economic slowdown only partially offset by the supply-driven price rally in the iron ore and nickel markets. Oil prices rebounded sharply at the beginning of the year, surpassing $71 a barrel in April,[1] driven by positive momentum in financial markets, supply cuts, and declining US crude oil stockpiles. Since then, however, oil prices have retrenched substantially due to record-high production growth in the United States and subdued global economic growth (especially in emerging markets). In response to the price decline, OPEC and non-OPEC oil exporters (including Russia) in July agreed to extend their December 2018 production cuts to the end of the first quarter of 2020. Coal and natural gas prices decreased amid a decline in industrial activity and power generation across regions.

Oil Prices in a Narrow Range amid Energy Prices' Decline and Heightened Uncertainty

Oil prices have been relatively stable, trading within a narrow range this year despite heightened geopolitical uncertainty. In April, they surpassed $71, their highest for 2019, and hit their recent bottom of $55 in August before rebounding back above $60 in September. Initially, prices were pushed higher by the recovery of financial conditions as well as outages in Venezuela and US tensions with Iran. But in late spring a weaker global economy raised concern about the strength of global oil demand, which was amplified by a buildup of US crude oil stockpiles.

Supply outages and geopolitical tensions, however, masked the oil demand weakness and, so, temporarily supported prices. Venezuela suffered production loss after a power outage in March, and Russian oil exports were partially halted in May because of pipeline contamination. Although these outages were temporary, they helped balance the market, resulting in lower US inventories in early spring. In addition, in May, previously issued US waivers to eight major importers of Iranian crude oil were not extended. Moreover, geopolitical tensions in the Middle East rose because of several attacks on Saudi oil infrastructures and oil tankers near the Strait of Hormuz; given that about 20 percent of global crude oil trade passes through the Strait, the fear of a conflict in that area drives up precautionary oil demand and insurance costs. On September 14, an attack on two key oil facilities in Saudi Arabia knocked out 5.7 million barrels per day of production for a few days (that is, about half of Saudi Arabia's total production, or 5 percent of global oil production), raising initially the fear of disruptions in the physical crude oil market and further escalating tensions. Further support for oil prices came from OPEC and non-OPEC oil exporters (including Russia), which, on July 1, 2019, agreed to extend their crude oil production cuts beyond their initial six-month period for an additional nine months until March 2020, by 0.8 million barrels a day (mbd) and 0.4 mbd, respectively.

On the demand side, weaker global economic fundamentals have contributed to lower prices.

The authors of this special feature are Christian Bogmans, Lama Kiyasseh, Akito Matsumoto, Andrea Pescatori (team leader), and Julia Xueliang Wan, with research assistance from Lama Kiyasseh, Claire Mengyi Li, and Julia Xueliang Wang.

[1]Oil price in this document refers to the IMF average petroleum spot price, which is based on UK Brent, Dubai Fateh, and West Texas Intermediate, equally weighted, unless specified otherwise.

Figure 1.SF.1. Commodity Market Developments

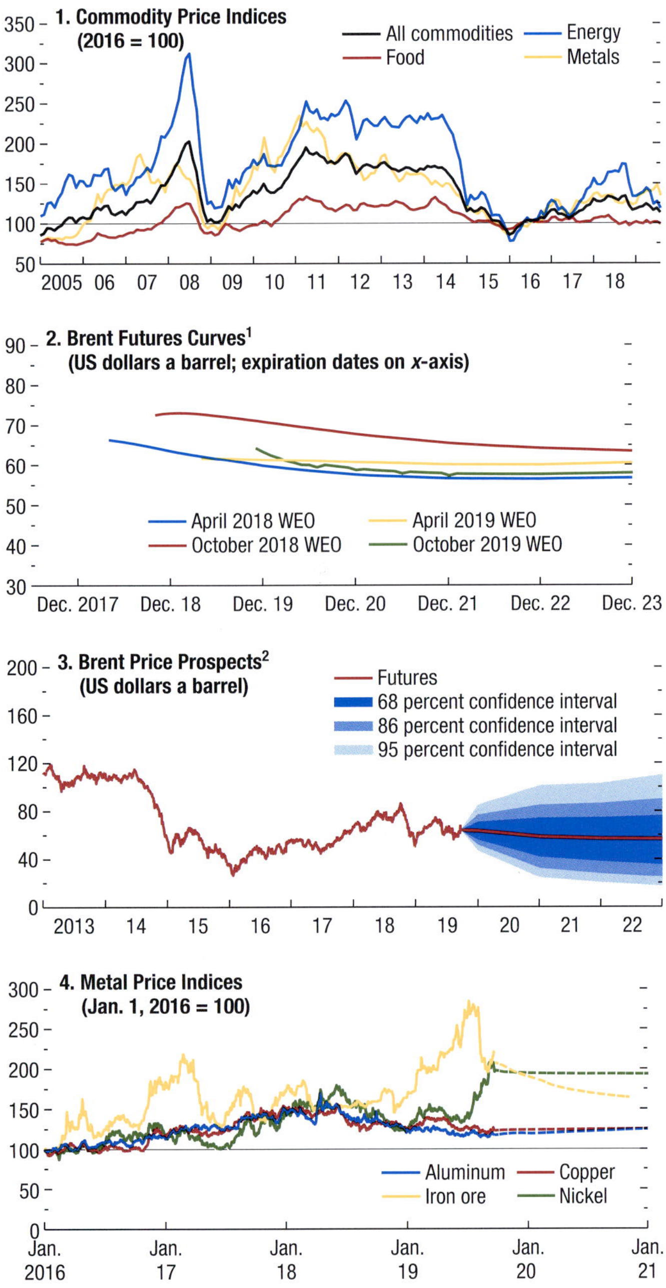

Sources: Bloomberg Finance L.P.; IMF, Primary Commodity Price System; Thomson Reuters Datastream; and IMF staff estimates.
Note: WEO = *World Economic Outlook.*
[1]WEO futures prices are baseline assumptions for each WEO and are derived from futures prices. October 2019 WEO prices are based on September 17, 2019, closing.
[2]Derived from prices of futures options on September 17, 2019.

The IMF's October downward revision of the global growth forecast—by 0.3 percent to 3.0 percent and by 0.2 percent to 3.4 percent for 2019 and 2020, respectively, from its April forecast—illustrates a slowdown in global activity, driven in particular by emerging markets and the euro area. In line with this slowdown, the International Energy Agency revised its oil demand growth forecast as of September for this year down to 1.1 mbd from 1.4 mbd in February.

In the natural gas market, spot prices have been declining in recent months amid increased production and higher stock levels due to lower global power demand. Coal prices have decreased in tandem because of declining power generation. Further downward pressure followed last year's record retirement of US coal-fired power capacity. Its replacement by cheaper gas-fired power plants, as part of a global trend, has lowered the share of coal in US power generation. Despite the ongoing decarbonization of the power sector in the United States and the rest of the world, however, global greenhouse gas emissions increased again in 2018 following strong global growth (see Box 1.SF.1).

As of late September 2019, oil futures contracts indicate that Brent prices will gradually decline to $55 over the next five years (Figure 1.SF.1, panel 2). Baseline assumptions, also based on futures prices, suggest average annual prices of $61.8 a barrel in 2019—a decrease of 9.6 percent from the 2018 average—and $57.9 a barrel in 2020 for the IMF's average petroleum spot prices. Despite the weaker demand outlook, risks are tilted to the upside in the near term but balanced in the medium term (Figure 1.SF.1, panel 3). Upside risks to prices in the short term include ongoing geopolitical events in the Middle East disrupting oil supply and contributing to rising insurance and shipping costs of oil cargoes. Downside risks include higher US production and exports thanks to new Permian pipelines coming online, noncompliance among OPEC and non-OPEC members, and a downturn in petrochemical demand. Further, a rise in trade tensions and other risks to global growth could decelerate global activity and reduce oil demand in the medium term.

Metal Prices Mixed

Base metal prices declined slightly by 0.9 percent between February 2019 and August 2019 as continued trade policy uncertainty and fears of a global economic slowdown—especially in China—were only partially offset by supply-driven price increases in iron ore and nickel. Precious metal prices rose, reflecting in part increased expectations of monetary easing in the United States and a flight to safety amid trade tensions.

Iron ore prices increased 6.7 percent between February 2019 and August 2019. Widespread disruptions—including the Vale dam collapse in Brazil and tropical cyclone Veronica in Australia—coupled with record-high steel output in China pushed iron ore prices to five-year highs during the first half of 2019. However, the normalization of previously disrupted operations and escalating trade tensions between the United States and China triggered a sharp correction in August, partially offsetting the gains since the beginning of the year. The price of nickel, a key input for stainless steel and batteries in electric vehicles, gained 24.1 percent between February 2019 and August 2019 on supply concerns as Indonesia, the world's largest nickel producer, introduced a complete ban on exports of raw nickel ore beginning in January 2020.

Other base metal prices suffered from a weaker global economy, however. Copper prices declined 9.4 percent on global trade uncertainty despite recent production cuts in the Republic of Congo, a labor dispute in Chuquicamata (Chile), and increasing extraction costs in Indonesia's Grasberg mine. The price of aluminum fell by 6.6 percent because of overcapacity in China and weakening demand from the vehicle market there. The price of zinc, which is used mainly to galvanize steel, decreased 16 percent from February to August 2019 as steel demand prospects deteriorated. The price of cobalt continued its downward trend and declined by 6.1 percent, reflecting a supply glut after production was ramped up in the Democratic Republic of the Congo.

The IMF annual base metals price index is projected to increase by 4.3 percent in 2019 (relative to its average in 2018) and decrease by 6.2 percent in 2020. Major downside risks to the outlook include prolonged trade negotiations and a further slowdown of industrial activity globally. Upside risks are supply disruptions and more stringent environmental regulations in major metal producing countries.

Meat Prices Higher Following Animal Disease Outbreaks

The IMF's food and beverage price index has decreased slightly, by 1.3 percent, as price declines of cereals, vegetables, vegetable oils, and sugar overwhelmed a large, 13.2 percent increase in the meat index.

Following the rapid spread of African swine fever across China (the world's largest producer and consumer of pork) and other parts of Southeast Asia, prices of pork jumped by 42.8 percent. News of disease outbreaks and animal culling have raised uncertainty regarding Chinese pork supplies in the near future. The outbreak has also led to tighter supplies and higher prices in Europe and the United States as domestic producers increased exports to China. In the wake of the crisis, prices of some other animal proteins surged too, with beef, for example, rising by 8.3 percent.

Record rainfall in the Midwest of the United States delayed corn and soybean-planting in May and June, introducing a high weather premium into grain markets. This premium then left the markets between late July and end of August, however, as US corn acreage and yields surpassed expectations. Strong global production also weighed on corn prices, which ultimately decreased by 3.6 percent between February and August. Soybeans experienced a net loss of 5.9 percent as trade tensions and the African swine fever outbreak in China continued to depress animal feed demand.

Cocoa prices decreased by 2.7 percent following favorable weather conditions in west Africa during July and August. Palm oil prices declined, by 2.6 percent, given that inventories are expected to increase and global demand in 2019–20 may shrink for the first time in two decades, following environmental concerns in some importing countries and rising competition from other vegetable oils.

Food prices are projected to decrease by 3.4 percent a year in 2019, mainly because of higher prices in the first half of 2018, and then increase by 2.8 percent in 2020. Weather conditions have been unusual in recent months and additional weather disruptions remain an upside risk to the forecast. On August 9, 2019, the US National Oceanic and Atmospheric Administration announced that El Niño climate conditions that started last September are now officially over. A resolution of the trade conflict between the United States—the world's largest food exporter—and China remains the largest source of upside potential for prices.

Precious Metals

What determines fluctuations in the prices of precious metals? What are they used for primarily? Are gold and other precious metals the ultimate haven and hedging instruments against the loss of monetary discipline, or is their role as a store of value overstated? This section tries to answer these questions by offering a brief historical overview, then investigating the basic characteristics of precious metals, including the geographical distribution of their production, and, finally, through an econometric analysis to test some possible answers to these questions.

Coinage, Money, and Precious Metals: A Brief Historical Overview

Since ancient times, luster, ductility, rarity, and remarkable chemical stability have conferred high value on precious metals (that is, gold and silver and, later, platinum and palladium, which share similar physical properties).[2] The first use of gold and silver for ornaments, rituals, and to signal social status dates to prehistoric times and was widespread across cultures and civilizations (Green 2007). The combination of these unique characteristics made precious metals excellent *stores of value* and probably was crucial in fostering the introduction of *coins*—a fundamental innovation in the history of money and a transition in the development of civilization itself (Mundell 2002). Coinage, in turn, inextricably connected precious metals to money and currencies for centuries.[3]

Thanks also to their density, gold and silver coins were strongly favored as medium of exchange relative to other metals (such as copper), especially for (sizable) international transactions. As a result, some gold and silver coins minted by reliable entities gained wide international acceptance (for example, gold florins and ducats in the Middle Ages and silver pesos in modern times)—facilitating and stimulating trade across kingdoms and civilizations (Vilar 1976).[4]

Mixed metallic standards, in which government or central bank notes are convertible into metal coins at a fixed price, were a natural evolution to overcome some of the obvious limitations of pure coin standards (Officer 2008). After centuries of widespread bimetallism, in which the gold–silver ratio is given by the mint price, in the third quarter of the 19th century, following the lead of Britain, monometallic gold standards prevailed across the major economic powers of that time—possibly stimulating global trade.[5] As silver was demonetized across the world, silver prices declined substantially, especially after the 1873 Coinage Act (also known as the "Crime of '73"; Friedman 1990). Hence, after thousands of years of relative stability, the silver–gold price ratio became volatile and shot up from 16:1 in the mid-1800s to almost 100:1 in subsequent decades (Figure 1.SF.2, panel 2).[6]

The stability of gold purchasing power was quite remarkable—with the exception of the world wars and the Great Depression—until the suspension of dollar-gold convertibility in 1971, which two years

[2]Gold and silver belong to the seven metals of antiquity (with copper, tin, lead, iron, and mercury). Today 86 metals are known. The first European reference to platinum appears in 1557 in the writings of the Italian humanist Giulio Cesare della Scala. Only at the end of 18th century, however, did platinum gain appreciation as a precious metal. Palladium was discovered by William Hyde Wollaston in 1802 (curiously named after the asteroid 2 Pallas) and has been used as a precious metal in jewelry since 1939 as an alternative to platinum in alloys called "white gold." (The naturally white color of palladium does not require rhodium plating.) Other precious metals, in addition to those analyzed, include the platinum group metals: ruthenium, rhodium, osmium, and iridium, which are, however, not widely traded.

[3]The introduction of coinage is still shrouded in mystery, but it seems likely that the first coin (the *electrum*, a mix of gold and silver) was minted in Lydia around 600 BCE, and it rapidly spread throughout the Mediterranean area. The Lydian electrum coins were overvalued, yielding profit or seigniorage to the issuer. This overvaluation indicates that the issuing state must have been strong enough to enforce a monopoly of coinage, inhibiting entry by means of drastic prohibitions (Mundell 2002).

[4]By 500 BCE, after Darius conquered Lydia, Persia embraced coinage (opting for a bimetallic monetary standard) and struck massive quantities of Persian *sigloi* (a silver coin), which became the international currency of its time, along with two other Anatolian coins (that is, the gold coins of Lampsacus and the electrum coins of Cyzicus) (Mundell 2002). After the Roman *aureum*, in the middle ages, the gold Florentine florins and Venetian ducats became accepted across Europe, while the silver peso (also known as the "piece of eight"), minted in the Spanish Empire, was the international currency of modern times, the antecedent of the US dollar, and was legal tender in the United States until the Coinage Act of 1857 (Vilar 1976).

[5]Some studies have found that the rise of the classical gold standard, between 1870 and 1913, could account for 20 percent of the increase in global trade between 1880 and 1910—strongly supporting the idea that commodity money regime coordination and currency unions were an important catalyst for 19th century globalization (Lopez-Cordova and Meissner 2003).

[6]Silver was demonetized first in the United Kingdom in 1819, later during the 1870s in Germany, France, the Scandinavian Union, the Netherlands, Austria, Russia, and in the Latin Monetary Union (Belgium, Italy, and Switzerland), and in the United States with the 1973 Coinage Act. By the late 1870s, China and India were the only major countries effectively on a silver standard.

Figure 1.SF.2. Gold and Silver Prices

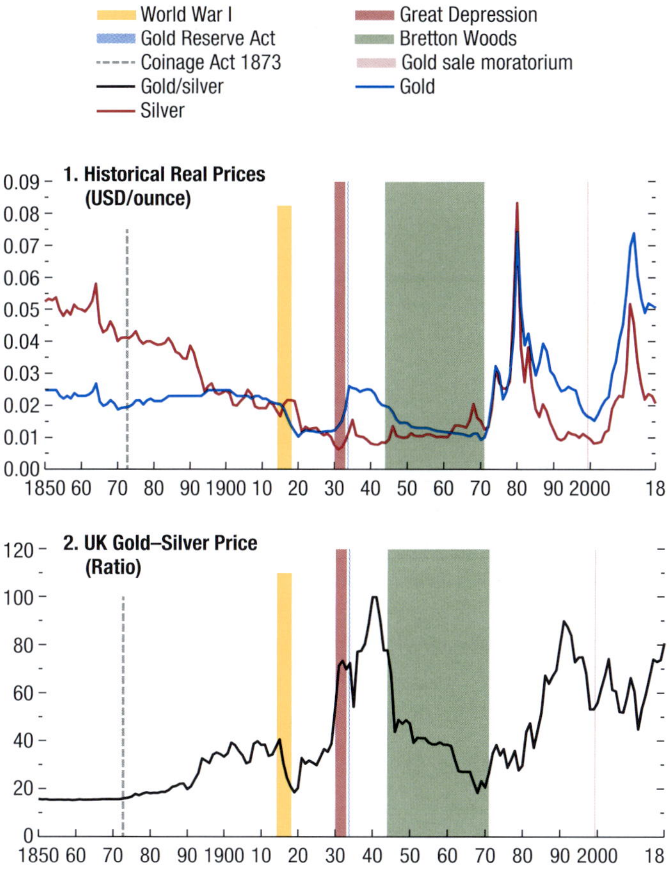

Sources: Measuringworth.com; Minneapolis Federal Reserve; and IMF staff calculations.
Note: USD = US dollars.

later led to the collapse of the system, inaugurating a new era of fluctuating gold prices and indefinitely severing the link between precious metals and currencies (Figure 1.SF.2).

Even today in a world of fiat currencies, the legacy of gold-currency convertibility is visible as official holdings of gold—mostly held by central banks and international institutions such as the IMF and the Bank for International Settlements—still represent a large share of the total stock of the precious metals of official reserves and, sometimes, even of a country's public debt (Table 1.SF.1).

The next section investigates the current role of precious metals in the global economy, looking at their production volumes and values (sizable for various countries) and their usage.

Basic Facts about Precious Metals

The Production of Precious Metals and Its Geographical Distribution

The production of precious metals, especially platinum and palladium, is concentrated in a few places. The global flow of production for gold was about 3,260 metric tons in 2018, equivalent to about $134 billion. The top five producers (China, Australia, Russia, United States, Canada) make up more than 40 percent of production. The value of gold production is bigger than copper and dwarfs other precious metals. Global production of silver, palladium, and platinum was $13 billion, $9 billion, and $4 billion in 2018, respectively. Their production, however, is much more concentrated; for example, the two largest silver producers (Mexico and Peru) represent almost 40 percent of global production. Similarly, Russia and South Africa account for three-quarters of global palladium production, while South Africa alone accounts for more than two-thirds of global platinum production (Table 1.SF.2).

Taken as a group, total production and reserves of precious metals represent a nonnegligible share of GDP (exports) for various countries (Figure 1.SF.3), especially for medium and small low-income countries (for example, Burkina Faso, Ghana, Mali, Suriname). Fluctuations in prices may, thus, induce significant income and wealth effects on a wide variety of countries.

The mining of precious metals is relatively inelastic to prices, as a price boom in the mid-2000s showed (Erb and Harvey 2013). Precious metal production ratios exhibit no clear trend over a long period, and the gold–silver ratio was, surprisingly, barely affected by the American silver production boom of the 16th and 17th centuries (Table 1.SF.3).[7] In addition, silver–gold production and price ratios have shown no obvious relationship in the past decade, suggesting that the relative supply of precious metals has not been a significant source of price fluctuations.

The Use of Precious Metals

Demand for precious metals can be classified as follows: industrial, jewelry, and investment and net official purchases by central banks and

[7]Interestingly, while the production volume of precious metals has increased about 500 times since 1500, global GDP and population have increased 50 and 15 times, respectively (Malanima 2009). Over the same period, the purchasing power of gold and silver has not declined (Erb and Harvey 2013).

Table 1.SF.1. Official Gold Reserves

	Tons						Value ($ billions)	Percent of Reserves	Percent of Public Debt
	1970	1980	1990	2000	2010	2019		2019	
United States	9,839	8,221	8,146	8,137	8,133	8,133	332	75	2
Germany	3,537	2,960	2,960	3,469	3,407	3,368	137	70	6
International Monetary Fund	3,856	3,217	3,217	3,217	2,934	2,814	115	–	#N/A
Italy	2,565	2,074	2,074	2,452	2,452	2,452	100	66	4
France	3,139	2,546	2,546	3,025	2,435	2,436	99	61	4
Russian Federation	–	–	–	343	710	2,183	88	19	39
China	–	398	395	395	1,054	1,900	77	2	1
Switzerland	2,427	2,590	2,590	2,538	1,040	1,040	42	5	15
Japan	473	754	754	754	765	765	31	2	0
India	216	267	333	358	558	613	25	65	5
Netherlands	1,588	1,367	1,367	912	612	612	25	6	1
European Central Bank	–	–	–	747	501	505	21	28	#N/A
Taiwan Province of China	73	98	421	421	424	424	17	4	8
Portugal	802	689	492	607	383	383	16	60	5
Kazakhstan	–	–	–	56	67	367	15	56	40
Uzbekistan	–	–	–	–	–	355	14	53	136
Saudi Arabia	106	142	143	143	323	323	13	3	9
United Kingdom	1,198	586	589	563	310	310	13	8	1
Turkey	113	117	127	–	–	296	12	14	5
Lebanon	255	287	287	287	287	287	12	23	14

Sources: IMF, *International Financial Statistics*; World Gold Council; and IMF staff calculations.
Note: 2019 values are as of March.

Table 1.SF.2. Precious Metals Production, 2016–18

Gold	Value ($ billions)	Cumulative World Share (Percent)	Silver	Value ($ billions)	Cumulative World Share (Percent)
China	13.1	11	Mexico	3.1	21
Australia	9.3	18	Peru	2.3	37
Russia	8.5	26	China	1.7	48
Kazakhstan	8.4	32	Chile	0.7	53
United States	7.4	39	Russia	0.7	58
Ghana	7.4	45	Poland	0.7	63
Peru	6.2	50	Australia	0.7	67
Canada	6.2	55	Bolivia	0.7	72
Brazil	5.6	59	Kazakhstan	0.6	76
Papua New Guinea	4.7	63	Argentina	0.6	80
South Africa	4.5	67	United States	0.5	84
Mexico	4.2	71	Other Countries	2.4	100
Other Countries	35.6	100	World	14.8	
World	121.3				
Palladium	**Value ($ billions)**	**Cumulative World Share (Percent)**	**Platinum**	**Value ($ billions)**	**Cumulative World Share (Percent)**
Russia	2.2	39	South Africa	3.9	70
South Africa	2.1	75	Russia	0.7	82
Canada	0.5	83	Zimbabwe	0.4	89
United States	0.4	90	Canada	0.3	95
Zimbabwe	0.3	95	United States	0.1	97
Other Countries	0.3	100	Other Countries	0.2	100
World	5.8		World	5.6	

Sources: IMF, Primary Commodity Price System; United States Geological Survey; and IMF staff calculations.
Note: Three-year average (2016–18) of both prices and production.

Figure 1.SF.3. Macro Relevance of Precious Metals
(Percent)

Sources: IMF, Primary Commodity Price System; S&P Global Market Intelligence; Thomson Reuters Datastream; UN, COMTRADE; United States Geological Survey; World Bank, World Development Indicators; and IMF staff calculations.
Note: Data labels use International Organization for Standardization (ISO) country codes.

international organizations. More than half of newly mined gold is used in jewelry (Figure 1.SF.4). Silver, instead, has various industrial applications, which account for half of silver consumption, while only 25 percent of silver demand is for jewelry. Investment demand for gold and silver (in the form of coins and bars or holdings in exchange-traded funds) varies significantly as it is more sensitive to prices.[8] Industrial use is more important for platinum and, especially, palladium—which are used in catalytic converters by the car industry.

Official sector gold holdings are large, accounting for about 30 percent of the global stock of gold. Their sale can disrupt the market and therefore has been limited to 400 metric tons a year.[9] The declining role of gold in the balance sheets of central banks in advanced economies, however, has been more than offset by a recent surge in emerging market gold reserves (Table 1.SF.1). The next section will take a financial investment perspective on precious metals by looking at them as an asset class, analyzing their major price determinants, and paying attention to their safe haven and hedging properties during market turmoil and against high inflation.

Price Properties of Precious Metals

Precious metals can be considered an asset class of their own. Their returns show a high correlation among themselves, especially gold, silver, and platinum, consistent with their respective ranking in industrial use (Figure 1.SF.5). At monthly frequencies, gold and silver have the highest correlation, 0.72, while palladium and gold have the lowest, at 0.33. At lower frequencies, palladium prices are more related to industrial metals (such as copper) than to gold, but the highest correlation for palladium is still with its close substitute, platinum. Movements in global industrial production have, however, minor implications for precious metal prices, even for palladium and platinum (Table 1.SF.5).

The relationship between precious metals and inflation throughout history has changed with the monetary system in place. In historical metallic regimes, in

[8]The exchange-traded fund GLD holds 20 percent of total stock scattered in warehouses across the world. Scrap metal is another significant, price-sensitive source of supply, which for gold is almost half of mining production.

[9]The central bank moratorium on gold sales, in September 1999, led the price of gold to rise by 25 percent within a month. There have since been three further agreements, in 2004, 2009, and 2014, limiting the amount of gold that signatories can sell in any one year.

Table 1.SF.3. Relative Rarity
(Production ratios of volume)

		American Silver Production Boom									
	Early 1500s	1500s	1600s	1700s	1800s	1900–10	1995–99	2000–04	2005–09	2010–14	2015–18
Silver (volume in metric tons)	47	233	373	570	2,223	5,655	16,260	19,280	21,120	24,920	26,775
Silver to Platinum							104	102	100	132	144
Silver to Palladium							119	105	104	126	124
Silver to Gold	8.1	32.7	40.8	30.0	11.9	10.2	7.0	7.6	8.8	9.1	8.5
Silver to Copper							0.0014	0.0014	0.0014	0.0015	0.0013
Gold–Silver Price Ratio	11.0	11.3	13.5	15.0	19.2	35.7	64.8	64.2	57.9	56.9	75.4

Sources: Broadberry and Gupta (2006); United States Geological Survey; Vilar (1976); and IMF staff calculations.
Note: Historical production ratios are century averages.

which a currency was pegged to metals, such as under the Bretton Woods system, an increase in price was associated with a decline in the real price of metals (Figure 1.SF.6). This result is, however, reversed in contemporary fiat currency regimes.

Bekaert and Wang (2010) proposes testing whether an asset is a good inflation hedge by simply regressing its nominal return on inflation, arguing that if the regression slope (inflation beta) is 1 then the asset is a good inflation hedge. Averages of precious metals' inflation betas calculated across a broad set of countries during 1978–2019[10] are below 1 at monthly frequencies but get close to 1 as the horizon increases, especially for gold and silver (Table 1.SF.4). However, the regression fit is usually modest, and betas vary substantially across countries (see Online Annex Table 1.SF.1), suggesting that precious metals, including gold and silver, are not a reliable and robust inflation hedge.[11] This result, however, is not that surprising, given that the volatility of precious metal prices increased substantially after the end of the Bretton Woods agreements, even for gold. It does, however, suggest that gold prices peaked in 1980 and 2012, two periods during which there was fear, justified or not, of a globally widespread wave of high inflation.[12] This observation would call

Figure 1.SF.4. Share of Total Demand
(Percent)

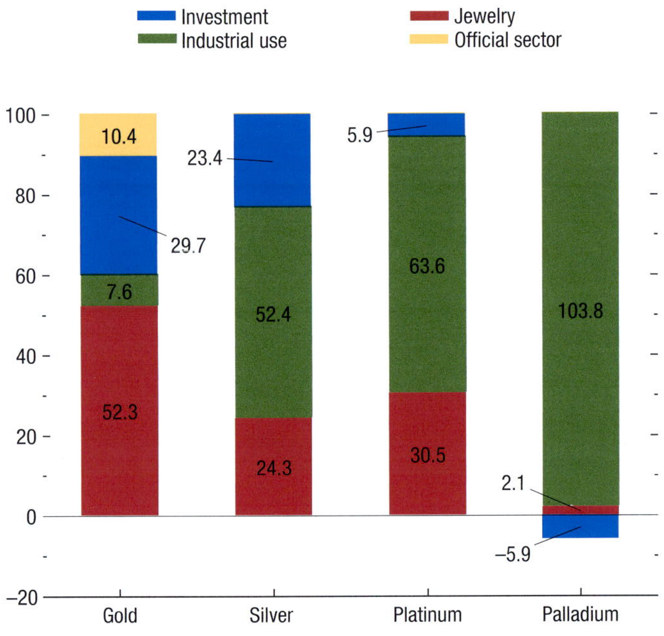

Sources: 2018 World Silver Survey; PGM Market Report; and World Gold Council.
Note: Investment includes coins, bars, and exchange traded funds' inventory changes; for silver, jewelry includes silverware; for platinum and palladium, industrial use includes autocatalysts; 2015–17 averages.

[10]Executive Order 6102, issued in 1933, prohibited hoarding of gold coins, gold bullion, and gold certificates in the continental United States. The limitation on gold private ownership in the United States was repealed in 1974, leading to a resumption of gold bullion trading in spot and futures markets in 1975.

[11]A similar conclusion is obtained when testing for the presence of a unit root in the real price of precious metals over a long time span. Most of the tests are inconclusive, suggesting that metal prices are not an obvious inflation hedge. In fact, even though long-term real returns are close to zero, fluctuations in the real price of precious metals can be very persistent, especially in local currency.

[12]In early 1980 US consumer price inflation peaked at almost 15 percent. By 2012 many central banks around the world had embarked on quantitative easing; the Federal Reserve balance sheet doubled in size while consumer price inflation in the United States had peaked at almost 4 percent in the previous year. Bekaert and Wang (2010) argues that the "recent crisis has made market observers and economists wonder whether inflation will rear its ugly head again in years to come. Central banks across the world have injected substantial amounts of liquidity in the financial system, and public debt has surged everywhere. It is not hard to imagine that inflationary pressures may resurface with a vengeance once the economy rebounds." In both episodes, however, concerns were probably overplayed given that inflation declined in the subsequent years (in most advanced economies).

Figure 1.SF.5. Correlation: Precious Metals, Copper, and Oil

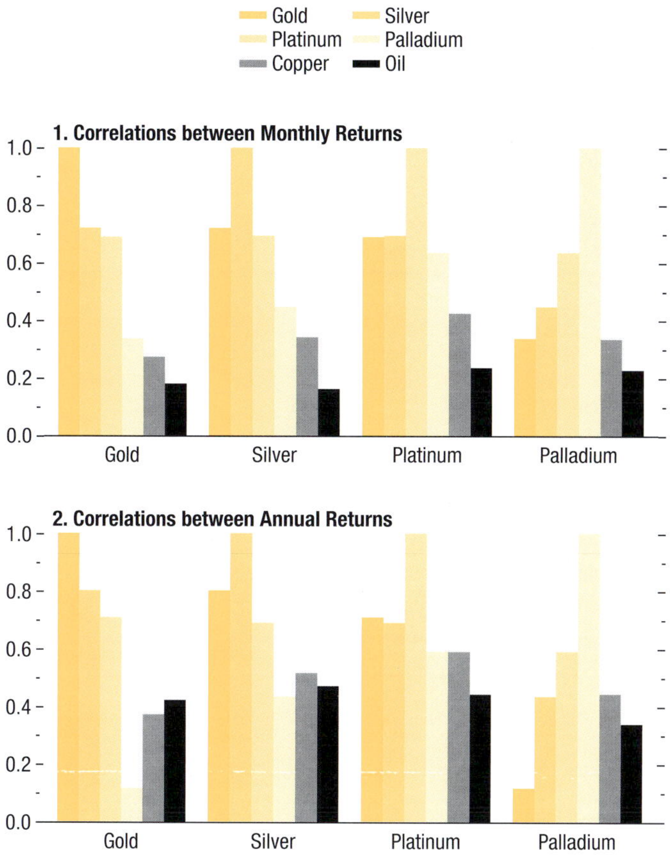

Sources: IMF, Primary Commodity Price System; and IMF staff calculations.
Note: Sample period of gold, silver, copper, and oil is from 1970:M1 to 2019:M5; Platinum starts in 1976; Palladium starts in 1987.

Figure 1.SF.6. Precious Metals versus Consumer Price Index Inflation

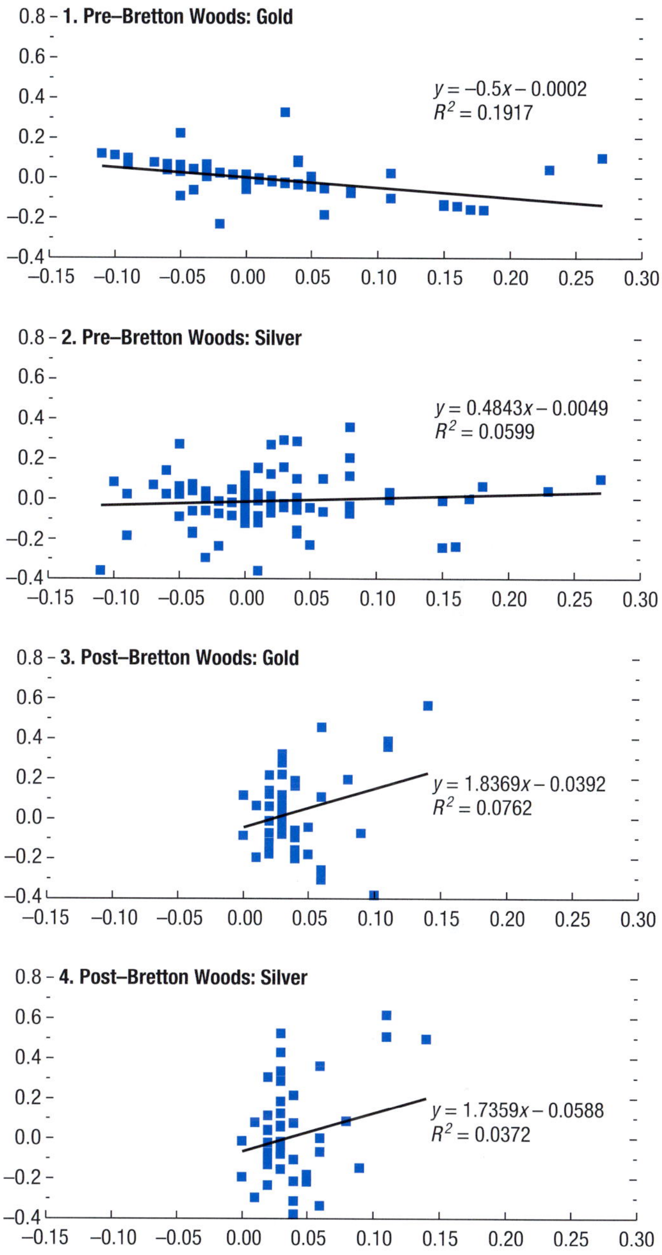

Sources: Measuringworth.com; Minneapolis Federal Reserve; and IMF staff calculations.
Note: A regression of annual real gold price change (silver) on US consumer price index inflation shows a negative coefficient before 1973 but positive thereafter.

for testing precious metals' ability to hedge against tail events, such as the collapse of major fiat currency systems—a daunting task, however, given that that has never happened.

A more viable alternative is to regress precious metal prices on a measure of inflation risk (such as past inflation volatility or inflation forecast dispersion) and a set of control variables (Table 1.SF.5). Results of the analysis support the view that precious metal prices react to inflation concerns. The analysis uses monthly data starting in 1978 and controlling for the exchange rate (traditionally, an important determinant), Treasury yields (a proxy for carrying costs), mean reversion, and expected and surprise inflation. An increase in inflation uncertainty by one standard deviation tends, within a month, to raise the price of gold by 0.8 percent and silver by 1.6 percent. A decline in inflation uncertainty can explain half of the observed gold price decline of the 1990s and one-third of the price rise after 2008.

The role of inflation uncertainty is, instead, positive but not significant for platinum and palladium, yet irrelevant for copper. Interestingly, because of dollar invoicing, an appreciation of the US dollar has a similar strong negative effect on all metals tested, including copper. What is more surprising is a coefficient above

Table 1.SF.4. World Average Inflation Betas

Horizon	Gold	Silver	Platinum	Palladium
1 Month	0.42	0.48	0.44	0.40
6 Months	0.77	0.81	0.77	0.66
12 Months	0.90	0.89	0.82	0.61
5 Years	1.05	1.05	0.89	0.72

Sources: IMF, *International Financial Statistics*; IMF, Primary Commodity Price System; Newey and West (1987); and IMF staff calculations.

Note: The betas reported are weighted averages across all countries (weight = the inverse of the Newey–West standard errors). For each country, betas come from regressions between log difference of 1-month, 6-month, 12-month, and 5-year nominal precious metal prices in local currency and inflation corresponding to the same horizon.

unity, suggesting that metal prices are excessively sensitive to the US dollar.[13]

In addition to tail events in the monetary sphere, precious metals have been considered safe assets during sharp movements in economic and policy uncertainty, as proxied by stock price changes. Table 1.SF.6 shows that gold and (to a lesser extent) silver returns do not correlate during days of high stock market swings: the top 30 stock market booms are associated with a stable gold price, on average, while the top 30 stock market declines are associated with an average slight increase in gold prices (there is still-sizable uncertainty around the average reaction). This safe haven property—which stands out for gold and, to a lesser extent, silver but is not present for platinum nor, especially, palladium—is shared by the US dollar and Treasury notes, typical safe haven assets. It is not shared by other base metals. Finally, cryptocurrencies, which have some similarities to gold

[13]Capie, Mills, and Wood (2005) and Sjaastad (2008) examine the hedge property of gold with respect to changes of the US dollar and show that dollar exchange rates and gold prices are inversely related. This result has also been found for oil prices (Kilian and Zhou 2019).

Table 1.SF.5. Determinants of One-Month Return on Precious Metals

	(1) Gold	(2) Silver	(3) Platinum	(4) Palladium	(5) Copper
Industrial Production	0.095	−0.018	0.487	1.049	1.993***
	(0.26)	(−0.03)	(0.94)	(1.43)	(3.79)
Inflation Surprise	2.583*	2.690	3.117*	0.407	1.297
	(2.24)	(1.32)	(2.41)	(0.22)	(1.06)
Lag of Inflation Expectation	0.406	−0.086	−0.128	−2.235**	−0.062
	(0.86)	(−0.10)	(−0.24)	(−3.29)	(−0.15)
Oil Price	−0.001	0.002	0.002	0.00292*	0.00371***
	(−0.74)	(1.14)	(1.59)	(2.01)	(3.98)
US Treasury Bill	−17.210	5.885	0.061	60.04*	−5.640
	(−1.87)	(0.31)	(0.01)	(2.15)	(−0.74)
Lag of US Treasury Bill	12.330	−10.760	−2.681	−53.170	4.101
	(1.34)	(−0.59)	(−0.32)	(−1.86)	(0.52)
Lag of Precious Metal Real Price	−0.0163**	−0.0341***	−0.0286**	−0.012	−0.013
	(−3.31)	(−3.43)	(−3.06)	(−1.24)	(−1.69)
Exchange Rate	−1.219***	−1.437***	−1.456***	−0.561	−1.365***
	(−6.93)	(−4.17)	(−6.19)	(−1.68)	(−4.99)
Inflation Volatility	0.909*	2.373**	0.821	1.327	0.254
	(2.34)	(2.8)	(1.55)	(1.62)	(0.57)
Constant	0.0293**	−0.0792**	0.0654**	0.0456*	0.049
	(2.62)	(−3.28)	(3.22)	(2.02)	(1.85)
Sample Start Date	1980m1	1980m1	1980m1	1987m2	1980m1
Sample End Date	2018m12	2018m12	2018m12	2018m12	2018m12
R^2	0.18	0.15	0.21	0.15	0.26

Sources: Consensus Economics Forecast; IMF, Primary Commodity Price System; Thomson Reuters Datastream; University of Michigan, Survey of Consumers; and IMF staff calculations.

Note: Variables are in logarithmic scale. Industrial Production and Oil Price are in log difference. Lag of Precious Metal Real Price = real price of dependent variable in US dollars. Exchange Rate = exchange rate constructed to be orthogonal to other independent variables using nominal effective exchange rate. Inflation Volatility = rolling standard deviation of inflation over 36-month window. t statistics in parentheses.

$^{*}p < 0.05$, $^{**}p < 0.01$, $^{***}p < 0.001$

Table 1.SF.6. Asset Returns Associated with Largest Single-Day Changes in the S&P 500 Index
(Percent change)

	S&P 500	Gold	Silver	Platinum	Palladium	US dollar	10Y Yield	Metals	Bitcoin
Top 30	5.3 (4.3,5.5)	0.0 (–1.1,1)	–0.2 (–2.5,0.9)	0.1 (–1.2,1.6)	0.7 (–1.2,3.7)	–0.3 (–0.8,0.3)	4.9 (–2.9,11.2)	0.5 (–1.7,2.3)	1.2 (–1.2,1.7)
Top 50	4.7 (3.8,4.9)	–0.4 (–1.3,0.7)	–0.6 (–2.5,0.6)	0.2 (–0.9,1.7)	0.3 (–1.5,2.2)	–0.2 (–0.6,0.5)	5.3 (–2.5,12.8)	0.4 (–1.4,2.1)	0.9 (–0.8,2.5)
Top 100	3.9 (3.1,4.2)	–0.3 (–0.7,0.5)	–0.4 (–1.6,0.7)	0.3 (–0.7,1.5)	0.3 (–0.8,1.4)	–0.1 (–0.6,0.5)	5.6 (–0.9,12.2)	0.6 (–0.4,1.8)	0.0 (–3.9,0.9)
Bottom 30	–6.0 (–6.9,–4.8)	0.6 (–0.8,1.8)	0.2 (–0.4,0.7)	–0.5 (–1.5,0.9)	–0.9 (–2,1.3)	0.3 (–0.2,0.8)	–9.2 (–17.7,–3)	–2.7 (–4,–1.8)	–0.3 (–2.5,4.1)
Bottom 50	–5.2 (–6,–3.9)	0.5 (–0.8,1.8)	0.1 (–0.6,0.6)	–0.4 (–1.6,1.1)	–1.0 (–2.2,0.9)	0.1 (–0.5,0.8)	–9.1 (–14.2,–3.4)	–2.0 (–3.8,–0.4)	–2.6 (–4.3,4.2)
Bottom 100	–4.2 (–4.6,–3.1)	0.3 (–0.6,1.2)	0.0 (–1,1.1)	–0.4 (–1.4,1.1)	–0.9 (–2.1,0.8)	0.1 (–0.5,0.7)	–7.5 (–11.7,–3.6)	–1.5 (–2.7,–0.1)	–1.4 (–4,3.7)

Sources: Thomson Reuters Datastream; and IMF staff calculations.
Note: Numbers represent asset returns (percent change) associated with large changes in the S&P 500. For example, Top 30 and Bottom 30 refer to the average percent change of the 30 largest single-day increases and decreases, respectively, of the S&P 500. Data for all asset returns are sorted based on S&P 500. 10Y Yield is the daily basis point difference on 10-year US bond yields. For all other indicators, data are daily growth rates. For Bitcoin, the time period is August 18, 2011, to August 19, 2019. Metals is the IMF base metals index. For all other indicators, the time interval is January 1, 1998, to August 19, 2019. Bitcoin numbers are adjusted by multiplying by the ratio of the S&P 500 movements over the aforementioned time intervals. Data in the parenthesis are the interquartile range.

and silver, do not appear to be safe havens during stock market routs.[14,15] Moreover, unlike gold and silver, they do not have intrinsic value.

Conclusions

Precious metals are macrorelevant (more so for some low-income countries) and have relevant industrial use, especially platinum and palladium—even though their price is only mildly affected by global activity. Gold and silver can function as inflation hedges, but this property should not be overstated, especially when changes in inflation are modest. Instead, given their historical role in monetary systems and purchasing power stability, gold and silver seem to have been buoyed at times by the (possibly irrational) fear of a collapse of major fiat currency systems. The safe haven properties of precious metals have probably been more apparent during some (but not all) major economic and policy shocks, proxied by stock market swings, that triggered or reversed investor flight to safety—with gold standing out as a safe asset, much like US Treasury notes. Crypto assets do not seem to share this property, so far.

[14]Cryptocurrency prices, proxied by Bitcoin, are calculated for 2011–19.

[15]As is true of gold and silver, the supply of some cryptocurrencies is limited. Cryptocurrencies also appeal to users and investors because of their decentralized nature and anonymity.

Box 1.SF.1. What's Happening with Global Carbon Emissions?

To slow the pace of climate change, carbon emissions need to be reduced. But how have emissions changed over the past decade? And which countries are driving those changes? Although global carbon emissions were flat between 2014 and 2016, they alarmingly rebounded in 2017 and 2018 (Figure 1.SF.1.1).

China has been a key driver of emission growth since the turn of the century, but its impact has diminished in recent years as economic reforms have picked up pace. India and other emerging markets, instead, are partially filling the gap. In 2018 emissions decreased in all Group of Seven economies besides the United States, whose emissions increased because of a resurgence of industrial production and bad weather (see BP 2019).

The authors of this box are Christian Bogmans, Akito Matsumoto, and Andrea Pescatori.

It is possible to decompose total emissions E as a product of carbon intensity c (carbon emissions per unit of energy), energy intensity e (energy per unit of GDP), GDP per capita y, and human population P (Kaya and Yokobori 1997):

$$E = \frac{E}{Energy} * \frac{Energy}{GDP} * \frac{GDP}{P} P = c * e * y * P.$$

The contribution of income growth to the growth of carbon emissions is larger, on average, and more cyclical than that of population growth (Figure 1.SF.1.2). Declining energy intensity has consistently helped reduce emission growth, but in 2018 its contribution was lower, possibly because of a cyclical pickup in global industrial production. In 2018 decarbonization was the most important mitigation force as wind, solar, and natural gas slowly replaced coal as the energy source of choice in the power sectors of all major emitters.

Figure 1.SF.1.1. Contribution to World Emissions, by Location

(Percent change)

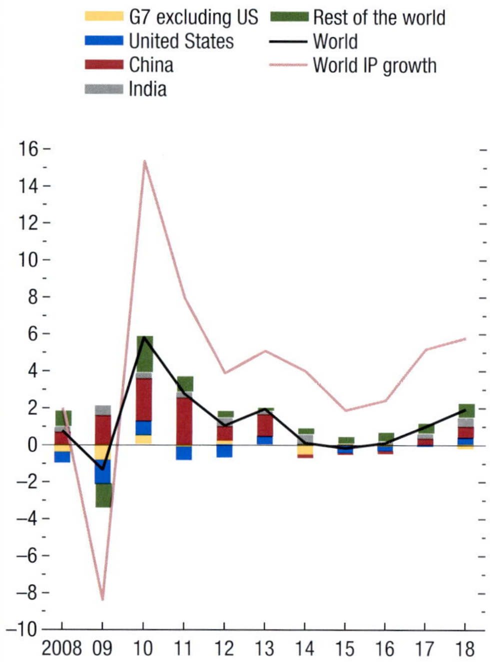

Sources: British Petroleum; International Energy Agency; and IMF staff calculations.
Note: G7 = Group of Seven; IP = industrial production.

Figure 1.SF.1.2. Contribution to World Emissions, by Source

(Percent change)

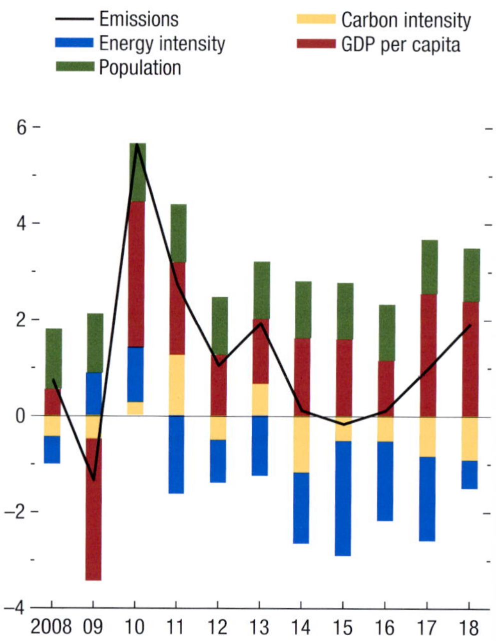

Sources: British Petroleum; International Energy Agency; World Bank, World Development Indicators; and IMF staff calculations.

Annex Table 1.1.1. European Economies: Real GDP, Consumer Prices, Current Account Balance, and Unemployment

(Annual percent change, unless noted otherwise)

	Real GDP			Consumer Prices[1]			Current Account Balance[2]			Unemployment[3]		
		Projections			Projections			Projections			Projections	
	2018	2019	2020	2018	2019	2020	2018	2019	2020	2018	2019	2020
Europe	**2.3**	**1.4**	**1.8**	**3.3**	**3.2**	**2.8**	**2.5**	**2.5**	**2.2**	...	...	...
Advanced Europe	**1.9**	**1.2**	**1.5**	**1.9**	**1.4**	**1.5**	**2.7**	**2.7**	**2.6**	**7.1**	**6.7**	**6.6**
Euro Area[4,5]	1.9	1.2	1.4	1.8	1.2	1.4	2.9	2.8	2.7	8.2	7.7	7.5
Germany	1.5	0.5	1.2	1.9	1.5	1.7	7.3	7.0	6.6	3.4	3.2	3.3
France	1.7	1.2	1.3	2.1	1.2	1.3	–0.6	–0.5	–0.5	9.1	8.6	8.4
Italy	0.9	0.0	0.5	1.2	0.7	1.0	2.5	2.9	2.9	10.6	10.3	10.3
Spain	2.6	2.2	1.8	1.7	0.7	1.0	0.9	0.9	1.0	15.3	13.9	13.2
Netherlands	2.6	1.8	1.6	1.6	2.5	1.6	10.9	9.8	9.5	3.8	3.3	3.3
Belgium	1.4	1.2	1.3	2.3	1.5	1.3	–1.3	–1.1	–0.8	6.0	5.5	5.5
Austria	2.7	1.6	1.7	2.1	1.5	1.9	2.3	1.6	1.8	4.9	5.1	5.0
Ireland	8.3	4.3	3.5	0.7	1.2	1.5	10.6	10.8	9.6	5.8	5.5	5.2
Portugal	2.4	1.9	1.6	1.2	0.9	1.2	–0.6	–0.6	–0.7	7.0	6.1	5.6
Greece	1.9	2.0	2.2	0.8	0.6	0.9	–3.5	–3.0	–3.3	19.3	17.8	16.8
Finland	1.7	1.2	1.5	1.2	1.2	1.3	–1.6	–0.7	–0.5	7.4	6.5	6.4
Slovak Republic	4.1	2.6	2.7	2.5	2.6	2.1	–2.5	–2.5	–1.7	6.6	6.0	5.9
Lithuania	3.5	3.4	2.7	2.5	2.3	2.2	1.6	1.1	1.1	6.1	6.1	6.0
Slovenia	4.1	2.9	2.9	1.7	1.8	1.9	5.7	4.2	4.1	5.1	4.5	4.5
Luxembourg	2.6	2.6	2.8	2.0	1.7	1.7	4.7	4.5	4.5	5.0	5.2	5.2
Latvia	4.8	2.8	2.8	2.6	3.0	2.6	–1.0	–1.8	–2.1	7.4	6.5	6.7
Estonia	4.8	3.2	2.9	3.4	2.5	2.4	1.7	0.7	0.3	5.4	4.7	4.7
Cyprus	3.9	3.1	2.9	0.8	0.7	1.6	–7.0	–7.8	–7.5	8.4	7.0	6.0
Malta	6.8	5.1	4.3	1.7	1.7	1.8	9.8	7.6	6.2	3.7	3.8	4.0
United Kingdom	1.4	1.2	1.4	2.5	1.8	1.9	–3.9	–3.5	–3.7	4.1	3.8	3.8
Switzerland	2.8	0.8	1.3	0.9	0.6	0.6	10.2	9.6	9.8	2.5	2.8	2.8
Sweden	2.3	0.9	1.5	2.0	1.7	1.5	1.7	2.9	2.7	6.3	6.5	6.7
Czech Republic	3.0	2.5	2.6	2.2	2.6	2.3	0.3	–0.1	–0.2	2.2	2.2	2.3
Norway	1.3	1.9	2.4	2.8	2.3	1.9	8.1	6.9	7.2	3.9	3.6	3.5
Denmark	1.5	1.7	1.9	0.7	1.3	1.5	5.7	5.5	5.2	5.0	5.0	5.0
Iceland	4.8	0.8	1.6	2.7	2.8	2.5	2.8	3.1	1.6	2.7	3.3	3.6
San Marino	1.1	0.8	0.7	1.5	1.3	1.5	0.4	0.4	0.2	8.0	8.1	8.1
Emerging and Developing Europe[6]	**3.1**	**1.8**	**2.5**	**6.2**	**6.8**	**5.6**	**1.7**	**1.6**	**0.6**	...	...	...
Russia	2.3	1.1	1.9	2.9	4.7	3.5	6.8	5.7	3.9	4.8	4.6	4.8
Turkey	2.8	0.2	3.0	16.3	15.7	12.6	–3.5	–0.6	–0.9	11.0	13.8	13.7
Poland	5.1	4.0	3.1	1.6	2.4	3.5	–0.6	–0.9	–1.1	3.8	3.8	3.8
Romania	4.1	4.0	3.5	4.6	4.2	3.3	–4.5	–5.5	–5.2	4.2	4.3	4.6
Ukraine[7]	3.3	3.0	3.0	10.9	8.7	5.9	–3.4	–2.8	–3.5	9.0	8.7	8.2
Hungary	4.9	4.6	3.3	2.8	3.4	3.4	–0.5	–0.9	–0.6	3.7	3.5	3.4
Belarus	3.0	1.5	0.3	4.9	5.4	4.8	–0.4	–0.9	–3.4	0.4	0.5	0.9
Bulgaria[5]	3.1	3.7	3.2	2.6	2.5	2.3	4.6	3.2	2.5	5.3	4.9	4.8
Serbia	4.3	3.5	4.0	2.0	2.2	1.9	–5.2	–5.8	–5.1	13.3	13.1	12.8
Croatia	2.6	3.0	2.7	1.5	1.0	1.2	2.5	1.7	1.0	9.9	9.0	8.0

Note: Data for some countries are based on fiscal years. Please refer to Table F in the Statistical Appendix for a list of economies with exceptional reporting periods.
[1]Movements in consumer prices are shown as annual averages. Year-end to year-end changes can be found in Tables A6 and A7 in the Statistical Appendix.
[2]Percent of GDP.
[3]Percent. National definitions of unemployment may differ.
[4]Current account position corrected for reporting discrepancies in intra-area transactions.
[5]Based on Eurostat's harmonized index of consumer prices except for Slovenia.
[6]Includes Albania, Bosnia and Herzegovina, Kosovo, Moldova, Montenegro, and North Macedonia.
[7]See country-specific note for Ukraine in the "Country Notes" section of the Statistical Appendix.

Annex Table 1.1.2. Asian and Pacific Economies: Real GDP, Consumer Prices, Current Account Balance, and Unemployment

(Annual percent change, unless noted otherwise)

	Real GDP			Consumer Prices[1]			Current Account Balance[2]			Unemployment[3]		
		Projections			Projections			Projections			Projections	
	2018	2019	2020	2018	2019	2020	2018	2019	2020	2018	2019	2020
Asia	5.5	5.0	5.1	2.4	2.4	2.6	1.3	1.5	1.3	. . .	. . .	. . .
Advanced Asia	**1.8**	**1.3**	**1.3**	**1.3**	**1.0**	**1.3**	**4.0**	**3.9**	**3.6**	**3.2**	**3.2**	**3.2**
Japan	0.8	0.9	0.5	1.0	1.0	1.3	3.5	3.3	3.3	2.4	2.4	2.4
Korea	2.7	2.0	2.2	1.5	0.5	0.9	4.4	3.2	2.9	3.8	4.0	4.2
Australia	2.7	1.7	2.3	2.0	1.6	1.8	–2.1	–0.3	–1.7	5.3	5.1	5.1
Taiwan Province of China	2.6	2.0	1.9	1.5	0.8	1.1	12.2	11.4	10.8	3.7	3.8	3.8
Singapore	3.1	0.5	1.0	0.4	0.7	1.0	17.9	16.5	16.6	2.1	2.2	2.2
Hong Kong SAR	3.0	0.3	1.5	2.4	3.0	2.6	4.3	5.5	5.1	2.8	2.9	3.0
New Zealand	2.8	2.5	2.7	1.6	1.4	1.9	–3.8	–4.1	–4.3	4.3	4.3	4.5
Macao SAR	4.7	–1.3	–1.1	3.0	2.4	2.7	35.2	35.7	35.3	1.8	1.8	1.8
Emerging and Developing Asia	**6.4**	**5.9**	**6.0**	**2.6**	**2.7**	**3.0**	**–0.1**	**0.4**	**0.2**	. . .	. . .	. . .
China	6.6	6.1	5.8	2.1	2.3	2.4	0.4	1.0	0.9	3.8	3.8	3.8
India[4]	6.8	6.1	7.0	3.4	3.4	4.1	–2.1	–2.0	–2.3	. . .	. . .	. . .
ASEAN-5	**5.2**	**4.8**	**4.9**	**2.8**	**2.4**	**2.6**	**0.2**	**0.4**	**0.1**	. . .	. . .	. . .
Indonesia	5.2	5.0	5.1	3.2	3.2	3.3	–3.0	–2.9	–2.7	5.3	5.2	5.0
Thailand	4.1	2.9	3.0	1.1	0.9	0.9	6.4	6.0	5.4	1.2	1.2	1.2
Malaysia	4.7	4.5	4.4	1.0	1.0	2.1	2.1	3.1	1.9	3.3	3.4	3.4
Philippines	6.2	5.7	6.2	5.2	2.5	2.3	–2.6	–2.0	–2.3	5.3	5.2	5.1
Vietnam	7.1	6.5	6.5	3.5	3.6	3.7	2.4	2.2	1.9	2.2	2.2	2.2
Other Emerging and Developing Asia[5]	**6.3**	**6.3**	**6.2**	**5.0**	**5.3**	**5.3**	**–3.1**	**–2.8**	**–2.9**	. . .	. . .	. . .
Memorandum												
Emerging Asia[6]	6.4	5.9	6.0	2.5	2.6	2.9	0.0	0.5	0.3	. . .	. . .	. . .

Note: Data for some countries are based on fiscal years. Please refer to Table F in the Statistical Appendix for a list of economies with exceptional reporting periods.
[1]Movements in consumer prices are shown as annual averages. Year-end to year-end changes can be found in Tables A6 and A7 in the Statistical Appendix.
[2]Percent of GDP.
[3]Percent. National definitions of unemployment may differ.
[4]See country-specific note for India in the "Country Notes" section of the Statistical Appendix.
[5]Other Emerging and Developing Asia comprises Bangladesh, Bhutan, Brunei Darussalam, Cambodia, Fiji, Kiribati, Lao P.D.R., Maldives, Marshall Islands, Micronesia, Mongolia, Myanmar, Nauru, Nepal, Palau, Papua New Guinea, Samoa, Solomon Islands, Sri Lanka, Timor-Leste, Tonga, Tuvalu, and Vanuatu.
[6]Emerging Asia comprises the ASEAN-5 (Indonesia, Malaysia, Philippines, Thailand, Vietnam) economies, China, and India.

Annex Table 1.1.3. Western Hemisphere Economies: Real GDP, Consumer Prices, Current Account Balance, and Unemployment

(Annual percent change, unless noted otherwise)

	Real GDP			Consumer Prices[1]			Current Account Balance[2]			Unemployment[3]		
		Projections			Projections			Projections			Projections	
	2018	2019	2020	2018	2019	2020	2018	2019	2020	2018	2019	2020
North America	**2.7**	**2.1**	**2.0**	**2.7**	**2.0**	**2.3**	**–2.4**	**–2.4**	**–2.4**	...	...	...
United States	2.9	2.4	2.1	2.4	1.8	2.3	–2.4	–2.5	–2.5	3.9	3.7	3.5
Canada	1.9	1.5	1.8	2.2	2.0	2.0	–2.6	–1.9	–1.7	5.8	5.8	6.0
Mexico	2.0	0.4	1.3	4.9	3.8	3.1	–1.8	–1.2	–1.6	3.3	3.4	3.4
Puerto Rico[4]	–4.9	–1.1	–0.7	1.3	–0.1	1.0	...	...	...	9.2	9.2	9.4
South America[5]	**0.4**	**–0.2**	**1.8**	**7.1**	**9.2**	**8.6**	**–1.8**	**–1.6**	**–1.4**	...	...	...
Brazil	1.1	0.9	2.0	3.7	3.8	3.5	–0.8	–1.2	–1.0	12.3	11.8	10.8
Argentina	–2.5	–3.1	–1.3	34.3	54.4	51.0	–5.3	–1.2	0.3	9.2	10.6	10.1
Colombia	2.6	3.4	3.6	3.2	3.6	3.7	–4.0	–4.2	–4.0	9.7	9.7	9.5
Chile	4.0	2.5	3.0	2.3	2.2	2.8	–3.1	–3.5	–2.9	7.0	6.9	6.9
Peru	4.0	2.6	3.6	1.3	2.2	1.9	–1.6	–1.9	–2.0	6.7	6.7	6.7
Venezuela	–18.0	–35.0	–10.0	65,374.1	200,000	500,000	6.4	7.0	1.5	35.0	47.2	50.5
Ecuador	1.4	–0.5	0.5	–0.2	0.4	1.2	–1.4	0.1	0.7	3.7	4.3	4.7
Paraguay	3.7	1.0	4.0	4.0	3.5	3.7	0.5	–0.1	1.3	5.6	6.1	5.9
Bolivia	4.2	3.9	3.8	2.3	1.7	3.1	–4.9	–5.0	–4.1	3.5	4.0	4.0
Uruguay	1.6	0.4	2.3	7.6	7.6	7.2	–0.6	–1.7	–3.0	8.4	8.6	8.1
Central America[6]	**2.6**	**2.7**	**3.4**	**2.6**	**2.7**	**3.0**	**–3.2**	**–2.7**	**–2.6**	...	...	...
Caribbean[7]	**4.7**	**3.3**	**3.7**	**3.7**	**2.8**	**4.4**	**–1.6**	**–1.8**	**–2.2**	...	...	...
Memorandum												
Latin America and the Caribbean[8]	1.0	0.2	1.8	6.2	7.2	6.7	–1.9	–1.6	–1.5	...	...	...
Eastern Caribbean Currency Union[9]	4.0	3.6	3.4	1.3	1.5	2.0	–8.4	–7.9	–7.7	...	...	...

Note: Data for some countries are based on fiscal years. Please refer to Table F in the Statistical Appendix for a list of economies with exceptional reporting periods.

[1]Movements in consumer prices are shown as annual averages. Aggregates exclude Venezuela. Year-end to year-end changes can be found in Tables A6 and A7 in the Statistical Appendix.

[2]Percent of GDP.

[3]Percent. National definitions of unemployment may differ.

[4]Puerto Rico is a territory of the United States but its statistical data are maintained on a separate and independent basis.

[5]Includes Guyana and Suriname. See country-specific notes for Argentina and Venezuela in the "Country Notes" section of the Statistical Appendix.

[6]Central America comprises Belize, Costa Rica, El Salvador, Guatemala, Honduras, Nicaragua, and Panama.

[7]The Caribbean comprises Antigua and Barbuda, Aruba, The Bahamas, Barbados, Dominica, Dominican Republic, Grenada, Haiti, Jamaica, St. Kitts and Nevis, St. Lucia, St. Vincent and the Grenadines, and Trinidad and Tobago.

[8]Latin America and the Caribbean comprises Mexico and economies from the Caribbean, Central America, and South America. See country-specific notes for Argentina and Venezuela in the "Country Notes" section of the Statistical Appendix.

[9]Eastern Caribbean Currency Union comprises Antigua and Barbuda, Dominica, Grenada, St. Kitts and Nevis, St. Lucia, and St. Vincent and the Grenadines as well as Anguilla and Montserrat, which are not IMF members.

Annex Table 1.1.4. Middle East and Central Asia Economies: Real GDP, Consumer Prices, Current Account Balance, and Unemployment

(Annual percent change, unless noted otherwise)

	Real GDP			Consumer Prices[1]			Current Account Balance[2]			Unemployment[3]		
		Projections			Projections			Projections			Projections	
	2018	2019	2020	2018	2019	2020	2018	2019	2020	2018	2019	2020
Middle East and Central Asia	**1.9**	**0.9**	**2.9**	**9.9**	**8.2**	**9.1**	**2.7**	**–0.4**	**–1.4**	**. . .**	**. . .**	**. . .**
Oil Exporters[4]	**0.6**	**–0.7**	**2.3**	**8.5**	**6.9**	**8.0**	**5.9**	**1.6**	**0.1**	**. . .**	**. . .**	**. . .**
Saudi Arabia	2.4	0.2	2.2	2.5	–1.1	2.2	9.2	4.4	1.5	6.0	. . .	. . .
Iran	–4.8	–9.5	0.0	30.5	35.7	31.0	4.1	–2.7	–3.4	14.5	16.8	17.4
United Arab Emirates	1.7	1.6	2.5	3.1	–1.5	1.2	9.1	9.0	7.1	. . .	. . .	. . .
Iraq	–0.6	3.4	4.7	0.4	–0.3	1.0	6.9	–3.5	–3.7	. . .	. . .	. . .
Algeria	1.4	2.6	2.4	4.3	2.0	4.1	–9.6	–12.6	–11.9	11.7	12.5	13.3
Kazakhstan	4.1	3.8	3.9	6.0	5.3	5.2	0.0	–1.2	–1.5	4.9	4.9	4.9
Qatar	1.5	2.0	2.8	0.2	–0.4	2.2	8.7	6.0	4.1	. . .	. . .	. . .
Kuwait	1.2	0.6	3.1	0.6	1.5	2.2	14.4	8.2	6.8	1.3	1.3	1.3
Oman	1.8	0.0	3.7	0.9	0.8	1.8	–5.5	–7.2	–8.0	. . .	. . .	. . .
Azerbaijan	1.0	2.7	2.1	2.3	2.8	3.0	12.9	9.7	10.0	5.0	5.0	5.0
Turkmenistan	6.2	6.3	6.0	13.2	13.4	13.0	5.7	–0.6	–3.0	. . .	. . .	. . .
Oil Importers[5]	**4.4**	**3.8**	**3.9**	**12.7**	**10.7**	**11.3**	**–6.6**	**–6.0**	**–5.3**	**. . .**	**. . .**	**. . .**
Egypt	5.3	5.5	5.9	20.9	13.9	10.0	–2.4	–3.1	–2.8	10.9	8.6	7.9
Pakistan	5.5	3.3	2.4	3.9	7.3	13.0	–6.3	–4.6	–2.6	6.1	6.1	6.2
Morocco	3.0	2.7	3.7	1.9	0.6	1.1	–5.4	–4.5	–3.8	9.8	9.2	8.9
Uzbekistan	5.1	5.5	6.0	17.5	14.7	14.1	–7.1	–6.5	–5.6	. . .	. . .	. . .
Sudan	–2.2	–2.6	–1.5	63.3	50.4	62.1	–13.6	–7.4	–12.5	19.5	22.1	21.0
Tunisia	2.5	1.5	2.4	7.3	6.6	5.4	–11.1	–10.4	–9.4	15.4	. . .	. . .
Jordan	1.9	2.2	2.4	4.5	2.0	2.5	–7.0	–7.0	–6.2	18.3	. . .	. . .
Lebanon	0.2	0.2	0.9	6.1	3.1	2.6	–25.6	–26.4	–26.3	. . .	. . .	. . .
Afghanistan	2.7	3.0	3.5	0.6	2.6	4.5	9.1	2.0	0.2	. . .	. . .	. . .
Georgia	4.7	4.6	4.8	2.6	4.2	3.8	–7.7	–5.9	–5.8	12.7	. . .	. . .
Tajikistan	7.3	5.0	4.5	3.8	7.4	7.1	–5.0	–5.8	–5.8	. . .	. . .	. . .
Armenia	5.2	6.0	4.8	2.5	1.7	2.5	–9.4	–7.4	–7.4	18.2	17.7	17.5
Kyrgyz Republic	3.5	3.8	3.4	1.5	1.3	5.0	–8.7	–10.0	–8.3	6.6	6.6	6.6
Memorandum												
Caucasus and Central Asia	4.2	4.4	4.4	8.3	7.6	7.6	0.3	–1.3	–1.7	. . .	. . .	. . .
Middle East, North Africa, Afghanistan, and Pakistan	1.6	0.5	2.7	10.1	8.3	9.3	2.9	–0.3	–1.4	. . .	. . .	. . .
Middle East and North Africa	1.1	0.1	2.7	11.0	8.4	8.9	3.8	0.1	–1.3	. . .	. . .	. . .
Israel[6]	3.4	3.1	3.1	0.8	1.0	1.3	2.7	2.4	2.5	4.0	4.0	4.0
Maghreb[7]	3.0	1.4	2.7	4.3	2.3	3.7	–7.3	–8.6	–9.1	. . .	. . .	. . .
Mashreq[8]	4.8	5.0	5.4	18.8	12.5	9.1	–6.7	–6.9	–6.2	. . .	. . .	. . .

Note: Data for some countries are based on fiscal years. Please refer to Table F in the Statistical Appendix for a list of economies with exceptional reporting periods.
[1]Movements in consumer prices are shown as annual averages. Year-end to year-end changes can be found in Tables A6 and A7 in the Statistical Appendix.
[2]Percent of GDP.
[3]Percent. National definitions of unemployment may differ.
[4]Includes Bahrain, Libya, and Yemen.
[5]Includes Djibouti, Mauritania, and Somalia. Excludes Syria because of the uncertain political situation.
[6]Israel, which is not a member of the economic region, is included for reasons of geography but is not included in the regional aggregates.
[7]The Maghreb comprises Algeria, Libya, Mauritania, Morocco, and Tunisia.
[8]The Mashreq comprises Egypt, Jordan, and Lebanon. Syria is excluded because of the uncertain political situation.

Annex Table 1.1.5. Sub-Saharan African Economies: Real GDP, Consumer Prices, Current Account Balance, and Unemployment
(Annual percent change, unless noted otherwise)

	Real GDP			Consumer Prices[1]			Current Account Balance[2]			Unemployment[3]		
		Projections			Projections			Projections			Projections	
	2018	2019	2020	2018	2019	2020	2018	2019	2020	2018	2019	2020
Sub-Saharan Africa	**3.2**	**3.2**	**3.6**	**8.5**	**8.4**	**8.0**	**–2.7**	**–3.6**	**–3.8**	**. . .**	**. . .**	**. . .**
Oil Exporters[4]	**1.3**	**2.0**	**2.4**	**13.0**	**11.4**	**11.4**	**1.9**	**–0.1**	**–0.3**	**. . .**	**. . .**	**. . .**
Nigeria	1.9	2.3	2.5	12.1	11.3	11.7	1.3	–0.2	–0.1	22.6	. . .	. . .
Angola	–1.2	–0.3	1.2	19.6	17.2	15.0	6.1	0.9	–0.7	. . .	. . .	. . .
Gabon	0.8	2.9	3.4	4.8	3.0	3.0	–2.4	0.1	0.9	. . .	. . .	. . .
Republic of Congo	1.6	4.0	2.8	1.2	1.5	1.8	6.7	6.8	5.3	. . .	. . .	. . .
Chad	2.4	2.3	5.4	4.0	3.0	3.0	–3.4	–6.4	–6.1	. . .	. . .	. . .
Middle-Income Countries[5]	**2.8**	**2.8**	**2.9**	**4.6**	**4.6**	**5.2**	**–3.6**	**–3.6**	**–3.9**	**. . .**	**. . .**	**. . .**
South Africa	0.8	0.7	1.1	4.6	4.4	5.2	–3.5	–3.1	–3.6	27.1	27.9	28.4
Ghana	6.3	7.5	5.6	9.8	9.3	9.2	–3.1	–3.6	–3.8	. . .	. . .	. . .
Côte d'Ivoire	7.4	7.5	7.3	0.4	1.0	2.0	–4.7	–3.8	–3.8	. . .	. . .	. . .
Cameroon	4.1	4.0	4.2	1.1	2.1	2.2	–3.7	–3.7	–3.5	. . .	. . .	. . .
Zambia	3.7	2.0	1.7	7.0	9.9	10.0	–2.6	–3.6	–3.4	. . .	. . .	. . .
Senegal	6.7	6.0	6.8	0.5	1.0	1.5	–8.8	–8.5	–11.1	. . .	. . .	. . .
Low-Income Countries[6]	**6.2**	**5.3**	**5.9**	**7.6**	**9.2**	**7.4**	**–7.0**	**–7.9**	**–8.0**	**. . .**	**. . .**	**. . .**
Ethiopia	7.7	7.4	7.2	13.8	14.6	12.7	–6.5	–6.0	–5.3	. . .	. . .	. . .
Kenya	6.3	5.6	6.0	4.7	5.6	5.3	–5.0	–4.7	–4.6	. . .	. . .	. . .
Tanzania	7.0	5.2	5.7	3.5	3.6	4.2	–3.7	–4.1	–3.6	. . .	. . .	. . .
Uganda	6.1	6.2	6.2	2.6	3.2	3.8	–8.9	–11.5	–10.5	. . .	. . .	. . .
Democratic Republic of the Congo	5.8	4.3	3.9	29.3	5.5	5.0	–4.6	–3.4	–4.2	. . .	. . .	. . .
Mali	4.7	5.0	5.0	1.7	0.2	1.3	–3.8	–5.5	–5.5	. . .	. . .	. . .
Madagascar	5.2	5.2	5.3	7.3	6.7	6.3	0.8	–1.6	–2.7	. . .	. . .	. . .
Memorandum												
Sub-Saharan Africa Excluding South Sudan	3.2	3.2	3.6	8.2	8.3	8.0	–2.7	–3.6	–3.8	. . .	. . .	. . .

Note: Data for some countries are based on fiscal years. Please refer to Table F in the Statistical Appendix for a list of economies with exceptional reporting periods.
[1]Movements in consumer prices are shown as annual averages. Year-end to year-end changes can be found in Table A7 in the Statistical Appendix.
[2]Percent of GDP.
[3]Percent. National definitions of unemployment may differ.
[4]Includes Equatorial Guinea and South Sudan.
[5]Includes Botswana, Cabo Verde, Eswatini, Lesotho, Mauritius, Namibia, and Seychelles.
[6]Includes Benin, Burkina Faso, Burundi, the Central African Republic, Comoros, Eritrea, The Gambia, Guinea, Guinea-Bissau, Liberia, Malawi, Mali, Mozambique, Niger, Rwanda, São Tomé and Príncipe, Sierra Leone, Togo, and Zimbabwe.

Annex Table 1.1.6. Summary of World Real per Capita Output

(Annual percent change; in international currency at purchasing power parity)

	Average									Projections		
	2001–10	2011	2012	2013	2014	2015	2016	2017	2018	2019	2020	2024
World	**2.4**	**3.0**	**2.0**	**2.2**	**2.3**	**2.1**	**2.1**	**2.5**	**2.4**	**1.8**	**2.3**	**2.5**
Advanced Economies	**1.1**	**1.2**	**0.7**	**0.9**	**1.6**	**1.8**	**1.2**	**2.0**	**1.8**	**1.3**	**1.3**	**1.2**
United States	0.8	0.8	1.5	1.1	1.8	2.2	0.9	1.7	2.3	1.8	1.5	1.1
Euro Area[1]	0.8	1.3	–1.2	–0.5	1.2	1.8	1.6	2.4	1.8	1.0	1.3	1.2
Germany	1.0	3.9	0.2	0.2	1.8	0.9	1.4	2.1	1.2	0.5	1.2	1.3
France	0.6	1.7	–0.2	0.1	0.4	0.7	0.8	2.0	1.6	1.1	1.0	1.1
Italy	–0.2	0.2	–3.2	–2.3	–0.3	0.9	1.3	1.8	1.0	0.2	0.7	0.9
Spain	0.8	–1.4	–3.0	–1.3	1.7	3.8	3.2	3.0	2.5	1.7	1.4	1.2
Japan	0.6	–0.3	1.7	2.2	0.5	1.3	0.6	2.1	1.0	1.1	0.8	1.0
United Kingdom	1.0	0.8	0.8	1.4	2.2	1.5	1.0	1.2	0.8	0.6	0.9	1.1
Canada	0.8	2.1	0.7	1.3	1.8	–0.1	0.1	1.7	0.5	0.3	0.8	0.8
Other Advanced Economies[2]	2.7	2.5	1.3	1.7	2.1	1.4	1.6	2.2	1.9	0.9	1.2	1.7
Emerging Market and Developing Economies	**4.6**	**4.8**	**3.6**	**3.6**	**3.2**	**2.8**	**3.1**	**3.3**	**3.2**	**2.5**	**3.3**	**3.5**
Emerging and Developing Asia	7.2	6.7	5.9	5.9	5.8	5.7	5.7	5.6	5.5	5.0	5.1	5.1
China	9.9	9.0	7.4	7.3	6.7	6.4	6.1	6.2	6.2	5.8	5.5	5.3
India[3]	5.9	5.2	4.1	5.0	6.0	6.6	6.8	5.8	5.4	4.7	5.6	5.9
ASEAN-5[4]	3.7	3.1	4.7	3.7	3.3	3.6	3.8	4.2	4.1	3.7	3.8	4.2
Emerging and Developing Europe	4.4	5.6	2.7	2.7	1.6	0.4	1.6	3.7	2.9	1.6	2.4	2.4
Russia	5.1	5.0	3.5	1.5	–1.1	–2.4	0.1	1.6	2.3	1.1	1.9	2.0
Latin America and the Caribbean	1.9	3.4	1.7	1.7	0.2	–0.9	–1.8	0.2	0.1	–0.9	1.1	1.9
Brazil	2.5	3.1	1.0	2.1	–0.3	–4.4	–4.1	0.3	0.3	0.2	1.4	1.7
Mexico	0.2	2.4	2.4	0.2	1.7	2.2	1.8	1.1	1.0	–0.6	0.4	1.6
Middle East and Central Asia	2.2	3.7	0.9	0.4	0.5	0.4	2.8	–0.2	–0.1	–1.2	1.0	1.4
Saudi Arabia	0.3	6.8	2.5	–0.1	2.5	1.7	–0.6	–3.3	0.0	–1.8	0.2	0.5
Sub-Saharan Africa	2.9	2.5	1.5	2.4	2.4	0.4	–1.3	0.3	0.6	0.6	0.9	1.5
Nigeria	6.1	2.1	1.5	2.6	3.5	0.0	–4.2	–1.8	–0.7	–0.3	–0.1	0.1
South Africa	2.1	1.7	0.7	0.9	0.3	–0.3	–1.1	–0.1	–0.7	–0.9	–0.4	0.2
Memorandum												
European Union	1.2	1.6	–0.6	0.0	1.6	2.1	1.8	2.5	2.0	1.3	1.5	1.4
Low-Income Developing Countries	3.8	3.6	1.7	3.6	3.7	1.9	1.2	2.4	2.8	2.7	2.9	3.2
Middle East and North Africa	1.9	6.1	0.3	–0.3	–0.2	0.0	3.1	–1.1	–1.1	–2.1	0.8	0.8

Note: Data for some countries are based on fiscal years. Please refer to Table F in the Statistical Appendix for a list of economies with exceptional reporting periods.
[1]Data calculated as the sum of individual euro area countries.
[2]Excludes the G7 (Canada, France, Germany, Italy, Japan, United Kingdom, United States) and euro area countries.
[3]See country-specific note for India in the "Country Notes" section of the Statistical Appendix.
[4]Indonesia, Malaysia, Philippines, Thailand, Vietnam.

References

Abbritti, Mirko, and Stephan Fahr. 2013. "Downward Wage Rigidity and Business Cycle Asymmetries." *Journal of Monetary Economics* 60: 871–86.

Adrian, Tobias, and Maurice Obstfeld. 2017. "Why International Financial Cooperation Remains Essential." IMF Blog, March 23.

Aiyar, Shekhar, and Simon Voigts. 2019. "The Negative Mean Output Gap." IMF Working Paper 19/183, International Monetary Fund, Washington, DC.

Baker, Scott R., Nicholas Bloom, and Steven J. Davis. 2016. "Measuring Economic Policy Uncertainty." *Quarterly Journal of Economics* 131 (4): 1593–636.

Banque Centrale du Luxembourg (BCL). 2019. Bulletin 2019 (2).

Bekaert, Geert, and Xiaozheng Wang. 2010. "Inflation Risk and the Inflation Risk Premium." *Economic Policy* 25 (64): 755–806.

Bems, Rudolf, Robert C. Johnson, and Key-Mu Yi. 2011. "Vertical Linkages and the Collapse of Global Trade." *American Economic Review, Papers and Proceedings* 101 (3) 308–12.

British Petroleum (BP). 2019. "Statistical Review of World Energy." https://www.bp.com/content/dam/bp/business-sites/en/global/corporate/pdfs/energy-economics/statistical-review/bp-stats-review-2019-full-report.pdf.

Broadberry, Stephen, and Bishnupriya Gupta. 2006. "The Early Modern Great Divergence: Wages, Prices, and Economic Development in Europe and Asia, 1500–1800." *The Economic History Review* 59 (1): 2–31.

Caldara, Dario, and Matteo Iacoviello. 2018. "Measuring Geopolitical Risk." International Finance Discussion Papers 1222, Board of Governors of the Federal Reserve System.

Caliendo, Lorenzo, Robert C. Feenstra, John Romalis, and Alan Taylor. 2017. "Tariff Reductions, Entry, and Welfare: Theory and Evidence for the Last Two Decades." NBER Working Paper 21768, National Bureau of Economic Research, Cambridge, MA.

Capie, Forrest, Terence Mills, and Geoffrey Wood. 2005. "Gold as a Hedge against the Dollar." *Journal of International Financial Markets* 15 (4): 343–52.

Damgaard, Jannick, and Thomas Elkjaer. 2017. "The Global FDI Network: Searching for Ultimate Investors." IMF Working Paper 17/258, International Monetary Fund, Washington, DC.

De Nederlandsche Bank (DNB). 2019. "Statistical News Release: Current Account Surplus Contracts in First Quarter." https://www.dnb.nl/en/news/news-and-archive/Statistischnieuws2019/dnb384751.jsp.

Dupraz, Stéphane, Emi Nakamura, and Jón Steinsson. 2019. "A Plucking Model of Business Cycle." mimeo.

Erb, Claude, and Campbell Harvey. 2013. "The Golden Dilemma." NBER Working Paper 18706, National Bureau of Economic Research, Cambridge, MA.

European Central Bank (ECB). 2019. "What the Maturing Tech Cycle Signals for the Global Economy." ECB Economic Bulletin 3/2019. https://www.ecb.europa.eu/pub/economic-bulletin/focus/2019/html/ecb.ebbox201903_01~4e6e0fcef6.en.html.

Friedman, Milton. 1964. "Monetary Studies of the National Bureau." In *The National Bureau Enters Its 45th Year*, 44th Annual Report: 7–25. http://www.nber.org/nberhistory/annualreports.html.

———. 1990. "Bimetallism Revisited." *Journal of Economic Perspectives* 4 (4): 85–104.

———. 1993. "The Plucking Model of Business Fluctuations Revisited." *Economic Inquiry* 31: 171–77.

Green, Timothy. 2007. *The Ages of Gold: Mines, Markets, Merchants, and Goldsmiths from Egypt to Troy, Rome to Byzantium, and Venice to the Space Age*. GFMS Limited.

Gruss, Bertrand. 2014. "After the Boom—Commodity Prices and Economic Growth in Latin America and the Caribbean." IMF Working Paper 14/154, International Monetary Fund, Washington, DC.

International Monetary Fund (IMF). 2018. "Final Report of the Task Force on Special Purpose Entities." IMF Committee on Balance of Payments Statistics (BOCPOM), BOPCOM-18/03 (https://www.imf.org/external/pubs/ft/bop/2018/pdf/18-03.pdf).

———. 2019. "Fiscal Policies for Paris Climate Strategies—From Principle to Practice." Policy Paper 19/010.

Kaya, Yoichi, and Keiichi Yokobori, eds. 1997. *Environment, Energy, and Economy: Strategies for Sustainability*. Tokyo: United Nations University Press.

Kilian, Lutz, and Xiaoqing Zhou. 2019. "Oil Prices, Exchange Rates and Interest Rates." Manuscript, University of Michigan: Michigan. https://drive.google.com/file/d/1SAz_WsNhsHJ5OCxi12HcFyhDYfUjzyw6/view.

Lane, Philip, and Gian Maria Milesi Ferretti. 2018. "The External Wealth of Nations Revisited: International Financial Integration in the Aftermath of the Global Financial Crisis." *IMF Economic Review* 66 (1): 189–222.

Lopez-Cordova, Ernesto, and Christopher Meissner. 2003. "The Globalization of Trade and Democracy, 1870–2000." NBER Working Paper 11117, National Bureau of Economic Research, Cambridge, MA.

Malanima, Paolo. 2009. *Pre-Modern European Economy: One Thousand Years (10th–19th Centuries)*. Boston: Brill.

Mian, Atif, and Amir Sufi. 2012. "The Effects of Fiscal Stimulus: Evidence from the 2009 Cash for Clunkers Program." *Quarterly Journal of Economics* 127 (3): 1107–142.

Mundell, Robert A. 2002. "The Birth of Coinage." Columbia University Department of Economics Discussion Paper Series 0102–08, New York, NY.

Newey, Whitney, and Kenneth West. 1987. "A Simple, Positive Semi-Definite, Heteroskedasticity, and Autocorrelation Consistent Covariance Matrix." *Econometrica* 55 (3): 703–08.

Nieuwenhuis, Paul, and Peter Wells, eds. 2015. *The Global Automotive Industry*. John Wiley and Sons.

Officer, Lawrence. 2008. "Gold Standard." In *The New Palgrave Dictionary of Economics*, 2501–507.

Schultz, M., K. Dziczek, Y. Chen, and B. Swiechi. 2019. *US Consumer & Economic Impacts of US Automotive Trade Policies*. Center for Automotive Research, Ann Arbor, Michigan.

Setser, Brad. 2019. "$500 Billion in Dividends Out of the Double Irish with a Dutch Twist (with a Bit of Help from Bermuda)." Blog, Council of Foreign Relations, August 12.

Sjaastad, Larry H. 2008. "The Price of Gold and the Exchange Rates: Once Again." *Resources Policy* 33: 118–24.

Smolyansky, Michael, Gustavo Suarez, and Alexandra Tabova. 2019. "US Corporations' Repatriation of Offshore Profits: Evidence from 2018." FEDS Notes, Board of Governors of the Federal Reserve System, Washington, DC, August 6. https://doi.org/10.17016/2380-7172.2396.

Swiss National Bank (SNB). 2019. "Swiss Balance of Payments and International Investment Position: Q4 2018 and Review of the Year 2018." https://www.snb.ch/en/mmr/reference/pre_20190325/source/pre_20190325.en.pdf.

Timmer, Marcel P., Erik Dietzenbacher, Bart Los, Robert Stehrer and Gaaitzen J. de Vries. 2015. "An Illustrated User Guide to the World Input-Output Database: The Case of Global Automotive Production." *Review of International Economics* 23 (3): 575–605.

Vilar, Pierre. 1976. *A History of Gold and Money: 1450–1920*. Translated by Judith White. London: New Left Books.

CHAPTER 2

CLOSER TOGETHER OR FURTHER APART? WITHIN-COUNTRY REGIONAL DISPARITIES AND ADJUSTMENT IN ADVANCED ECONOMIES

Subnational—within-country—regional disparities in real output, employment, and productivity in advanced economies have attracted greater interest in recent years against a backdrop of growing social and political tensions. Regional disparities in the average advanced economy have risen since the late 1980s, reflecting gains from economic concentration in some regions and relative stagnation in others. On average, lagging regions have worse health outcomes, lower labor productivity, and greater employment shares in agriculture and industry sectors than other within-country regions. Moreover, adjustment in lagging regions is slower, with adverse shocks having longer-lived negative effects on economic performance. Although much discussed, trade shocks—in particular greater import competition in external markets—do not appear to drive the differences in labor market performance between lagging and other regions, on average. By contrast, technology shocks—proxied by declines in the relative costs of machinery and equipment capital goods—raise unemployment in regions that are more vulnerable to automation, with more exposed lagging regions particularly hurt. National policies that reduce distortions and encourage more flexible and open markets, while providing a robust social safety net, can facilitate regional adjustment to adverse shocks, dampening rises in unemployment. Place-based policies targeted at lagging regions may also play a role, but they must be carefully calibrated to ensure they help rather than hinder beneficial adjustment.

Introduction

Disparities in economic activity across subnational regions in the average advanced economy have been gradually creeping upward since the late 1980s, undoing some of the marked decline over the previous three decades and mirroring trends in overall income inequality in many advanced economies (Figure 2.1, panel 1).[1,2] Real GDP per capita in the advanced economy region at the 90th percentile is now, on average, 70 percent higher than that in the region at the 10th percentile. Such a wide disparity means that within-country regional differences in economic activity in a number of advanced economies are larger than the average differences between peer countries (Figure 2.2). By contrast, average subnational regional (simply regional hereafter) disparities in emerging market economies have trended down since 2010, after rising from the early 2000s (Figure 2.1, panel 3). On average, though, they remain about double those in advanced economies. In parallel, the average speed of regional convergence in advanced economies has slowed to less than one-half percent per year, while picking up to more than 1 percent in emerging market economies (Figure 2.1, panels 2 and 4).

Slowing regional convergence and rising disparities in some advanced economies, alongside regional labor market and productivity developments, have attracted much interest in recent years, in part because of evidence that poor regional performance within a country can fuel discontent and political polarization, erode social trust, and threaten national cohesion.[3]

The authors of this chapter are John Bluedorn (co-lead), Zsóka Kóczán (co-lead), Weicheng Lian, Natalija Novta, and Yannick Timmer, with support from Christopher Johns, Evgenia Pugacheva, Adrian Robles Villamil, and Yuan Zeng. The chapter also benefited from discussions with Philip Engler, Antonio Spilimbergo, and Jiaxiong Yao, and from comments from internal seminar participants.

[1]For evidence on trends in overall income inequality in advanced economies, see Dabla-Norris and others (2015); the October 2017 *Fiscal Monitor*; and Nolan, Richiardi, and Valenzuela (2019), among others. Immervoll and Richardson (2011) argues that declining fiscal redistribution accounts for some of this rise.

[2]Subnational regions are the TL2 regions as defined in OECD (2018) unless otherwise indicated. These are typically the first-level administrative units within a country, corresponding roughly to US states or German Länder. Consequently, the geographic extents of TL2 regions are not homogenous across or within countries. Alternative geographic aggregates (for example, higher resolution areal or metropolitan aggregates or different administrative classifications) may generate different findings. Subnational regional real GDP per capita is purchasing power parity (PPP) adjusted for cross-country comparability, although not adjusted for within-country regional price differences. Box 2.1 discusses some of the issues with measuring regional real GDP per capita and its link to welfare.

[3]See Algan and Cahuc (2014) and Guriev (2018) on social trust, regional performance, and rising political polarization. Looking at Europe, Winkler (2019) presents evidence that regional income inequality engenders greater political polarization in regions. Rajan (2019) argues that lack of attention to peripheral regions is fostering despair and a backlash, destabilizing societies.

Figure 2.1. Subnational Regional Disparities and Convergence over Time

Subnational regional disparities in the average advanced economy have risen over the past three decades, while regional convergence has slowed. Disparities in emerging market economies are typically larger but have been coming down, while within-country average convergence has picked up.

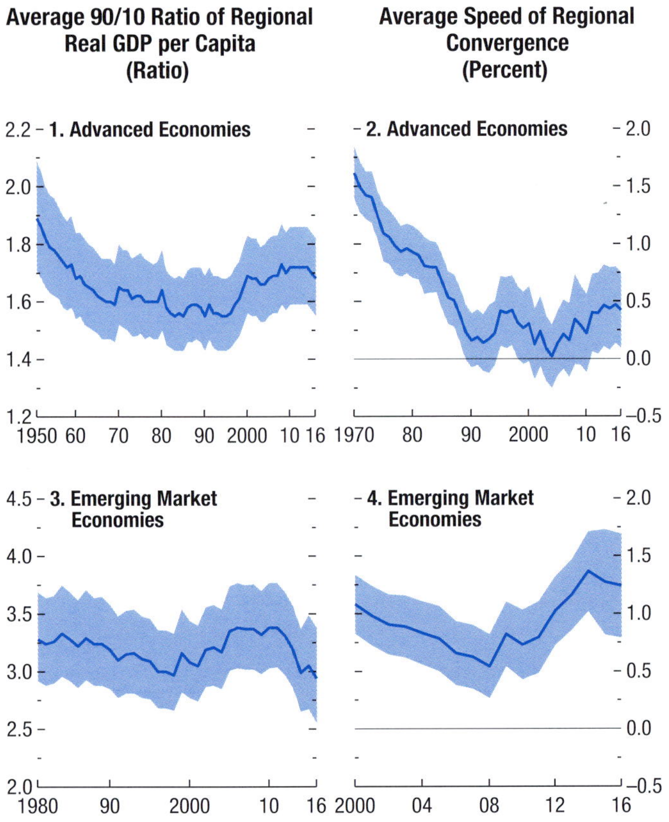

Sources: Gennaioli and others (2014); Organisation for Economic Co-operation and Development Regional Database; and IMF staff calculations.
Note: The regional 90/10 ratio for a country is defined as real GDP per capita in the region at the 90th percentile of the country's regional real GDP per capita distribution over that of the region at the 10th percentile. The solid line in panels 1 and 3 shows the year fixed effects from a regression of regional 90/10 ratios from the indicated sample on year fixed effects and country fixed effects to account for entry and exit during the period and level differences in the 90/10 regional GDP ratios. Blue shaded areas indicate the associated 90 percent confidence interval. Panels 2 and 4 show the coefficient on initial log real GDP per capita from a cross-sectional regression of average real purchasing power parity GDP per capita growth on initial log real GDP per capita, estimated over 20-year rolling windows (plotted at the last year of the window). The regression includes country fixed effects, so it indicates average within-country regional convergence. The coefficient is expressed in annualized terms, indicating the average annual speed of convergence. See Online Annex 2.1 for the country samples.

Figure 2.2. Distribution of Subnational Regional Disparities in Advanced Economies
(Density, 2013)

Many advanced economies have larger within-country regional disparities than exist between advanced economies.

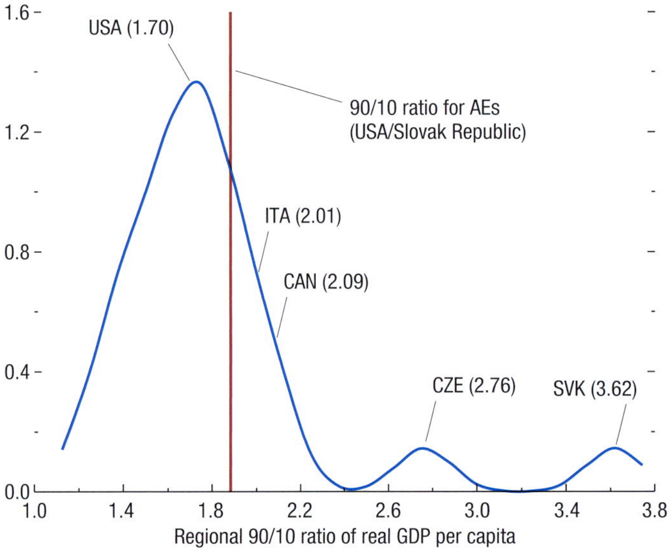

Sources: Organisation for Economic Co-operation and Development Regional Database; and IMF staff calculations.
Note: The figure plots the kernel density of the country-level regional 90/10 ratio across advanced economies (the ratio of real GDP per capita, PPP-adjusted, of the 90th percentile subnational region to the 10th percentile subnational region, calculated for each country). The vertical line indicates the national 90/10 ratio within the same group of advanced economies (that is, the ratio of real GDP per capita, PPP-adjusted of the country at the 90th percentile to the country at the 10th percentile). Selected countries' positions in the distribution are indicated by their International Organization for Standardization (ISO) codes and corresponding regional 90/10 value in parentheses. See Online Annex 2.1 for the country sample. PPP = purchasing power parity.

More generally, a recurring theme in the latest economic research is that local conditions play an essential role in shaping individual opportunities and social mobility—in other words, place can be primal.[4]

Aside from their political and social ramifications, are disparities in regional economic activity a macroeconomic concern? To be sure, increases in

[4]For example, see Chetty and Hendren (2018a, 2018b) on how place-of-birth has profound and long-lasting effects on an individual's lifetime economic opportunities, even accounting for family background and other influences. Durlauf and Seshadri (2018) argues that causation flows from economic inequality to lower social mobility, rather than the reverse. Drawing on other evidence from the United States, Chetty, Hendren, and Katz (2016) contends that geographic mobility is a key means by which social mobility—improved lifetime incomes and opportunities—can be achieved. See also Conolly, Corak, and Haeck (2019) for similar analyses and evidence from Canada.

disparities between regions of a country can be a normal feature of growth. Increasing specialization and agglomeration—the phenomenon in which the increasing spatial density of economic activity makes trade and exchange more efficient—can boost productivity and lead to a greater concentration of economic activity in some regions within a country, causing them to pull away from others.[5] Growth in core regions can nonetheless eventually spread outward to peripheral regions, generating catch-up.[6]

However, persistently large or increasing regional disparities can also be a sign that some regions are not adjusting to changing economic circumstances and are falling behind. Failure to adjust to adverse shocks—contributing to high regional unemployment and persistent shortfalls in productivity—could reflect barriers to labor and capital moving to regions and firms where their returns would be higher. Indeed, long-term unemployment rates tend to be higher in worse-performing regions within advanced economies, suggesting some persistent inefficiencies may be at work (Figure 2.3).

Consistent with the notion that regional disparities can drive social and political discontent, lagging regions in advanced economies—those failing to converge toward richer regions of the same country over the past couple of decades—tend to do worse than other regions, on average, on key measures of well-being, including health, human capital, and labor market outcomes (Figure 2.4).[7] The age profiles of populations in lagging regions may explain part of their overall lower employment rate—lagging regions have significantly lower prime age (ages 25–54) population shares and skew significantly younger (under age 25) than other regions. But these demographic characteristics are not the complete story for lagging regions, as seen by their higher overall unemployment rate and higher youth inactivity rate (share of youth not in employment, education, or training), on average. Given the importance of employment status for life satisfaction, independent of its effect on income, improving regional labor market performance can generate welfare gains beyond those that can be achieved through income redistribution.[8]

Motivated by these considerations and taking into account the greater recent rise in disparities in advanced economies alongside data availability constraints, this chapter examines regional disparities and labor market adjustment in advanced economies, with a focus on the

Figure 2.3. Subnational Regional Unemployment and Economic Activity in Advanced Economies, 1999–2016

Regional long-term unemployment rates tend to be higher where economic activity per person is lower, suggesting the existence of greater inefficiencies in lagging regions.

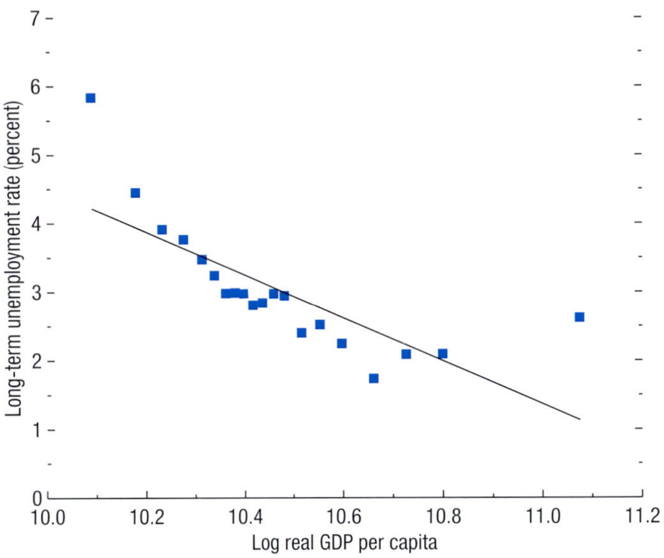

Sources: Organisation for Economic Co-operation and Development Regional Database; and IMF staff calculations.
Note: The figure illustrates the regression slope for the relationship between regional long-term unemployment rates and log regional real GDP per capita after controlling for country-year fixed effects. Dots show the binned underlying data from the regression, based on the method from Chetty, Friedman, and Rockoff (2014). See Online Annex 2.1 for the country sample.

[5]The underlying impetus for these dynamics may be simple geography (less costly access to trading partners and inputs), natural resource booms, or the persistent effects of historical factors. See Krugman (1991), Davis and Weinstein (2002), Duranton and Puga (2004), Moretti (2011), and Nunn (2014) for further discussion of these mechanisms and drivers.

[6]See Coe, Kelly, and Yeung (2007) and WB (2009) for evidence on these spillovers.

[7]Specifically, lagging regions are defined as those whose real GDP per capita in 2000 was below the country's regional median and whose growth was slower than the country's average from 2000–16. Similar patterns for human capital and labor market outcomes also hold if lagging regions are defined by predetermined criteria, such as below median initial real GDP per capita and initial service sector employment share. Nunn, Parsons, and Shambaugh (2018) finds that US counties that had initially low human capital, were less diversified in production, and were more dependent on manufacturing, had worse health, income, and labor market outcomes. It is important to note that the findings for lagging regions hold, on average; it is possible for a given region to differ from that average behavior. Moreover, due to data availability constraints, as noted, the classification is based on real GDP per capita data from 2000–16. See Online Annex 2.1 for further details. All annexes are available at www.imf.org/en/Publications/WEO.

[8]See Clark and Oswald (1994); Grün, Hauser, and Rhein (2010); and Clark (2018), among others, for evidence on the positive link between employment and happiness, independent of income and job quality.

Figure 2.4. Demographics, Health, Human Capital, and Labor Market Outcomes in Advanced Economies: Lagging versus Other Regions
(Percentage point difference, unless otherwise noted)

Lagging regions tend to have worse health, education, and labor market outcomes than other regions.

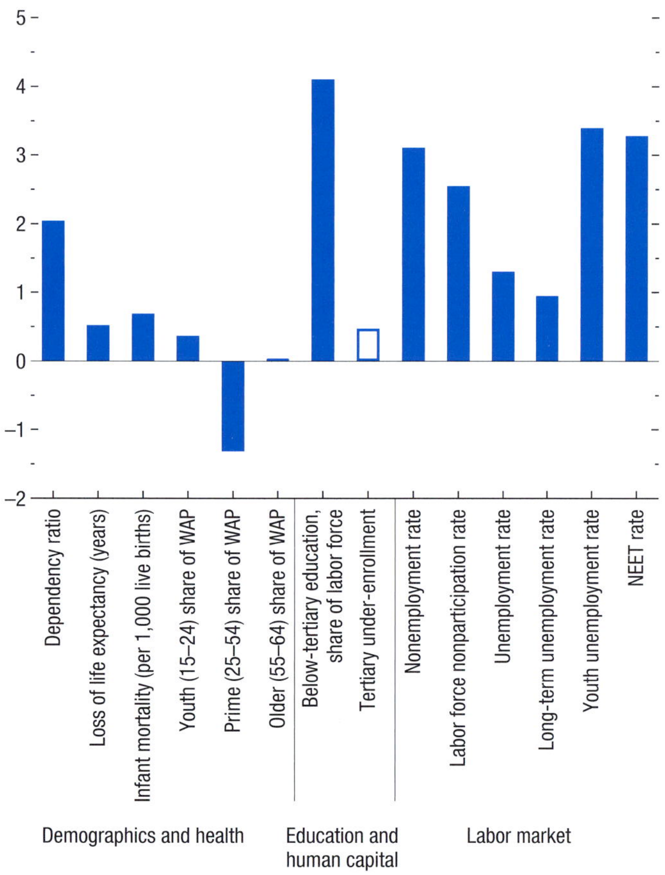

Sources: Organisation for Economic Co-operation and Development Regional Database; and IMF staff calculations.
Note: Bars show the difference in lagging regions versus other regions for each of the variables. Results are based on regressions of each variable on an indicator for whether a region is lagging or not, controlling for country-year fixed effects and with standard errors clustered at the country-year level. Solid bars indicate that the estimated coefficient on the lagging indicator is statistically significant at the 10 percent level. Variables are defined so that positive estimated coefficients indicate worse performance by lagging regions. Tertiary under-enrollment is the difference in the percent of population enrolled in tertiary education in other regions versus lagging regions. The nonemployment rate is defined as 100 minus the employment rate (in percent). The labor force nonparticipation rate is defined as 100 minus the labor force participation rate of the working-age (ages 15–64) population (in percent). The unemployment rate is the share of the working-age labor force that is unemployed. The long-term unemployment rate is the share of the working-age labor force that has been unemployed for one year or more. The youth unemployment rate is the share of the youth (ages 15–24) labor force that is unemployed. The NEET rate is the percent of the youth population that is not in education, employment, or training. Lagging regions are defined as those with real GDP per capita below their country median in 2000 and with average growth below the country's average over 2000–16. NEET = not in education, employment, or training; WAP = working-age population. See Online Annex 2.1 for the country sample.

characteristics and dynamics of lagging regions since 2000. It also explores whether differences in national policies related to labor and product market functioning influence regional disparities and adjustment. Specifically, the chapter investigates the following questions:

- How different are advanced economies in the extent of their regional disparities in economic activity? How do regional differences in sectoral production account for variation in labor productivity across regions within countries? How do lagging regions compare with other regions in their sectoral mix of employment and productivity? How effective have lagging regions been in responding to trends in the sectoral reallocation of labor?
- What are the regional labor market effects of local labor demand shocks—in particular trade and technology shocks—in advanced economies? Is adjustment to these shocks in lagging regions different from that in other regions?
- Do national policies and distortions play a role in regional disparities and adjustment in advanced economies?

The chapter's main findings are the following:

- The extent of regional disparities differs markedly across advanced economies—with the 90/10 ratios for regional real GDP per capita ranging from about 1.3 to more than 3. Underlying these disparities are regional differences in sectoral labor productivities and the sectoral employment mix, with lagging regions, on average, being systematically less productive and more specialized in agriculture and industry.
  - o Intrinsic sectoral productivity differences across regions tend to drive most regional labor productivity differences within a country. But for lagging regions, the employment mix matters more than it does for other regions.
  - o Even controlling for differences in trends across countries, lagging regions' employment is more concentrated in agriculture (suggesting that some are more rural) and industry, and less in services. Moreover, labor productivity across sectors is systematically lower in lagging regions than in others.
  - o From the early 2000s to the mid-2010s, one-third of the increase in the overall labor productivity gap between lagging and other regions appears to have reflected relatively ineffective sectoral labor market adjustment in lagging regions, with the rest attributed to growing sectoral productivity differences.

- Adverse trade and technology shocks affect more exposed regional labor markets, but only technology shocks tend to have lasting effects, with even larger unemployment rises for vulnerable lagging regions, on average.
  - Increases in import competition in external markets associated with the rise of China's productivity do not have marked effects on regional unemployment, although labor force participation falls in the near term, but quickly abates. Conditions in lagging regions do not look very different from other regions after such shocks.
  - By contrast, differences in vulnerability to automation across regions translate into noticeable differences in labor market responses to capital goods prices. When machinery and equipment prices fall, more vulnerable regions see more persistent rises in unemployment and declines in labor force participation than do less vulnerable regions. More vulnerable lagging regions have even larger rises in unemployment rates. Out-migration from more vulnerable lagging regions also appears to drop, suggesting that adjustment to technology shocks through labor mobility may be weaker in lagging regions that are more vulnerable to automation pressures.
- National structural policies that encourage more open and flexible markets are associated with improved regional adjustment to shocks and a lower dispersion of firms' efficiencies in allocating capital, which may narrow regional disparities.
  - Less stringent employment protection regulations and less generous unemployment benefits are associated with milder unemployment effects of trade and technology shocks.
  - National policies that encourage more open and flexible product markets are associated with lower variability in firms' capital allocative efficiencies, which is associated with lower regional disparities.

This chapter documents patterns and associations between regional disparities and adjustment and national policies in advanced economies. This is intended to help inform debate and discussion, complementing the vast literature examining regional differences on a country-by-country basis.[9] Much of the chapter's analysis focuses on the relatively short period since 2000 for which broad, cross-country regional data are available, enabling a look at labor market adjustment but precluding study of longer-term regional development dynamics. Furthermore, regions in the analysis are typically defined as countries' first-level administrative units, which are economically and politically meaningful within countries and for which good data coverage is available (see also footnote 2). However, this means that regions as diverse in size as Texas and Rhode Island in the United States are pooled together, despite the very different potential extents of their within-region markets for adjustment. Although the analysis attempts to account for this diversity through the inclusion of a variety of controls, alternative levels of geographic aggregation could generate different findings. Robustness checks are undertaken to confirm that the stylized facts and analysis results hold excluding capital-intensive, resource-rich regions. Finally, given that national policies may be affected by many different variables, their estimated effects on regional adjustment should be interpreted as associational rather than causal.

Although regional differences in economic activity and labor market outcomes are substantial within advanced economies, analysis of overall household-level inequality in disposable incomes at the country-level suggests that its regional component is small (Figure 2.5; see also Box 2.1 for a discussion of the measurement of regional economic activity and welfare).[10] For the subset of advanced economies and years since 2008 for which the decomposition can be calculated, the regional component of household disposable income inequality ranges from less than 1 percent in Austria to about 15 percent in Italy. This means that for advanced economies, further reducing differences in average disposable income across regions would typically have only moderate effects on income inequality in a country. However, there are some important exceptions. If, for example, average regional differences were eliminated in Italy, its income inequality could drop to levels seen in the early 1990s, which

[9]For a selection of work examining or leveraging regional economic differences in specific countries, see, for example, Kaufman, Swagel, and Dunaway (2003) and Breau and Saillant (2016) on Canadian provincial differences; Bande, Fernández, and Montuenga (2008), IMF (2018), and Liu (2018) on Spanish regional differences; Felice (2011), Giordano and others (2015), and Boeri and others (2019) on Italian regional differences.

[10]See Shorrocks and Wan (2005), Novotný (2007), and Cowell (2011), which come to broadly similar conclusions with alternative personal income concepts and multiple decomposable income inequality metrics. A similar finding holds using pretax and pretransfer household income. Note that household disposable income differs from GDP in that it incorporates factor income flows to/from elsewhere and the effects of fiscal redistribution.

Figure 2.5. Inequality in Household Disposable Income within Advanced Economies
(Indexes)

The regional component of income inequality in most advanced economies is relatively small, accounting for only about 5 percent of overall country inequality, on average.

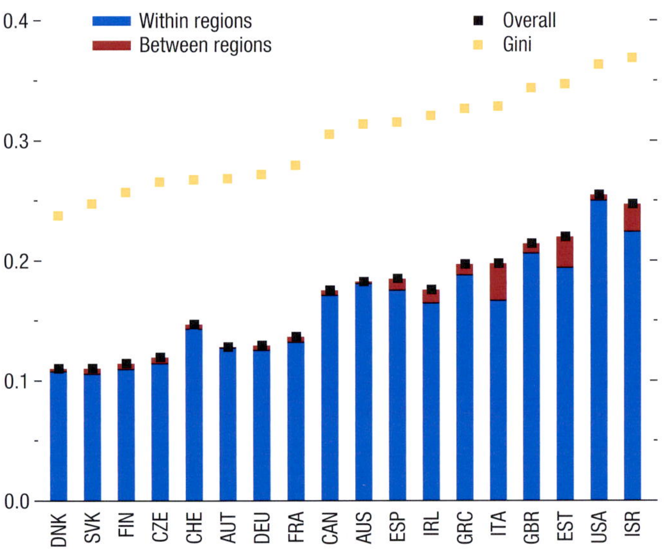

Sources: Luxembourg Income Study; and IMF staff calculations.
Note: The overall index shown is the generalized entropy index, also known as Theil's L, or the mean log deviation index of inequality. The income measure used is equivalized household disposable income (household income after tax and transfers transformed to account for household size differences), by country in the latest available year after 2008. The height of the bar indicates the overall level of the income inequality index, which is then decomposed into two components: (1) inequality attributable to average income differences across regions (the between component), and (2) inequality attributable to income differences across households within regions, after adjusting for average regional income differences (the within component). The Gini index of income inequality is also shown for comparison, as a more familiar inequality measure (but that is not decomposable). Data labels use International Organization for Standardization (ISO) country codes.

were the lowest since the 1970s.[11] But, as discussed above, reducing regional disparities and improving performance in economic activity and employment can have important consequences beyond current income. Moreover, some evidence indicates that countries with larger regional disparities may experience lower long-term growth (Che and Spilimbergo 2012).

The chapter begins with a brief discussion of how to think about regional development and adjustment. The subsequent section presents evidence on patterns of regional disparities in advanced economies and how lagging regions differ from others. Then, the regional responses to local labor demand shocks arising from trade and technology shocks are examined, focusing on how lagging regions differ and how national labor market policies may influence regional adjustment. The chapter then presents some evidence on labor mobility and the effects of national policies on regional disparities in the effectiveness of factor reallocation. Finally, a summary and concluding thoughts consider the potential implications for policies, including place-based policies.

Regional Development and Adjustment: A Primer

As in the large body of literature on the drivers of cross-country economic differences, the causes of persistent regional disparities within countries are hotly debated.[12] However, unlike countries, regions within a country are typically subject to the same overarching institutional structure (both political and economic) and common, national policies, with free exchange of goods and services and no legal impediments to the movements of capital and labor across the country.[13] Under perfectly competitive output and input markets and no market frictions (such as barriers to cross-regional factor movements), capital and labor would flow within and across regions to equalize marginal returns of capital and

[11]Based on the historical path of Italy's Gini coefficient from Atkinson and others (2017) and the assumption that the Gini would decline in proportion to the decline in the mean log deviation or generalized entropy index (Theil's L; which is a decomposable income inequality measure) if the regional component were eliminated.

[12]The development accounting framework (Caselli 2005; Hsieh and Klenow 2010) is often used to organize the potential drivers of regional differences within a country into proximate (physical capital, labor and human capital, and total factor productivity) and other intermediate and ultimate determinants (such as policies, culture, institutions, geography, climate, luck). Based on the analysis of global samples, Acemoglu and Dell (2010) and Gennaioli and others (2013, 2014) argue for the critical importance of human capital for development. Lessmann and Seidel (2017) also points to the importance of mobility and trade openness for regional development. Hsieh and Moretti (2019) contends that economies arising from regional agglomeration are substantial and that regional zoning restrictions lowered US aggregate output growth by one-third from the 1960s through the 2000s. Rodríguez-Pose and Storper (2019) pushes back against Hsieh and Moretti's (2019) contention, arguing that housing price differences across regions are not the primary drivers of regional migration. Rodríguez-Pose and Ketterer (forthcoming) asserts that regional differences in governance quality within-country lead to persistent differences in regional development and performance. See also OECD (2016b; 2018) for further analysis and evidence on broad patterns and drivers of persistent regional disparities across a wide range of countries.

[13]There are exceptions—often in federal states—where free exchange and movement within countries are inhibited. For example, Canadian provinces and territories differ in their standards and regulations for some goods and services, de facto restricting interprovincial trade (Alvarez, Krznar, and Tombe 2019).

labor within a country, even if differences in regional total factor productivity were persistent. For instance, workers would move to regions with the highest returns to labor, and hence wages, pushing down wages in the destination region over time. At the same time, lower labor supply in source regions where wages are relatively low would, in turn, help raise wage rates there, facilitating convergence of labor productivities.

Nonetheless, such an efficient allocation of factors across regions can be consistent with differences in regional real GDP per capita if, for example, labor is differentiated by skill level.[14] In practice though, markets may be neither perfectly competitive nor friction-free across regions, leading to diminished efficiency, misallocation of factors across regions, and hampered adjustment to shocks. Labor mobility may be constrained or evident only among the highly skilled, leading to more persistent regional unemployment in response to adverse shocks.[15]

The propensities for economic activity to cluster in space (agglomeration economies) and for productivity to rise with the density of skilled workers (human capital externalities) can also generate divergence if differences in production costs and the concentration of skills across regions are large enough.[16] Although these features may suggest the presence of market failures (that is, inefficient barriers to regions growing even more concentrated), their implications for optimal policies are ambiguous.[17] Overall social welfare could actually be larger if lagging regions were given help to create their own virtuous cycles of growing agglomeration economies, rather than be depopulated through population shifts to leading regions. Given these ambiguities and the more general difficulty of quantifying the relative importance of efficient versus inefficient allocation in driving regional disparities, the chapter focuses on lagging regions and their characteristics and adjustment.

Patterns of Regional Disparities in Advanced Economies

The extent of regional disparities in economic activity varies widely across advanced economies (Figure 2.6). For example, Japan's regional differences are relatively narrow, with real GDP per capita of the region at the 90th percentile only about 30 percent higher than

Figure 2.6. Subnational Regional Disparities in Real GDP per Capita

(Ratio to regional median times 100, 2013)

The extent of regional disparities differs widely across advanced economies.

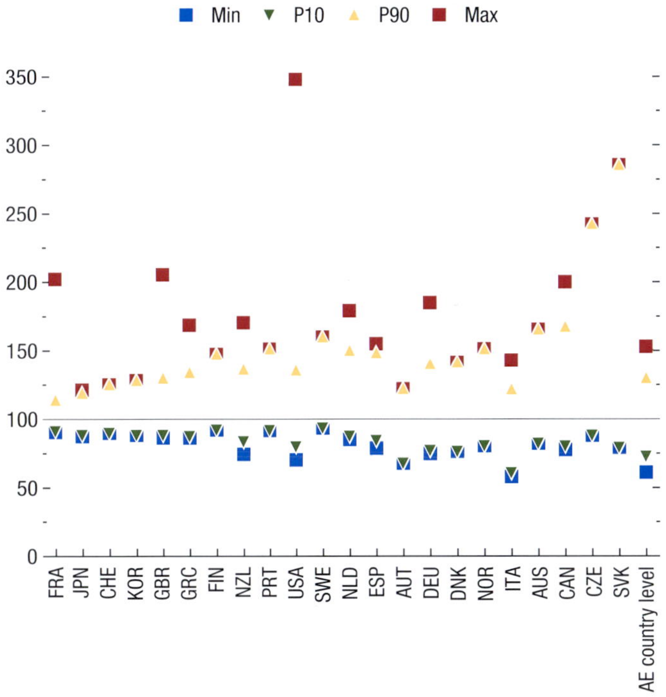

Sources: Organisation for Economic Co-operation and Development (OECD) Regional Database; and IMF staff calculations.
Note: P10(50, 90) indicates the 10(50, 90)th percentile of the regional real GDP per capita (purchasing power parity-adjusted) distribution within the country. Countries are sorted by the ratio of the within-country 90th percentile to the 10th percentile of regional real GDP per capita. Regional medians (P50) by country are normalized to 100, with other percentiles and the maximum and minimum shown relative to the median by country. Underlying regions are OECD territorial level 2 entities. The sample includes 22 advanced economies (all countries with four or more regions). The AE country level shows the corresponding quantiles calculated over the country-level sample of advanced economies. AE = advanced economies. Data labels use International Organization for Standardization (ISO) country codes.

[14]For example, if labor and human capital are differentiated (such as high skill/low skill), then total factor productivity differences may entail differences in the human capital composition of the workforce, affecting output per worker. If technology differs across regions, this may also lead to differences in output per worker across regions even if marginal returns to factors are equalized.

[15]See Kim (2008) and Duranton and Venables (2018) for evidence and arguments.

[16]See Krugman and Venables (1995); Fujita, Krugman, and Venables (1999); and Gennaioli and others (2013) on how increasing returns from agglomeration economies and human capital externalities can manifest in spatial economic models.

[17]See Austin, Glaeser, and Summers (2018) for further discussion of the ambiguous implications of agglomeration economies. As noted earlier, Hsieh and Moretti (2019) argues that housing and zoning restrictions present substantial barriers to beneficial agglomeration in the United States, lowering welfare and increasing spatial wage dispersion. However, Giannone (2018) suggests that the bulk of the increase in spatial wage dispersion in the United States over the past 40 years is due to skill-biased technological change rather than agglomeration.

that of the 10th percentile region. France has a similar 90/10 ratio, but with a notable better-performing outlier region (centered on the capital Paris) that has about double the real GDP per capita of the median French region. The United States has a 90/10 ratio which is about average for advanced economies, but it also shows greater dispersion in the tails of the distribution, with even more extreme regional outcomes than average (the District of Columbia's regional real GDP per capita is more than three times that of the median US region, while Mississippi's is about one-third lower than the median). Among the advanced economies with larger regional differences are Canada and Italy, with 90/10 ratios at about 2.

Regional labor productivity—output per worker—is closely related to regional real GDP per capita. A shift-share analysis of regional labor productivity provides insights into the relative importance of differences in sectoral labor productivities, sectoral employment shares, and the allocation of workers to more or less productive sectors in accounting for regional disparities within a country (Figure 2.7).[18] For most advanced economies, the bulk of regional variation in labor productivity appears to be due to sectoral labor productivity differences across regions rather than the sectoral employment mix—in other words, intrinsic sectoral productivity differences across regions tend to be the most important. However, Greece, Italy, Korea, and Portugal are notable examples in which other components explain the overall regional variation. In these cases, simply reallocating regional employment across sectors (holding sectoral productivity differences constant) could substantially lower regional variability in labor productivity.

The greater presence of lagging regions does not appear to be systematically related to differences in the drivers of regional variation across countries. About 20 percent of regions in advanced economies are classified as lagging, with the distribution differing across countries. That said, analysis suggests that the sectoral employment mix has been more influential in driving regional differences for lagging regions compared to others, consistent with the view that labor markets in lagging regions may be reallocating employment across sectors less effectively than other regions.[19]

Figure 2.7. Shift-Share Variance Decomposition, by Country, 2003–14

(Share of overall average regional variance)

For most advanced economies, much of the regional variation in labor productivity can be attributed to differences in sector productivity across regions.

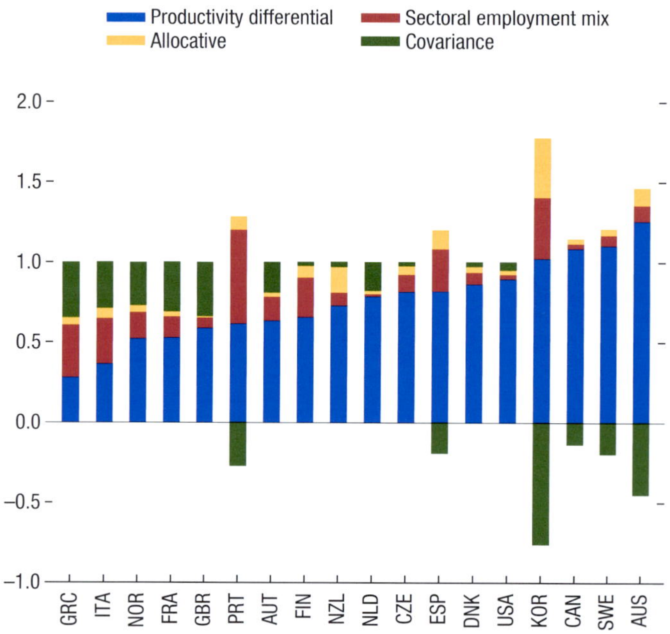

Sources: Organisation for Economic Co-operation and Development (OECD) Regional Database; and IMF staff calculations.

Note: The figure illustrates the shift-share analysis and variance decomposition for regional differences by country from Esteban (2000), sorted according to the share of the overall average regional variance explained by regional productivity differentials across sectors. For further details, see Online Annex 2.3. The sample includes 18 advanced economies (all countries with five or more regions at the OECD territorial level 2), from 2003–14. For all countries, the 10-sector ISIC Revision 4 classification of the OECD regional database is used (see Online Annex 2.1 for details). Bars sum up to 1 (overall average regional variance by country). Data labels use International Organization for Standardization (ISO) country codes.

Lagging regions also have significantly lower labor productivities across sectors than do other regions (Figure 2.8, panel 1). These range from about 5 percent less in public services, to about 15 percent less in industry and finance and professional services. This lower productivity for lagging regions could reflect a mix of poorer characteristics, such as lower human capital—something highlighted as essential in much work on regional development, including Acemoglu and Dell 2010 and Gennaioli and others 2013, 2014—and less efficient labor allocation across sectors. It may also reflect poorer quality of complements to labor in lagging regions, such as connective infrastructure, which has been identified as important in development in some

[18]For the variance decomposition of the shift-share analysis, there is an additional fourth term equal to the sum of the covariances across the three components described here. See Esteban (2000) and Online Annex 2.3 for further details on the calculation.

[19]See Online Annex 2.3 for further details.

Figure 2.8. Sectoral Labor Productivity and Employment Shares: Lagging versus Other Regions

Lagging regions tend to have lower labor productivity across sectors and higher shares of employment in agriculture and industry sectors, with lower shares of employment in services.

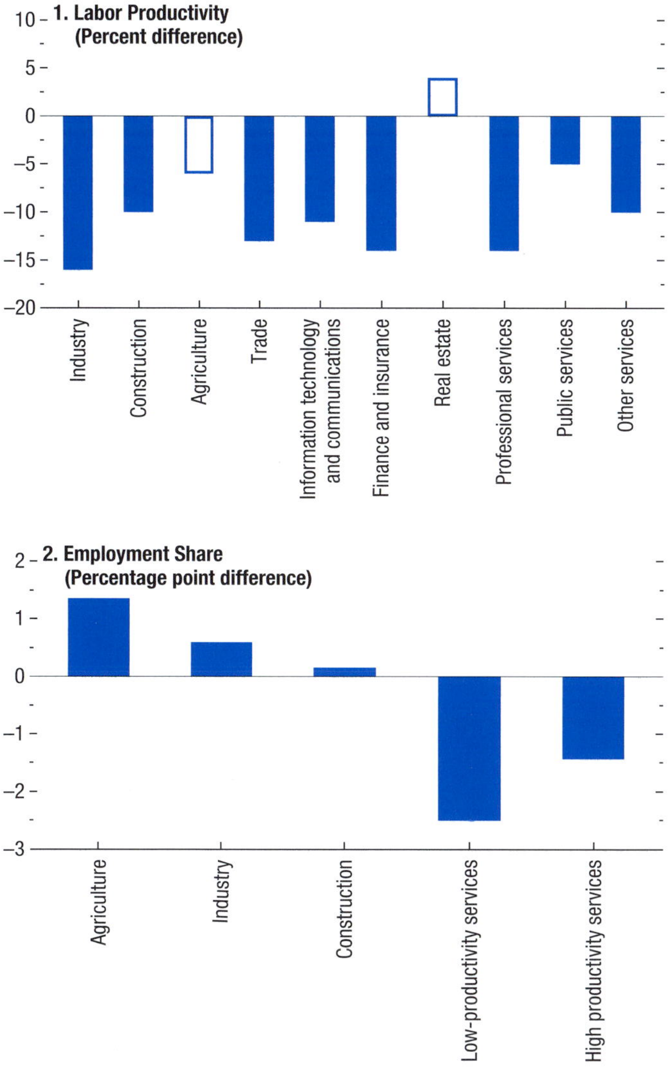

Sources: Organisation for Economic Co-operation and Development Regional Database; and IMF staff calculations.
Note: Lagging regions in a country are defined as those with real GDP per capita below the country's regional median in 2000 and with average growth below the country's average over 2000–16. Panel 1 shows the estimated difference in sectoral labor productivity in lagging versus other regions. All models control for country-year fixed effects with standard errors clustered at the country-year level. Solid bars indicate statistical significance at the 10 percent level while hollow bars do not. Panel 2 shows the estimated difference in sectoral employment shares between lagging and other regions. High productivity service sectors are finance and insurance, information technology and communications, and real estate. All other service sectors are low-productivity service sectors. See Online Annex 2.1 for the country sample.

studies (Allen and Arkolakis 2014; Donaldson and Hornbeck 2016). Box 2.2 presents evidence that local climate also plays a role, and that climate change may exacerbate differences in productivity between lagging and other regions in advanced economies.

In addition to being less productive, lagging regions, on average, are also significantly likelier to have employment more concentrated in agriculture and industry than in services, including the high productivity growth service sectors of information technology and communications and finance (Figure 2.8, panel 2). In other words, lagging regions, on average, tend to be more rural and have employment more reliant on sectors with lower potential for productivity growth.[20]

A simple counterfactual exercise supports the view that sectoral labor allocation plays an important role in the relative performance of regions (Figure 2.9). In advanced economies from 2002 to 2014, the average labor productivity of lagging regions as a percentage of the labor productivity of other regions declined by about 5 percent, reflecting the evolution of both sectoral labor productivities and employment shares. If only sectoral labor productivity changes were operative, with no change in employment shares, the ratio would still have declined, but by about one-third less than it did. In other words, rather than mitigating the relative decline in overall labor productivity for lagging regions, the shift in sectoral labor allocation appears to have exacerbated it.

Regional Labor Market Adjustment in Advanced Economies

To get a better sense of how differences in regional performance may reflect differences in shocks and responses to shocks, the chapter investigates the effects of adverse local labor demand shocks on regional unemployment and migration.[21] If sectoral

[20]See Chapter 3 of the April 2018 *World Economic Outlook* (WEO) for how structural change in advanced economies and the (in)ability to shift into highly productive service sectors may impact inequality.

[21]There has been a host of work in this vein, inspired by Blanchard and Katz's (1992) early work on US regional labor market dynamics and convergence. Decressin and Fatás (1995) contrasts US and European regional dynamics, finding less of a common component for employment and less migration in response to shocks in Europe. More recently, Dao, Furceri, and Loungani (2017) updates the analysis by Blanchard and Katz (1992) for the United States with improved and more recent data, finding that labor mobility has declined.

Figure 2.9. Labor Productivity: Lagging versus Other Regions
(Ratio)

The overall productivity difference between lagging and other regions has grown, with about one-third due to poor allocation of labor across sectors and the rest to worsening sectoral productivity differences.

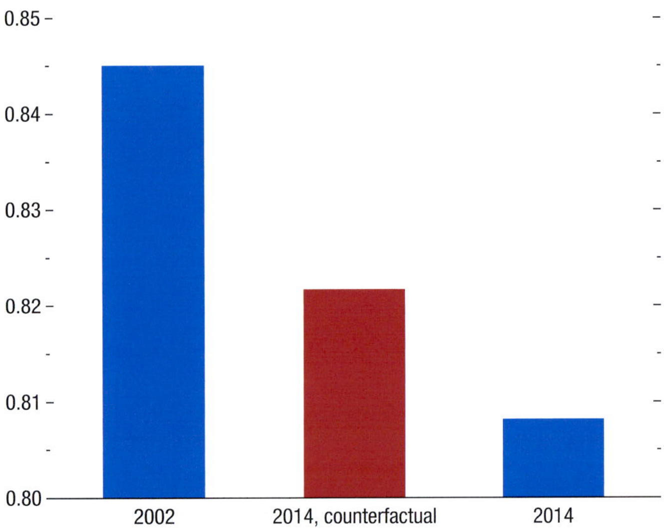

Sources: Organisation for Economic Co-operation and Development Regional Database; IMF staff calculations.
Note: Bars show the average country ratio of labor productivity (defined as real gross value-added per worker) in lagging regions to that of other regions in 2002 and 2014 across advanced economies. In the counterfactual scenario, sectoral employment shares are held constant at their 2002 levels while sectoral productivities are set at their realized values. Lagging regions in a country are defined as those with real GDP per capita below the country's regional median in 2000 and with average growth below the country's average over 2000–16. See Online Annex 2.1 for the country sample and Online Annex 2.4 for further details on the calculation.

labor reallocation in a region functions effectively, regional unemployment and participation should be largely shielded from adverse shocks, while migration flows and within-region sectoral employment shifts to absorb them. The critical insight that regional differences in the preexisting sectoral employment mix translate into regional differences in exposure to external shocks enables region-level shocks to be constructed.[22] Two particular types of local labor demand shocks are considered. They attempt to capture some of the much-discussed drivers of trade and technology:[23]

- A shock from increased import competition in external markets that is associated with the rise of China's productivity (Autor, Dorn, and Hanson 2013a, 2013b).[24]
- A shock based on the interaction between a region's vulnerability to automation and the costs of machinery and equipment capital goods (building upon Autor and Dorn 2013; Chapter 3 of the April 2017 WEO; Das and Hilgenstock 2018; and Lian and others 2019).

In general, the findings point to regional labor markets having sluggish adjustment and reallocation in response to negative shocks in advanced economies.[25] Moreover, even though the incidence of these shocks is actually somewhat lower for lagging than other regions (see Online Annex 2.5), some evidence, detailed below, suggests that lagging regions do suffer more in response to some shocks.

Shocks from increasing import competition in external markets from China's economic rise do not have marked average effects on regional unemployment in a broad sample of advanced economies, although they do tend to reduce labor force participation after one year, but this quickly abates (Figure 2.10). The responses of

[22]First conceptualized and used by Bartik (1991), this insight for the construction of plausibly exogenous regional shocks based on preexisting regional differences in exposure to aggregate drivers was then popularized in the field of regional development and adjustment by Blanchard and Katz (1992) and for trade by Topalova (2010). Goldsmith-Pinkham, Sorkin, and Swift (2019) presents a critical evaluation of these kind of instruments.

[23]For recent work on the roles of trade and technology in driving disparities and other trends, see Jaumotte, Lall, and Papageorgiou (2013); Karabarbounis and Neiman (2014); Dabla-Norris and others (2015); Autor, Dorn, and Hanson (2015); Helpman (2016); Abdih and Danninger (2017); Dao and others (2017); and Chapter 2 of the April 2018 WEO, among others.

[24]Although the trade shock associated with China's rising productivity has been well studied, it is by no means the only trade shock for advanced economies. In general, advanced economies have faced increasing competition as emerging market economies have become more productive and engaged in international markets.

[25]See Online Annex 2.5 for further details on the construction of the shocks and the regression model specification and estimation. The dynamic responses of regional unemployment and labor force participation rates, and inward and outward migration, are estimated using the local projection method (Jordà 2005), controlling for lagged regional real GDP per capita, lagged regional population density (helping to capture the degree of urbanization), lagged country real GDP per capita, and region-specific and year fixed effects. Although the analysis controls for many regional characteristics through region-specific fixed effects (capturing time-invariant characteristics of regions, including geography and membership in a federation) and lagged regional real GDP per capita (proxying for many aspects of regional development), unobserved time-varying regional variables, such as the extent of cross-regional fiscal redistribution, may also impact adjustment and reallocation. The findings therefore represent the average effects of the shocks within the sample, given the existing distribution of unobservables. Changes in the distribution of unobservables could entail changes in the effects of the shocks.

Figure 2.10. Regional Effects of Import Competition Shocks

Greater competition in external markets tends to raise unemployment in the near term for exposed regions, with little difference between lagging and other regions. But this rise unwinds as regions adjust relatively quickly.

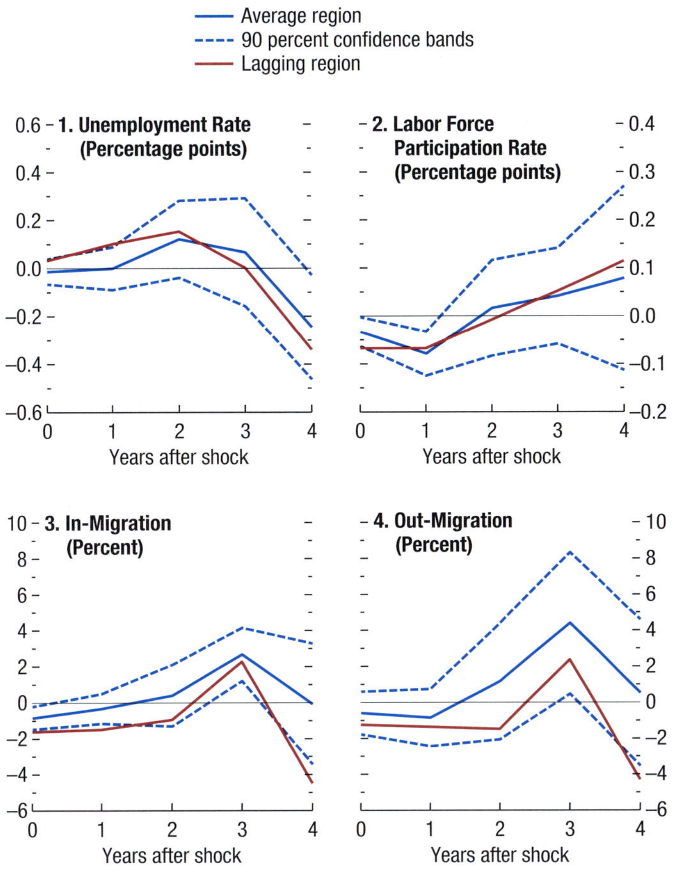

Source: IMF staff estimations.
Note: The blue and red solid lines plot the impulse responses of the indicated variable to a one standard deviation import competition shock, defined as the growth of Chinese imports per worker in external markets weighted by the lagged regional employment mix. Impulse responses are estimated using the local projection method of Jordà (2005). Horizon 0 is the year of the shock. Lagging regions in a country are defined as those with real GDP per capita below the country's regional median in 2000 and with average growth below the country's average over 2000–16. See Online Annex 2.1 for the country sample and Online Annex 2.5 for further details about the shock definition and econometric specification.

lagging regions do not look very different from those of other regions. This stands in contrast to recent literature examining more highly localized labor markets in specific countries. For example, Autor, Dorn, and Hanson (2013a) finds significant adverse local effects on employment for the United States from a similarly defined shock. Applying a similar approach over a similar period, Dauth, Findeisen, and Suedekum (2014) estimates an overall positive net employment effect of the rise in trade for Germany. These studies suggest that the regional effects of trade may vary across countries. However, the results presented here are not inconsistent with these studies, given that they reflect the average regional effect within countries for the group of advanced economies, rather than country-specific responses. Moreover, the analysis here is undertaken at a higher level of regional aggregation and over a later period (post-1999).

By contrast, adverse shocks to local labor demand arising from technological change have noticeable and persistent effects on labor markets (Figure 2.11). Although there is little sign of an impact effect, unemployment rates in regions more vulnerable to automation rise steadily over the following four years—a pattern consistent with a gradual substitution of capital for labor. The absence of much change in gross migration flows over the near term indicates that labor mobility across regions is low after automation shocks. For lagging regions that are more vulnerable to automation, the rise in unemployment rates is even larger and statistically significantly different from that of other regions. Moreover, unlike other regions, more vulnerable lagging regions see a persistent and statistically significant drop in out-migration after an automation shock, suggesting that workers in these regions may find it harder to move than if they were in other regions. Box 2.3 studies the regional effects of automotive manufacturing plant closures, which may ultimately be driven by trade or technology shocks, finding similarly persistent increases in unemployment, which tend to be worse in regions where gross migration flows are lower.

Can national labor market policies and distortions inhibit regional labor market adjustment? They might if they contribute to more rigid regional labor markets, leading adverse shocks to have more long-lived effects on unemployment and participation.[26] The following discussion examines how the calibration of two national labor market policies—the stringency of employment protection regulations and the generosity of unemployment insurance schemes—influence regional labor market responses to local shocks. More stringent employment protection regulation will tend to reduce job destruction, dampening the likelihood of layoffs, but also job creation and the hiring rate, as employers recognize that new hires come with the potential cost of more sluggish adjustment in

[26]An example of a national structural policy that alters the functioning of regional labor markets is presented in Boeri and others (2019), which compares the regional effects of Italy's and Germany's national collective bargaining systems.

Figure 2.11. Regional Effects of Automation Shocks

Falling machinery and equipment prices tend to raise unemployment in regions where production is more vulnerable to automation, with exposed lagging regions hurt even more. Out-migration stalls or drops for more exposed lagging regions.

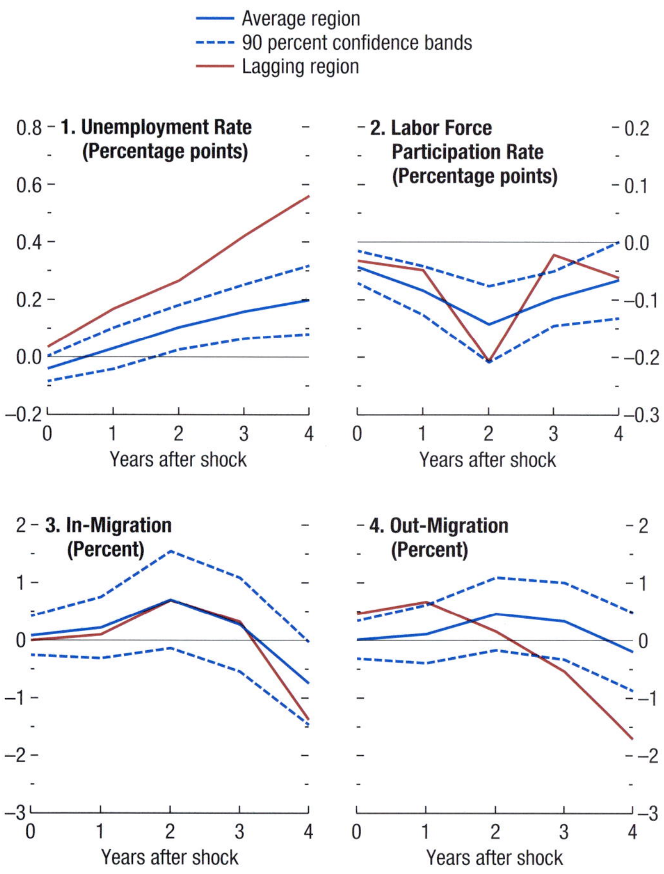

Source: IMF staff estimations.
Note: The blue and red solid lines plot the impulse responses of the indicated variable to an automation shock, defined as a one standard deviation decline in machinery and equipment capital price growth for a region that experiences a one standard deviation rise in its vulnerability to automation (Autor and Dorn 2013; Lian and others 2019). Horizon 0 is the year of the shock. Lagging regions in a country are defined as those with real GDP per capita below the country's regional median in 2000 and with average growth below the country's average over 2000–16. See Online Annex 2.1 for the country sample and Online Annex 2.5 for further details about the shock definition and econometric specification.

downturns. Whether unemployment rises in response to adverse shocks depends on which of these two forces dominates, which is theoretically ambiguous (Pissarides 2001). Unemployment insurance provides security against income shocks from job loss, but can also impact the dynamics of unemployment through its impacts on an individual's job search efforts and job quality with reemployment (Chetty 2008; Tatsiramos and van Ours 2014; Schmieder, von Wachter, and Bender 2016).

Analysis suggests that national policies do matter for regional labor market adjustment—they may exacerbate or dampen adverse unemployment effects, although their impact varies across outcomes and shocks (Figure 2.12). Moreover, the findings should be interpreted as associational, given that national policies are only considered one-by-one, rather than jointly. That means that the change in regional responses associated with national employment protection and unemployment benefits policies may incorporate the influence of correlated national policies that are not included in the analysis.

More stringent national employment protection is associated with greater regional unemployment effects from import competition and automation shocks. Automation shocks are also associated with higher unemployment in the near term, where benefits are greater, suggesting that the incentive effects of greater benefits do make unemployment more persistent, although the difference vanishes at longer horizons. Responses to import competition shocks meanwhile show little difference between more versus less generous unemployment benefit regimes. The overall takeaway from these findings is that national policies that encourage more flexible labor markets may ease adjustment and reallocation in regional labor markets, improving their resilience to shocks.

Regional Labor Mobility and Factor Allocation: Individual and Firm-Level Evidence

As noted, regional adjustment to shocks depends on the effectiveness of factor reallocation—the ability of capital and labor to move across sectors, firms, and space, toward their most productive use. Where factor mobility within and across regions is hampered or reallocation ineffective, negative shocks may have prolonged effects, contributing to poorer performance in some regions and exacerbating disparities within a country. This section examines differences in labor mobility between lagging regions and others, the characteristics of regional migrants, and the differences across regions in the efficiency with which firms allocate capital—the sensitivity of their investments to the marginal returns to capital.

Lagging regions, on average, have lower gross migration flows (inward or outward) than other regions. This suggests that their labor reallocation mechanisms are less powerful, given that lagging regions are actually less likely than other regions to experience

Figure 2.12. Regional Effects of Trade and Technology Shocks Conditional on National Policies
(Percentage points)

Regional adjustment to adverse trade and technology shocks tends to be faster in countries with policies supporting more flexible labor markets.

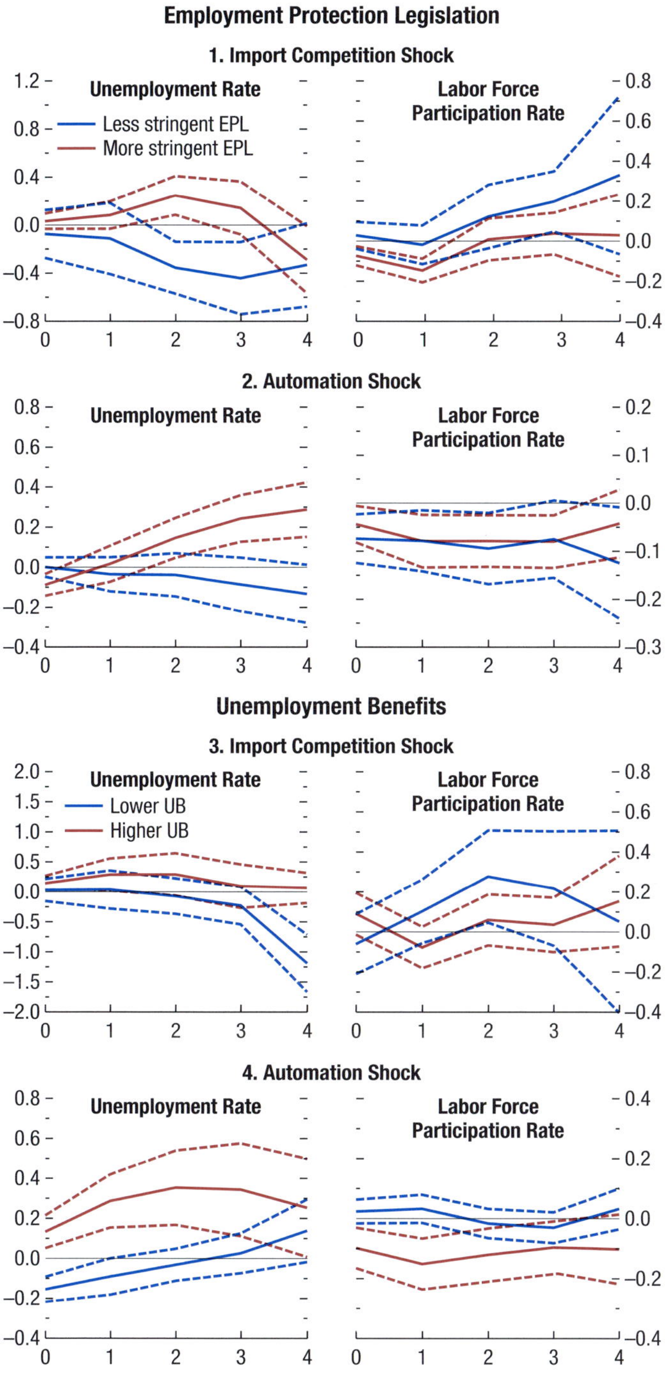

Source: IMF staff estimations.
Note: Years after impact on *x*-axis. Less (more) stringent/low (high) = 25th (75th) percentile of the indicated variable. EPL = Index of employment protection legislation; UB = gross replacement rate of unemployment benefits. Dashed lines indicate the 90 percent confidence bands. See Figures 2.10 and 2.11 for definitions of the import competition and automation shocks. See Online Annex 2.5 for detailed definitions of import competition and automation shocks and Online Annex 2.1 for country samples.

shocks (Figure 2.13, panel 1).[27] The better educated (either upper secondary or tertiary education) or employed are more likely to move within countries (Figure 2.13, panels 2 and 3). Those facts are consistent with migration being more constrained in lagging regions, where unemployment tends to be higher and education and skills lower.

For another perspective on factor allocation across regions within a country, differences in firms' allocative efficiency across regions of a country are analyzed. Allocative efficiency is measured at the firm level by the responsiveness of their investment (capital growth) to the firm's marginal return on an additional unit of capital (captured by the marginal revenue product of capital), after accounting for a host of region-sector-country-year differences. These firm-level estimates are then mapped to the region-country-sector-year, enabling the construction of their distribution across regions by country, sector, and year. Analysis shows that greater variability in firms' allocative efficiency across regions within a country—as captured by the ratio of the standard deviation to the mean allocative efficiency by country-sector-year—is correlated with greater regional disparities in economic activity. In essence, when regional differences in firms' responsiveness to marginal returns to capital are large, the spread in regional performance also tends to be wider.[28]

As with regional adjustment dynamics, national-level structural policies and distortions may affect the variability in firms' allocative efficiencies across regions of a country by creating incentives for more or less efficient firm choices. The analysis indicates that national policies that support greater flexibility and openness in product markets are associated with lower variability of firms' allocative efficiency across regions of a country (Figure 2.14). In particular, countries with less stringent product market regulation (related to the level of protection for incumbent firms), lower administrative costs for starting a business, and greater trade openness, are all associated with lower variability in capital allocative efficiency across regions. These associations might reflect the selective effects of more competitive and contestable markets on firms, pushing allocative efficiency across regions closer together, and of the beneficial effects of greater flexibility for factors to be reallocated by individual firms and also across firms.

[27]See Online Annex 2.5 for further details on the incidence of import competition from China and automation shocks for lagging versus other regions.

[28]See Online Annex 2.6 for further details on the construction of the measure. The ratio of the standard deviation to the mean of a distribution is also known as the coefficient of variation.

Figure 2.13. Subnational Regional Migration and Labor Mobility

Gross migration flows tend to be smaller in lagging regions. The better educated and employed are more likely to migrate within a country.

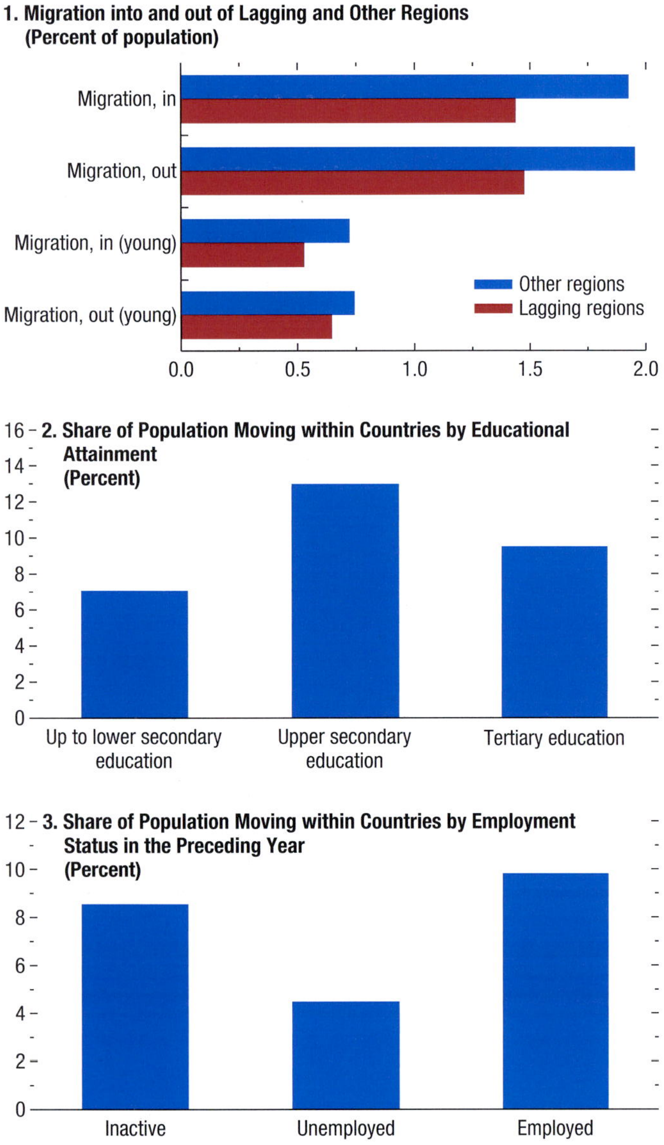

Sources: Organisation for Economic Co-operation and Development Regional Database; European Union (EU) Labor Force Survey; and IMF staff calculations.
Note: Panel 1 shows migration into and out of lagging regions versus other regions between 2000–16, defined as gross inflows and outflows of migrants divided by the population in the previous period in the region. Lagging regions in a country are defined as those with real GDP per capita below country regional median in 2000 and with average growth below the country's average over 2000–16. Panel 2 plots the share of the population who moved within the past year by education level, based on individual worker level data from the EU Labor Force Survey between 2000–16. Lower secondary education indicates educational attainment less than 9 years, upper secondary education between 9 and 12 years, and tertiary education greater than 12 years. Panel 3 plots the share of the population who moved within the past year by employment status, based on individual worker level data from the EU Labor Force Survey between 2000–16. See Online Annex 2.1 for the country sample.

Figure 2.14. Effects of National Structural Policies on Subnational Regional Dispersion of Capital Allocative Efficiency
(Response to one standard deviation increase in indicated policy variable)

The regional dispersion of firms' allocative efficiency—the responsiveness of their investment to capital returns—tends to be lower in countries where national policies support more open markets.

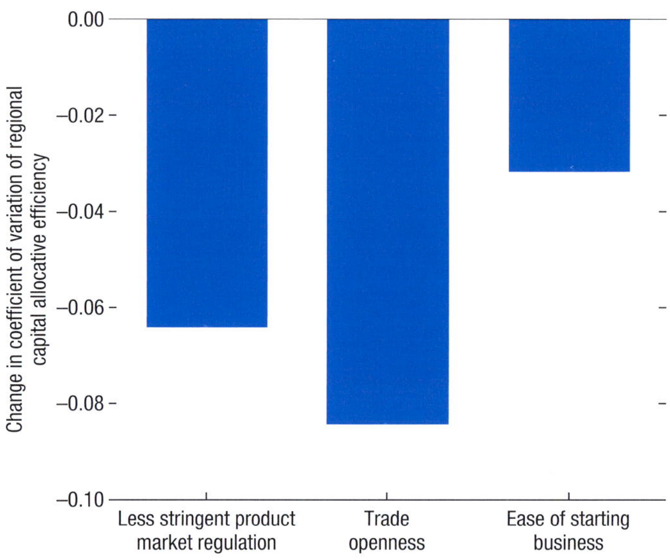

Source: IMF staff calculations.
Note: Bars show the associated average change in the coefficient of variation of regional capital allocative efficiency, calculated by country-sector-year, for a one standard deviation change in the indicated structural policy variable. All effects shown are statistically significant at the 10 percent level. Regression controls for country-sector and sector-year fixed effects, with standard errors clustered at the country-year level. See Online Annex 2.1 for the country sample and Online Annex 2.6 for further details on the econometric methods.

Summary and Policy Implications

The regional dimension of economic performance has generated much interest in recent years, reflecting the perception that increasing regional differences in growth and employment opportunities in advanced economies are stoking social unease and distrust, as some regions and peoples are left behind. The chapter shows that while there is a grain of truth in these contentions, the size and scope of regional disparities differs markedly across economies. Regional disparities are closely associated with differences in the sectoral composition of employment and levels of sectoral productivity. Lagging regions of a country are more likely to have lower labor productivity across sectors and to be more concentrated in agriculture and industry than in services (and particularly high productivity growth service sectors, such as information technology and communications). They also tend to have smaller populations of prime-age workers than other regions, which may contribute further to their poorer productivity performance (Feyrer 2007; Adler and others 2017).

Regional adjustment to adverse local labor demand shocks generally takes time and is associated with higher unemployment, reflecting frictions in shifting production and employment across sectors and labor mobility. Lagging regions do not appear more likely to be hit by these shocks, but they do appear to suffer more in response to some—in particular shocks related to differences in exposure to technological changes—suggesting that adjustment mechanisms in lagging regions may be more obstructed than in other regions.

How might policies reduce these disparities and promote improved regional adjustment? The analyses here and in earlier literature suggest several possible actions. As noted earlier, the consensus is that human capital plays a pivotal role in driving regional development. Boosting educational and training quality and opportunities where there are gaps, as well as introducing more broad-based educational reforms to improve learning outcomes and adapt to the changing world of work, would disproportionately benefit lagging regions (see also Coady and Dizioli 2017 and WB 2018, 2019a). Similarly, deploying more active labor market policies to create jobs, retrain the displaced, and find new job matches for the unemployed could also help lift lagging regions and ease adjustment. However, the design of active labor market policies matters enormously for their success. They must be carefully tailored to address the labor market failures specific to a region's context and assessed and improved regularly (Card, Kluve, and Weber 2018).

National labor and product market policies and distortions also affect regional adjustment and factor reallocation (Dabla-Norris and others 2015; Boeri and others 2019). Evidence presented here suggests that the appropriate calibration of employment protection regulations and unemployment insurance regimes can facilitate regional labor market adjustment, dampening the unemployment effects of adverse shocks. Greater flexibility can also be helpfully accompanied by stronger retraining and other forms of job assistance to help ensure displaced workers achieve any necessary reskilling and reemployment rapidly (Aiyar and others 2019).[29] Product markets that are more open—through lower barriers to entry and greater trade openness—are associated with lower variability in the capital allocative efficiencies of firms across the regions of a country, which is in turn associated with lower regional disparities. More competitive markets within a country are associated with greater efficiency in the reallocation of capital, both in and across regions.

Although not a focus of the analysis here owing to data constraints, spatially targeted, place-based fiscal policies and investments may also help lagging regions, but only when need is spatially concentrated and individual-level targeting has been less effective (Box 2.4 explores place-based policies and offers more in-depth discussion). There is evidence that greater fiscal decentralization, which effectively enables more spatially differentiated policies, may also help reduce regional disparities (Lessmann 2009; Kappeler and others 2013; Blöchliger, Bartolini, and Stossberg 2016). Austin, Glaeser, and Summers (2018) argues that explicit spatial targeting may also be justified if some regions are more sensitive to fiscal interventions than others—for example, if an area has greater labor market slack because local demand conditions are depressed. However, place-based policies must be carefully designed to ensure that beneficial adjustment is encouraged rather than resisted (Kline and Moretti 2014) and to avoid interfering with the continued success of leading regions (Barca, McCann, and Rodríguez-Pose 2012; Pike, Rodríguez-Pose, and Tomaney 2017; Rodríguez-Pose 2018).

[29]For example, see the Danish model of "flexicurity," which accompanies great flexibility in hiring and firing, with retraining, job matching, and unemployment benefits that are subject to strong monitoring and conditionality (OECD 2016a).

Box 2.1. Measuring Subnational Regional Economic Activity and Welfare

Although real GDP per capita has many shortcomings as a measure of individual well-being and social welfare, it remains a touchstone in much economic analysis and cross-country comparisons.[1] Recent research suggests that it is also still useful as a broad metric for cross-country comparisons, finding it highly correlated for a large set of indicators based on various aspects of human welfare (including subjective well-being, mortality, inequality, and leisure).[2] However, in the case of within-country regional comparisons, two issues arise that can complicate the welfare interpretation of patterns of real GDP per capita—regional price or cost-of-living differences and the effects on personal income of fiscal redistribution and income flows to and from elsewhere.

Although real GDP per capita is typically corrected for average cross-country differences in cost-of-living (purchasing power parity adjustments), regional differences in the cost-of-living are often not fully reflected in regional real GDP per capita measures, largely because regional price indexes are not broadly available.[3] Gennaioli and others (2014) attempts to correct for this for a subset of countries in its global data set, using housing cost differences as a proxy for the cost of living. The study finds that, although the size of regional disparities fell, they remained substantial. Gbohoui, Lam, and Lledo (2019) undertakes a similar calculation using more recent data. As shown in Figure 2.1.1, it also finds that regional disparities (as captured by the ratio of real GDP per capita in the 75th to the 25th percentile region within-country) narrowed with the correction, but remained significant, with the ratio going from 1.34 to 1.26, on average. Hence, although regional price differences are part of the picture, they do not account for all regional disparities in economic activity.

Real GDP per capita is a measure of real output or economic activity occurring within a territory over a given period (UN 2009). It is not a measure of an individual's or household's income available for their consumption and investment, which would be a more direct measure of welfare. This is more properly captured by disposable income—the sum of labor compensation and investment income after taxes and transfers.[4] Given that disposable income incorporates income streams from elsewhere, such as capital income from geographically diversified portfolios, it can better capture interregional risk sharing and result in narrower regional disparities.[5] Fiscal

Figure 2.1.1. Subnational Regional Disparities: Before and after Regional Price Adjustment

(Ratio for the interquartile range of real GDP per capita across subnational regions by country during 2010–14)

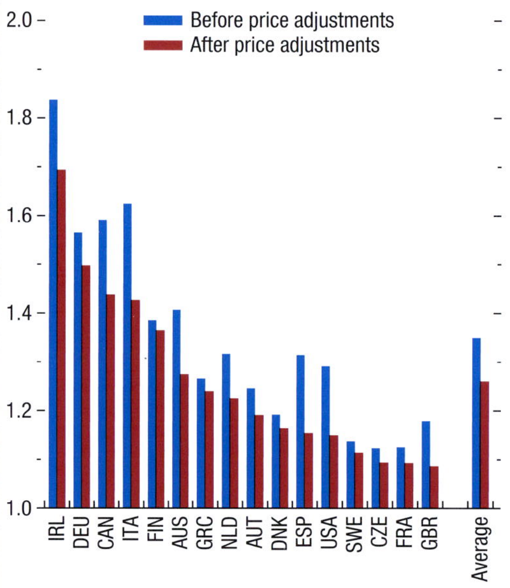

Source: Gbohoui, Lam, and Lledo (2019).
Note: Constructed from Organisation for Economic Co-operation and Development Regional Database, Gennaioli and others (2014), and Luxembourg Income Study for available years. The price adjustment is based on the housing deflator. Data labels use International Organization for Standardization (ISO) country codes.

The author of this box is John Bluedorn, with contributions from William Gbohoui, W. Raphael Lam, and Victor Lledo.

[1]See Fleurbaey (2009); Coyle (2015); Feldstein (2017); and Stiglitz, Fitoussi, and Durand (2018), among others.

[2]See Stevenson and Wolfers (2008) and Jones and Klenow (2016) for evidence.

[3]See Feenstra, Inklaar, and Timmer (2015) for a discussion of the purchasing power parity adjustment of GDP measures and OECD (2018) for details on the construction in the OECD Regional Database.

[4]See OECD (2013, 2018) for further details on disposable income and its construction and availability at the region-level.

[5]Asdrubali, Sørensen, and Yosha (1996) leverages this fact to estimate the extent of interregional risk-sharing within the United States.

Box 2.1 *(continued)*

redistribution through taxes and transfers within and across regions can provide a further channel for narrowing income differences across regions.[6] For the limited countries and years for which data on regional disposable income per capita are available, regional differences are smaller than they are as measured by real GDP per capita differences, but again, can be substantial (OECD 2018). For example, the top income regions in the United States had average disposable income per capita more than 50 percent higher than the national average.

With its wider availability across time and countries, regional real GDP per capita remains the best measure for assessing the extent and evolution of regional differences in economic activity. However, recognizing its drawbacks as a measure of welfare and motivated by the extensive evidence on the pivotal role of employment in individual's life satisfaction, the chapter's analysis focuses more on regional labor market outcomes and adjustment, paralleling some of the latest research (Austin, Glaeser, and Summers 2018).

[6]See Obstfeld and Peri (1998) and Boadway and Shah (2007) for a discussion of the role of fiscal redistribution in facilitating adjustment.

Box 2.2. Climate Change and Subnational Regional Disparities

Climate change may further exacerbate subnational regional disparities in many advanced economies by the end of the 21st century. This conclusion is based on two findings. First, estimates of the effect of temperature increases on sectoral labor productivity—agriculture, industry, and services—at the subnational level indicate that agriculture and industry are likely to suffer, even in advanced economies. Second, because lagging regions tend to specialize in agriculture and industry (see Figure 2.9), the negative effect of global warming on labor productivity may be larger in lagging regions, therefore pushing them to fall behind even more by the end of the 21st century.[1]

Analysis at the country-level, presented in Chapter 3 of the October 2017 *World Economic Outlook*, already establishes that a 1.0°C increase in temperature lowers labor productivity in heat-exposed industries (mostly agriculture and industry), while there is no negative effect on non-heat-exposed industries (mostly services).[2] It also shows little adaptation to climate change, except in advanced economies. Because the analysis in this box focuses only on the advanced economies, which have already invested in climate adaptation, any negative effects uncovered here are likely to be at the lower bound of estimates in a global sample.

In general, temperature has a nonlinear effect on economic activity—in very cold regions, warming may bring economic benefits. Beyond a certain "optimal" level, temperature increases hurt economic output and labor productivity. However, there is significant heterogeneity in the relationship between temperature and labor productivity across sectors, as Figure 2.2.1 demonstrates.[3] For example, for a median lagging region, which has an average annual temperature of 12°C in this sample, an increase in temperature by 1°C would reduce labor productivity in the agriculture and industry sectors and have no effect on the service sector. In contrast, because the median non-lagging region is at 10.5°C, an increase in average annual temperature by 1°C would raise productivity in the service sector, lower it in the industry sector, and have no statistically significant effect on the agriculture sector.

The author of this box is Natalija Novta.

[1]See also the October 2019 *Fiscal Monitor* for analysis examining how climate change mitigation policies may differentially impact regions within a country, depending on their industry mix.

[2]Heat-exposed industries include forestry, fishing and hunting, construction, mining, transportation, utilities, and manufacturing, following the classification by Graff Zivin and Neidell (2014).

[3]Based on the estimates in Figure 2.2.1, the optimal temperature is about 14°C for the service sector, but only 5°C and 9°C for industry and agriculture sectors, respectively.

Figure 2.2.1. Marginal Effect of 1°C Increase in Temperature on Sectoral Labor Productivity

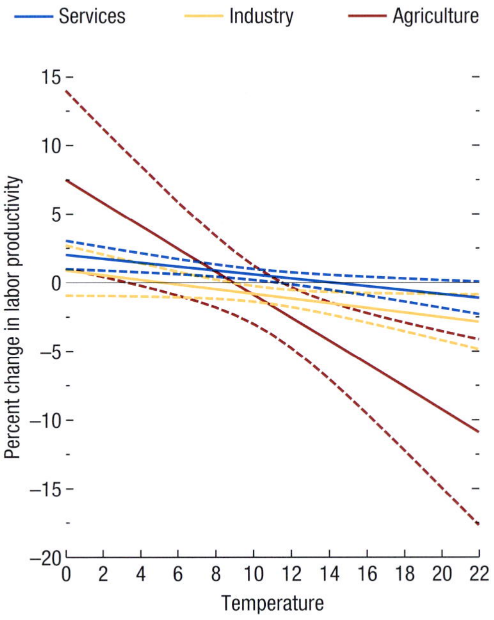

Sources: Organisation for Economic Co-operation and Development (OECD) Regional Database; University of East Anglia, Climate Research Unit; and IMF staff calculations.
Note: The figure shows the contemporaneous effect of a 1°C increase in temperature on sectoral labor productivity. Because temperature has a nonlinear effect, its marginal effect is shown at each level of regional average annual temperature. The baseline specification mirrors that of Chapter 3 of the October 2017 *World Economic Outlook* but is reestimated in a sample of subnational regions within advanced economies with a population of at least a quarter million. The industry sector includes industry, manufacturing, and construction from the OECD classification (ISIC Revision 4). Sectoral labor productivity is defined as sectoral gross value added divided by the number of employees in that sector. The dependent variable is the growth of sectoral labor productivity, and it is regressed on average annual population-weighted temperature, temperature squared, precipitation, and precipitation squared, controlling for one-year lags of all the climate variables, a lag of the dependent variable and subnational regional fixed effects. The solid lines show the point estimates for each sector, and the dashed lines show 90 percent confidence intervals. Standard errors are clustered at the level of subnational regions.

Box 2.2 *(continued)*

Given these findings, it is not surprising that lagging (warmer) regions might be expected to fall further behind in the coming decades. In the early 2000s, labor productivity in lagging regions was, on average, at about 85 percent of that in other regions (Figure 2.9). Under an unmitigated climate change scenario (Representative Concentration Pathway (RCP) 8.5),[4] labor productivity in lagging regions could fall by about 2–3 percentage points in Italy, Spain, and the United States by 2100 (Figure 2.2.2). This is similar to the decline in relative labor productivity of the lagging regions between 2002 and 2014 (Figure 2.9). Under a milder scenario, which assumes emissions peaking around 2050 (RCP 4.5), the decline in labor productivity of lagging regions would be smaller, at about 1.5 percentage points.

Historical weather patterns may have already contributed to some regions falling behind. An increase in a region's average annual temperature by 1°C increases the probability of being lagging by about 2 percentage points or about 10 percent relative to the baseline likelihood of about 20 percent, even after controlling for country-year fixed effects. This means that a hypothetical move from the coolest to the warmest region within a country, which have a median temperature difference of about 5.5°C, is associated with about an 11 percentage point higher chance of being lagging.

Finally, it is important to note that, even though climate change is a relatively slow process, it is very persistent and its negative effects have historically been extremely hard to eliminate. Therefore, even the seemingly small absolute effects demonstrated here should be a cause for concern, especially because they appear in the context of advanced economies that are relatively well-adapted and tend to have temperate climates.

[4]As constructed by the Intergovernmental Panel on Climate Change.

Figure 2.2.2. Change in Labor Productivity of Lagging versus Other Regions Due to Projected Temperature Increases between 2005 and 2100
(Percentage points)

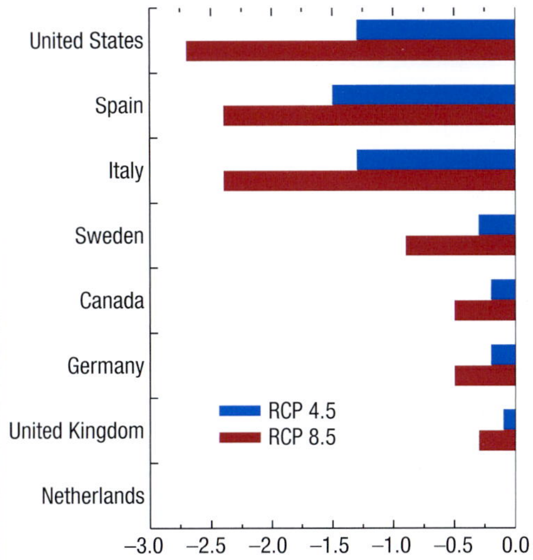

Sources: National Aeronautics and Space Administration temperature projections for scenarios RCP 4.5 and 8.5; Organisation for Economic Co-operation and Development Regional Database; and IMF staff calculations.
Note: To construct the figure, the following procedure is followed: first, for 2005, the ratio of labor productivity in lagging regions relative to other regions is calculated as the weighted average of labor productivities in agriculture, industry, and services; second, the mean projected temperature increases for 2005–2100 under RCP scenarios 4.5 and 8.5 and the estimated sectoral labor productivities are used to project sectoral labor productivity at the level of subnational regions in 2100 under each of the two RCP scenarios; and, finally, the difference between the projected labor productivity of lagging regions (relative to others) in 2100 and actual labor productivity of lagging regions (relative to others) in 2005 is calculated. Representative Concentration Pathways (RCP) are scenarios of greenhouse gas concentrations, constructed by the Intergovernmental Panel on Climate Change (IPCC 2014). RCP 4.5 is an intermediate scenario, which assumes emissions peaking around 2050 and declining thereafter. RCP 8.5 is an unmitigated scenario in which emissions continue to rise throughout the 21st century.

Box 2.3. The Persistent Effects of Local Shocks: The Case of Automotive Manufacturing Plant Closures

The declining share of manufacturing jobs in overall employment over the past decades has attracted attention in recent years due to concerns that manufacturing might play a role as a catalyst for productivity growth and income convergence and be a source of well-paid jobs for less-skilled workers (Chapter 3 of the April 2018 *World Economic Outlook* presents in-depth analysis of this contention). Factory closures have accompanied this trend, with job losses sometimes concentrated in particular regions within countries. A large literature exists on the local labor market impacts of factory closures, with most early studies focused on closures affecting heavy industry, such as coal, steel, and shipbuilding.[1] In more recent years, the effects of automotive manufacturing plant closures have become the focus of more studies, although most examine the effects for a single country or of a specific closure.[2]

With these in mind, this box looks at the impact of automotive manufacturing plant closures—events caused by forces originating outside the immediate region—on the regional labor markets for a sample of six advanced economies for which historical data on automotive factory closures are available.[3] The box compares unemployment rates in regions that experienced car factory closures during 2000–16 and in regions in the same country that did not experience such shocks. If regions of a country were adept at reallocating labor and capital, they could absorb shocks, including permanent shocks, and show no persistent effects on local activity and employment and little difference between the two groups of regions.

The analysis suggests that regions that experienced car factory closures typically had bigger increases in unemployment rates after the closures than comparator regions in the same countries, with the difference being statistically significant. Regressing regional unemployment rates on a dummy variable for whether the region experienced at least one plant closure points to significant and persistent effects, even after controlling for differences between regions' employment shares in industry, initial real GDP per capita, population density, and dependency ratios (Figure 2.3.1, full sample). Unemployment rates in regions with car factory closures increase for three years after the shock as the initial impact of the closure is magnified by local spillover effects to other sectors.[4]

Out-migration is expected to be a key adjustment mechanism after automotive factory closures, if other local employment options are insufficient.

Figure 2.3.1. Associations between Automotive Manufacturing Plant Closures and Unemployment Rates
(Percentage point change in unemployment rate)

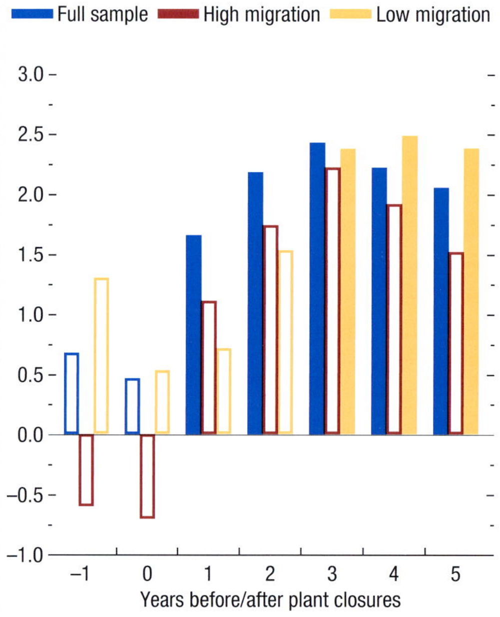

Sources: Organisation for Economic Co-operation and Development Regional Database; and IMF staff calculations.
Note: The figure shows coefficient estimates from regressions of the unemployment rate on a dummy variable for whether the region experienced at least one plant closure, controlling for initial GDP per capita, population density, share of employment in industry, and the dependency ratio. Solid bars indicate statistical significance at the 10 percent level while hollow bars do not. High and low migration refer to gross migration flows split at the sample median.

The author of this box is Zsóka Kóczán.

[1]See Martin and Rowthorn (1986); Pinch and Mason (1991); Hinde (1994); Kirkham and Watts (1998); Tomaney, Pike, and Cornford (1999); Shutt, Henderson, and Kumi-Ampofo (2003); and Henderson and Shutt (2004); among others.

[2]See Chapain and Murie (2008), Ryan and Campo (2013), Bailey and others (2014), and Stanford (2017) for recent examples.

[3]The sample of countries includes Australia, Canada, Germany, Italy, the United Kingdom, and the United States, covering 2000–16. Over the period, 30 closures were recorded in these countries.

[4]See Goldstein (2017) for vivid descriptions of such effects.

Box 2.3 *(continued)*

To examine the role of migration, the regressions in this study are repeated separately for regions with high and low gross migration flows. The persistent unemployment effects are driven by regions with low gross migration flows. The negative effects of closures are not statistically significant in regions with high gross migration flows (Figure 2.3.1, high and low migration subsamples). The highly persistent effects of permanent automotive factory closures are consistent with adjustment being stuck in some regions, particularly those where mobility is low, potentially due to the more constrained and selective nature of migration.[5] Endogenous local demand effects and expectations about the future development of a place hit by factory closures could further reinforce the effects of such local shocks, exacerbating regional disparities within countries.

[5]See Kim (2008) and Duranton and Venables (2018) for discussions of the nature of mobile labor.

Box 2.4. Place-Based Policies: Rethinking Fiscal Policies to Tackle Inequalities within Countries

Policymakers deploy a variety of tools to reduce economic inequality, including fiscal redistribution through taxes and transfers and growth-friendly policies to improve education, health care, infrastructure, and affordable housing (October 2017 *Fiscal Monitor*). Most national policies have been spatially blind, targeting individuals based on their circumstances and characteristics, regardless of their residency. Examples of such policy measures include national disability and unemployment payments in the United States and unemployment benefits in France and Spain, which are targeted to individuals in need or who are unemployed, irrespective of their location. However, persistent and growing regional economic disparities in some countries have increased interest in place-based or spatially targeted fiscal policies as a further way to tackle inequality.

Place-based policies intend to promote regional equity and inclusive growth and to insure against region-specific shocks (Kim and Dougherty 2018). Examples of such policies include the European Union's Regional Development Funds that support naturally disadvantaged (remote, less-developed, or disaster-stricken) subnational regions; Canada's Regional Development Agencies, which provide support to diversify regional economies and foster community development; and US enterprise zones, which provide tax credits to generate new jobs and investment. As shown in Table 2.4.1, spatially targeted interventions can differ according to their proximate objectives, spatial coverage, and fiscal instruments. The decision on what to use will depend on the nature of the underlying regional issues.

Place-based policies can boost the success of existing fiscal policies in reducing inequality if (1) the intended recipients, such as low-income households or the unemployed, are geographically concentrated; and (2) traditional nationwide means-testing approaches have limited coverage, are less progressive, or are difficult to enforce (Coady, Grosh, and Hoddinott 2004; October 2017 *Fiscal Monitor*).[1] Place-based policies may also have merit if fiscal interventions are expected to have stronger impacts on the disadvantaged in certain regions, for example, in the case of hiring incentives that might be more effective in creating jobs and growth in regions with higher unemployment rates (Austin, Glaeser, and Summers 2018). Place-based policies should ensure that interventions facilitate convergence and sectoral reallocation in response to shocks, rather than create new barriers. But policymakers should also be mindful that such policies may raise horizontal equity concerns, as individuals with

The authors of this box are William Gbohoui, W. Raphael Lam, and Victor Lledo.

[1]Limited coverage refers to the fact that, in most countries, only a portion of the households that meet the criteria to receive a transfer (for example, means-tested) actually receive the transfer. Coverage is calculated as the percent of eligible households that in fact receive the transfer.

Table 2.4.1. Examples of Place-Based Policies

Aims	Instruments	Country Programs	Coverage
Enterprise zones: attract firms to create jobs and invest	Tax incentives on investment, job creation, and corporate income taxes; streamlined regulations	US Federal Empowerment Zones	Zones and communities within the region
Cluster promotion: agglomeration of high-tech firms and research institutions	Tax incentives; public research and development spending; grants	France's Local Productive System; "High-tech Offensive" programs in Bavaria, Germany	Region at large; communities within the region
Relocation programs: Compensate people to live/relocate in selected regions	Tax exemptions on personal income tax; grants and transfers	US low-income housing tax credit; Spain's income tax credits for unemployed that relocate for jobs; Canadian Northern Economic Development initiative to retain youth in northern regions	Low-income neighborhoods

Sources: Neumark and Simpson (2014); WB (2009); and IMF staff estimates.

Box 2.4 *(continued)*

the same status, but living in different regions, may receive different treatment.

Drawing on individual household income surveys for a selected sample of countries, illustrative simulations suggest that combining spatial targeting with conventional means-testing programs could improve the effectiveness of fiscal redistribution—as captured by the size of the decline in income inequality—by 7–10 percent, without increasing fiscal costs (see Figure 2.4.1 and Gbohoui, Lam, and Lledo 2019 for further details). For example, because France and the United Kingdom have highly progressive social safety nets and are successful at reaching a high percentage of households eligible for transfers, the potential gains from spatial targeting are relatively small (at about 7–8 percent). But improvements are larger (about 10 percent) in the United States, where poorer households are more concentrated in lagging regions and a higher percentage of eligible households end up not receiving transfers (that is, coverage is worse).

When designing and implementing place-based policies, it is important to assign responsibilities to the appropriate level of government. The choice should be sensitive to intergovernmental fiscal arrangements within a country (for example, a unitary or federal state) and the associated revenue-raising capacity and scope for intergovernmental transfers. As a general principle, the central government should take the lead on overall policy design and monitoring, given that it can account for possible externalities and spillovers across states and provinces. Subnational governments could be more involved in the implementation, as they are more attuned to local needs and preferences. For example, in federal or highly decentralized countries, such as the United States, subnational governments have greater autonomy to determine income and property tax rates, and spending on education and health care.

Figure 2.4.1. Effects of Fiscal Redistribution by Conventional versus Spatially Targeted Means-Tested Transfers

(Reduction in Gini points, unless otherwise noted)

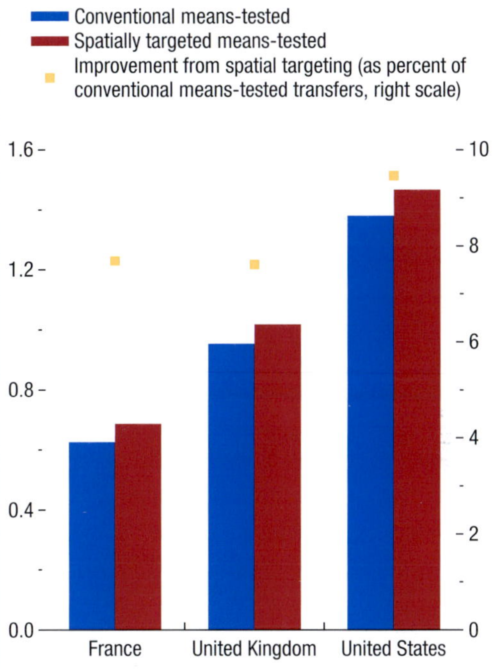

Sources: Luxembourg Income Study; and IMF staff calculations.

Note: The figure is based on an illustrative exercise that compares conventional (spatially blind) means-tested transfers with spatially targeted means-testing. Conventional means-tested transfers have limited coverage; that is, some percentage of eligible households do not receive the transfer (see October 2017 *Fiscal Monitor*). Spatially targeted means-testing can enhance the coverage at the same fiscal cost. The fiscal redistribution effect is defined as the difference in nationwide income inequality (Gini coefficient) before and after taxes and transfers, and is calculated separately for conventional and spatially targeted means-tested transfers. The improvement is calculated as the difference in Gini reduction, expressed as a percentage of the fiscal redistribution under conventional means-tested transfers.

References

Abdih, Yasser, and Stephan Danninger. 2017. "What Explains the Decline of the US Labor Share of Income? An Analysis of State and Industry Level Data." IMF Working Paper 17/167, International Monetary Fund, Washington, DC.

Acemoglu, Daron, and Melissa Dell. 2010. "Productivity Differences between and within Countries." *American Economic Journal: Macroeconomics* 2 (1): 169–88.

Adler, Gustavo, Romain Duval, Davide Furceri, Sinem Kiliç Çelik, and Marcos Poplawski-Ribeiro. 2017. "Gone with the Headwinds: Global Productivity." IMF Staff Discussion Note 17/04, International Monetary Fund, Washington, DC.

Aiyar, Shekhar, John Bluedorn, Romain Duval, Davide Furceri, Daniel Garcia-Macia, Yi Ji, Davide Malacrino, Haonan Qu, Jesse Siminitz, and Aleksandra Zdzienicka. 2019. "Strengthening the Euro Area: The Role of National Structural Reforms in Enhancing Resilience." IMF Staff Discussion Note 19/05, International Monetary Fund, Washington, DC.

Algan, Yann, and Pierre Cahuc. 2014. "Trust, Growth, and Well-Being: New Evidence and Policy Implications." Chapter 2 in *Handbook of Economic Growth* 2, edited by Philippe Aghion and Steven N. Durlauf: 49–120. North Holland: Elsevier.

Allen, Treb, and Costas Arkolakis. 2014. "Trade and the Topography of the Spatial Economy." *Quarterly Journal of Economics* 129 (3): 1085–140.

Alvarez, Jorge, Ivo Krznar, and Trevor Tombe. 2019. "Internal Trade in Canada: Case for Liberalization." IMF Working Paper 19/158, International Monetary Fund, Washington, DC.

Asdrubali, Pierfederico, Bent E. Sørensen, and Oved Yosha. 1996. "Channels of Interstate Risk Sharing: United States 1963–1990." *Quarterly Journal of Economics* 111 (4): 1081–110.

Atkinson, Tony, Joe Hasell, Salvatore Morelli, and Max Roser. 2017. *The Chartbook of Economic Inequality*. Institute for New Economic Thinking, Oxford, United Kingdom.

Austin, Benjamin, Edward Glaeser, and Lawrence H. Summers. 2018. "Jobs for the Heartland: Place-Based Policies in 21st Century America." *Brooking Papers on Economic Activity*, Spring: 151–255.

Autor, David H., and David Dorn. 2013. "The Growth of Low-Skill Service Jobs and the Polarization of the US Labor Market." *American Economic Review* 103 (5): 1553–597.

Autor, David H., David Dorn, and Gordon H. Hanson. 2013a. "The China Syndrome: Local Labor Market Effects of Import Competition in the United States." *American Economic Review* 103 (6): 2121–168.

———. 2013b. "The Geography of Trade and Technology Shocks in the United States." *American Economic Review* 103 (3): 220–25.

———. 2015. "Untangling Trade and Technology: Evidence from Local Labour Markets." *Economic Journal* 125 (584): 621–46.

Bailey, David, Gill Bentley, Alex de Ruyter, and Stephen Hall. 2014. "Plant Closures and Taskforce Responses: An Analysis of the Impact of and Policy Response to MG Rover in Birmingham." *Regional Studies, Regional Science* 1 (1): 60–78.

Bande, Roberto, Melchor Fernández, and Victor Montuenga. 2008. "Regional Unemployment in Spain: Disparities, Business Cycle and Wage Setting." *Labour Economics* 15 (5): 885–914.

Barca, Fabrizio, Philip McCann, and Andrés Rodríguez-Pose. 2012. "The Case for Regional Development Intervention: Place-Based versus Place-Neutral Approaches." *Journal of Regional Science* 52 (1): 134–52.

Bartik, Timothy J. 1991. "Who Benefits from State and Local Economic Development Policies?" W. E. Upjohn Institute for Employment Research, Kalamazoo, MI.

Blanchard, Olivier Jean, and Lawrence F. Katz. 1992. "Regional Evolutions." *Brookings Papers on Economic Activity* 1: 1–75.

Blöchliger, Hansjorg, David Bartolini, and Sibylle Stossberg. 2016. "Does Fiscal Decentralisation Foster Regional Convergence?" OECD Economic Policy Paper 17, Organisation for Economic Co-operation and Development, Paris.

Boadway, Robin, and Anwar Shah, eds. 2007. *Intergovernmental Fiscal Transfers: Principles and Practice*. Public Sector Governance and Accountability Series. World Bank Group, Washington, DC.

Boeri, Tito, Andrea Ichino, Enrico Moretti, and Johanna Posch. 2019. "Wage Equalization and Regional Misallocation: Evidence from Italian and German Provinces." NBER Working Paper 25612, National Bureau of Economic Research, Cambridge, MA.

Breau, Sébastien, and Richard Saillant. 2016. "Regional Income Disparities in Canada: Exploring the Geographical Dimensions of an Old Debate." *Regional Studies, Regional Science* 3 (1): 463–81.

Card, David, Jochen Kluve, and Andrea Weber. 2018. "What Works? A Meta Analysis of Recent Active Labor Market Program Evaluations." *Journal of the European Economic Association* 16 (3): 894–931.

Caselli, Francesco. 2005. "Accounting for Cross-Country Income Differences." Chapter 9 in *Handbook of Economic Growth* 1a, edited by Philippe Aghion and Steven N. Durlauf. Old Holland: Elsevier. 679–741.

Chapain, Caroline, and Alan Murie. 2008. "The Impact of Factory Closure on Local Communities and Economies: The Case of the MG Rover Longbridge Closure in Birmingham." *Policy Studies* 29 (3): 305–17.

Che, Natasha X., and Antonio Spilimbergo. 2012. "Structural Reforms and Regional Convergence." IMF Working Paper 12/106, International Monetary Fund, Washington, DC.

Chetty, Raj. 2008. "Moral Hazard versus Liquidity and Optimal Unemployment Insurance." *Journal of Political Economy* 116 (2): 173–234.

Chetty, Raj, John N. Friedman, and Jonah E. Rockoff. 2014. "Measuring the Impacts of Teachers II: Teacher Value-Added and Student Outcomes in Adulthood." *American Economic Review* 104 (9): 2633–79.

Chetty, Raj, and Nathaniel Hendren. 2018a. "The Impacts of Neighborhoods on Intergenerational Mobility I: Childhood Exposure Effects." *Quarterly Journal of Economics* 133 (3): 1107–62.

———. 2018b. "The Impacts of Neighborhoods on Intergenerational Mobility II: County-Level Estimates." *Quarterly Journal of Economics* 133 (3): 1163–228.

Chetty, Raj, Nathaniel Hendren, and Lawrence F. Katz. 2016. "The Effects of Exposure to Better Neighborhoods on Children: New Evidence from the Moving to Opportunity Experiment." *American Economic Review* 106 (4): 855–902.

Clark, Andrew E. 2018. "Four Decades of the Economics of Happiness: Where Next?" *Review of Income and Wealth* 64 (2): 245–69.

Clark, Andrew E., and Andrew J. Oswald. 1994. "Unhappiness and Unemployment." *Economic Journal* 104 (424): 648–59.

Coady, David, and Allan Dizioli. 2017. "Income Inequality and Education Revisited: Persistence, Endogeneity, and Heterogeneity." IMF Working Paper 17/126, International Monetary Fund, Washington, DC.

Coady, David, Margaret Grosh, and John Hoddinott. 2004. *Targeting of Transfers in Developing Countries: Review of Lessons and Experience*. Washington, DC: World Bank Group.

Coe, Neil M., Philip F. Kelly, and Henry W. C. Yeung. 2007. *Economic Geography: A Contemporary Introduction*. Oxford: Blackwell Publishing.

Conolly, Marie, Miles Corak, and Catherine Haeck. 2019. "Intergenerational Mobility between and within Canada and the United States." *Journal of Labor Economics* 37 (S2): S595–S641.

Cowell, Frank. 2011. *Measuring Inequality*. Third edition. Oxford: Oxford University Press.

Coyle, Diane. 2015. *GDP: A Brief but Affectionate History*. Revised and expanded edition. Princeton, NJ: Princeton University Press.

Dabla-Norris, Era, Kalpana Kochhar, Nujin Suphaphiphat, Frantisek Ricka, and Evridiki Tsounta. 2015. "Causes and Consequences of Income Inequality: A Global Perspective." IMF Staff Discussion Note 15/13, International Monetary Fund, Washington, DC.

Dao, Mai Chi, Mitali Das, Zsóka Kóczán, and Weicheng Lian. 2017. "Why Is Labor Receiving a Smaller Share of Global Income? Theory and Empirical Evidence." IMF Working Paper 17/169, International Monetary Fund, Washington, DC.

Dao, Mai, Davide Furceri, and Prakash Loungani. 2017. "Regional Labor Market Adjustment in the United States: Trend and Cycle." *Review of Economics and Statistics* 99 (2): 243–57.

Das, Mitali, and Benjamin Hilgenstock. 2018. "The Exposure to Routinization: Labor Market Implications for Developed and Developing Economies." IMF Working Paper 18/135, International Monetary Fund, Washington, DC.

Dauth, Wolfgang, Sebastian Findeisen, and Jens Suedekum. 2014. "The Rise of the East and the Far East: German Labor Markets and Trade Integration." *Journal of the European Economic Association* 12 (6): 1643–75.

Davis, Donald R., and David E. Weinstein. 2002. "Bones, Bombs, and Break Points: The Geography of Economic Activity." *American Economic Review* 92 (5): 1269–89.

Decressin, Jörg, and Antonio Fatás. 1995. "Regional Labor Market Dynamics in Europe." *European Economic Review* 39: 1627–55.

Díez, Federico, Jiayue Fan, and Carolina Villegas-Sánchez. 2018. "Global Declining Competition." IMF Working Paper 19/82, International Monetary Fund, Washington, DC.

Donaldson, Dave, and Richard Hornbeck. 2016. "Railroads and American Economic Growth: A 'Market Access' Approach." *Quarterly Journal of Economics* 131 (2): 799–858.

Duranton, Gilles, and Diego Puga. 2004. "Micro-Foundations of Urban Agglomeration Economies." Chapter 48 in *Handbook of Regional and Urban Economics* 4, edited by J. Vernon Henderson and Jacques-François Thisse. North Holland: Elsevier. 2063–3073.

Duranton, Gilles, and Anthony J. Venables. 2018. "Place-Based Policies for Development." NBER Working Paper 24562, National Bureau of Economic Research, Cambridge, MA.

Durlauf, Steven N., and Ananth Seshadri. 2018. "Understanding the Great Gatsby Curve." Chapter 4 in *NBER Macroeconomics Annual 2017* 32, edited by Martin Eichenbaum and Jonathan A. Parker. Cambridge, MA: National Bureau of Economic Research. 333–93.

Esteban, J. 2000. "Regional Convergence in Europe and the Industry Mix: A Shift-Share Analysis." *Regional Science and Urban Economics* 30 (3): 353–64.

Feenstra, Robert C., Robert Inklaar, and Marcel P. Timmer. 2015. "The Next Generation of the Penn World Table." *American Economic Review* 105 (10): 3150–82.

Feldstein, Martin. 2017. "Underestimating the Real Growth of GDP, Personal Income, and Productivity." *Journal of Economic Perspectives* 31 (2): 145–64.

Felice, Emanuele. 2011. "Regional Value Added in Italy, 1891–2001, and the Foundation of a Long-Term Picture." *Economic History Review* 64 (3): 929–50.

Feyrer, James. 2007. "Demographics and Productivity." *Review of Economics and Statistics* 89 (1): 100–09.

Fleurbaey, Marc. 2009. "Beyond GDP: The Quest for a Measure of Social Welfare." *Journal of Economic Literature* 47 (4): 1029–75.

Fujita, Masahisa, Paul Krugman, and Anthony J. Venables. 1999. *The Spatial Economy: Cities, Regions, and International Trade*. Cambridge, MA: MIT Press.

Gal, Peter. 2013. "Measuring Total Factor Productivity at the Firm Level Using OECD-ORBIS." OECD Economics Department Working Paper 1049, Organisation for Economic Co-operation and Development, Paris.

Gandhi, Amit, Salvador Navarro, and David Rivers. 2018. "On the Identification of Gross Output Production Functions." University of Western Ontario, Centre for Human Capital and Productivity Working Papers, London, Ontario, Canada.

Gbohoui, William, W. Raphael Lam, and Victor Lledo. 2019. "The Great Divide: Regional Inequality and Fiscal Policy." IMF Working Paper 19/88, International Monetary Fund, Washington, DC.

Gennaioli, Nicola, Rafael La Porta, Florencio Lopez-de-Silanes, and Andrei Schleifer. 2013. "Human Capital and Regional Development." *Quarterly Journal of Economics*, February 128 (1): 105–64.

———. 2014. "Growth in Regions." *Journal of Economic Growth* 19 (3): 259–309.

Giannone, Elisa. 2018. "Skill-Biased Technical Change and Regional Convergence." 2017 Meeting Papers, 190, Society for Economic Dynamics, Stonybrook, NY.

Giordano, Raffaela, Sergi Lanau, Pietro Tommasino, and Petia Topalova. 2015. "Does Public Sector Inefficiency Constrain Firm Productivity: Evidence from Italian Provinces." IMF Working Paper 15/168, International Monetary Fund, Washington, DC.

Goldsmith-Pinkham, Paul, Isaac Sorkin, and Henry Swift. 2019. "Bartik Instruments: What, When, Why, and How." NBER Working Paper 24408, National Bureau of Economic Research, Cambridge, MA.

Goldstein, Amy. 2017. *Janesville: An American Story*. New York: Simon and Schuster.

Gopinath, Gita, Şebnem Kalemli-Özcan, Loukas Karabarbounis, and Carolina Villegas-Sánchez. 2017. "Capital Allocation and Productivity in South Europe." *Quarterly Journal of Economics* 132 (4): 1915–967.

Graff Zivin, Joshua, and Matthew Neidell. 2014. "Temperature and the Allocation of Time: Implications for Climate Change." *Journal of Labor Economics* 32 (1): 1–26.

Grün, Carola, Wolfgang Hauser, and Thomas Rhein. 2010. "Is Any Job Better than No Job? Life Satisfaction and Re-employment." *Journal of Labor Research* 31 (3): 285–306.

Guriev, Sergei. 2018. "Economic Drivers of Populism." *American Economic Review: Papers and Proceedings* 108: 200–03.

Harris, I., Philip D. Jones, Timothy J. Osborn, and David H. Lister. 2014. "Updated High-Resolution Grids of Monthly Climatic Observations—the CRU TS3.10 Dataset." *International Journal of Climatology* 34 (3): 623–42. Version 3.24.01.

Helpman, Elhanan. 2016. "Globalization and Wage Inequality." NBER Working Paper 22944, National Bureau of Economic Research, Cambridge, MA.

Henderson, Roger, and John Shutt. 2004. "Responding to a Coalfield Closure: Old Issues for a New Regional Development Agency?" *Local Economy* 19 (1): 25–37.

Hinde, Kevin. 1994. "Labor Market Experiences Following Plant Closures: Sunderland's Shipyard Workers." *Regional Studies* 28 (7): 713–24.

Hsieh, Chang-Tai, and Peter J. Klenow. 2010. "Development Accounting." *American Economic Journal: Macroeconomics* 2 (1): 207–23.

Hsieh, Chang-Tai, and Enrico Moretti. 2019. "Housing Constraints and Spatial Misallocation." *American Economic Journal: Macroeconomics* 11 (2): 1–39.

Immervoll, Herwig, and Linda Richardson. 2011. "Redistribution Policy and Inequality Reduction in OECD Countries: What Has Changed in Two Decades?" OECD Social, Employment and Migration Working Paper 122, Organisation for Economic Co-operation and Development, Paris.

Intergovernmental Panel on Climate Change (IPCC). 2014. "Climate Change 2014: Impacts, Adaptation, and Vulnerability. Part A: Global and Sectoral Aspects." Contribution of Working Group II to the *Fifth Assessment Report of the Intergovernmental Panel on Climate Change*. Cambridge University Press: Cambridge, United Kingdom and New York.

International Monetary Fund (IMF). 2018. "Spain: Selected Issues." IMF Country Report 18/331, Washington, DC.

Jakubik, Adam, and Victor Stolzenburg. 2018. "The 'China Shock' Revisited: Insights from Value Added Trade Flows." WTO Staff Working Paper ERSD-2018–10.

Jaumotte, Florence, Subir Lall, and Chris Papageorgiou. 2013. "Rising Income Inequality: Technology, or Trade and Financial Globalization?" *IMF Economic Review* 61 (2): 271–309.

Jones, Charles I., and Peter J. Klenow. 2016. "Beyond GDP? Welfare across Countries and Time." *American Economic Review* 106 (9): 2426–57.

Jordà, Òscar. 2005. "Estimation and Inference of Impulse Responses by Local Projections." *American Economic Review* 95 (1): 161–82.

Kalemli-Özcan, Şebnem, Bent Sorensen, Carolina Villegas-Sánchez, Vadym Volosovych, and Sevcan Yesiltas. 2015. "How to Construct Nationally Representative Firm Level Data from the ORBIS Global Database." NBER Working Paper 21558, National Bureau of Economic Research, Cambridge, MA.

Kappeler, Andreas, Albert Solé-Ollé, Andreas Stephan, and Timo Välilä. 2013. "Does Fiscal Decentralization Foster Regional Investment in Productive Infrastructure?" *European Journal of Political Economy* 31: 15–25.

Karabarbounis, Loukas, and Brent Neiman. 2014. "The Global Decline of the Labor Share." *Quarterly Journal of Economics* 129 (1): 61–103.

Kaufman, Martin, Phillip Swagel, and Steven Dunaway. 2003. "Regional Convergence and the Role of Federal Transfers in Canada." IMF Working Paper 03/97, International Monetary Fund, Washington, DC.

Kim, Junghun, and Sean Dougherty, eds. 2018. *Fiscal Decentralisation and Inclusive Growth*. OECD Fiscal Federalism Studies, OECD Publishing, Paris/KIPF, Seoul.

Kim, Sukkoo. 2008. "Spatial Inequality and Economic Development: Theories, Facts and Policies." Commission on Growth and Development Working Paper 16, World Bank Group, Washington, DC.

Kirkham, Janet D., and Hugh D. Watts. 1998. "Multi-Locational Manufacturing Organisations and Plant Closures in Urban Areas." *Urban Studies* 35 (9): 1559–75.

Klein Goldewijk, Kees, Arthur Beusen, Jonathan Doelman, and Elke Stehfest. 2017. "Anthropogenic Land-Use Estimates for the Holocene – HYDE 3.2." *Earth System Science Data*, 9: 924–53.

Kline, Patrick, and Enrico Moretti. 2014. "People, Places, and Public Policy: Some Simple Welfare Economics of Local Economic Development Programs." *Annual Review of Economics* 6 (1): 629–62.

Krugman, Paul. 1991. "Increasing Returns and Economic Geography." *Journal of Political Economy* 99 (3): 483–99.

Krugman, Paul, and Anthony J. Venables. 1995. "Globalization and the Inequality of Nations." *Quarterly Journal of Economics* 110 (4): 857–80.

Lessmann, Christian. 2009. "Fiscal Decentralization and Regional Disparity: Evidence from Cross-Section and Panel Data." *Environment and Planning A: Economy and Space* 41(10): 2455–73.

Lessmann, Christian, and André Seidel. 2017. "Regional Inequality, Convergence, and its Determinants: A View from Outer Space." *European Economic Review* 92: 110–32.

Lian, Weicheng, Natalija Novta, Evgenia Pugacheva, Yannick Timmer, and Petia B. Topalova. 2019. "The Price of Capital Goods: A Driver of Investment under Threat." IMF Working Paper 19/134, International Monetary Fund, Washington, DC.

Liu, Lucy Qian. 2018. "Regional Labor Mobility in Spain." IMF Working Paper 18/282, International Monetary Fund, Washington, DC.

Luxembourg Income Study (LIS) Database. Multiple years. http://www.lisdatacenter.org (multiple countries). Luxembourg.

Martin, Ron, and Bob Rowthorn. 1986. *The Geography of De-Industrialisation*. London: Macmillan.

Moretti, Enrico. 2011. "Local Labor Markets." Chapter 14 in *Handbook of Labor Economics* 4b, edited by David Card and Orley Ashenfelter. North Holland: Elsevier. 1237–313.

Neumark, David, and Helen Simpson. 2015. "Place-Based Policies." Chapter 18 in *Handbook of Regional and Urban Economics* 5, edited by Gilles Duranton, J. Vernon Henderson, and William C. Strange. North Holland: Elsevier. 1197–287.

Nolan, Brian, Matteo G. Richiardi, and Luis Valenzuela. 2019. "The Drivers of Income Inequality in Rich Countries." *Journal of Economic Surveys*, early view: 1–40.

Novotný, Josef. 2007. "On the Measurement of Regional Inequality: Does Spatial Dimension of Income Inequality Matter?" *Annals of Regional Science* 41 (3): 563–80.

Nunn, Nathan. 2014. "Historical Development." Chapter 7 in *Handbook of Economic Growth* 2, edited by Philippe Aghion and Steven N. Durlauf, North Holland: Elsevier. 347–402.

Nunn, Ryan, Jana Parsons, and Jay Shambaugh. 2018. "The Geography of Prosperity." In *Place-Based Policies for Shared Economic Growth,* edited by Jay Shambaugh and Ryan Nunn. Washington, DC: Hamilton Project, Brookings Institution.

Obstfeld, Maurice, and Giovanni Peri. 1998. "Regional Non-Adjustment and Fiscal Policy." *Economic Policy* 13 (26): 205–59.

Organisation for Economic Co-operation and Development (OECD). 2013. *Understanding National Accounts*. Second edition. Paris: OECD Publishing.

———. 2016a. *Back to Work: Denmark: Improving the Re-Employment Prospects of Displaced Workers*. Paris: OECD Publishing.

———. 2016b. *OECD Regional Outlook 2016: Productive Regions for Inclusive Societies*. Paris: OECD Publishing.

———. 2018. *OECD Regions and Cities at a Glance 2018*. Paris: OECD Publishing.

Pike, Andy, Andrés Rodríguez-Pose, and John Tomaney. 2017. *Local and Regional Development*. Second edition. New York: Routledge.

Pinch, Steven, and Colin Mason. 1991. "Redundancy in an Expanding Labour Market: A Case-Study of Displaced Workers from Two Manufacturing Plants in Southampton." *Urban Studies* 28 (5): 735–57.

Pissarides, Christopher A. 2001. "Employment Protection." *Labour Economics* 8 (2): 131–59.

Rajan, Raghuram. 2019. *The Third Pillar: How Markets and the State Leave the Community Behind*. New York: Penguin Press.

Rodríguez-Pose, Andrés. 2018. "The Revenge of the Places that Don't Matter (and What to Do About it)." *Cambridge Journal of Regions, Economy and Society* 11 (1): 189–209.

Rodríguez-Pose, Andrés, and Tobias Ketterer. Forthcoming. "Institutional Change and the Development of Lagging Regions in Europe." *Regional Studies*.

Rodríguez-Pose, Andrés, and Michael Storper. 2019. "Housing, Urban Growth, and Inequalities: The Limits to Deregulation and Upzoning in Reducing Economic and Spatial Inequality." CEPR Discussion Paper DP 13713, Center for Economic Policy Research, Washington, DC.

Ryan, Brent D., and Daniel Campo. 2013. "Autopia's End: The Decline and Fall of Detroit's Automotive Manufacturing Landscape." *Journal of Planning History* 12 (2): 95–132.

Schmieder, Johannes F., Till von Wachter, and Stefan Bender. 2016. "The Effect of Unemployment Benefits and Nonemployment Durations on Wages." *American Economic Review* 106 (3): 739–77.

Shorrocks, Anthony. 1980. "The Class of Additively Decomposable Inequality Measures." *Econometrica* 48 (3): 613–25.

Shorrocks, Anthony, and Guanghua Wan. 2005. "Spatial Decomposition of Inequality." *Journal of Economic Geography* 5 (1): 59–81.

Shutt, John, Roger Henderson, and Felix Kumi-Ampofo. 2003. "Responding to a Regional Economic Crisis: An Impact and Regeneration Assessment of the Selby Coalfield Closure on the Yorkshire and Humber Region." Paper delivered to the Regional Studies Association International Conference. Pisa, Italy, April 2003.

Stanford, Jim. 2017. “When an Auto Industry Disappears: Australia’s Experience and Lessons for Canada.” *Canadian Public Policy* 43 (S1): S57–S74.

Stevenson, Betsey, and Justin Wolfers. 2008. “Economic Growth and Subjective Well-Being: Reassessing the Easterlin Paradox.” *Brookings Papers on Economy Activity* 2008 (1): 1–102.

Stiglitz, Joseph E., Jean-Paul Fitoussi, and Martine Durand. 2018. *Beyond GDP: Measuring What Counts for Economic and Social Performance.* Paris: OECD Publishing.

Tatsiramos, Konstantinos, and Jan C. van Ours. 2014. “Labor Market Effects of Unemployment Insurance Design.” *Journal of Economic Surveys* 28 (2): 284–311.

Timmer, Marcel P., Erik Dietzenbacher, Bart Los, Robert Stehrer, and Gaaitzen J. de Vries. 2015. “An Illustrated User Guide to the World Input–Output Database: The Case of Global Automotive Production.” *Review of International Economics* 23 (3): 575–605.

Tomaney, John, Andy Pike, and James Cornford. 1999. “Plant Closure and the Local Economy: The Case of Swan Hunter on Tyneside.” *Regional Studies* 33 (5): 401–11.

Topalova, Petia. 2010. “Factor Immobility and Regional Impacts of Trade Liberalization: Evidence on Poverty from India.” *American Economic Journal: Applied Economics* 2 (4): 1–41.

United Nations (UN). 2009. *System of National Accounts 2008.* New York: United Nations.

Winkler, Hernan. 2019. “The Effect of Income Inequality on Political Polarization: Evidence from European Regions, 2002–2014.” *Economics and Politics* 31 (2): 137–62.

World Bank (WB). 2009. *World Development Report 2009: Reshaping Economic Geography.* Washington, DC.

———. 2018. *World Development Report 2018: Learning to Realize Education’s Promise.* Washington, DC.

———. 2019a. *World Development Report 2019: The Changing Nature of Work.* Washington, DC.

———. 2019b. Doing Business Database. Washington, D.C.

CHAPTER 3

REIGNITING GROWTH IN LOW-INCOME AND EMERGING MARKET ECONOMIES: WHAT ROLE CAN STRUCTURAL REFORMS PLAY?

The pace of structural reforms in emerging market and developing economies was strong during the 1990s, but it has slowed since the early 2000s. Using a newly constructed database on structural reforms, this chapter finds that a reform push in such areas as governance, domestic and external finance, trade, and labor and product markets could deliver sizable output gains in the medium term. A major and comprehensive reform package might double the speed of convergence of the average emerging market and developing economy to the living standards of advanced economies, raising annual GDP growth by about 1 percentage point for some time. At the same time, reforms take several years to deliver, and some of them—easing job protection regulation and liberalizing domestic finance—may entail greater short-term costs when carried out in bad times; these are best implemented under favorable economic conditions and early in authorities' electoral mandate. Reform gains also tend to be larger when governance and access to credit—two binding constraints on growth—are strong, and where labor market informality is higher—because reforms help reduce it. These findings underscore the importance of carefully tailoring reforms to country circumstances to maximize their benefits.

Introduction

Emerging market and developing economies have enjoyed good growth over the past two decades. Living standards have been converging toward those in advanced economies at a fast pace in the aggregate. However, for many countries, the speed of income convergence remains modest. The typical (median) emerging market has been closing its (purchasing-power-parity-adjusted) income per capita gap with the United States by about 1.3 percent a year since the 2008 financial crisis, while the equivalent speed for a typical low-income developing country is 0.7 percent (Figure 3.1). At these rates, it would take more than 50 years for a typical emerging market economy, and 90 years for a typical low-income developing country, to close half of their current gaps in living standards. Furthermore, convergence has been highly heterogeneous; while some countries have been converging fast (mostly Asian economies and, during the 2000s, some commodity producers), others have stagnated or—in the case of almost a quarter of economies—even diverged. For the latter, disasters (crises, wars, disease outbreaks, extreme climatic events) played a role in some cases, but there is also broader concern about weak underlying trends in income per capita growth.

Subdued and uneven growth, concerns about policies and growth prospects in advanced economies—a key driver of growth in emerging market and developing economies (April 2017 *World Economic Outlook* (WEO)), waning chances of a new commodity price boom, and shrinking macroeconomic—primarily fiscal policy (April 2019 *Fiscal Monitor*)—space have revived emerging market and developing economy policymakers' interest in structural reforms. There is also a sense that reform efforts waned after the liberalization wave that followed the economic crises of the 1990s, leaving much scope for improving the functioning of (financial, labor, product) markets and for improving the quality of other government-influenced drivers of economic growth—such as education, health care, and infrastructure. In some areas, such as, for example, labor markets, automation and globalization put existing regulations that protect jobs rather than workers under pressure, further strengthening the case for reform.

At the same time, broad uncertainty surrounds the potential scope for, and gains to be reaped from, structural reforms in emerging market and developing economies. Individual countries' experience with reforms have been mixed.[1] Some prominent reformers over one

The authors of this chapter are Gabriele Ciminelli, Romain Duval (co-lead), Davide Furceri (co-lead), Guzman Gonzalez-Torres Fernandez, Joao Jalles, Giovanni Melina, and Cian Ruane, with contributions from Zidong An, Hites Ahir, Jun Ge, Yi Ji, and Qiaoqiao Zhang, and supported by Luisa Calixto, Grey Ramos, and Ariana Tayebi. Funding from the UK Department of International Development (DFID) is gratefully acknowledged. The views expressed in this chapter do not necessarily represent those of DFID.

[1]Zettelmeyer (2006) provides an overview of reform experiences in Latin America and a comprehensive discussion of existing explanations for why gains may have undershot expectations.

Figure 3.1. Speed of Income-per-Capita Convergence in Emerging Markets and Low-Income Developing Countries
(Percent)

The average speed of convergence to living standards in advanced economies has been rather modest among EMDEs.

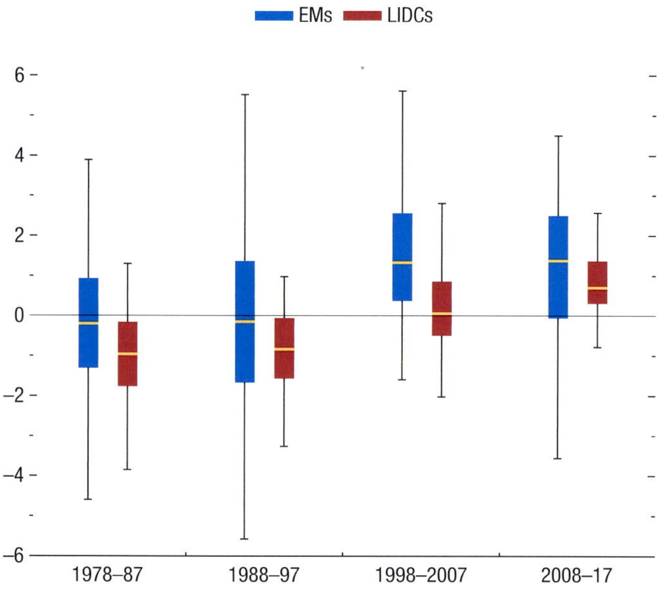

Sources: Penn World Tables; and IMF staff calculations.
Note: For each country, the speed of convergence for each decade is computed as the ratio between average annual real per capita GDP growth relative to the United States and the percent difference between the US real per capita GDP and that of each country at the beginning of each decade at purchasing power parity. The horizontal line inside each box represents the median; the upper and lower edges of each box show the top and bottom quartiles, respectively; and the top and bottom markers denote the maximum and the minimum, respectively.
EMs = emerging markets; EMDEs = emerging market and developing economies; LIDCs = low-income developing countries.

Figure 3.2. Reform Intensity and Speed of Income-per-Capita Convergence in Selected Economies
(Percent)

Some top reformers have enjoyed strong subsequent income growth and convergence while others have not.

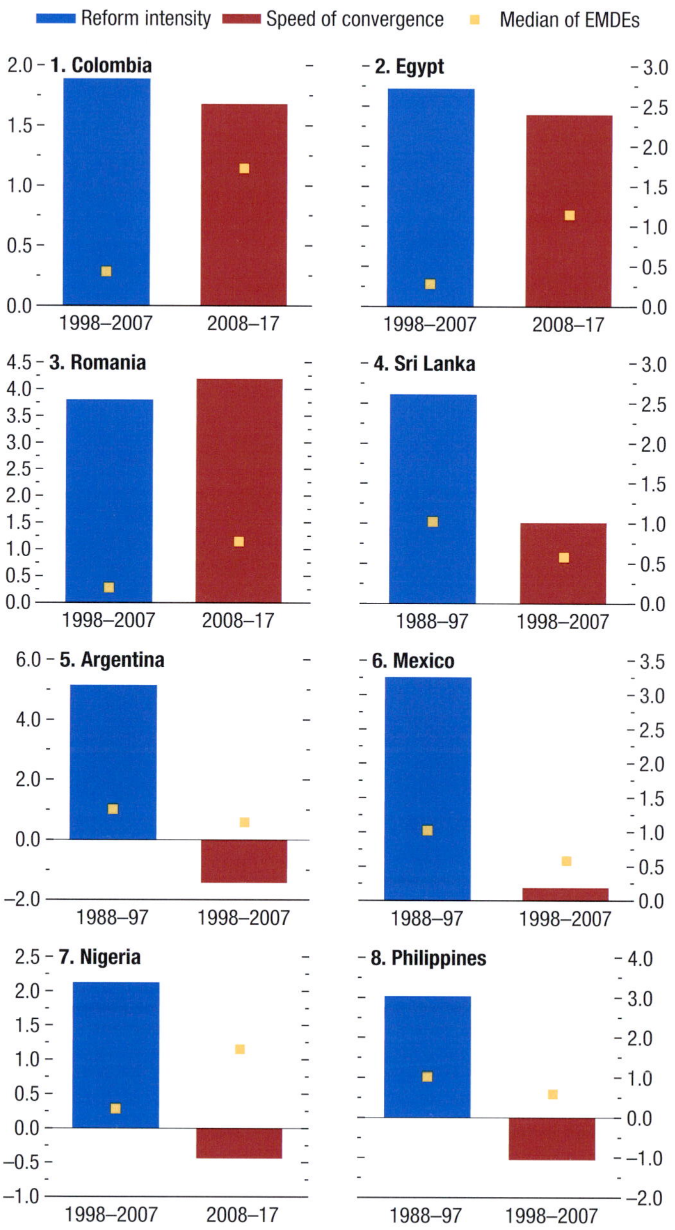

Sources: Alesina and others (forthcoming); Penn World Tables; and IMF staff calculations.
Note: For each country, the speed of convergence for each decade is computed as the ratio between average annual real per capita purchasing power parity GDP growth relative to the United States and the percent difference between the US real per capita GDP and that of each country at the beginning of each decade. Reform intensity is computed as the average annual change in each decade (multiplied by 100) of the average reform index. The average reform index is computed as the arithmetic average of indicators capturing liberalizations in five areas: domestic finance, external finance, trade, product market, and labor market. The index ranges from 0 to 1, with higher values denoting greater liberalization. EMDEs = emerging market and developing economies.

particular decade, such as Sri Lanka during 1988–97, or Colombia, Egypt, and Romania during 1998–2007, have seen their per capita incomes converge fast toward that of the United States (and other advanced economies) during the subsequent decade (Figure 3.2). But other major reformers, such as Argentina, Mexico, and the Philippines during 1988–97, and Nigeria during 1998–2007, failed to converge over the subsequent decade. In some cases, such as Mexico, this could reflect disappointing payoffs from reforms because of pervasive microeconomic distortions that have encouraged informality (Levy 2018). In other cases, it may be that reform gains were negated by adverse events, such as macroeconomic shocks or misguided policies. Examples include the exchange rate overvaluation and the collapse of the currency board in the early 2000s in Argentina—which also led to a reversal of earlier reforms; the 2016 recession driven by the decline in global oil prices, delayed policy adjustment and oil production disruptions in Nigeria; and the hit from the 1997 Asian crisis in the Philippines, which then recovered quickly and grew rapidly beginning in the early 2000s. Macroeconomic shocks can entail persistent or even permanent income losses (Cerra and Saxena 2008), especially when their impact is amplified by specific macroeconomic and structural vulnerabilities (for example, high public debt mostly denominated in foreign currency, or an unsustainable exchange rate peg). This underscores the importance—and difficulty—of disentangling the effects of reforms from those of other drivers of economic growth, such as macroeconomic shocks and policies.

Mixed experience with past reforms could also reflect a given reform's different effects across countries, depending on their specific characteristics. In particular, reforms may pay off only if strong core institutions are in place (Acemoglu, Johnson, and Robinson 2005). Key among these may be laws and institutions that deliver strong governance; for example, reducing border or behind-the-border barriers to competition may not lead to much new firm entry, innovation, and productivity growth if property rights are not well defined and enforced or incumbent domestic firms continue to benefit from tacit government support. More broadly, given the many market imperfections in most emerging market and developing economies, addressing one may not necessarily help the economy if other market distortions are not remedied (Hausmann, Rodrik, and Velasco 2005). For example, opening up the capital account may trigger fickle and poorly allocated capital inflows if the domestic financial system is insufficiently developed, regulated, and supervised to mediate these inflows safely, and so weakens the benefits from capital flow liberalization. Likewise, raising female labor supply through support for childcare or stronger legal protections against discrimination may not fully translate into formal employment gains if labor market institutions, such as stringent job protection legislation for formal workers, make firms less willing to hire. This points to the need to uncover some of the important factors that may account for cross-country differences in the impact of reforms.

A more practical difficulty in assessing the case for structural reforms is the lack of recent comprehensive data and analysis. Although information on structural policies is up to date for selected areas (for example, governance or the cost of doing business, as assessed in Kaufmann, Kraay, and Mastruzzi 2010 and WB 2019), and for a broader range of areas for a few larger emerging market economies (for example, OECD 2018), comprehensive cross-country time-series information is lacking. Partly reflecting these data limitations, there has also been little recent cross-country evidence regarding the growth impact of past reforms, with some exceptions, including earlier IMF work based on indicators constructed in the late 2000s (Christiansen, Schindler, and Tressel 2013; Prati, Onorato, and Papageorgiou 2013).

To assess the macroeconomic effects of structural reforms, this chapter builds on a new IMF reform data set covering regulations for many emerging market economies and low-income developing countries during 1973–2014 in five areas (Alesina and others, forthcoming): trade (tariffs); domestic finance (credit and interest rate controls, entry barriers, public ownership, quality of supervision in the domestic financial system); external finance (capital account openness, encompassing regulations governing international transactions); labor market regulation (stringency of job protection legislation); and product market regulation (stringency of regulations and public ownership in two large network industries—namely, electricity and telecommunications). These new data are supplemented by the World Governance Indicators (Kaufmann, Kraay, and Mastruzzi 2010).[2] The growth impact of regulatory changes in each of the six areas is then explored through empirical analysis, supplemented by model-based analysis that provides alternative quantification of the impact of reforms and sheds light on the channels through which they affect the economy, including the role of informality. Specifically, the chapter tackles the following questions:

- How has structural reform progress evolved over the past couple of decades? Has the pace of reform slowed in emerging market and developing economies in recent years? What is the remaining scope for reform, and how does it vary across regulatory areas and countries?
- What are the short- to medium-term effects of reforms on economic activity? To what extent could such reforms speed up the convergence of emerging market economies and low-income developing countries to living standards in advanced economies?

[2]While the database covers 90 economies around the world, the analysis in this chapter excludes those classified as advanced economies at the beginning of the sample; as such, it covers the 41 current emerging markets, seven former emerging markets, and 20 low-income developing countries.

- What are the channels through which reforms affect the economy? For example, do reforms affect primarily productivity or employment? How do they affect informality, which is often associated with poor firm productivity?
- When should reforms be implemented? Do they pay off less, or more, in bad times?
- Do the effects of reforms vary across economies, and, if so, why? Are there particular reforms that could magnify the gains from others? More broadly, should reforms be implemented as packages, or should policymakers focus on the most binding constraint(s) to growth and, if so, which one(s)?

In addressing these questions, the chapter reaches the following conclusions:

- After the major liberalization waves of the late 1980s and the 1990s, reform in emerging market and developing economies slowed in the 2000s. Although this reflects in part gradual narrowing of the scope for further deregulation, there is still ample room for a renewed reform push, particularly in low-income developing countries—notably, across sub-Saharan Africa and, to a lesser extent, in the Middle East and North Africa and Asia and Pacific regions.
- Reforms can yield sizable payoffs in the medium term, even though gains vary across different types of regulations. For the average emerging market and developing economy, empirical analysis suggests that major simultaneous reforms across all six areas considered in this chapter could raise output by more than 7 percent over a six-year period. This would increase annual GDP growth by more than 1 percentage point and double the average current speed of income-per-capita convergence to advanced economy levels from about 1 percent to more than 2 percent. Model-based analysis points to output gains about twice as large in the longer term.
- Reducing informality, which helps boost firms' productivity and capital investment, is one important channel through which reforms raise output. Given that reforms facilitate formalization, they tend to pay off more in countries where informality is higher, all else equal to start with.
- However, reforms generally take time to deliver. It typically takes at least three years for significant positive effects on output to materialize, although some reforms—such as product market deregulation—pay off more quickly. Possibly reflecting this delay, the political cost of reform—in the executive power's electoral prospects—is lowest when measures are enacted early in the government's political mandate.
- The timing of reform matters—some reforms are best implemented in good times. In normal times, the reforms studied in this chapter are not found to entail short-term macroeconomic costs. However, when macroeconomic conditions are weak, easing job protection legislation or deregulating domestic finance does not pay off and may even lower employment and output in the short term, possibly because stimulating labor or credit supply fails to elicit much response when the demand for labor or credit is depressed.
- Getting reform packaging and sequencing right can also make a difference. Reforms typically deliver larger gains in countries where governance is stronger. This means that strengthening governance can support economic growth and income convergence, not just directly by incentivizing more productive formal firms to invest and recruit, but also indirectly by magnifying the payoff from reforms in other areas. Therefore, there are advantages to combining trade, financial, labor, and product market reforms with, or implementing them after, concrete actions to improve governance. Such concrete actions include streamlined and transparent public spending and tax administration procedures and stronger protection and enforcement of property and contractual rights, for example. Reforms that incentivize formal firms to grow—such as lower administrative burdens or easier labor regulations—also tend to work better when there is better access to credit, which makes it possible for firms to expand. This underscores the importance of domestic finance liberalization, supported by a strong regulatory and supervisory framework. More broadly, identifying binding constraints on growth and specific reform complementarities is key.

Three other important issues that go beyond the scope of this analysis should be borne in mind when considering, prioritizing, and designing reforms. First, this chapter considers reforms essentially aimed at improving the functioning of (financial, labor, product) markets. It ignores others that seek, instead, to directly facilitate the accumulation of productive factors—physical and human capital and labor. Key reforms in this regard involve improving education and health systems, public infrastructure spending frameworks, and laws and regulations that obstruct women's participation in the labor force. Second, in the long term, reforms could entail larger gains than found here by (1) enabling economies to be not just more efficient but also more innovative, leading to more persistent effects on economic growth, and (2) enhancing the reforming economies' resilience to, and thereby alleviating permanent output losses from, economic and financial crises (Aiyar and others 2019). Third, policymakers should factor in and implement up-front complementary reforms to mitigate any adverse effects of reforms on income distribution. Absent any redistribution through the tax-benefit system, some of the reforms considered in this chapter might yield highly uneven gains across the population (Fabrizio and others 2017; Furceri, Loungani, and Ostry, forthcoming). Tackling inequality issues is an important policy objective, but it also matters for the ultimate impact of reform on economic growth (Ostry, Berg, and Kothari 2018). The poor have fewer opportunities for education and less financial access and therefore are less likely to reap the benefits of market reform. More fundamentally, reforms whose gains are captured only by a small fraction of society risk losing support and stalling, or being undone, down the road (Alesina and others, forthcoming).

The next section examines reform patterns in emerging market and developing economies over the past four decades. It also identifies remaining scope for reform and existing differences across geographic regions and countries. The subsequent section analyzes the effects of reforms on growth and the channels through which they materialize. After that, the investigation turns to the drivers of differences in the effects of reforms across countries and over time. In particular, it looks at whether the effects of reforms vary depending on business conditions and explores reform complementarities. The final section discusses the main takeaways and policy implications.

Structural Policy and Reform Patterns in Emerging Market and Developing Economies

This chapter relies on a new IMF database on economic regulations that identifies structural policies and reforms in trade (tariffs), domestic finance (regulation and supervision), external finance (capital account openness), labor market regulation (job protection legislation), and product market regulation (in electricity and telecommunications, two large network industries) in 90 advanced and emerging market and developing economies—of which 48 are current and former emerging markets and 20 are low-income developing countries—during 1973–2014 (see Online Annex 3.1 for details about the indicators and country coverage). The database was compiled through a systematic reading and coding of policy actions documented in various sources, including national laws and regulations as well as in IMF staff reports (for more details see Alesina and others, forthcoming). While the indices capture the stringency of regulations in each area, they need not imply that all such regulations are unwarranted; indeed, whether full deregulation is optimal depends on individual countries' circumstances and the availability of alternative policy tools to meet governments' policy objectives—as discussed in IMF (2012) regarding capital account liberalization, for example. These data on market regulations and reforms are complemented by a composite indicator of the quality of governance (political stability, government effectiveness, strength of rule of law, control of corruption) based on the Worldwide Governance Indicators (WGIs).[3] All indices are normalized to vary continuously between 0 and 1, with 0 indicating the most restrictive regulations in a given policy area and 1 indicating the most unrestricted. For the governance indicator, higher scores denote stronger governance frameworks.

These indicators have several limitations. First, the new IMF data capture de jure regulations. As such, they may not always fully capture de facto changes in intended outcomes—even though indicator scores in domestic finance, external finance, and trade correlate rather well with related outcomes, such as the share of credit in GDP, financial openness, and trade openness (see Online Annex 3.1). Second, indicator scores are comparable across time and countries within each individual policy area, but they are not comparable across different policy areas.[4] Therefore, while useful to study broad reform trends, the overall reform index, constructed as a simple average of the five IMF indicators, should be interpreted with caution. Third, the WGIs

[3]The analysis in the chapter uses a composite governance indicator rather than all its individual components because the latter are highly correlated. Empirical analysis based on each indicator considered in isolation yields qualitatively similar findings.

[4]For instance, if a country has a higher score in the area of domestic finance than in product market regulation, it cannot be concluded that the country has a more liberalized financial than product market.

are perception indices summarizing the views of many businesses, citizens, and expert survey respondents on the quality of governance in a country; the quality of underlying data can vary across countries and data sources.[5] Therefore, individual country rankings based on these indicators should be avoided. Fourth, the scope of reforms studied in this chapter is limited to the six areas mentioned earlier, which relate mainly to the functioning of markets. There are, however, several other important reforms that could facilitate the accumulation of capital and labor, such as improving education and health care systems, strengthening public infrastructure spending frameworks, or changing laws and regulations that obstruct women's participation in the labor force. Finally, within each reform area, the scope of regulations covered by the corresponding indicator is also limited. For example, the indicator for product market regulations focuses on two important network industries—that is, electricity and telecommunications—but it does not cover other industries or broader administrative burdens on companies. Likewise, the domestic finance indicator captures regulations in the banking system, but does not cover nonbank financial institutions.

After the major liberalization waves in the late 1980s and—most important—the 1990s, the pace of structural reform slowed in emerging market and developing economies in the late 2000s, especially in low-income developing countries (Figure 3.3). This was the result of some stabilization of policy in (domestic and external) finance, trade, and product markets after the significant deregulation of the previous decades. Deregulation included phasing out of credit and interest rate controls in banking sectors; liberalization of foreign capital inflows and outflows; external tariff reductions, including from multilateral trade liberalization rounds; and reduced entry barriers as well as privatization in network industries (Figure 3.4). In turn, stabilization during the 2000s in part reflects a gradual narrowing of the scope for further reforms, but also waning reform efforts, notably in the sub-Saharan Africa and Middle East and North Africa regions. Labor market regulation differs from other areas: it has been far more stable for the average emerging market and developing economy, without any noticeable deregulation trend since the 1970s—and roughly in line with the experience in advanced economies (Chapter 3 of the April 2016 WEO). This may be because labor market regulations importantly aim to protect workers from the risk of income loss—even though this may be best pursued by shifting from stringent employment protection legislation, which is the dimension considered in this chapter, toward unemployment insurance (Duval and Loungani 2019). Finally, over the past two decades, there has been no noticeable improvement in governance in the average emerging market and developing economy.[6]

Figure 3.3. Overall Reform Trends
(Scale, 0–1; higher score indicates greater liberalization)

Regulatory convergence has stalled in the past decade, especially in low-income developing economies.

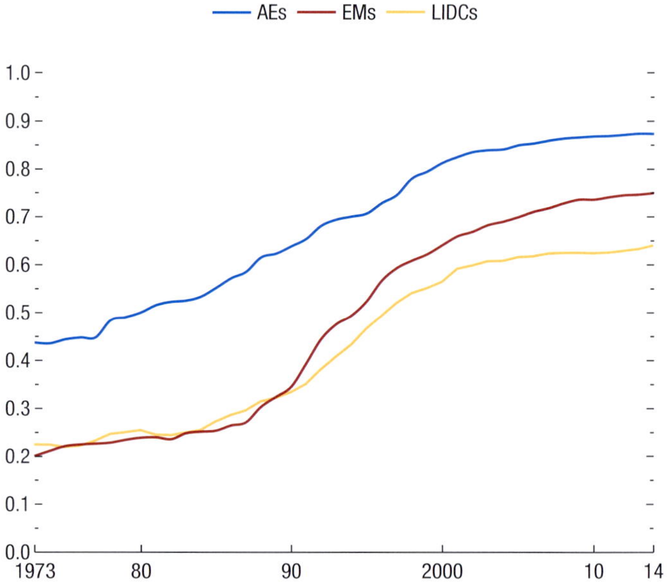

Sources: Alesina and others, forthcoming; and IMF staff calculations.
Note: The average reform index is computed as the arithmetic average of indicators capturing liberalizations in five areas: domestic finance, external finance, trade, product market, and labor market. It excludes the governance indicator due to its lower time coverage. The index ranges from 0 to 1, with higher values denoting greater liberalization. AEs = advanced economies; EMs = emerging markets; LIDCs = low-income developing countries.

[5]WGIs do not reflect the official views of the World Bank and are not used by the World Bank Group to allocate resources.

[6]Figure 3.4 does not report the evolution of the governance indicator because the WGIs are not comparable across different time periods, given that they are normalized to keep the world average constant over time. However, based on the underlying data sources, there seems to be little evidence of a systematic improvement in governance over time (https://info.worldbank.org/governance/wgi/#home).

Figure 3.4. Reform Trends, by Area
(Scale, 0–1; higher score indicates greater liberalization)

Reform trends have been heterogenous across areas, with deregulation mostly taking place in trade, finance, and product markets.

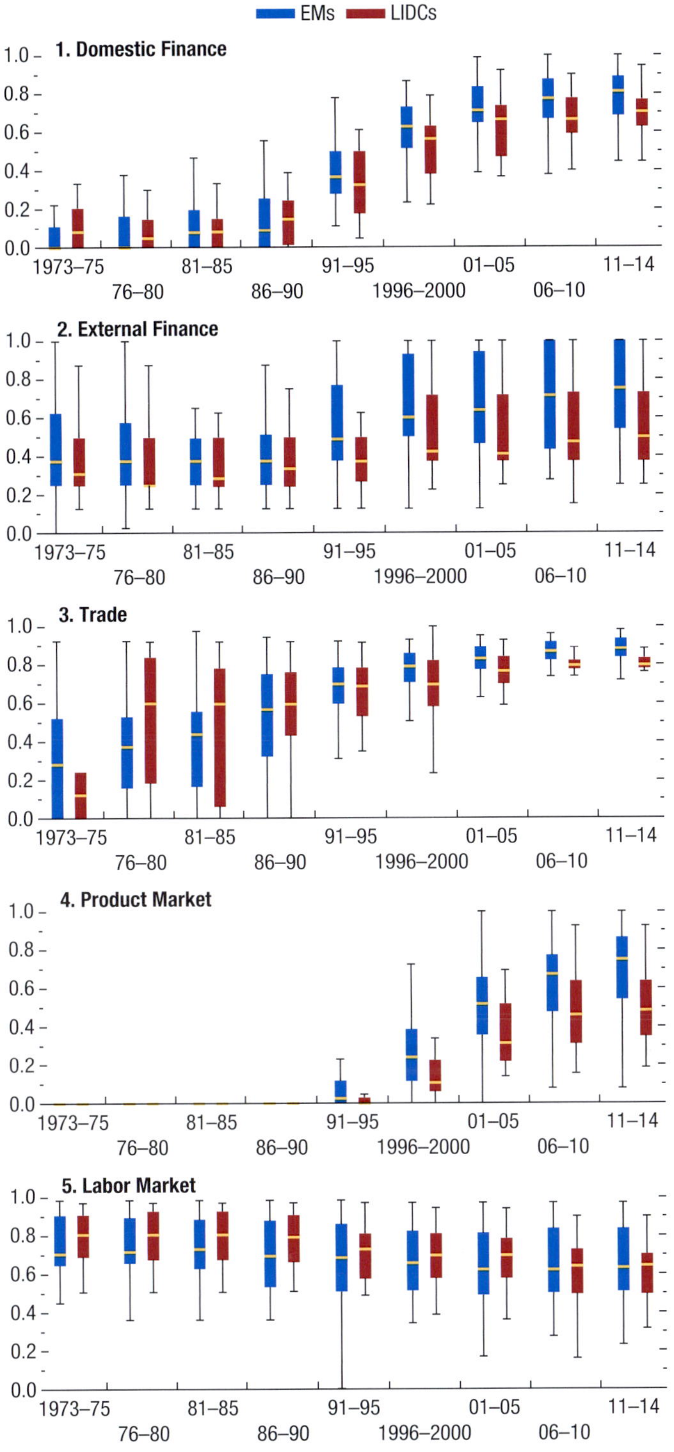

Sources: Alesina and others (forthcoming); and IMF staff calculations.
Note: The horizontal line inside each box represents the median; the upper and lower edges of each box show the top and bottom quartiles, respectively; and the top and bottom markers denote the maximum and the minimum, respectively. EMs = emerging markets; LIDCs = low-income developing countries.

Reforms have been generally more far-reaching in emerging markets than in low-income developing countries over the past few decades. Exceptions include international trade—widespread international trade liberalization has led to tariff convergence toward low levels around the world—and labor laws—there is no evidence of a trend toward labor market deregulation and, in fact, there has even been tightening in recent years. In product markets and in domestic and external finance, regulation was strict for both the average emerging market economy and low-income developing country until the 1990s but, since then, liberalization has sped up, particularly in emerging markets. These average patterns mask considerable heterogeneity, however. Among both emerging markets and low-income developing countries, some economies have undergone far-reaching liberalization while others have maintained stringent restrictions, most strikingly on international capital flows (external finance). For example, since the early 1990s, emerging market economies that have substantially improved their structural indicator scores include, among others, Estonia and Latvia (domestic finance); Peru and Romania (external finance); Chile and Colombia (product markets); China and Egypt (labor markets); and South Africa and Uruguay (international trade). Among low-income countries, examples of major reformers over the same period include Madagascar and Tanzania (domestic finance); Kenya and Uganda (external finance); Nicaragua and Senegal (product markets); Cameroon and Côte d'Ivoire (labor markets); and Bolivia and Ghana (international trade). A few emerging market economies have achieved significant improvements in governance (Albania and Georgia, for example), as have some low-income developing countries (Cameroon and Ethiopia, for example).

Broad differences in reform trends have also been observed across and within regions. Overall, reform efforts have been greater among emerging market and developing economies in Europe and in the Latin America and Caribbean region than across sub-Saharan Africa and, to a lesser extent, the Middle East and North Africa and Asia and Pacific regions (Figure 3.5). The European integration process after the collapse of the Soviet Union played a key role for Europe, while for Latin American emerging market and developing economies the crises of the 1980s and 1990s were contributing factors. Again, there have been wide differences across countries in these reform trends. Within

Figure 3.5. Overall Reform Trends across Different Geographical Regions
(Scale, 0–1; higher score indicates greater liberalization)

Reforms have been, on average, more far-reaching in Europe and the Latin America and the Caribbean region than they have been in the Middle East and North Africa, Asia-Pacific, and sub-Saharan Africa regions.

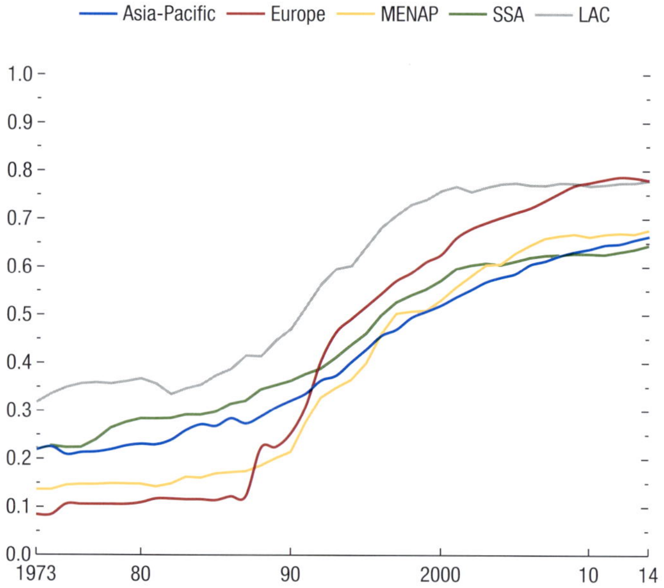

Sources: Alesina and others (forthcoming); and IMF staff calculations.
Note: Each region includes only EMDEs. The average reform index is computed as the arithmetic average of indicators capturing liberalizations in five areas: domestic finance, external finance, trade, product market, and labor market. It excludes the governance indicator due to its lower time coverage.
EMDEs = emerging market and developing economies; LAC = Latin America and the Caribbean; MENAP = Middle East, North Africa, Afghanistan, and Pakistan; SSA = sub-Saharan Africa.

Figure 3.6. Regulatory Indices, by Country Income Groups
(Scale, 0–1; higher score indicates greater liberalization)

There remains ample scope for further reforms in most areas across emerging market and low-income developing economies.

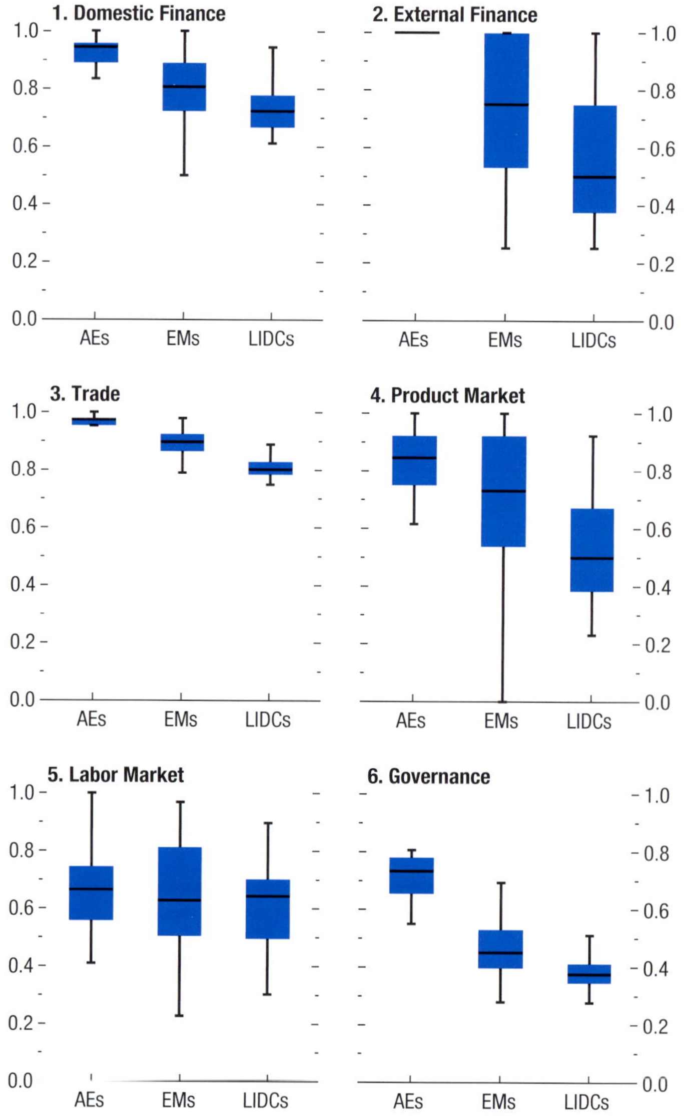

Sources: Alesina and others (forthcoming); and IMF staff calculations.
Note: Bars represent the 2014 value of each index (2013 for the governance index). The horizontal line inside each box represents the median; the upper and lower edges of each box show the top and bottom quartiles, respectively; and the top and bottom markers denote the maximum and the minimum, respectively.
AEs = advanced economies; EMs = emerging markets; LIDCs = low-income developing countries.

each broad geographic region, significant reformers across the five market regulation areas over the past decades have included, among others, China and the Philippines (Asia), Bulgaria and Hungary (Europe), Argentina and Peru (Latin America), Egypt and Jordan (Middle East and North Africa), and South Africa and Uganda (sub-Saharan Africa).

Past reforms have not exhausted the scope for deregulation, which remains sizable in most emerging market and developing economies, and particularly in low-income developing countries. Except for labor market regulation—an area in which many advanced economies also could benefit from employment protection legislation reform (Chapter 3 of the April 2016 WEO)—emerging market and developing economies retain significantly more restrictive market regulations than advanced economies; they also lag on governance (Figure 3.6). Regarding international trade, over and above cutting remaining tariffs, much room exists for reducing nontariff barriers to trade, which are not captured by the indicator considered here.[7] Overall, the Middle East and North Africa, Asia and the Pacific, and, to a greater extent, sub-Saharan Africa, on average, have the most room for reforms, although there are broad differences across countries within each region (Figure 3.7).

The Macroeconomic Effects of Reforms in Emerging Market and Developing Economies

This section quantifies the macroeconomic effects of reforms, focusing on average effects in the average emerging market and developing economy. Three complementary approaches are followed. The first is country time-series empirical analysis of the short- to medium-term response of key macroeconomic outcomes—primarily output, but also investment and employment—to reforms in each of the six areas considered in the chapter. Special care is taken to control for other drivers of output growth that may obscure the actual impact of reforms (omitted variable bias) and to address the impact that expected growth may have on decisions to undertake reform itself (reverse causality).[8] Second, to provide additional insight into

[7]Although they can differ in nature, nontariff barriers to trade tend to be pervasive in both advanced and emerging market economies and in low-income developing countries (see, for example, Ederington and Ruta 2016).

[8]The statistical method follows the approach proposed by Jordà (2005). The baseline specifications control for past economic growth and past reforms, as well as country and time-fixed effects. A possible concern regarding the analysis is that the probability of structural reform is influenced not only by past economic growth and the occurrence of recessions, but also by contemporaneous economic developments and expectations of future growth. However, this is unlikely to be a major issue, given long lags associated with the implementation of structural reforms and that information about future growth is likely to be largely embedded in past economic activity. Most important, controlling for expectations of current and future growth delivers very similar results to, and not different with statistical significance from, those reported in this chapter. Similar results for the medium-term effects are also obtained when controlling for current economic growth. Another possible concern regarding the analysis is that the results may suffer from omitted variable bias, as reforms may occur across different areas at the same time or because they are undertaken within the context of broader macroeconomic stabilization packages. However, including all the reforms simultaneously in the estimated equation, and controlling for macroeconomic policies aimed at reducing inflation and public debt, does not substantially alter the magnitude and statistical significance of the results. See the discussion later in the chapter and in Online Annex 3.2 for details.

Figure 3.7. Regulatory Indices, by Geographical Regions
(Scale, 0–1; higher score indicates greater liberalization)

The scope for further reforms is largest in the Middle East and North Africa and sub-Saharan Africa regions, although there is also wide cross-country heterogeneity within each geographical region.

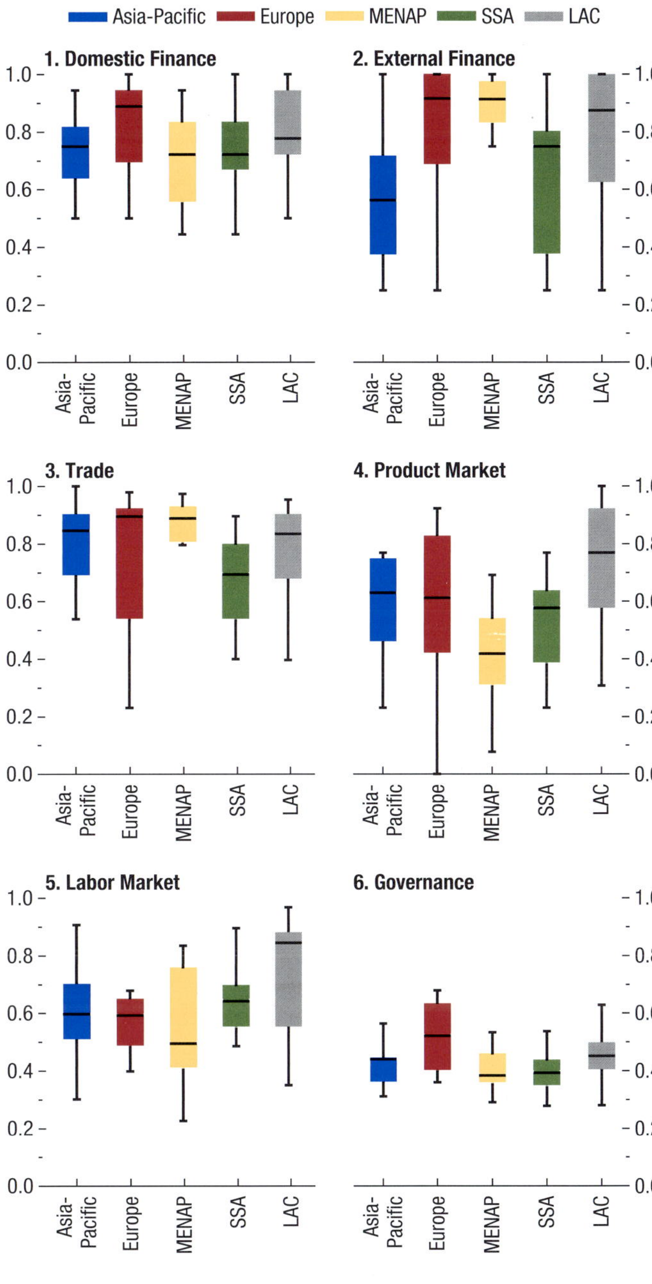

Sources: Alesina and others (forthcoming); and IMF staff calculations.
Note: Each region includes only EMDEs. Bars represent the 2014 value of each index (2013 for the governance index). The horizontal line inside each box represents the median; the upper and lower edges of each box show the top and bottom quartiles, respectively; and the top and bottom markers denote the maximum and the minimum, respectively. LAC = Latin America and the Caribbean; MENAP = Middle East, North Africa, Afghanistan, and Pakistan; SSA = sub-Saharan Africa.

the channels through which reforms affect economic activity, and to deal with some of the limitations of the country time-series approach, industry-level empirical analysis is carried out. This analysis exploits the fact that reforms benefit some industries more than others—for example, job protection reform that makes it easier for firms to hire and lay off workers is expected to offer more benefit for industries that typically need high job turnover. The third approach, adopted to analyze the effects of reforms and shed light on transmission channels—the role of informality, in particular—is to use a model that captures key regulations and other features of a "typical" emerging market and developing economy.

Figure 3.8. Average Effects of Reforms
(Percent; effect on output, unless noted otherwise)

Empirical estimates point to sizable average effects of reforms that materialize only gradually.

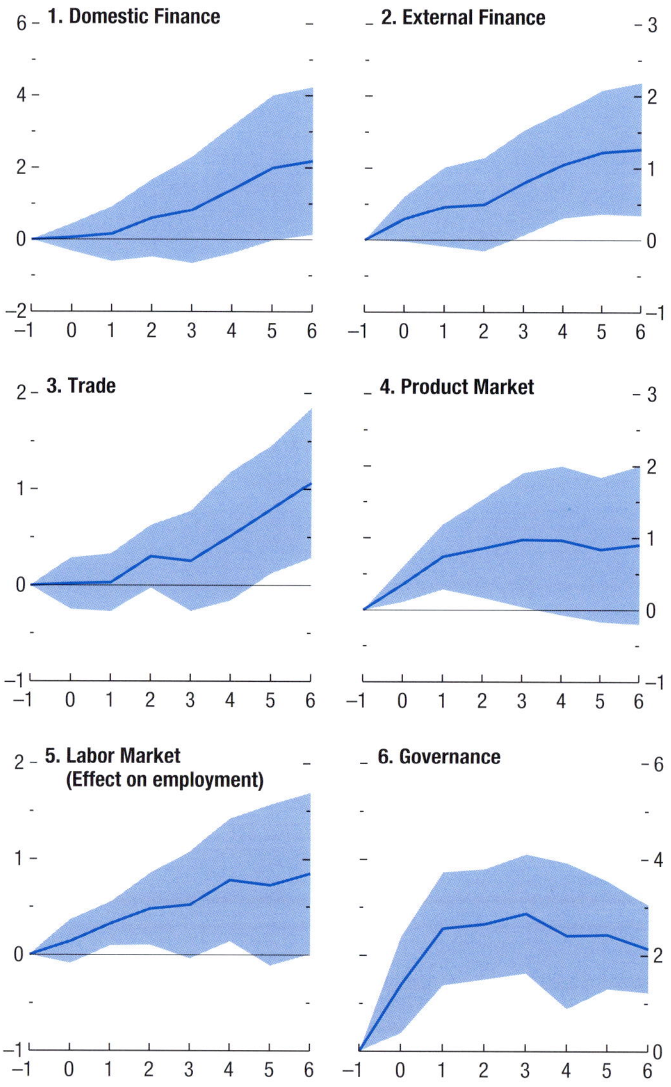

Source: IMF staff calculations.
Note: *x*-axes in years; $t = 0$ is the year of the shock. The lines denote the response to a major historical reform (two standard deviations). The shaded areas denote 90 percent confidence bands.

Country-Level Results

Major historical reforms have had sizable average positive effects on output over the medium term (Figure 3.8).[9] In normal times, the reforms studied in this chapter do not appear to entail short-term macroeconomic costs. However, with some exceptions, such as product market deregulation, which pays off rather quickly, it takes some time—typically at least three years—for reform gains to become economically and statistically significant. In addition, wide confidence bands around point estimates are indicative of significant cross-country differences in the effects of past reforms. Some important aspects of this heterogeneity are explored in the next section.

The quantitative effects vary across historical major reforms:[10]

- For *domestic finance* (Figure 3.8, panel 1), a major liberalization event—for example, a reform of the size that took place in Egypt in 1992—leads to a statistically significant increase in output of about 2 percent on average six years after reform implementation.[11] Estimates suggest that domestic finance liberalization also increases investment and employment, although to a smaller extent. The weak impact on investment is consistent with existing literature that fails to find an unambiguous positive relationship between domestic finance reforms and the quantity of savings and investment (for example, Bandiera and others 2000). In contrast, the main channel at play seems to be that of an improvement in the

[9]Major historical reforms correspond to those associated with a change in the relevant indicator above two standard deviations of the distribution (of annual changes in the relevant indicator across the whole sample).

[10]As stressed earlier, the magnitudes of historical reforms are not comparable across different policy areas.

[11]The reform in Egypt involved easing bank entry restrictions and improving banking supervision and regulation.

allocative efficiency of financial markets (see, for example, Abiad, Oomes, and Ueda 2008).[12]

- For *external finance* (Figure 3.8, panel 2), a major liberalization—of the type carried out by Romania in 2003, for example—is found to lead to a statistically significant increase in the output level of more than 1 percent six years after the reform.[13] Estimates also suggest that one of the channels underpinning this increase is higher investment. In contrast, external finance reforms do not have a large or statistically significant effect on employment (see, for example, Furceri, Loungani, and Ostry, forthcoming). This implies that the positive output impact of liberalization largely reflects increases in labor productivity.[14]
- For *international trade* (Figure 3.8, panel 3), a large tariff cut—for example, similar to that in Kenya in 1994—is estimated to increase output by an average of about 1 percent six years later. Labor productivity, which rises by about 1.4 percent after six years, is the key transmission channel, in line with extensive literature on the productivity gains from trade liberalization (for example, Ahn and others 2019 and references therein). These aggregate effects on real activity bolster the traditional view against protectionism (Furceri and others 2018).
- In *product markets* (Figure 3.8, panel 4), major deregulation—such as, for example, the adoption of the Law on Regulators of Public Utilities in Latvia in 2001—leads to a statistically significant increase in output of about 1 percent three years after the reform. This is a remarkable effect considering that the analysis is restricted to deregulation in only two key network industries, namely electricity and telecommunications. The gains from broader reforms across a wider range of protected industries would therefore be expected to be larger. Further estimates suggest that product market deregulation increases employment and investment as well as productivity, in the medium term.
- In *labor markets* (Figure 3.8, panel 5), a major easing of job protection legislation—along the lines of the labor code revisions in Kazakhstan in 2000, which facilitated dismissal procedures and lowered severance pay—is found to increase employment by almost 1 percent, on average, in the medium term. Also, investment is positively impacted, possibly reflecting higher (marginal) returns on capital as employment rises and profitability increases. However, the short- to medium-term output and productivity effects of job protection deregulation are not found to be statistically significant at conventional levels (Duval and Furceri 2018 has a similar finding for advanced economies).
- As regards *governance* (Figure 3.8, panel 6), an improvement of a magnitude similar to that achieved by Ghana when it adopted its anti-corruption laws in 2006, for example, increases output by about 2 percent after six years.[15] The main transmission channel is investment (IMF 2018), although the reform also has a (smaller) positive and statistically significant effect on employment and labor productivity.

Summarizing, the results of the empirical analysis suggest that a very ambitious and comprehensive reform agenda involving simultaneous major reforms across all six areas considered—that is, summing up the effects of each individual reform, and abstracting from possible complementarities between them, which are explored in the next section—might raise output in the average emerging market and developing economy by more than 7 percent over a six-year period.[16] This would raise annual GDP growth more than 1 percentage point and double the current speed of income-per-capita convergence to advanced economy levels from about 1 percent to more than 2 percent. An even larger increase in annual GDP growth, exceeding 1.25 and 2 percentage points in the average emerging market economy and low-income developing country, respectively, would be possible under an even more ambitious scenario in

[12]Furthermore, the increase in output is larger than the increase in employment, which implies an increase in labor productivity. At a six-year horizon, the productivity increase amounts to 1.4 percent and the effect is statistically significant.

[13]The reform in Romania included the liberalization of capital movements related to the performance of insurance contracts and other capital flows with significant influence on the real economy, such as lifting restrictions concerning the access of nonresidents to bank deposits.

[14]This is in line with recent cross-country studies finding that financial openness affects growth primarily through higher productivity (Bonfiglioli 2008; Bekaert and others 2011).

[15]The index is computed as the arithmetic average of six WGIs (see Online Annex 3.1 for details).

[16]Summing up the effects of each individual reform implicitly assumes that reforms do not entail major complementarity—which would imply a larger gain from a package than from the sum of each individual reform undertaken in isolation—or substitutability. As discussed in detail in the next section, while not all reforms are complementary, some of them are. As a result, the potential gain from a comprehensive reform package may be even larger than reported here.

which all emerging market and developing economies align their policies in each area with those of the currently most liberalized emerging market economies.

Sector-Level Results

As a robustness check for the economy-wide results, and to shed further light on transmission channels, country-industry-level analysis explores how reforms affect within-country differences in the response of output between industries.[17] For domestic and external finance, the empirical approach follows the methodology proposed by Rajan and Zingales (1998), which assesses the long-term effect of financial depth on industry growth according to differences in external finance dependence across industries.[18] For labor market reforms, the approach follows Duval, Furceri, and Jalles (2019), which examines the effect of job protection deregulation on industry-level employment in advanced economies depending on differences in "natural" layoff rates across industries—that is, the natural propensity of firms in a given industry to adjust their workforce to idiosyncratic shocks.[19]

The industry-level analysis confirms the findings of the aggregate country-level analysis for domestic and external finance reforms. The difference in medium-term output effects of major domestic finance liberalization between industries with high and low dependence on external finance (at the 75th and 25th percentiles of the cross-industry distribution of external financial dependence) is estimated to be about 6 percentage points (Figure 3.9, panel 1). Comparable results are obtained for external finance reforms (Figure 3.9, panel 2)—even though the magnitude and the precision of the point estimates decline in the medium term. For labor market reforms, the analysis does not find a statistically significant difference, on average, in the impact of deregulation between industries with high turnover and low turnover. However, as discussed in the next section, this insignificant effect masks considerable heterogeneity depending on whether the reform was undertaken in good or bad times.

Figure 3.9. Industry-Level Effect of Domestic and External Finance Reforms on Output
(Percent)

Financial reforms have stronger effects in industries with greater dependence on external sources of financing.

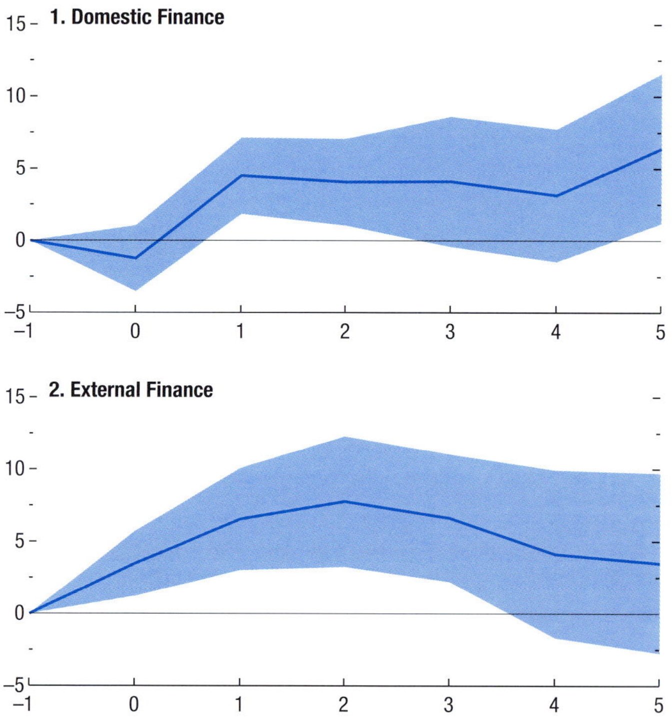

Source: IMF staff calculations.
Note: *x*-axes in years; $t = 0$ is the year of the shock. The shock represents a major historical reform (two standard deviations); the lines denote the differential impact in percent between the sector at the 75th percentile of the degree of dependence on external finance versus the sector at the 25th percentile; the shaded areas denote 90 percent confidence bands. External finance dependence in each industry is measured as the median across all US firms, in each industry, of the ratio of total capital expenditures minus the current cash flow to total capital expenditure.

[17]The analysis focuses on the manufacturing sector and explores the differential effects of reforms across different industries using an unbalanced panel of 19 manufacturing industries at the 2-digit level in 66 emerging market and developing economies from 1973 to 2014. Like the country-level analysis, the industry-level analysis also relies on the local projection method, but reforms are identified at the industry level by interacting the (country-level) reform variable with relevant industry-specific characteristics that capture each industry's exposure to reform. The main advantage of this approach is that it is less prone to endogeneity concerns and thereby to enhance the causal interpretation of the chapter's findings (see Online Annex 3.2 for technical details).

[18]Following Rajan and Zingales (1998), the degree of dependence on external finance in each industry is measured as the median across all US firms, in each industry, of the ratio of total capital expenditures minus current cash flows to total capital expenditures.

[19]The measure of "natural" industry-specific layoff rates is the ratio of the number of workers dismissed for business reasons to total employment in the United States, following the methodology proposed by Micco and Pagés (2006) and Bassanini, Nunziata, and Venn (2009). Data on laid-off workers and employed individuals come from the US Current Population Survey covering 2003–07. Because of the quasi absence of employment protection legislation, the United States provides the closest empirical example of a frictionless labor market and, as a result, its industries can be seen as exhibiting "natural" layoff rates.

Model-Based Results

The empirical estimates are complemented by use of a structural general equilibrium model that brings three key benefits for assessments of reform impacts.[20] First, it allows for quantification of reform gains over a longer horizon than considered in the empirical analysis—the medium to long term, once the effects of reforms on the economy fully play out. Second, while the effects of historical reforms may have varied, depending on the quality of their implementation and other prevailing circumstances that might not be fully controlled for in the empirical setup, model-based analysis is, by design, free of such limitations. Third, it sheds light on the transmission channels of reforms. This is because the model captures several key features of many emerging market and developing economies—their large informal sectors (La Porta and Shleifer 2008, 2014), financial constraints on firm growth (Midrigan and Xu 2014), large sunk costs of registering in the formal sector (Djankov and others 2002), employment protection laws that raise formal sector labor costs (Alesina and others, forthcoming), and weak governance that acts as a tax on the output of formal sector firms (Mauro 1995; IMF 2018).[21] Another important model feature is that the formal sector is both more capital intensive and more productive than the informal sector, and only firms in the formal sector have access to external finance (La Porta and Shleifer 2008, 2014).

The model-based analysis points to three key channels through which reforms can increase output: they facilitate entry from the informal sector to the formal sector, incentivize formal firms to invest and grow, and can reduce misallocation of resources between formal firms.[22] In particular, product market and financial market reforms make it easier for informal firms to enter the formal sector—the former by reducing entry costs and the latter by enabling firms to finance such costs. Formalization, in turn, leads to capital deepening, higher aggregate productivity, and increased output.[23] Improving governance or easing job protection legislation increases the profitability of formal sector firms directly; this encourages them to grow, increasing investment and reallocating resources from the less productive informal sector. Domestic finance reforms have qualitatively similar effects, given that they relax credit constraints on formal sector firms and so enable them to grow rapidly to their optimal size.[24]

The reforms are found to yield larger—twice as large, on average—output gains in the long term than those estimated in the empirical analysis for the medium term (Figure 3.10).[25] Two key factors help explain the higher long-term gains predicted by the model. First, firm formalization and capital accumulation typically take place over a longer horizon than is considered in the empirical analysis. Second, the model represents an ideal reform scenario, while average empirical estimates also reflect cases of imperfect reform implementation. These effects are those for an average emerging market and developing economy, given that the model is calibrated to match a large set of average microeconomic and macroeconomic characteristics across a large sample of emerging market and developing economies.

[20]The model is an extension of Midrigan and Xu (2014). Online Annex 3.3 provides a technical description of the model.

[21]It is important to note that data limitations mean that the costs of governance are simply modeled as a fraction of formal sector output that is lost (potentially due to corruption and weak rule of law). The model therefore abstracts from many other channels through which governance can affect GDP, including through informal firms (see Online Annex 3.3 for further discussion).

[22]The model is calibrated to account for the distortions created by regulations studied in the empirical analysis, such as productivity differentials between sectors and financial market distortions, based on the observed values of key variables such as the private sector debt-to-GDP ratio and the share of employment in the informal sector, across a large set of emerging market and developing economies between 2013 and 2018. The size of reforms considered in the analysis is designed to be as comparable as possible to the size of reforms presented in the empirical analysis. The results are qualitatively robust to, and quantitatively stable across, alternative calibrations (see Online Annex 3.3 for further details).

[23]The productivity gain from doing business in the formal sector is consistent with the large gap in value added per worker between informal and formal firms reported in La Porta and Shleifer (2008, 2014). Drivers of this gap may include, among others, better access to intermediate inputs (Amiti and Konings 2007), access to export markets (De Loecker 2007), and higher-skilled workers (Ulyssea 2018). Aggregate capital deepening follows from the formal sector's greater access to credit markets and capital intensity. Martin, Nataraj, and Harrison (2017) finds that product market deregulation in India between 2000 and 2007 led to increases in district-level capital, as well as in output and employment.

[24]By contrast, resource misallocation across formal firms does not constitute an important source of output gains from these reforms in the model, compared with the gains from formalization and increased investment. This is partly because restricted access to credit is the only regulation that affects different formal firms differently—and therefore the only one that generates misallocation—in this version of the model (see Online Annex 3.3 for details).

[25]Reforms simulated with the model are designed to be comparable in magnitude to those considered in the empirical section (see Online Annex 3.3 for details). These are large reforms in practice; for example, the size of the domestic finance reform considered in Figure 3.10 would enable Mexican firms to increase their leverage, raising the corporate sector debt-to-GDP ratio to the level observed in Poland.

Figure 3.10. Output Gains from Major Historical Reforms: Model-Based versus Empirical Estimates
(Percent of GDP)

Model-based analysis generally predicts larger output gains in the long term than those found in the empirical analysis for the medium term.

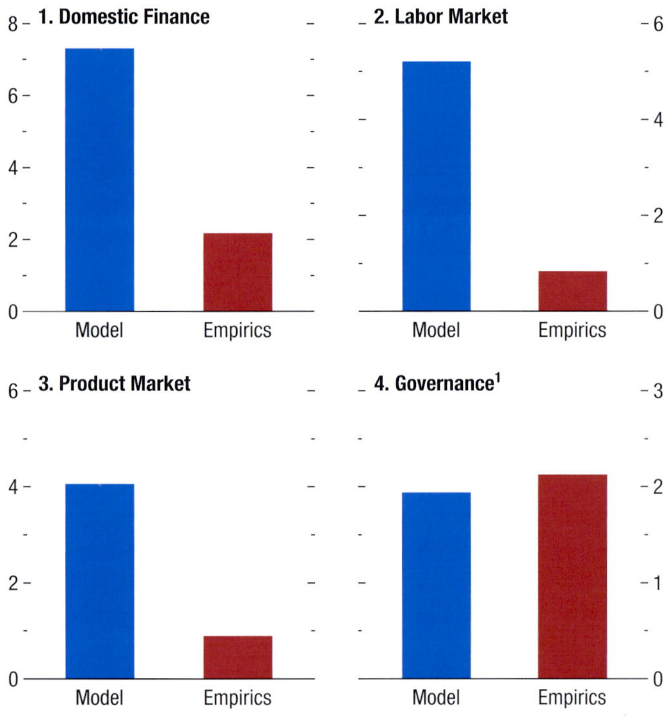

Source: IMF staff calculations.
Note: Bars represent the percent increase in aggregate output from a reduction in the corresponding friction at the benchmark calibration. The size of the reforms is designed to be in line with a major reform in the reform indices ($\Delta Reform$: $\Delta Targeted\ Moment = (2\sigma_{\Delta Reform\ Index}/\sigma_{Reform\ Index}) \cdot \sigma_{Targeted\ Moment}$). For example, in the case of domestic finance reform, the parameter representing the financial friction is changed such that the credit-to-GDP ratio shifts across the distribution (of the credit-to-GDP ratios across countries) the same way the domestic finance regulation indicator does across the distribution (of this indicator across countries) after a major reform in the empirical analysis.
[1]"Governance" is modeled as a reduction in an implicit tax on formal firms' revenue. While conventional, this modeling choice ignores other potential gains from strengthening governance, such as lower costs of doing business in the informal sector, lower operational uncertainty, and reduced misallocation across firms in the formal sector—to the extent that these might suffer to different degrees from poor governance.

Accounting for Differences across Countries

While past reforms have delivered sizable average gains, wide confidence intervals around these estimated impacts point to substantial differences across countries. So do the mixed experiences of past reformers, even within given regions. For example, reforms in Latin American economies during the 1980s and 1990s were followed by growth spurts in some cases (such as Chile), but not in others (such as Argentina or Mexico). Likewise, while most reforming countries in central and eastern Europe converged fast to advanced economies' living standards after the collapse of the Soviet Union in the early 1990s, most reforming economies of the Commonwealth of Independent States did not.

This section investigates some of the drivers of that heterogeneity by asking the following question: Which country characteristics tend to be associated with larger gains from reforms? In doing so, it highlights the influence of business conditions at the time of reform and—focusing more on longer-term effects—the importance of informality and interactions across reform areas.[26]

Role of Business Conditions

Prevailing business conditions may affect an economy's short- to medium-term response to reforms in certain areas. For example, liberalizing credit supply may not elicit much credit and output growth when demand for credit is weak, as would be the case in a depressed economy. Likewise, easing job protection legislation in a recession may not induce firms to recruit but, instead, incentivize them to lay off workers, so further reducing aggregate employment and output in the short term (Cacciatore and others 2016). The role of business conditions is explored empirically using state-dependent regressions in which the state of the economy at the time of reform is captured by a smooth-transition function of the GDP growth rate (Auerbach and Gorodnichenko 2012) or, alternatively, by a dummy variable for crisis.[27]

Although the effects of most reforms do not appear to differ significantly, whether passed in good or bad times, domestic finance liberalization appears to pay off far more when implemented in an expansionary

[26]Another open question is whether reform priorities should differ according to the level of development, including between emerging market economies and low-income developing countries. While there is generally a strong case for tailoring reform priorities along these lines, no evidence could be found that the effects of reforms considered in this chapter vary systematically depending on the level of income per capita or across country income groups. Likewise, a comprehensive analysis of interactions across reforms, performed by conditioning the impact of reform in one area on the regulatory stance in other areas, did not provide systematic evidence of complementarity (or substitutability) between reforms. One exception is the importance of strong governance for other reforms' payoffs, which is discussed below.
[27]For technical details, see Online Annex 3.2.

phase of the business cycle (Figure 3.11, panels 1 and 2). Under very strong business conditions, the estimated impact of reform on output is found to be three times larger than it would be in normal times, consistent with a stronger response of credit demand to credit supply deregulation during an economic boom. By contrast, point estimates suggest that financial liberalization can be contractionary if passed when economic conditions are weak, although this negative effect is not statistically distinguishable from zero. One interpretation of this result is that increasing competition in the financial sector at a time of weak credit demand may push certain financial intermediaries out of business, further weakening the economy.

Likewise, job protection deregulation appears to deliver short-term gains in good times, but not in bad times (Figure 3.11, panels 3 and 4). This is in line with previous IMF evidence for advanced economies (Duval and Furceri 2018; Duval, Furceri, and Jalles 2019) and reflects the fact that when it is easier to hire and fire workers, firms tend to increase primarily hires when they face strong demand for their goods and services—while they tend to increase primarily layoffs when facing weak demand. Job protection deregulation, when implemented during strong economic conditions, is estimated to raise employment three times as much as when enacted in normal times. If undertaken during a financial crisis, it may even be contractionary, although the estimated negative effect is not statistically distinguishable from zero. Industry-level results are consistent with these country-level estimates (Figure 3.11, panels 5 and 6). When the labor market is liberalized in good times, employment rises significantly in industries with high natural layoff rates—that is, those where stringent job protection legislation is likely to be more binding—relative to those with low layoff rates. The reverse holds when the reform is implemented during bad times: employment in industries with high layoff rates falls more than in industries with low layoff rates. These results suggest that accompanying macroeconomic policies that boost aggregate demand could magnify the effects of certain structural reforms.[28]

[28]For example, further analysis not reported here suggests that labor market reforms are more effective at raising output when implemented together with expansionary fiscal policy. This is in line with previous IMF analysis for advanced economies (Chapter 3 of the April 2016 WEO; Duval, Furceri, and Jalles 2019).

Figure 3.11. Effects of Reforms: The Role of Macroeconomic Conditions
(Percent)

Some reforms do not pay off when undertaken in bad times.

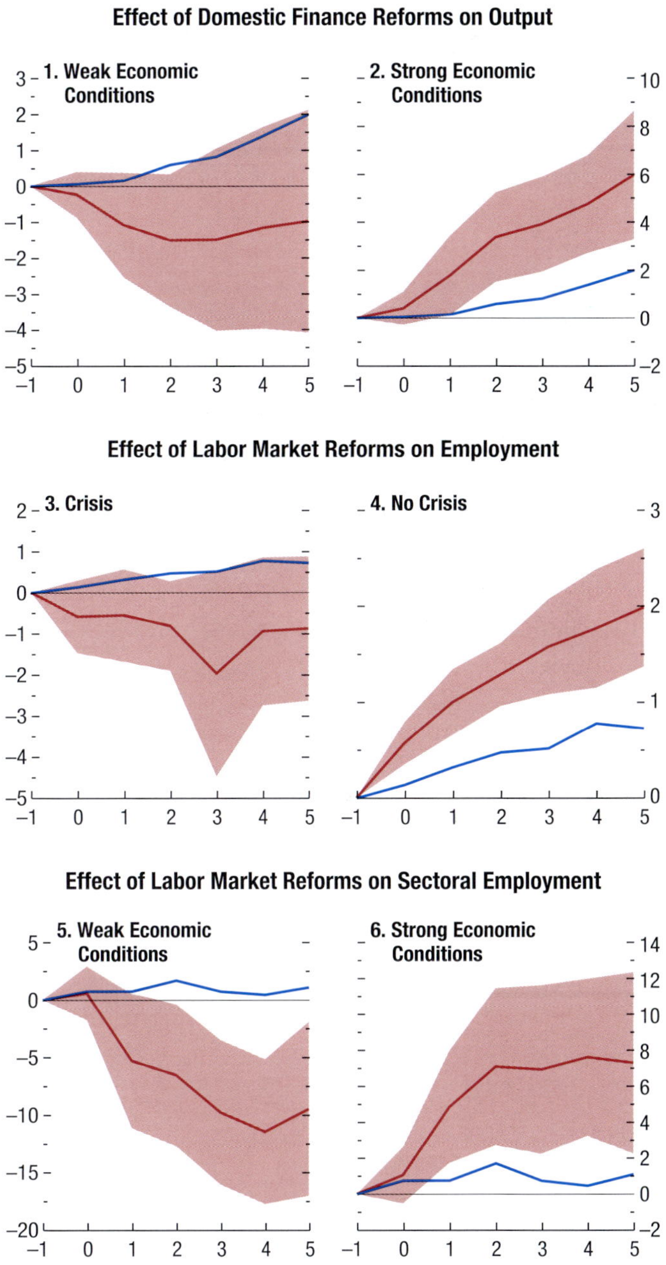

Source: IMF staff calculations.
Note: *x*-axes in years; $t = 0$ is the year of the shock. Red lines denote the percent response to a major historical reform (two standard deviations). Shaded areas denote 90 percent confidence bands. Blue lines represent the unconditional result.

Role of Informality

The role of individual country characteristics for the impact of reform is investigated using both empirical and model-based analyses. On the empirical side, the chapter uses a flexible approach to explore sources of parameter heterogeneity across units (countries): the Bayesian hierarchical empirical model along the lines of Boz, Gopinath, and Plagborg-Møller (2017). This method makes it possible to estimate flexibly the country-specific impact of each reform conditional on observed individual country characteristics such as the weight of the informal sector in the economy (see Online Annex 3.2 for technical details).[29] On the model side, the impact of a given reform is simulated under alternative sets of regulations and characteristics, such as under low versus high barriers to entry in the formal sector—that is, under high versus low informality.[30]

Among the many possible country characteristics that could shape the impact of reforms, informality appears particularly important. Empirical findings suggest that, in most areas (domestic finance, product and labor market regulations, governance), reforms have larger effects when informality is high (Figure 3.12, panels 1–4). At a five-year horizon, the gain from reform is typically twice as large in a country with a high degree of informality (at the 75th percentile of the cross-country distribution of informality rates) as in a country with low informality (at the 25th percentile of the distribution). Model-based analysis also points to larger reform gains in an economy with a higher initial level of informality (such as India) than in one with lower informality (such as South Africa or Panama), as shown in Figure 3.13.

Reforms tend to pay off more when informality is higher because one of the effects of reforms is precisely to reduce informality, which in turn benefits the economy. This channel is generally more powerful when informality is high to start with. For example, cutting barriers to entry in the formal sector, or explicit (labor) and implicit (corruption) taxes on formal firms, induces some informal firms to become formal. In turn, formalization boosts output by increasing productivity and capital accumulation; for example, becoming formal can help firms invest by enhancing their access to credit and improve their productivity by giving them access to better intermediate inputs or export markets. Empirical analysis confirms that this formalization channel is important. Applying the local projection method to study the impact on informality of a change in the average regulation indicator (across the areas studied in this chapter) suggests

Figure 3.12. Effects of Reforms on Output: The Role of Informality
(Percent)

Gains from past reforms have been larger in economies with higher informality.

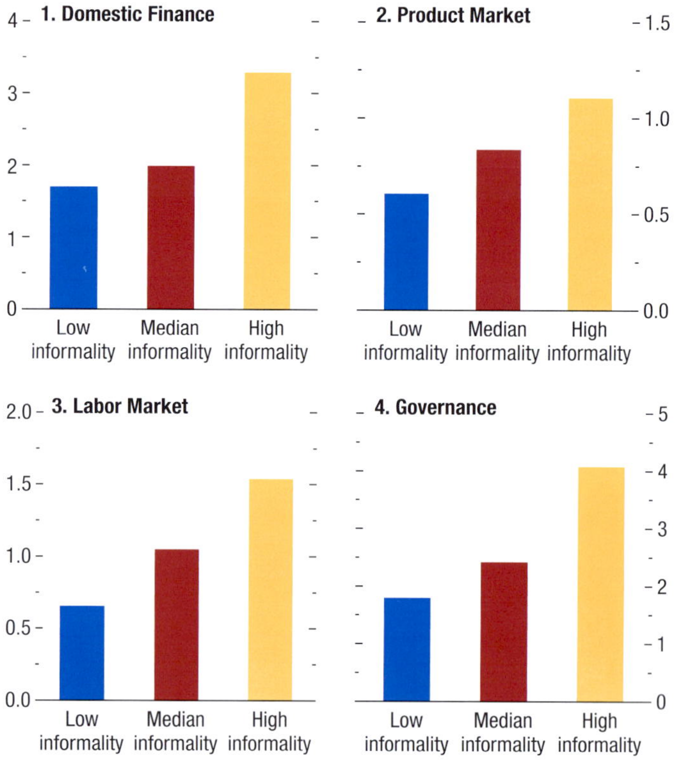

Source: IMF staff calculations.
Note: Bars denote the five-year-ahead output response to a major historical reform (two standard deviations). Low (high) informality refers to a level of informality equal to the 25th (75th) percentile of the distribution of the informality index.

[29]The main advantage of this approach over the more conventional use of multiplicative interactions is that it does not impose any functional form on the interaction between the country characteristic of interest (for example, the level of informality) and the reform coefficient, but instead uses a nonparametric specification for the distribution of the coefficient conditional on the country characteristic.

[30]In the model, the size of the informal sector is determined by all the structural features of the economy, including regulations. Here, the lower-informality economy is one in which entry costs into the formal sector are lower than in the baseline case—they are set equal to the 25th percentile of the cross-country distribution of entry costs. The higher-informality economy is the baseline economy.

Figure 3.13. Model-Implied Gains from Reforms: The Role of Informality
(Percent)

Model simulations imply that economies with larger informal sectors benefit somewhat more from reforms.

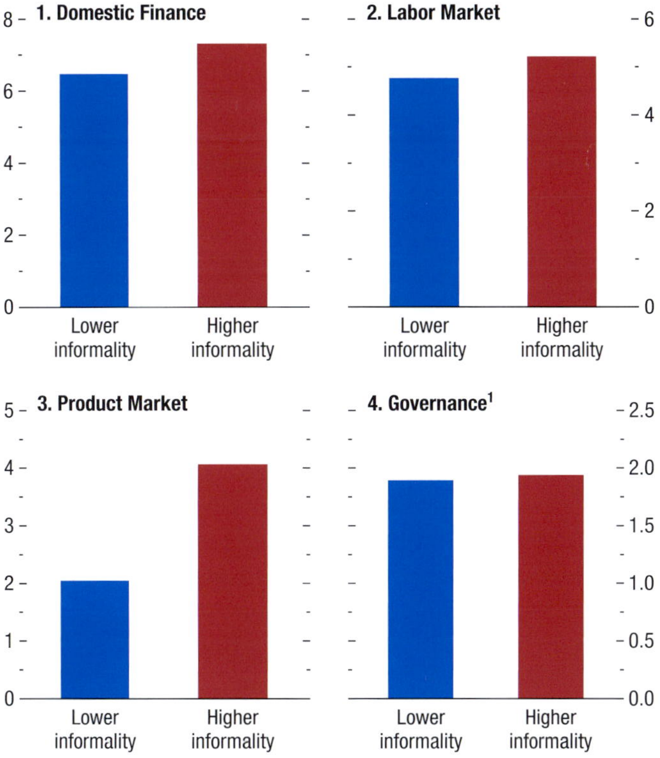

Source: IMF staff calculations.
Note: Bars represent the percent increase in aggregate output from a reduction in the corresponding friction at either the lower informality or higher informality benchmark calibration. The higher informality calibration is the benchmark calibration for the median economy. The lower informality calibration is constructed by reducing the entry regulation friction to its 25th percentile in the data. The size of the reforms is designed to be in line with a two-standard-deviation change in the reform indices.
[1]"Governance" is modeled as a reduction in an implicit tax on formal firms' revenue. While conventional, this modeling choice ignores other potential gains from strengthening governance, such as lower costs of doing business in the informal sector, lower operational uncertainty, and reduced misallocation across firms in the formal sector—to the extent that these might suffer to different degrees from poor governance.

Figure 3.14. Effect of Reforms on Informality
(Percent)

A major reform across the areas covered in the empirical analysis is associated with a subsequent reduction in informality.

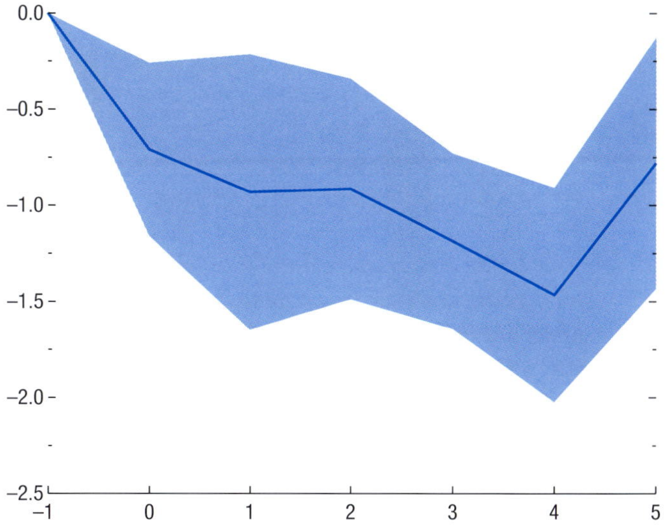

Source: IMF staff calculations.
Note: *x*-axis in years; $t = 0$ is the year of the shock. The lines denote the response of the informality indicator to an average reform of size two standard deviations. The shaded areas denote 90 percent confidence bands.

that a major broad-based reform is associated with a statistically significant decrease in informality of about 1 percentage point at a five-year horizon (Figure 3.14). This is consistent with evidence reported in microeconomic studies.[31]

Reform Complementarities

Reforms do not always entail complementarity (or substitutability), in the sense that a package combining multiple reforms does not necessarily yield a larger (or smaller) gain than the sum of the effects of each reform taken in isolation. This is confirmed by rather inconclusive empirical analysis (using the Bayesian procedure mentioned earlier) of whether countries reaped larger gains from a given reform when they had already deregulated other areas; in general, reforms are not found to have widely different effects across different countries with different regulations. Model analysis confirms that reforms need not always be complementary, and it also explains why. For example, as reforms

[31]See McCaig and Pavcnik (2018) for the effects of liberalizations in Vietnam; Martin, Nataraj, and Harrison (2017) for the same in India; and Paz (2014) for the same in Brazil. Benhassine and others (2018) provides experimental evidence on the impact of formalization reforms in Benin. Kaplan, Piedra, and Seira (2011) and Bruhn (2011) study the impact of deregulation on firms' market entry in Mexico. However, Mexico's experience highlights the variation in the response of informality across reform areas and its dependence on reform design. Despite major macroeconomic reforms during the 1990s, informality has since risen considerably (Levy 2018), coinciding with slow productivity growth. Levy (2008) argues that this increase in informality resulted from the introduction of new policies (such as changes in the relative benefits provided by contributory and noncontributory social insurance programs, among others) in the early 2000s that disincentivized firms and workers to formalize.

Figure 3.15. Effects of Reforms on Output: The Role of Governance
(Percent)

Stronger governance magnifies the impact of reforms.

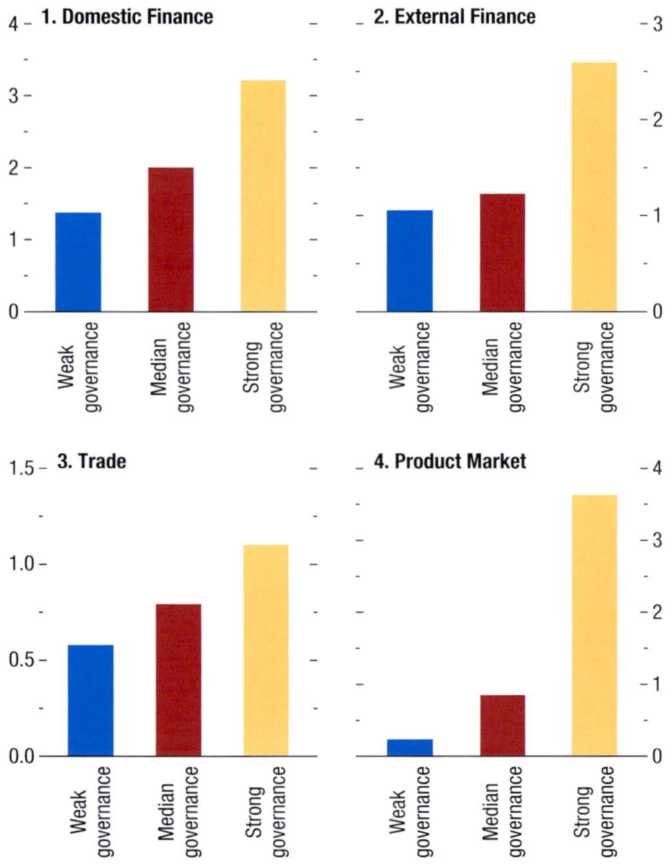

Sources: IMF reform data set; and IMF staff calculations.
Note: Bars denote the five-year-ahead output response to a major historical reform (two standard deviations). Weak (strong) governance refers to a level of governance equal to the 25th (75th) percentile of the distribution of the governance index.

are implemented, informality falls, reducing the scope for further declines in informality and thereby dampening potential gains from other reforms.

However, policymakers can exploit specific reform complementarities, notably by prioritizing improvements in governance. This may in part help explain the success in income convergence of some eastern European countries, such as Estonia, Latvia, and Romania, that joined the European Union and have carried out major reforms alongside improvements in governance since the 1990s. Bearing in mind the limitations of governance indicators mentioned above, the empirical analysis indicates that the impact of past reforms was most often larger in countries where the quality of governance was higher, while reforms yielded considerably smaller gains where governance was weaker (Figure 3.15, panel 4). The quality of governance matters particularly for the impact of product market deregulation; such reforms failed to pay off where governance was poor, but delivered larger gains where governance was strong. This is consistent with the view that reduced entry barriers in product markets foster new firm entry and push incumbent firms to be more efficient and innovative only if all firms are treated equally, which is easier to achieve when the rule of law is strong and property rights are strictly enforced. By the same token, strong governance can magnify the gains from other pro-competition reforms in finance or international trade.

Complementarities also exist between reforms that incentivize firms to grow and reforms that enable them to do so. Key among the growth-enabling reforms is domestic finance liberalization, which, by improving access to credit, can magnify the gains from reforms in other areas. As an illustration, model-based analysis highlights the complementarity between reforms that liberalize labor markets and financial markets simultaneously—as, for example, Bolivia did in 1985.[32] Labor market reform improves the profitability of the formal sector, inducing formal firms to expand and informal ones to formalize. Given that entrepreneurs need to finance their entry into the formal sector and their capital investment, improving access to credit through liberalization of domestic finance—alongside strengthened financial sector supervision[33]—amplifies the investment and output effects of labor market reform (Figure 3.16).[34]

Summary and Policy Implications

Key findings of this chapter make a strong case for a renewed structural reform push in emerging market and developing economies for two main reasons. First, even after the major liberalization wave of the 1990s, much scope generally remains for further reforms in

[32]In 1985 Bolivia removed directed credit by the government and liberalized interest rate controls. In addition, Supreme Decrees 7072, 9190, and 17610 were repealed, reestablishing the right of employers to dismiss workers according to previously existing provisions.

[33]While not captured by the model used here, sound supervision is key to alleviating risks of a buildup in financial sector vulnerabilities following domestic finance liberalization (Johnston and Sundararajan 1999).

[34]See Online Annex 3.3 for further technical details.

Figure 3.16. Gain from Packaging Domestic Finance and Labor Market Reforms
(Additional percent gain from packaging reforms)

Packaging labor market reform with domestic finance deregulation entails complementarities and amplifies aggregate output gains.

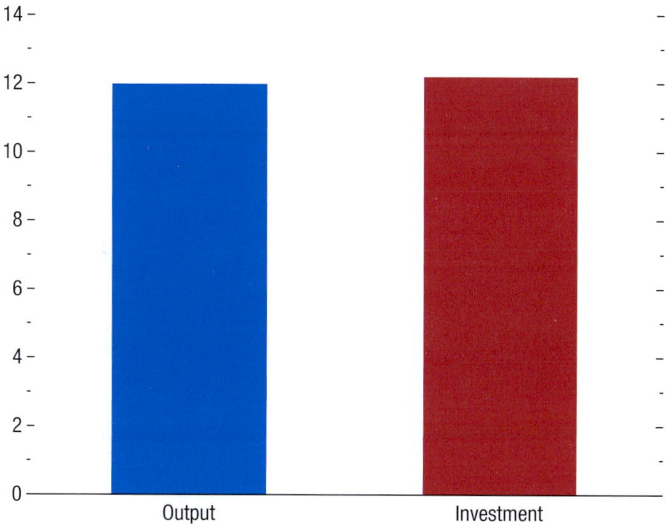

Source: IMF staff calculations.
Note: Bars represent the difference between the impact from a package combining both reforms and the sum of the impacts from each reform in isolation, in percent.

the areas covered in this chapter: domestic and external finance, international trade, labor and product market regulations, and governance. This holds true particularly for low-income developing countries—notably across sub-Saharan Africa and, to a lesser extent, in the Middle East and North Africa and Asia and Pacific regions. Second, the reforms studied in this chapter are not found to entail short-term macroeconomic costs—except for some of them when implemented in bad times—and they can yield sizable output and employment gains in the medium to long term: for a typical emerging market and developing economy, major simultaneous reforms across the areas listed above could raise annual economic growth by about 1 percentage point over five to 10 years, doubling the current speed of income-per-capita convergence to advanced economy levels over the next decade. In countries where informality is comparatively high, reform gains could be even larger, all else equal. In addition, these estimates do not factor in further potential gains from other growth-oriented policies not covered in this chapter, such as improving education and health care systems, public infrastructure spending frameworks, and laws and regulations that impede women's labor force participation.

At the same time, reform in one area has different effects across economies, depending on their existing regulations in other areas and prevailing business conditions at the time of reform. This suggests that getting reform packaging, sequencing, and prioritizing right is key to maximizing payoffs. Concrete actions to improve governance and facilitate access to credit by firms are often an important step to remove binding constraints on growth and amplify reform gains. In countries where economic conditions are weak, priority should also be given to reforms—such as cutting barriers to international trade or firm entry in domestic nonmanufacturing industries—whose gains do not depend on prevailing economic conditions. Reforms, such as easing job protection legislation and deregulating the domestic financial sector, that do not pay off in bad times, would be best enacted with a credible provision that they will take effect later, when economic conditions are stronger. If it is not possible to delay when they take effect (for labor market reforms), reforms can be grandfathered—that is, new rules would apply only to new beneficiaries—although this comes at the cost of delaying the full gains from reform. In addition, job protection deregulation should be accompanied by some strengthening of social safety nets (Duval and Loungani 2019). In countries with credible medium-term fiscal frameworks and available fiscal space, countercyclical fiscal policy could also alleviate short-term costs of reforms.

Reform strategies should also internalize political economy considerations. Even if reforms deliver a net gain for society as a whole, they often produce hard-to-perceive gains that are spread broadly across the population, while losses are more visible and concentrated on small but sometimes powerful population groups (Olson 1971). Experience with past reforms highlights the need for careful design and prioritization, ownership, good communication, and transparency to ensure broad-based support.

There are also three more specific lessons from the past. First, given that reforms take time to deliver, government should act swiftly following an electoral victory to implement them during their political "honeymoon" period. This strategy will mitigate potential political costs (Box 3.1). Second, reforms are best implemented when economic conditions are favorable—that is, governments should "fix the roof while the sun is shining." In bad times, because voters are often unable to disentangle the effect of reform from that of poor economic conditions, reforms tend to be electorally costly. During recessions, macroeconomic policy support—where feasible—may reduce the political costs of reform. Third, policymakers should factor in, and implement up-front, complementary reforms to mitigate any adverse effects of reforms on income distribution. Strong social safety nets and active labor market programs that help workers move across jobs can help in this regard, given that reforms often lead simultaneously to new job creation and destruction. Reforms whose gains are captured only by a small fraction of society risk losing support and could stall, or be undone, down the road.

Box 3.1. The Political Effects of Structural Reforms

While the evidence presented in this chapter speaks strongly in favor of the economic benefits of structural reforms, their political benefits are much less clear, which has long been perceived as an obstacle to reform. One problem is that even if reforms deliver a net gain for society as whole, they often produce hard-to-perceive gains spread broadly across the population, and more visible losses that are concentrated on small but sometimes powerful population groups (Olson 1971). For example, cutting barriers to entry in a network industry—such as electricity or telecommunications, both of which are considered in this chapter—typically yields diffuse gains to consumers in the form of lower prices or better products, while incumbent firms and workers may lose much from the entry of new competitors and reduced profits. In these circumstances, politicians may hold back on reforms for fear they will be penalized at the ballot box by vocal losers from reform.

This box examines empirically whether fears of a political cost of reform are supported by historical experience. Specifically, it asks whether structural reforms lead to electoral losses or gains, and whether the timing of reform in the electoral cycle and the state of the economy matter for subsequent electoral outcomes.

To examine these issues, the analysis maps a new data set on electoral outcomes with the new reform data set presented in the chapter and estimates the effect of reforms on the change in the vote share of the incumbent party or coalition in the following election.[1] This dependent variable is especially useful in assessing the magnitude of electoral penalties or gains from reforms. A leader of the executive might remain in office, but with a much-reduced majority, or might be forced into a coalition government.

The key independent variable used in the analysis is the unweighted average of all the reform indices.[2]

The results of the analysis suggest that reforms entail electoral costs only when implemented in the year before an election; in this case, a major broad-based reform (defined in the rest of the chapter as a major change across all regulatory areas simultaneously) is associated with a decrease in the vote share of the coalition of about 3 percentage points. This effect is economically significant and is roughly equivalent to a 17 percentage point reduction in the likelihood of the incumbent leader of the coalition being reelected (Figure 3.1.1). In contrast, reforms earlier in an incumbent's term do not appear to affect election prospects. These results are suggestive of myopic behavior of the electorate and are also consistent with empirical evidence in this chapter that the economic gains from reforms take time to materialize.

These average results mask considerable differences across reformers, depending on whether measures were implemented in good or bad times (Figure 3.1.2). Reforms are not found to entail political costs when undertaken under strong economic conditions, but they tend to be politically costly when enacted in periods of weak economic activity, possibly because they lead to larger distributional costs (Alesina and others, forthcoming) and voters fail to disentangle the effects of reform from those of poor economic conditions. Because reforms have been predominantly undertaken under weak economic conditions (Box 3.2), their average impact on the vote share is also estimated to be negative (Figure 3.1.2).

These results hint at two ways reform strategies can helpfully internalize political-economy considerations and maximize chances of political success. First, because reforms take time to deliver, governments should act swiftly following an electoral victory to implement reforms during their political "honeymoon" period. Second, reforms are best implemented when economies are performing well.

This box was prepared by Davide Furceri and largely draws from Ciminelli and others (forthcoming) and Alesina and others (forthcoming).

[1]The electoral database in this study covers an unbalanced sample of democratic elections from 1973 (or the first year in which the country is characterized as a democratic regime) to 2014 for 66 advanced and developing economies.

[2]See Alesina and others (forthcoming) for additional details, including estimates for each individual reform indicator separately. The baseline specification includes the following set of control variables: (1) average GDP growth during the electoral term, (2) a developed country dummy (taking value 1 for continuous Organisation for Economic Co-operation and Development membership since 1963 and 0 otherwise), (3) a dummy variable for new democracies (taking value 1 for the first four elections after a year in which the country considered gets a negative Polity score on the −10 to 10 scale and 0 otherwise), (4) a dummy variable for a majoritarian political system (taking value 1 for countries with an electoral system that awards seats in winner-takes-all fashion in geographically based districts according to the Database of Political Institutions and 0 otherwise), (5) the initial average level of regulation across the areas considered, and (6) the level of the vote share in the previous election. See Online Annex 3.3 for further details on the empirical methodology.

Box 3.1 *(continued)*

Figure 3.1.1. The Effect of Reform on Electoral Outcomes
(Percentage points)

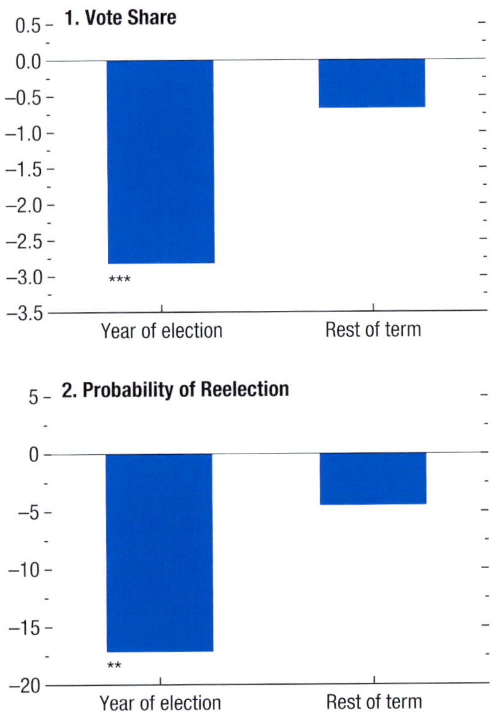

Source: IMF staff calculations.
Note: The bars denote the effect of a major reform event—defined as a change in the broad regulation indicator of two standard deviations (of the sample distribution of annual changes in the regulation indicator)—on electoral outcomes. ** and *** denote statistical significance at the 5 percent and 1 percent confidence levels, respectively.

Figure 3.1.2. The Effect of Reform on Vote Share: The Role of Economic Conditions
(Percentage points)

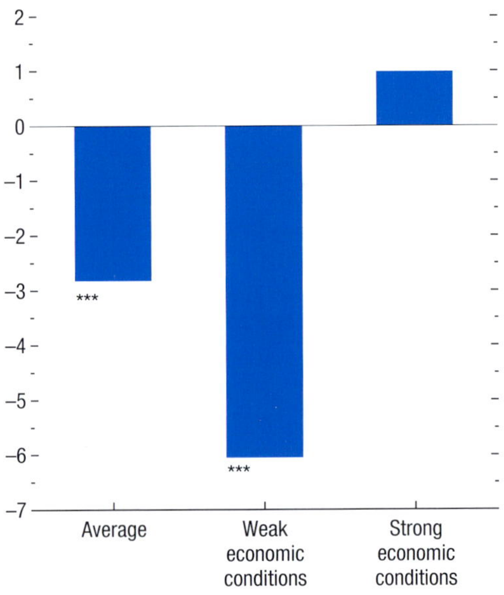

Source: IMF staff calculations.
Note: The bars denote the effect of a major reform event—defined as a change in the broad regulation indicator of two standard deviations (of the sample distribution of annual changes in the regulation indicator)—on electoral outcomes. *** denotes statistical significance at the 1 percent confidence level.

Box 3.2. The Impact of Crises on Structural Reforms

A broad range of political and economic factors can explain why and when reforms (do not) happen; one of these, which is particularly significant, is the presence of a crisis. Political factors may include government ideology, the type of political system (presidential versus parliamentary), the degree of political fragmentation, and the strength of democratic institutions (Ciminelli and others, forthcoming, and references therein). Economic factors may include prevailing business conditions, in particular. Crises can act as turning points and catalyze popular support for reform by increasing the cost of, and the support of incumbent workers and firms ("insiders") for, maintaining the status quo. At the same time, crises may lead to increased parliamentary fragmentation, which could weaken reform efforts (Mian, Sufi, and Trebbi 2014).

The relationship between crisis and reform may depend on whether the crisis is economic or financial, and it may also differ across regulatory areas. A collapse in domestic demand may lower opposition to trade liberalization from industries that usually rely on domestic demand (Lora and Olivera 2005). Similarly, periods of high unemployment may increase pressure on governments to enact reforms that ease labor market regulation in the hope of boosting employment (Duval, Furceri, and Miethe 2018). By contrast, a financial crisis after a period of deregulation could lead governments to reregulate the financial sector and the economy (Mian, Sufi, and Trebbi 2014; Gokmen and others 2017).

This box examines empirically the role of crises in fostering reforms using a vector autoregression (VAR) framework. This approach has two main advantages over a static framework. First, it allows investigation of the possibility that crises lead to reforms with long lags, an issue neglected in the empirical literature. Second, it makes it possible to account for feedback effects between changes in regulation in different areas. The set of structural reforms considered in the analysis is the same as in the rest of the chapter. As for crises, both economic recessions (defined as periods of negative real GDP growth) and systemic banking crises (defined in Laeven and Valencia 2008, 2012) are investigated.

Two VARs (one for each—economic or financial—type of crisis) are estimated according to the following model:

$$X_{i,t} = A^0 + \sum_{l=1}^{4} A^l X_{i,t-l} + \tau_t + \gamma_i + \varepsilon_{i,t}, \qquad (3.2.1)$$

in which the subscripts i and t refer to country and time. $X_{i,t}$ is a seven-variable vector containing the crisis dummy considered and the six structural reform indicators (in first differences); A^0 is a vector of constant terms; A^l is the vector of parameters to be estimated; τ_t and γ_i refer, respectively, to time- and country-fixed effects; and ε_{it} is the error term. Four lags of the dependent variables are included. The responses of reforms to crises are obtained using a Cholesky decomposition, with the crisis dummy ordered first; the implicit assumption is that the occurrence of a crisis in year t does not depend on reforms implemented in the same year.[1]

The results suggest that economic and banking crises have different effects on structural reforms (Figure 3.2.1). Economic recessions foster trade liberalization and, to a lesser extent, labor market and financial deregulation over the medium term. These results are supportive of the "crisis-induces-reform" hypothesis and consistent with the findings of Lora and Olivera (2004) and Duval, Furceri, and Miethe (2018). They suggest that governments respond to weaker external demand and higher unemployment by opening up to trade and liberalizing the labor market to foster employment. By contrast, banking crises are found to foster tighter regulation in the domestic finance and capital account areas. These effects are rather large and can be interpreted as an attempt by governments to control or mitigate perceived sources of financial instability.

This box was prepared by Gabriele Ciminelli and draws largely from Ciminelli and others (forthcoming).

[1]The ordering of the (reform) variables "below" the crisis dummy does not alter the results (for a formal derivation, see Christiano, Eichenbaum, and Evans 1999).

Box 3.2 *(continued)*

Figure 3.2.1. The Effect of Crises on Structural Reforms
(Reform indicator units)

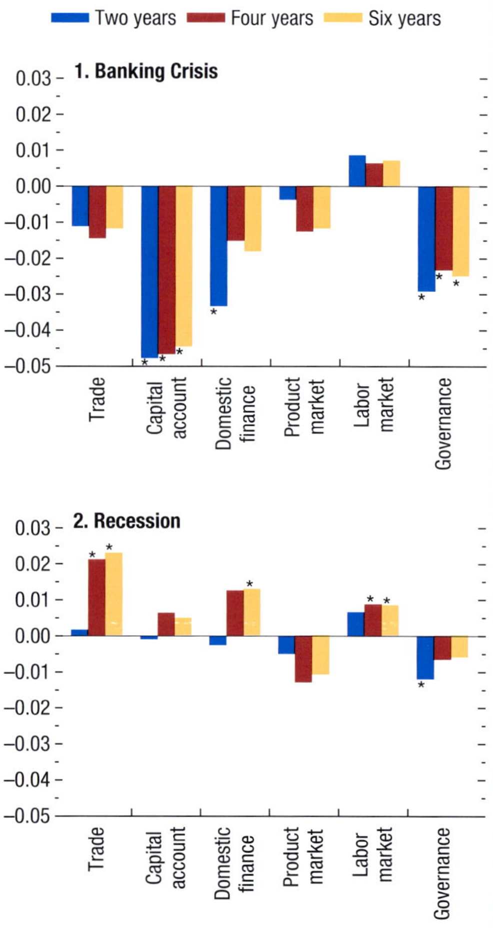

Source: IMF staff calculations.
Note: The figure reports the effects of banking crises (panel 1) and economic recessions (panel 2) on structural reforms over two-, four-, and six-year horizons. Each indicator ranges from 0 to 1. Bars with * denote statistical significance at least at 10 percent. Bars without * denote statistically insignificant results. Standard errors are computed via Monte Carlo simulations with 1,000 repetitions.

References

Abiad, Abdul, Enrica Detragiache, and Thierry Tressel. 2010. "A New Database of Financial Reforms." IMF Working Paper 08/266, International Monetary Fund, Washington, DC.

Abiad, Abdul, Nienke Oomes, and Kenichi Ueda. 2008. "The Quality Effect: Does Financial Liberalization Improve the Allocation of Capital?" *Journal of Development Economics* 87 (2): 270–82.

Acemoglu, Daron, Simon Johnson, and James Robinson. 2005. "Institutions as a Fundamental Cause of Long-Run Growth." In *Handbook of Economic Growth* 1A, edited by Philippe Aghion and Steven Durlauf. Amsterdam: Elsevier.

Ahn, Jaebin, Era Dabla-Norris, Romain Duval, Bingjie Hu, and Lamin Njie, 2019. "Reassessing the Productivity Gains from Trade Liberalization." *Review of International Economics* 27 (1): 130–54.

Aiyar, Shekhar, John Bluedorn, Romain Duval, Davide Furceri, Daniel Garcia-Macia, Yi Ji, Davide Malacrino, Haonan Qu, Jesse Siminitz, and Aleksandra. Zdzienicka. 2019. "Strengthening the Euro Area: The Role of National Reforms in Enhancing Resilience." IMF Staff Discussion Note 19/05, International Monetary Fund, Washington, DC.

Alesina, Alberto, Davide Furceri, Jonathan Ostry, Chris Papageorgiou, and Dennis Quinn. Forthcoming. "Structural Reforms and Electoral Outcomes: Evidence from a New Database of Regulatory Stances and Policy Changes." IMF Working Paper, International Monetary Fund, Washington, DC.

Amiti, Mary, and Jozef Konings. 2007. "Trade Liberalization, Intermediate Inputs, and Productivity." *American Economic Review* 97 (5): 1611–38.

Atkeson, Andrew, and Patrick J. Kehoe. 2007. "Modeling the Transition to a New Economy: Lessons from Two Technological Revolutions." *American Economic Review* 97 (1): 64–88.

Auerbach, Alan, and Youri Gorodnichenko. 2012. "Measuring the Output Responses to Fiscal Policy." *American Economic Journal: Economic Policy* 4 (2): 1–27.

Bandiera, Oriana, Gerard Caprio, Patrick Honohan, and Fabio Schiantarelli. 2000. "Does Financial Reform Raise or Reduce Saving?" *Review of Economics and Statistics* 82 (2): 239–63.

Bassanini, Andrea, Luca Nunziata, and Danielle Venn. 2009. "Job Protection Legislation and Productivity Growth in OECD Countries." *Economic Policy* 24 (58): 349–402.

Basu, Susanto, and John G. Fernald. 1997. "Returns to Scale in US Production: Estimates and Implications." *Journal of Political Economy* 105 (2): 249–83.

Bekaert, Geert, Campbell Harvey, Christian Lundblad, and Stephan Siegel. 2011 "What Segments Equity Markets?" *Review of Financial Studies* 24 (12): 3841–90.

Benhassine, Najy, David McKenzie, Victor Pouliquen, and Massimiliano Santini. 2018. "Does Inducing Informal Firms to Formalize Make Sense? Experimental Evidence from Benin." *Journal of Public Economics* 157: 1–14.

Bonfiglioli, Alessandra. 2008. "Financial Integration, Productivity and Capital Accumulation." *Journal of International Economics* 76 (2): 337–55.

Botero, Juan C., Simeon Djankov, Rafael La Porta, Florencio Lopez-de-Silanes, and Andrei Shleifer. 2004 "The Regulation of Labor." *Quarterly Journal of Economics* 119 (4): 1339–82.

Boz, Emine, Gita Gopinath, and Mikkel Plagborg-Møller. 2017. "Global Trade and the Dollar." IMF Working Paper 17/239. International Monetary Fund, Washington, DC.

Bruhn, Miriam. 2011. "License to Sell: The Effect of Business Registration Reform on Entrepreneurial Activity in Mexico." *Review of Economics and Statistics* 93 (1): 382–86.

Buera, Francisco J., and Yongseok Shin. 2017. "Productivity Growth and Capital Flows: The Dynamics of Reforms." *American Economic Journal: Macroeconomics* 9 (3): 147–85.

Cacciatore, Matteo, Romain Duval, Giuseppe Fiori, and Fabio Ghironi. 2016. "Market Reforms in the Time of Imbalance." *Journal of Economic Dynamics and Control* 72: 69–93.

Cerra, Valerie, and Sweta Saxena. 2008. "Growth Dynamics: The Myth of Economic Recovery." *American Economic Review* 102 (7): 3774–77.

Christiano, Lawrence J., Martin Eichenbaum, and Charles L. Evans. 1999. "Monetary Policy Shocks: What Have We Learned and to What End?" In *Handbook of Macroeconomics* 1 (1), edited by John. B. Taylor and Michael Woodford, 65–148. Amsterdam: Elsevier.

Christiansen, Lone, Martin Schindler, and Thierry Tressel. 2013. "Growth and Structural Reforms: A New Assessment." *Journal of International Economics* 89 (2): 347–56.

Ciminelli, Gabriele, Davide Furceri, Jun Ge, Jonathan D. Ostry, and Chris Papageorgiou. Forthcoming. "The Political Costs of Reforms: Fear or Reality?" IMF Staff Discussion Note. International Monetary Fund, Washington, DC.

De Loecker, Jan. 2007. "Do Exports Generate Higher Productivity? Evidence from Slovenia." *Journal of International Economics* 73 (1): 69–98.

Djankov, Simeon, Rafael La Porta, Florencio Lopez-de-Silanes, and Andrei Shleifer. 2002. "The Regulation of Entry." *Quarterly Journal of Economics* 117 (1): 1–37.

Duval, Romain, and Davide Furceri. 2018. "The Effects of Labor and Product Market Reforms: The Role of Macroeconomic Conditions and Policies." *IMF Economic Review* 66 (1): 31–69.

Duval, Romain, Davide Furceri, and Joao Jalles. 2019. "Job Protection Deregulation in Good and Bad Times." *Oxford Economic Papers* (July 21).

Duval, Romain, Davide Furceri, and Jakob Miethe. 2018. "The Needle in the Haystack: What Drives Labor and Product Market Reforms in Advanced Countries?" IMF Working Paper 18/101, International Monetary Fund, Washington, DC.

Duval, Romain, and Prakash Loungani. 2019. "Designing Labor Market Institutions in Emerging Market and Developing

Economies: Evidence and Policy Options." IMF Staff Discussion Note 19/04, International Monetary Fund, Washington, DC.

Ebell, Monique, and Christian Haefke. 2009. "Product Market Deregulation and the US Employment Miracle." *Review of Economic Dynamics* 12 (3): 479–504.

Ederington, Josh, and Michele Ruta. 2016. "Non-Tariff Measures and the World Trading System." World Bank Policy Research Paper 7661, World Bank, Washington, DC.

Fabrizio, Stefania, Davide Furceri, Rodrigo Garcia-Verdu, Bin G. Li, Sandra V. Lizarazo Ruiz, Marina Mendes Tavares, Futoshi Narita, and Adrian Peralta-Alva. 2017. "Macro-Structural Policies and Income Inequality in Low-Income Developing Countries." IMF Staff Discussion Note 17/01, International Monetary Fund, Washington, DC.

Furceri, Davide, Swarnali Hannan, Jonathan Ostry, and Andrew Rose. 2018. "Macroeconomic Consequences of Tariffs." NBER Working Paper 25402, National Bureau of Economic Research, Cambridge, MA.

Furceri, Davide, Prakash Loungani, and Jonanthan Ostry. Forthcoming. "The Aggregate and Distributional Effects of Financial Globalization: Evidence from Macro and Sectoral Data." *Journal of Money, Credit and Banking.*

Gokmen, Gunes, Massimiliano G. Onorato, Tommaso Nannicini, and Chris Papageorgiou. 2017. "Policies in Hard Times: Assessing the Impact of Financial Crises on Structural Reforms." IGIER Working Paper 605, Innocenzo Gasparini Institute for Economic Research, Bocconi University, Milan.

Granger, Clive, and Timo Teräsvirta. 1993. *Modelling Nonlinear Economic Relationships.* New York: Oxford University Press.

Hausmann, Ricardo, Dani Rodrik, and Andres Velasco. 2005. "Growth Diagnostics." John F. Kennedy School of Government, Harvard University, Cambridge, MA.

Hsieh, Chang-Tai, and Peter J. Klenow. 2009. "Misallocation and Manufacturing TFP in China and India." *Quarterly Journal of Economics* 124 (4): 1403–48.

International Monetary Fund (IMF). 2012. "The Liberalization of Management of Capital Flows: An Institutional View." IMF Policy Paper, Washington, DC.

———. 2018. "Review of 1997 Guidance Note on Governance—A Proposed Framework for Enhanced Fund Engagement." IMF Policy Paper 18/142, Washington, DC.

Johnston, R. Barry, and V. Sundararajan. 1999. *Sequencing Financial Sector Reforms.* Washington, DC: International Monetary Fund.

Jordà, Òscar. 2005. "Estimation and Inference of Impulse Responses by Local Projections." *American Economic Review* 95 (1): 161–82.

Kaplan, David S., Eduardo Piedra, and Enrique Seira. 2011. "Entry Regulation and Business Start-Ups: Evidence from Mexico." *Journal of Public Economics* 95 (11–12): 1501–15.

Kaufmann, Daniel, Aart Kraay, and Massimo Mastruzzi. 2010. "The Worldwide Governance Indicators: Methodology and Analytical Issues." World Bank Policy Research Working Paper 5430, World Bank, Washington, DC.

Laeven, Luc, and Fabian Valencia. 2008. "Systemic Banking Crises; A New Database." IMF Working Paper 08/224, International Monetary Fund, Washington, DC.

———. 2012. "Systemic Banking Crises: An Update." IMF Working Paper 12/163, International Monetary Fund, Washington, DC.

La Porta, Rafael, and Andrei Shleifer. 2008. "The Unofficial Economy and Economic Development." NBER Working Paper 1452, National Bureau of Economic Research, Cambridge, MA.

———. 2014. "Informality and Development." *Journal of Economic Perspectives* 28 (3): 109–26.

Levy, Santiago. 2008. *Good Intentions, Bad Outcomes.* Washington, DC: Brookings Institution.

———. 2018. *Unrewarded Efforts: The Elusive Quest for Prosperity in Mexico.* Washington, DC: Inter-American Development Bank.

Lora, Eduardo, and Mauricio Olivera. 2004. "What Makes Reforms Likely: Political Economy Determinants of Reforms in Latin America." *Journal of Applied Economics* 7 (1): 99–135.

———. 2005. "The Electoral Consequences of the Washington Consensus." *Economía* 5 (2): 1–61.

Martin, Leslie A., Shanthi Nataraj, and Ann E. Harrison. 2017. "In with the Big, Out with the Small: Removing Small-Scale Reservations in India." *American Economic Review* 107 (2): 354–86.

Mauro, Paulo. 1995. "Corruption and Growth." *Quarterly Journal of Economics* 110 (3): 681–712.

McCaig, Brian, and Nina Pavcnik. 2018. "Export Markets and Labor Allocation in a Low-Income Country." *American Economic Review* 108 (7): 1899–941.

Mian, Atif, Amir Sufi, and Francesco Trebbi. 2014. "Resolving Debt Overhang: Political Constraints in the Aftermath of Financial Crises." *American Economic Journal: Macroeconomics* 6 (2): 1–28.

Micco, Alejandro, and Carmen Pagés. 2006. "The Economic Effects of Employment Protection: Evidence from International Industry-Level Data." IZA Discussion Paper 2433, Institute of Labor Economics, Bonn.

Midrigan, Virgiliu, and Daniel Yi Xu. 2014. "Finance and Misallocation: Evidence from Plant-Level Data." *American Economic Review* 104 (2): 422–58.

Olson, Mancur. 1971. *The Logic of Collective Action: Public Goods and the Theory of Groups.* Cambridge, MA: Harvard University Press.

Organisation for Economic Co-operation and Development (OECD). 2018. *Economic Policy Reforms: Going for Growth.* Paris.

Ostry, Jonathan, Andrew Berg, and Siddharth Kothari. 2018. "Growth Equity Trade-Offs in Structural Reforms." IMF Working Paper 18/5, International Monetary Fund, Washington, DC.

Ostry, Jonathan David, Alessandro Prati, and Antonio Spilimbergo. 2009. "Structural Reforms and Economic Performance in Advanced and Developing Countries." IMF Occasional Paper 268, International Monetary Fund, Washington, DC.

Paz, Lourenço S. 2014. "The Impacts of Trade Liberalization on Informal Labor Markets: A Theoretical and Empirical Evaluation of the Brazilian Case." *Journal of International Economics* 92 (2): 330–48.

Prati, Alessandro, Massimiliano Gaetano Onorato, and Chris Papageorgiou. 2013. "Which Reforms Work and under Which Institutional Environment? Evidence from a New Data Set on Structural Reforms." *Review of Economics and Statistics* 95 (3): 946–68.

Quinn, Dennis. 1997. "The Correlates of Change in International Financial Regulation." *American Political Science Review* 91 (3): 531–51.

Quinn, Dennis P., and A. Maria Toyoda. 2008. "Does Capital Account Liberalization Lead to Economic Growth?" *Review of Financial Studies* 21 (3): 1403–49.

Rajan, Raghuram, and Luigi Zingales. 1998. "Financial Dependence and Growth." *American Economic Review* 88 (3): 559–86.

Ulyssea, Gabriel. 2018. "Firms, Informality and Development: Theory and Evidence from Brazil." *American Economic Review* 108 (8): 2015–47.

World Bank (WB). 2019. *Doing Business: Training for Reform.* Washington, DC: World Bank.

Zettelmeyer, Jeromin. 2006. "Growth and Reforms in Latin America: A Survey of Facts and Arguments." IMF Working Paper 06/210, International Monetary Fund, Washington, DC.

STATISTICAL APPENDIX

The Statistical Appendix presents historical data as well as projections. It comprises seven sections: Assumptions, What's New, Data and Conventions, Country Notes, Classification of Countries, Key Data Documentation, and Statistical Tables.

The assumptions underlying the estimates and projections for 2019–20 and the medium-term scenario for 2021–24 are summarized in the first section. The second section presents a brief description of the changes to the database and statistical tables since the April 2019 *World Economic Outlook* (WEO). The third section provides a general description of the data and the conventions used for calculating country group composites. The fourth section summarizes selected key information for each country. The fifth section summarizes the classification of countries in the various groups presented in the WEO. The sixth section provides information on methods and reporting standards for the member countries' national account and government finance indicators included in the report.

The last, and main, section comprises the statistical tables. (Statistical Appendix A is included here; Statistical Appendix B is available online at www.imf.org/en/Publications/WEO.)

Data in these tables have been compiled on the basis of information available through September 30, 2019. The figures for 2019 and beyond are shown with the same degree of precision as the historical figures solely for convenience; because they are projections, the same degree of accuracy is not to be inferred.

Assumptions

Real effective *exchange rates* for the advanced economies are assumed to remain constant at their average levels measured during the period July 26 to August 23, 2019. For 2019 and 2020, these assumptions imply average US dollar–special drawing right (SDR) conversion rates of 1.382 and 1.377, US dollar–euro conversion rates of 1.123 and 1.120, and yen–US dollar conversion rates of 108.2 and 104.5, respectively.

It is assumed that the *price of oil* will average $61.78 a barrel in 2019 and $57.94 a barrel in 2020.

Established *policies* of national authorities are assumed to be maintained. The more specific policy assumptions underlying the projections for selected economies are described in Box A1.

With regard to *interest rates*, it is assumed that the London interbank offered rate (LIBOR) on six-month US dollar deposits will average 2.3 percent in 2019 and 2.0 percent in 2020, that three-month euro deposits will average –0.4 percent in 2019 and –0.6 percent in 2020, and that six-month yen deposits will average 0.0 percent in 2019 and –0.1 percent in 2020.

As a reminder, in regard to the *introduction of the euro*, on December 31, 1998, the Council of the European Union decided that, effective January 1, 1999, the irrevocably fixed conversion rates between the euro and currencies of the member countries adopting the euro are as described in Box 5.4 of the October 1998 WEO. See Box 5.4 of the October 1998 WEO for details on how the conversion rates were established.

1 euro	=	13.7603	Austrian schillings
	=	40.3399	Belgian francs
	=	0.585274	Cyprus pound[1]
	=	1.95583	Deutsche marks
	=	15.6466	Estonian krooni[2]
	=	5.94573	Finnish markkaa
	=	6.55957	French francs
	=	340.750	Greek drachmas[3]
	=	0.787564	Irish pound
	=	1,936.27	Italian lire
	=	0.702804	Latvian lat[4]
	=	3.45280	Lithuanian litas[5]
	=	40.3399	Luxembourg francs
	=	0.42930	Maltese lira[1]
	=	2.20371	Netherlands guilders
	=	200.482	Portuguese escudos
	=	30.1260	Slovak koruna[6]
	=	239.640	Slovenian tolars[7]
	=	166.386	Spanish pesetas

[1]Established on January 1, 2008.
[2]Established on January 1, 2011.
[3]Established on January 1, 2001.
[4]Established on January 1, 2014.
[5]Established on January 1, 2015.
[6]Established on January 1, 2009.
[7]Established on January 1, 2007.

What's New

- Mauritania redenominated its currency in January 2018 by replacing 10 old Mauritanian ouguiya (MRO) with 1 new Mauritanian ouguiya (MRU). Local currency data for Mauritania are expressed in the new currency beginning with the October 2019 WEO database.
- São Tomé and Príncipe redenominated its currency in January 2018 by replacing 1,000 old São Tomé and Príncipe dobra (STD) with 1 new São Tomé and Príncipe dobra (STN). Local currency data for São Tomé and Príncipe are expressed in the new currency beginning with the October 2019 WEO database.
- Beginning with the October 2019 WEO, the regional group Commonwealth of Independent States (CIS) is discontinued. Four of the CIS economies (Belarus, Moldova, Russia, and Ukraine) are added to the regional group Emerging and Developing Europe. The remaining eight economies—Armenia, Azerbaijan, Georgia, Kazakhstan, Kyrgyz Republic, Tajikistan, Turkmenistan, and Uzbekistan, which comprise the regional subgroup Caucasus and Central Asia (CCA)—are combined with Middle East, North Africa, Afghanistan, and Pakistan (MENAP) to form the new regional group Middle East and Central Asia (MECA).

Data and Conventions

Data and projections for 194 economies form the statistical basis of the WEO database. The data are maintained jointly by the IMF's Research Department and regional departments, with the latter regularly updating country projections based on consistent global assumptions.

Although national statistical agencies are the ultimate providers of historical data and definitions, international organizations are also involved in statistical issues, with the objective of harmonizing methodologies for the compilation of national statistics, including analytical frameworks, concepts, definitions, classifications, and valuation procedures used in the production of economic statistics. The WEO database reflects information from both national source agencies and international organizations.

Most countries' macroeconomic data presented in the WEO conform broadly to the 2008 version of the *System of National Accounts* (SNA). The IMF's sector statistical standards—the sixth edition of the *Balance of Payments and International Investment Position Manual* (BPM6), the *Monetary and Financial Statistics Manual and Compilation Guide* (MFSMCG), and the *Government Finance Statistics Manual 2014* (GFSM 2014)—have been or are being aligned with the SNA 2008. These standards reflect the IMF's special interest in countries' external positions, financial sector stability, and public sector fiscal positions. The process of adapting country data to the new standards begins in earnest when the manuals are released. However, full concordance with the manuals is ultimately dependent on the provision by national statistical compilers of revised country data; hence, the WEO estimates are only partially adapted to these manuals. Nonetheless, for many countries, the impact on major balances and aggregates of conversion to the updated standards will be small. Many other countries have partially adopted the latest standards and will continue implementation over a period of years.[1]

The fiscal gross and net debt data reported in the WEO are drawn from official data sources and IMF staff estimates. While attempts are made to align gross and net debt data with the definitions in the GFSM, as a result of data limitations or specific country circumstances, these data can sometimes deviate from the formal definitions. Although every effort is made to ensure the WEO data are relevant and internationally comparable, differences in both sectoral and instrument coverage mean that the data are not universally comparable. As more information becomes available, changes in either data sources or instrument coverage can give rise to data revisions that can sometimes be substantial. For clarification on the deviations in sectoral or instrument coverage, please refer to the metadata for the online WEO database.

Composite data for country groups in the WEO are either sums or weighted averages of data for individual countries. Unless noted otherwise, multiyear averages of growth rates are expressed as compound annual rates of change.[2] Arithmetically weighted averages are used

[1] Many countries are implementing the SNA 2008 or European System of National and Regional Accounts (ESA) 2010, and a few countries use versions of the SNA older than that from 1993. A similar adoption pattern is expected for the BPM6 and GFSM 2014. Please refer to Table G, which lists the statistical standards adhered to by each country.

[2] Averages for real GDP and its components, employment, inflation, factor productivity, GDP per capita, trade, and commodity prices are calculated based on the compound annual rate of change, except in the case of the unemployment rate, which is based on the simple arithmetic average.

for all data for the emerging market and developing economies group—except data on inflation and money growth, for which geometric averages are used. The following conventions apply:

Country group composites for exchange rates, interest rates, and growth rates of monetary aggregates are weighted by GDP converted to US dollars at market exchange rates (averaged over the preceding three years) as a share of group GDP.

Composites for other data relating to the domestic economy, whether growth rates or ratios, are weighted by GDP valued at purchasing power parity as a share of total world or group GDP.[3] Annual inflation rates are simple percentage changes from the previous years, except in the case of emerging market and developing economies, for which the rates are based on logarithmic differences.

Composites for real GDP per capita in *purchasing power parity* terms are sums of individual country data after conversion to the international dollar in the years indicated.

Unless noted otherwise, composites for all sectors for the euro area are corrected for reporting discrepancies in intra-area transactions. Unadjusted annual GDP data are used for the euro area and for the majority of individual countries, except for Cyprus, Ireland, Portugal, and Spain, which report calendar-adjusted data. For data prior to 1999, data aggregations apply 1995 European currency unit exchange rates.

Composites for fiscal data are sums of individual country data after conversion to US dollars at the average market exchange rates in the years indicated.

Composite unemployment rates and employment growth are weighted by labor force as a share of group labor force.

Composites relating to external sector statistics are sums of individual country data after conversion to US dollars at the average market exchange rates in the years indicated for balance of payments data and at end-of-year market exchange rates for debt denominated in currencies other than US dollars.

Composites of changes in foreign trade volumes and prices, however, are arithmetic averages of percent changes for individual countries weighted by the US dollar value of exports or imports as a share of total world or group exports or imports (in the preceding year).

Unless noted otherwise, group composites are computed if 90 percent or more of the share of group weights is represented.

Data refer to calendar years, except in the case of a few countries that use fiscal years; Table F lists the economies with exceptional reporting periods for national accounts and government finance data for each country.

For some countries, the figures for 2018 and earlier are based on estimates rather than actual outturns; Table G lists the latest actual outturns for the indicators in the national accounts, prices, government finance, and balance of payments indicators for each country.

Country Notes

The consumer price data for *Argentina* before December 2013 reflect the consumer price index (CPI) for the Greater Buenos Aires Area (CPI-GBA), while from December 2013 to October 2015 the data reflect the national CPI (IPCNu). The government that took office in December 2015 discontinued the IPCNu, stating that it was flawed, and released a new CPI for the Greater Buenos Aires Area on June 15, 2016 (a new national CPI has been disseminated starting in June 2017). At its November 9, 2016, meeting, the IMF Executive Board considered the new CPI series to be in line with international standards and lifted the declaration of censure issued in 2013. Given the differences in geographical coverage, weights, sampling, and methodology of these series, the average CPI inflation for 2014, 2015, and 2016 and end-of-period inflation for 2015 and 2016 are not reported in the October 2019 WEO.

Argentina's authorities discontinued the publication of labor market data in December 2015 and released new series starting in the second quarter of 2016.

The fiscal series for the *Dominican Republic* have the following coverage: public debt, debt service, and the cyclically adjusted/structural balances are for the consolidated public sector (which includes central government, rest of the nonfinancial public sector, and the central bank); and the remaining fiscal series are for the central government.

India's real GDP growth rates are calculated as per national accounts: for 1998 to 2011, with base year 2004/05 and, thereafter, with base year 2011/12.

[3] See "Revised Purchasing Power Parity Weights" in the July 2014 WEO *Update* for a summary of the revised purchasing-power-parity-based weights, as well as Box A2 of the April 2004 WEO and Annex IV of the May 1993 WEO. See also Anne-Marie Gulde and Marianne Schulze-Ghattas, "Purchasing Power Parity Based Weights for the *World Economic Outlook*," in *Staff Studies for the World Economic Outlook* (Washington, DC: International Monetary Fund, December 1993), 106–23.

Against the backdrop of a civil war and weak capacity, the reliability of *Libya's* data, especially medium-term projections, is low.

Data for *Syria* are excluded from 2011 onward because of the uncertain political situation.

Trinidad and Tobago's growth estimates for 2018 are based on full-year energy sector data from the Ministry of Energy and Ministry of Finance, preliminary national accounts data for the first three quarters of the year from the Central Statistical Office, and staff projections for fourth-quarter nonenergy output based on available information. Growth projections from 2019 are unchanged from the April 2019 WEO in the absence of updates to published national accounts data.

Ukraine's revised national accounts data are available beginning in 2000 and exclude Crimea and Sevastopol from 2010.

Starting from October 2018 *Uruguay*'s public pension system has been receiving transfers in the context of a new law that compensates persons affected by the creation of the mixed pension system. These funds are recorded as revenues, consistent with the IMF's methodology. Therefore, data and projections for 2018–22 are affected by these transfers, which amounted to 1.3 percent of GDP in 2018 and are projected to be 1.2 percent of GDP in 2019, 0.9 percent of GDP in 2020, 0.4 percent of GDP in 2021, 0.2 percent of GDP in 2022, and zero percent of GDP thereafter. Please see IMF Country Report 19/64 for further details. The disclaimer about the public pension system applies only to the revenues and net lending/borrowing series.

The coverage of the fiscal data for *Uruguay* was changed from consolidated public sector (CPS) to nonfinancial public sector (NFPS) with the October 2019 WEO. In Uruguay, NFPS coverage includes central government, local government, social security funds, nonfinancial public corporations, and Banco de Seguros del Estado. Historical data were also revised accordingly. Under this narrower fiscal perimeter—which excludes the central bank—assets and liabilities held by the NFPS where the counterpart is the central bank are not netted out in debt figures. In this context, capitalization bonds issued in the past by the government to the central bank are now part of the NFPS debt. Gross and net debt estimates for the period 2008–11 are preliminary.

Projecting the economic outlook in *Venezuela*, including assessing past and current economic developments as the basis for the projections, is complicated by the lack of discussions with the authorities (the last Article IV consultation took place in 2004), incomplete understanding of the reported data, and difficulties in interpreting certain reported economic indicators given economic developments. The fiscal accounts include the budgetary central government; social security; FOGADE (insurance deposit institution); and a sample of public enterprises, including Petróleos de Venezuela, S.A. (PDVSA); and data for 2018 are IMF staff estimates. The effects of hyperinflation and the paucity of reported data mean that the IMF staff's estimated macroeconomic indicators need to be interpreted with caution. For example, nominal GDP is estimated assuming the GDP deflator rises in line with the IMF staff's estimated average inflation. Public external debt in relation to GDP is estimated using the IMF staff's estimate of the average exchange rate for the year. Wide uncertainty surrounds these projections. *Venezuela's* consumer prices are excluded from all WEO group composites.

Classification of Countries

Summary of the Country Classification

The country classification in the WEO divides the world into two major groups: advanced economies and emerging market and developing economies.[4] This classification is not based on strict criteria, economic or otherwise, and it has evolved over time. The objective is to facilitate analysis by providing a reasonably meaningful method of organizing data. Table A provides an overview of the country classification, showing the number of countries in each group by region and summarizing some key indicators of their relative size (GDP valued at purchasing power parity, total exports of goods and services, and population).

Some countries remain outside the country classification and therefore are not included in the analysis. Cuba and the Democratic People's Republic of Korea are examples of countries that are not IMF members, and their economies therefore are not monitored by the IMF.

[4] As used here, the terms "country" and "economy" do not always refer to a territorial entity that is a state as understood by international law and practice. Some territorial entities included here are not states, although their statistical data are maintained on a separate and independent basis.

General Features and Composition of Groups in the *World Economic Outlook* Classification

Advanced Economies

The 39 advanced economies are listed in Table B. The seven largest in terms of GDP based on market exchange rates—the United States, Japan, Germany, France, Italy, the United Kingdom, and Canada—constitute the subgroup of major advanced economies, often referred to as the Group of Seven (G7). The members of the euro area are also distinguished as a subgroup. Composite data shown in the tables for the euro area cover the current members for all years, even though the membership has increased over time.

Table C lists the member countries of the European Union, not all of which are classified as advanced economies in the WEO.

Emerging Market and Developing Economies

The group of emerging market and developing economies (155) includes all those that are not classified as advanced economies.

The regional breakdowns of emerging market and developing economies are emerging and developing Asia; emerging and developing Europe (sometimes also referred to as "central and eastern Europe"); Latin America and the Caribbean (LAC); Middle East and Central Asia (MECA, which comprises the regional subgroups Middle East, North Africa, Afghanistan, and Pakistan; and Caucasus and Central Asia); and sub-Saharan Africa (SSA).

Emerging market and developing economies are also classified according to *analytical criteria.* The analytical criteria reflect the composition of export earnings and a distinction between net creditor and net debtor economies. The detailed composition of emerging market and developing economies in the regional and analytical groups is shown in Tables D and E.

The analytical criterion *source of export earnings* distinguishes between the categories *fuel* (Standard International Trade Classification [SITC] 3) and *nonfuel* and then focuses on *nonfuel primary products* (SITCs 0, 1, 2, 4, and 68). Economies are categorized into one of these groups if their main source of export earnings exceeded 50 percent of total exports on average between 2014 and 2018.

The financial criteria focus on *net creditor economies, net debtor economies, heavily indebted poor countries* (HIPCs), and *low-income developing countries* (LIDCs). Economies are categorized as net debtors when their latest net international investment position, where available, was less than zero or their current account balance accumulations from 1972 (or earliest available data) to 2018 were negative. Net debtor economies are further differentiated on the basis of *experience with debt servicing.*[5]

The HIPC group comprises the countries that are or have been considered by the IMF and the World Bank for participation in their debt initiative known as the HIPC Initiative, which aims to reduce the external debt burdens of all the eligible HIPCs to a "sustainable" level in a reasonably short period of time.[6] Many of these countries have already benefited from debt relief and have graduated from the initiative.

The LIDCs are countries that have per capita income levels below a certain threshold (set at $2,700 in 2016 as measured by the World Bank's Atlas method), structural features consistent with limited development and structural transformation, and external financial linkages insufficiently close for them to be widely seen as emerging market economies.

[5] During 2014–18, 25 economies incurred external payments arrears or entered into official or commercial bank debt-rescheduling agreements. This group is referred to as *economies with arrears and/or rescheduling during 2014–18.*

[6] See David Andrews, Anthony R. Boote, Syed S. Rizavi, and Sukwinder Singh, "Debt Relief for Low-Income Countries: The Enhanced HIPC Initiative," IMF Pamphlet Series 51 (Washington, DC: International Monetary Fund, November 1999).

Table A. Classification by *World Economic Outlook* Groups and Their Shares in Aggregate GDP, Exports of Goods and Services, and Population, 2018[1]

(Percent of total for group or world)

	Number of Economies	GDP		Exports of Goods and Services		Population	
		Advanced Economies	World	Advanced Economies	World	Advanced Economies	World
Advanced Economies	**39**	**100.0**	**40.8**	**100.0**	**63.0**	**100.0**	**14.3**
United States		37.2	15.2	16.0	10.1	30.6	4.4
Euro Area	19	27.9	11.4	42.0	26.5	31.7	4.5
Germany		7.9	3.2	11.9	7.5	7.8	1.1
France		5.4	2.2	5.8	3.6	6.1	0.9
Italy		4.3	1.8	4.2	2.7	5.7	0.8
Spain		3.4	1.4	3.1	2.0	4.3	0.6
Japan		10.1	4.1	5.9	3.7	11.8	1.7
United Kingdom		5.5	2.2	5.4	3.4	6.2	0.9
Canada		3.3	1.4	3.5	2.2	3.5	0.5
Other Advanced Economies	16	15.9	6.5	27.2	17.1	16.1	2.3
Memorandum							
Major Advanced Economies	7	73.7	30.1	52.7	33.2	71.6	10.2
		Emerging Market and Developing Economies	World	Emerging Market and Developing Economies	World	Emerging Market and Developing Economies	World
Emerging Market and Developing Economies	**155**	**100.0**	**59.2**	**100.0**	**37.0**	**100.0**	**85.7**
Regional Groups							
Emerging and Developing Asia	30	56.2	33.2	48.6	18.0	56.3	48.2
China		31.5	18.7	28.8	10.7	21.8	18.7
India		13.1	7.7	5.9	2.2	20.8	17.9
ASEAN-5	5	9.4	5.5	12.3	4.6	8.8	7.6
Emerging and Developing Europe	16	12.1	7.2	16.5	6.1	5.9	5.1
Russia		5.3	3.1	5.5	2.0	2.3	2.0
Latin America and the Caribbean	33	12.6	7.5	13.7	5.1	9.7	8.4
Brazil		4.2	2.5	3.0	1.1	3.3	2.8
Mexico		3.2	1.9	5.2	1.9	1.9	1.7
Middle East and Central Asia	31	13.9	8.2	16.6	6.2	12.3	10.6
Saudi Arabia		2.3	1.4	3.4	1.3	0.5	0.4
Sub-Saharan Africa	45	5.2	3.0	4.6	1.7	15.7	13.5
Nigeria		1.5	0.9	0.7	0.3	3.1	2.6
South Africa		1.0	0.6	1.2	0.4	0.9	0.8
Analytical Groups[2]							
By Source of Export Earnings							
Fuel	27	17.1	10.1	22.1	8.2	11.6	10.0
Nonfuel	127	82.9	49.0	77.9	28.8	88.4	75.7
Of Which, Primary Products	35	5.1	3.0	5.2	1.9	9.0	7.7
By External Financing Source							
Net Debtor Economies	122	51.7	30.6	49.7	18.4	68.4	58.6
Net Debtor Economies by Debt-Servicing Experience							
Economies with Arrears and/or Rescheduling during 2014–18	25	3.4	2.0	2.8	1.0	5.8	4.9
Other Groups							
Heavily Indebted Poor Countries	39	2.5	1.5	2.0	0.7	11.8	10.1
Low-Income Developing Countries	59	7.3	4.3	7.0	2.6	23.0	19.8

[1]The GDP shares are based on the purchasing-power-parity valuation of economies' GDP. The number of economies comprising each group reflects those for which data are included in the group aggregates.

[2]Syria is omitted from the source of export earnings, and South Sudan and Syria are omitted from the net external position group composites because of insufficient data.

Table B. Advanced Economies by Subgroup

Major Currency Areas		
United States		
Euro Area		
Japan		
Euro Area		
Austria	Greece	Netherlands
Belgium	Ireland	Portugal
Cyprus	Italy	Slovak Republic
Estonia	Latvia	Slovenia
Finland	Lithuania	Spain
France	Luxembourg	
Germany	Malta	
Major Advanced Economies		
Canada	Italy	United States
France	Japan	
Germany	United Kingdom	
Other Advanced Economies		
Australia	Korea	Singapore
Czech Republic	Macao SAR[2]	Sweden
Denmark	New Zealand	Switzerland
Hong Kong SAR[1]	Norway	Taiwan Province of China
Iceland	Puerto Rico	
Israel	San Marino	

[1]On July 1, 1997, Hong Kong was returned to the People's Republic of China and became a Special Administrative Region of China.

[2]On December 20, 1999, Macao was returned to the People's Republic of China and became a Special Administrative Region of China.

Table C. European Union

Austria	Germany	Poland
Belgium	Greece	Portugal
Bulgaria	Hungary	Romania
Croatia	Ireland	Slovak Republic
Cyprus	Italy	Slovenia
Czech Republic	Latvia	Spain
Denmark	Lithuania	Sweden
Estonia	Luxembourg	United Kingdom
Finland	Malta	
France	Netherlands	

Table D. Emerging Market and Developing Economies by Region and Main Source of Export Earnings

	Fuel	Nonfuel Primary Products
Emerging and Developing Asia		
	Brunei Darussalam	Kiribati
	Timor-Leste	Lao P.D.R.
		Marshall Islands
		Papua New Guinea
		Solomon Islands
		Tuvalu
Emerging and Developing Europe		
	Russia	
Latin America and the Caribbean		
	Ecuador	Argentina
	Trinidad and Tobago	Bolivia
	Venezuela	Chile
		Guyana
		Paraguay
		Peru
		Suriname
		Uruguay
Middle East and Central Asia		
	Algeria	Afghanistan
	Azerbaijan	Mauritania
	Bahrain	Somalia
	Iran	Sudan
	Iraq	Tajikistan
	Kazakhstan	Uzbekistan
	Kuwait	
	Libya	
	Oman	
	Qatar	
	Saudi Arabia	
	Turkmenistan	
	United Arab Emirates	
	Yemen	
Sub-Saharan Africa		
	Angola	Burkina Faso
	Chad	Burundi
	Republic of Congo	Central African Republic
	Equatorial Guinea	Democratic Republic of the Congo
	Gabon	Côte d'Ivoire
	Nigeria	Eritrea
	South Sudan	Guinea
		Guinea-Bissau
		Liberia
		Malawi
		Mali
		Sierra Leone
		South Africa
		Zambia
		Zimbabwe

Table E. Emerging Market and Developing Economies by Region, Net External Position, and Status as Heavily Indebted Poor Countries and Low-Income Developing Countries

	Net External Position[1]	Heavily Indebted Poor Countries[2]	Low-Income Developing Countries
Emerging and Developing Asia			
Bangladesh	*		*
Bhutan	*		*
Brunei Darussalam	•		
Cambodia	*		*
China	•		
Fiji	*		
India	*		
Indonesia	*		
Kiribati	•		*
Lao P.D.R.	*		*
Malaysia	*		
Maldives	*		
Marshall Islands	*		
Micronesia	•		
Mongolia	*		
Myanmar	*		*
Nauru	*		
Nepal	•		*
Palau	•		
Papua New Guinea	*		*
Philippines	*		
Samoa	*		
Solomon Islands	*		*
Sri Lanka	*		
Thailand	*		
Timor-Leste	•		*
Tonga	*		
Tuvalu	•		
Vanuatu	*		
Vietnam	*		*
Emerging and Developing Europe			
Albania	*		
Belarus	*		
Bosnia and Herzegovina	*		
Bulgaria	*		
Croatia	*		
Hungary	*		
Kosovo	*		
Moldova	*		*
Montenegro	*		

	Net External Position[1]	Heavily Indebted Poor Countries[2]	Low-Income Developing Countries
North Macedonia	*		
Poland	*		
Romania	*		
Russia	•		
Serbia	*		
Turkey	*		
Ukraine	*		
Latin America and the Caribbean			
Antigua and Barbuda	*		
Argentina	•		
Aruba	*		
The Bahamas	*		
Barbados	*		
Belize	*		
Bolivia	*	•	
Brazil	*		
Chile	*		
Colombia	*		
Costa Rica	*		
Dominica	•		
Dominican Republic	*		
Ecuador	*		
El Salvador	*		
Grenada	*		
Guatemala	*		
Guyana	*	•	
Haiti	*	•	*
Honduras	*	•	*
Jamaica	*		
Mexico	*		
Nicaragua	*	•	*
Panama	*		
Paraguay	*		
Peru	*		
St. Kitts and Nevis	*		
St. Lucia	*		
St. Vincent and the Grenadines	*		
Suriname	*		
Trinidad and Tobago	•		
Uruguay	*		
Venezuela	•		

Table E. Emerging Market and Developing Economies by Region, Net External Position, and Status as Heavily Indebted Poor Countries and Low-Income Developing Countries ***(continued)***

	Net External Position[1]	Heavily Indebted Poor Countries[2]	Low-Income Developing Countries
Middle East and Central Asia			
Afghanistan	•	•	*
Algeria	•		
Armenia	*		
Azerbaijan	•		
Bahrain	•		
Djibouti	*		*
Egypt	*		
Georgia	*		
Iran	•		
Iraq	•		
Jordan	*		
Kazakhstan	*		
Kuwait	•		
Kyrgyz Republic	*		*
Lebanon	*		
Libya	•		
Mauritania	*	•	*
Morocco	*		
Oman	*		
Pakistan	*		
Qatar	•		
Saudi Arabia	•		
Somalia	*	*	*
Sudan	*	*	*
Syria[3]	. . .		
Tajikistan	*		*
Tunisia	*		
Turkmenistan	*		
United Arab Emirates	•		
Uzbekistan	•		*
Yemen	*		*
Sub-Saharan Africa			
Angola	*		
Benin	*	•	*
Botswana	•		
Burkina Faso	*	•	*
Burundi	*	•	*
Cabo Verde	*		
Cameroon	*	•	*
Central African Republic	*	•	*
Chad	*	•	*
Comoros	*	•	*
Democratic Republic of the Congo	*	•	*
Republic of Congo	*	•	*
Côte d'Ivoire	*	•	*
Equatorial Guinea	•		
Eritrea	*	*	*
Eswatini	•		
Ethiopia	*	•	*
Gabon	•		
The Gambia	*	•	*
Ghana	*	•	*
Guinea	*	•	*
Guinea-Bissau	*	•	*
Kenya	*		*
Lesotho	*		*
Liberia	*	•	*
Madagascar	*	•	*
Malawi	*	•	*
Mali	*	•	*
Mauritius	•		
Mozambique	*	•	*
Namibia	*		
Niger	*	•	*
Nigeria	*		*
Rwanda	*	•	*
São Tomé and Príncipe	*	•	*
Senegal	*	•	*
Seychelles	*		
Sierra Leone	*	•	*
South Africa	•		
South Sudan[3]	. . .		*
Tanzania	*	•	*
Togo	*	•	*
Uganda	*	•	*
Zambia	*	•	*
Zimbabwe	*		*

[1]Dot (star) indicates that the country is a net creditor (net debtor).
[2]Dot instead of star indicates that the country has reached the completion point, which allows it to receive the full debt relief committed to at the decision point.
[3]South Sudan and Syria are omitted from the net external position group composite for lack of a fully developed database.

Table F. Economies with Exceptional Reporting Periods[1]

	National Accounts	Government Finance
The Bahamas		Jul/Jun
Barbados		Apr/Mar
Bhutan	Jul/Jun	Jul/Jun
Botswana		Apr/Mar
Dominica		Jul/Jun
Egypt	Jul/Jun	Jul/Jun
Eswatini		Apr/Mar
Ethiopia	Jul/Jun	Jul/Jun
Haiti	Oct/Sep	Oct/Sep
Hong Kong SAR		Apr/Mar
India	Apr/Mar	Apr/Mar
Iran	Apr/Mar	Apr/Mar
Jamaica		Apr/Mar
Lesotho	Apr/Mar	Apr/Mar
Malawi		Jul/Jun
Marshall Islands	Oct/Sep	Oct/Sep
Mauritius		Jul/Jun
Micronesia	Oct/Sep	Oct/Sep
Myanmar	Oct/Sep	Oct/Sep
Namibia		Apr/Mar
Nauru	Jul/Jun	Jul/Jun
Nepal	Aug/Jul	Aug/Jul
Pakistan	Jul/Jun	Jul/Jun
Palau	Oct/Sep	Oct/Sep
Puerto Rico	Jul/Jun	Jul/Jun
St. Lucia		Apr/Mar
Samoa	Jul/Jun	Jul/Jun
Singapore		Apr/Mar
Thailand		Oct/Sep
Trinidad and Tobago		Oct/Sep

[1]Unless noted otherwise, all data refer to calendar years.

Table G. Key Data Documentation

		National Accounts					Prices (CPI)	
Country	Currency	Historical Data Source[1]	Latest Actual Annual Data	Base Year[2]	System of National Accounts	Use of Chain-Weighted Methodology[3]	Historical Data Source[1]	Latest Actual Annual Data
Afghanistan	Afghan afghani	NSO	2018	2002/03	SNA 1993		NSO	2018
Albania	Albanian lek	IMF staff	2018	1996	ESA 2010	From 1996	NSO	2018
Algeria	Algerian dinar	NSO	2018	2001	SNA 1993	From 2005	NSO	2018
Angola	Angolan kwanza	NSO and MEP	2018	2002	ESA 1995		NSO	2018
Antigua and Barbuda	Eastern Caribbean dollar	CB	2017	2006[6]	SNA 1993		NSO	2018
Argentina	Argentine peso	NSO	2018	2004	SNA 2008		NSO	2018
Armenia	Armenian dram	NSO	2018	2005	SNA 2008		NSO	2018
Aruba	Aruban Florin	NSO	2017	2000	SNA 1993	From 2000	NSO	2018
Australia	Australian dollar	NSO	2018	2015/16	SNA 2008	From 1980	NSO	2018
Austria	Euro	NSO	2018	2010	ESA 2010	From 1995	NSO	2018
Azerbaijan	Azerbaijan manat	NSO	2018	2005	SNA 1993	From 1994	NSO	2018
The Bahamas	Bahamian dollar	NSO	2018	2012	SNA 1993		NSO	2018
Bahrain	Bahrain dinar	NSO	2018	2010	SNA 2008		NSO	2018
Bangladesh	Bangladesh taka	NSO	2018	2005/06	SNA 1993		NSO	2018
Barbados	Barbados dollar	NSO and CB	2018	2010	SNA 1993		NSO	2018
Belarus	Belarusian ruble	NSO	2018	2014	SNA 2008	From 2005	NSO	2018
Belgium	Euro	CB	2018	2016	ESA 2010	From 1995	CB	2018
Belize	Belize dollar	NSO	2018	2000	SNA 1993		NSO	2018
Benin	CFA franc	NSO	2018	2015	SNA 1993		NSO	2018
Bhutan	Bhutanese ngultrum	NSO	2017/18	2000/01[6]	SNA 1993		CB	2017/18
Bolivia	Bolivian boliviano	NSO	2017	1990	SNA 2008		NSO	2018
Bosnia and Herzegovina	Bosnian convertible marka	NSO	2018	2010	ESA 2010	From 2000	NSO	2018
Botswana	Botswana pula	NSO	2018	2006	SNA 1993		NSO	2018
Brazil	Brazilian real	NSO	2018	1995	SNA 2008		NSO	2018
Brunei Darussalam	Brunei dollar	NSO and GAD	2018	2010	SNA 1993		NSO and GAD	2018
Bulgaria	Bulgarian lev	NSO	2018	2010	ESA 2010	From 1996	NSO	2018
Burkina Faso	CFA franc	NSO and MEP	2018	1999	SNA 1993		NSO	2018
Burundi	Burundi franc	NSO	2015	2005	SNA 1993		NSO	2017
Cabo Verde	Cabo Verdean escudo	NSO	2018	2007	SNA 2008	From 2011	NSO	2018
Cambodia	Cambodian riel	NSO	2018	2000	SNA 1993		NSO	2018
Cameroon	CFA franc	NSO	2017	2005	SNA 2008		NSO	2018
Canada	Canadian dollar	NSO	2018	2012	SNA 2008	From 1980	NSO	2018
Central African Republic	CFA franc	NSO	2017	2005	SNA 1993		NSO	2018
Chad	CFA franc	CB	2017	2005	SNA 1993		NSO	2017
Chile	Chilean peso	CB	2018	2013[6]	SNA 2008	From 2003	NSO	2018
China	Chinese yuan	NSO	2018	2015	SNA 2008		NSO	2018
Colombia	Colombian peso	NSO	2018	2015	SNA 1993	From 2005	NSO	2018
Comoros	Comorian franc	MEP	2016	2007	. . .	From 2007	NSO	2018
Democratic Republic of the Congo	Congolese franc	NSO	2018	2005	SNA 1993		CB	2018
Republic of Congo	CFA franc	NSO	2017	1990	SNA 1993		NSO	2018
Costa Rica	Costa Rican colón	CB	2018	2012	SNA 2008		CB	2018

Table G. Key Data Documentation *(continued)*

	Government Finance					Balance of Payments		
Country	Historical Data Source[1]	Latest Actual Annual Data	Statistics Manual in Use at Source	Subsectors Coverage[4]	Accounting Practice[5]	Historical Data Source[1]	Latest Actual Annual Data	Statistics Manual in Use at Source
Afghanistan	MoF	2018	2001	CG	C	NSO, MoF, and CB	2018	BPM 6
Albania	IMF staff	2018	1986	CG,LG,SS,MPC, NFPC	. . .	CB	2018	BPM 6
Algeria	MoF	2018	1986	CG	C	CB	2018	BPM 6
Angola	MoF	2018	2001	CG,LG	. . .	CB	2018	BPM 6
Antigua and Barbuda	MoF	2018	2001	CG	C	CB	2016	BPM 6
Argentina	MEP	2018	1986	CG,SG,SS	C	NSO	2018	BPM 6
Armenia	MoF	2018	2001	CG	C	CB	2018	BPM 6
Aruba	MoF	2018	2001	CG	Mixed	CB	2017	BPM 5
Australia	MoF	2017/18	2014	CG,SG,LG,TG	A	NSO	2018	BPM 6
Austria	NSO	2018	2001	CG,SG,LG,SS	A	CB	2018	BPM 6
Azerbaijan	MoF	2018	. . .	CG	C	CB	2018	BPM 6
The Bahamas	MoF	2017/18	2001	CG	C	CB	2018	BPM 5
Bahrain	MoF	2018	2001	CG	C	CB	2018	BPM 6
Bangladesh	MoF	2018	. . .	CG	C	CB	2018	BPM 6
Barbados	MoF	2018/19	1986	BCG	C	CB	2018	BPM 5
Belarus	MoF	2018	2001	CG,LG,SS	C	CB	2018	BPM 6
Belgium	CB	2018	ESA 2010	CG,SG,LG,SS	A	CB	2018	BPM 6
Belize	MoF	2018	1986	CG,MPC	Mixed	CB	2018	BPM 6
Benin	MoF	2018	1986	CG	C	CB	2017	BPM 6
Bhutan	MoF	2017/18	1986	CG	C	CB	2017/18	BPM 6
Bolivia	MoF	2017	2001	CG,LG,SS,NMPC, NFPC	C	CB	2017	BPM 6
Bosnia and Herzegovina	MoF	2018	2001	CG,SG,LG,SS	Mixed	CB	2018	BPM 6
Botswana	MoF	2018/19	1986	CG	C	CB	2018	BPM 6
Brazil	MoF	2018	2001	CG,SG,LG,SS, MPC,NFPC	C	CB	2018	BPM 6
Brunei Darussalam	MoF	2018	. . .	CG, BCG	C	NSO, MEP, and GAD	2018	BPM 6
Bulgaria	MoF	2018	2001	CG,LG,SS	C	CB	2018	BPM 6
Burkina Faso	MoF	2018	2001	CG	CB	CB	2017	BPM 6
Burundi	MoF	2015	2001	CG	A	CB	2016	BPM 6
Cabo Verde	MoF	2018	2001	CG	A	NSO	2018	BPM 6
Cambodia	MoF	2018	1986	CG,LG	Mixed	CB	2018	BPM 5
Cameroon	MoF	2017	2001	CG,NFPC	C	MoF	2017	BPM 6
Canada	MoF	2018	2001	CG,SG,LG,SS,other	A	NSO	2018	BPM 6
Central African Republic	MoF	2018	2001	CG	C	CB	2017	BPM 5
Chad	MoF	2017	1986	CG,NFPC	C	CB	2015	BPM 6
Chile	MoF	2018	2001	CG,LG	A	CB	2018	BPM 6
China	MoF	2018	. . .	CG,LG	C	GAD	2018	BPM 6
Colombia	MoF	2018	2001	CG,SG,LG,SS	. . .	CB and NSO	2018	BPM 6
Comoros	MoF	2018	1986	CG	Mixed	CB and IMF staff	2018	BPM 5
Democratic Republic of the Congo	MoF	2018	2001	CG,LG	A	CB	2018	BPM 5
Republic of Congo	MoF	2018	2001	CG	A	CB	2017	BPM 6
Costa Rica	MoF and CB	2018	1986	CG	C	CB	2018	BPM 6

Table G. Key Data Documentation *(continued)*

		National Accounts					Prices (CPI)	
Country	Currency	Historical Data Source[1]	Latest Actual Annual Data	Base Year[2]	System of National Accounts	Use of Chain-Weighted Methodology[3]	Historical Data Source[1]	Latest Actual Annual Data
Côte d'Ivoire	CFA franc	NSO	2016	2009	SNA 1993		NSO	2017
Croatia	Croatian kuna	NSO	2018	2010	ESA 2010		NSO	2018
Cyprus	Euro	NSO	2018	2010	ESA 2010	From 1995	NSO	2018
Czech Republic	Czech koruna	NSO	2018	2010	ESA 2010	From 1995	NSO	2018
Denmark	Danish krone	NSO	2018	2010	ESA 2010	From 1980	NSO	2018
Djibouti	Djibouti franc	NSO	2018	2013	SNA 1993		NSO	2018
Dominica	Eastern Caribbean dollar	NSO	2017	2006	SNA 1993		NSO	2016
Dominican Republic	Dominican peso	CB	2018	2007	SNA 2008	From 2007	CB	2018
Ecuador	US dollar	CB	2018	2007	SNA 1993		NSO and CB	2018
Egypt	Egyptian pound	MEP	2017/18	2011/12	SNA 2008		NSO	2017/18
El Salvador	US dollar	CB	2018	2014	SNA 2008		NSO	2018
Equatorial Guinea	CFA franc	MEP and CB	2017	2006	SNA 1993		MEP	2018
Eritrea	Eritrean nakfa	IMF staff	2018	2011	SNA 1993		NSO	2018
Estonia	Euro	NSO	2018	2015	ESA 2010	From 2010	NSO	2018
Eswatini	Swazi lilangeni	NSO	2017	2011	SNA 1993		NSO	2018
Ethiopia	Ethiopian birr	NSO	2017/18	2015/16	SNA 1993		NSO	2018
Fiji	Fijian dollar	NSO	2018	2014	SNA 1993		NSO	2018
Finland	Euro	NSO	2018	2010	ESA 2010	From 1980	NSO	2018
France	Euro	NSO	2018	2014	ESA 2010	From 1980	NSO	2018
Gabon	CFA franc	MoF	2018	2001	SNA 1993		NSO	2018
The Gambia	Gambian dalasi	NSO	2018	2013	SNA 1993		NSO	2018
Georgia	Georgian lari	NSO	2018	2010	SNA 1993	From 1996	NSO	2018
Germany	Euro	NSO	2018	2015	ESA 2010	From 1991	NSO	2018
Ghana	Ghanaian cedi	NSO	2018	2013	SNA 1993		NSO	2018
Greece	Euro	NSO	2018	2010	ESA 2010	From 1995	NSO	2018
Grenada	Eastern Caribbean dollar	NSO	2018	2006	SNA 1993		NSO	2018
Guatemala	Guatemalan quetzal	CB	2018	2001	SNA 1993	From 2001	NSO	2018
Guinea	Guinean franc	NSO	2018	2010	SNA 1993		NSO	2018
Guinea-Bissau	CFA franc	NSO	2018	2005	SNA 1993		NSO	2018
Guyana	Guyanese dollar	NSO	2017	2006[6]	SNA 1993		NSO	2018
Haiti	Haitian gourde	NSO	2017/18	1986/87	SNA 1993		NSO	2017/18
Honduras	Honduran lempira	CB	2017	2000	SNA 1993		CB	2018
Hong Kong SAR	Hong Kong dollar	NSO	2018	2017	SNA 2008	From 1980	NSO	2018
Hungary	Hungarian forint	NSO	2018	2005	ESA 2010	From 2005	IEO	2018
Iceland	Icelandic króna	NSO	2018	2005	ESA 2010	From 1990	NSO	2018
India	Indian rupee	NSO	2017/18	2011/12	SNA 2008		NSO	2017/18
Indonesia	Indonesian rupiah	NSO	2018	2010	SNA 2008		NSO	2018
Iran	Iranian rial	CB	2017/18	2011/12	SNA 1993		CB	2017/18
Iraq	Iraqi dinar	NSO	2017	2007	SNA 1968/93		NSO	2017
Ireland	Euro	NSO	2018	2017	ESA 2010	From 1995	NSO	2018
Israel	New Israeli shekel	NSO	2018	2015	SNA 2008	From 1995	NSO	2018
Italy	Euro	NSO	2018	2010	ESA 2010	From 1980	NSO	2018
Jamaica	Jamaican dollar	NSO	2018	2007	SNA 1993		NSO	2018

Table G. Key Data Documentation *(continued)*

Country	Government Finance: Historical Data Source[1]	Government Finance: Latest Actual Annual Data	Government Finance: Statistics Manual in Use at Source	Government Finance: Subsectors Coverage[4]	Government Finance: Accounting Practice[5]	Balance of Payments: Historical Data Source[1]	Balance of Payments: Latest Actual Annual Data	Balance of Payments: Statistics Manual in Use at Source
Côte d'Ivoire	MoF	2018	1986	CG	A	CB	2017	BPM 6
Croatia	MoF	2018	2001	CG,LG	A	CB	2018	BPM 6
Cyprus	NSO	2018	ESA 2010	CG,LG,SS	A	CB	2018	BPM 6
Czech Republic	MoF	2018	2001	CG,LG,SS	A	NSO	2018	BPM 6
Denmark	NSO	2018	2001	CG,LG,SS	A	NSO	2018	BPM 6
Djibouti	MoF	2018	2001	CG	A	CB	2018	BPM 5
Dominica	MoF	2018/19	1986	CG	C	CB	2018	BPM 6
Dominican Republic	MoF	2018	2014	CG,LG,SS,NMPC	A	CB	2018	BPM 6
Ecuador	CB and MoF	2018	1986	CG,SG,LG,SS,NFPC	Mixed	CB	2018	BPM 6
Egypt	MoF	2017/18	2001	CG,LG,SS,MPC	C	CB	2017/18	BPM 5
El Salvador	MoF and CB	2018	1986	CG,LG,SS	C	CB	2018	BPM 6
Equatorial Guinea	MoF and MEP	2017	1986	CG	C	CB	2017	BPM 5
Eritrea	MoF	2018	2001	CG	C	CB	2018	BPM 5
Estonia	MoF	2018	1986/2001	CG,LG,SS	C	CB	2018	BPM 6
Eswatini	MoF	2018/19	2001	CG	A	CB	2018	BPM 6
Ethiopia	MoF	2017/18	1986	CG,SG,LG,NFPC	C	CB	2017/18	BPM 5
Fiji	MoF	2018	1986	CG	C	CB	2018	BPM 6
Finland	MoF	2018	2001	CG,LG,SS	A	NSO	2018	BPM 6
France	NSO	2018	2001	CG,LG,SS	A	CB	2018	BPM 6
Gabon	IMF staff	2018	2001	CG	A	CB	2018	BPM 5
The Gambia	MoF	2018	1986	CG	C	CB and IMF staff	2018	BPM 5
Georgia	MoF	2017	2001	CG,LG	C	NSO and CB	2018	BPM 6
Germany	NSO	2018	2001	CG,SG,LG,SS	A	CB	2018	BPM 6
Ghana	MoF	2018	2001	CG	C	CB	2018	BPM 5
Greece	NSO	2018	2014	CG,LG,SS	A	CB	2018	BPM 6
Grenada	MoF	2018	2014	CG	CB	CB	2018	BPM 6
Guatemala	MoF	2018	2001	CG	C	CB	2018	BPM 6
Guinea	MoF	2018	2001	CG	C	CB and MEP	2018	BPM 6
Guinea-Bissau	MoF	2018	2001	CG	A	CB	2018	BPM 6
Guyana	MoF	2018	1986	CG,SS,NFPC	C	CB	2018	BPM 6
Haiti	MoF	2017/18	2001	CG	C	CB	2017/18	BPM 5
Honduras	MoF	2018	2014	CG,LG,SS,other	Mixed	CB	2018	BPM 6
Hong Kong SAR	NSO	2018/19	2001	CG	C	NSO	2018	BPM 6
Hungary	MEP and NSO	2018	ESA 2010	CG,LG,SS,NMPC	A	CB	2018	BPM 6
Iceland	NSO	2018	2001	CG,LG,SS	A	CB	2018	BPM 6
India	MoF and IMF staff	2017/18	1986	CG,SG	C	CB	2017/18	BPM 6
Indonesia	MoF	2018	2001	CG,LG	C	CB	2018	BPM 6
Iran	MoF	2017/18	2001	CG	C	CB	2017/18	BPM 5
Iraq	MoF	2017	2001	CG	C	CB	2017	BPM 6
Ireland	MoF and NSO	2018	2001	CG,LG,SS	A	NSO	2018	BPM 6
Israel	MoF and NSO	2017	2014	CG,LG,SS	. . .	NSO	2018	BPM 6
Italy	NSO	2018	2001	CG,LG,SS	A	NSO	2018	BPM 6
Jamaica	MoF	2018/19	1986	CG	C	CB	2017/18	BPM 5

Table G. Key Data Documentation *(continued)*

		National Accounts					Prices (CPI)	
Country	Currency	Historical Data Source[1]	Latest Actual Annual Data	Base Year[2]	System of National Accounts	Use of Chain-Weighted Methodology[3]	Historical Data Source[1]	Latest Actual Annual Data
Japan	Japanese yen	GAD	2018	2011	SNA 2008	From 1980	GAD	2018
Jordan	Jordanian dinar	NSO	2018	2016	SNA 2008		NSO	2018
Kazakhstan	Kazakhstani tenge	NSO	2018	2007	SNA 1993	From 1994	CB	2018
Kenya	Kenyan shilling	NSO	2018	2009	SNA 2008		NSO	2018
Kiribati	Australian dollar	NSO	2017	2006	SNA 2008		IMF staff	2017
Korea	South Korean won	CB	2018	2015	SNA 2008	From 1980	NSO	2018
Kosovo	Euro	NSO	2018	2016	ESA 2010		NSO	2018
Kuwait	Kuwaiti dinar	MEP and NSO	2017	2010	SNA 1993		NSO and MEP	2018
Kyrgyz Republic	Kyrgyz som	NSO	2018	2005	SNA 1993		NSO	2018
Lao P.D.R.	Lao kip	NSO	2018	2012	SNA 1993		NSO	2018
Latvia	Euro	NSO	2018	2010	ESA 2010	From 1995	NSO	2018
Lebanon	Lebanese pound	NSO	2017	2010	SNA 2008	From 2010	NSO	2017/18
Lesotho	Lesotho loti	NSO	2016/17	2012/13	SNA 2008		NSO	2018
Liberia	US dollar	CB	2018	1992	SNA 1993		CB	2018
Libya	Libyan dinar	MEP	2017	2007	SNA 1993		NSO	2017
Lithuania	Euro	NSO	2018	2010	ESA 2010	From 2005	NSO	2018
Luxembourg	Euro	NSO	2018	2010	ESA 2010	From 1995	NSO	2018
Macao SAR	Macanese pataca	NSO	2018	2017	SNA 2008	From 2001	NSO	2018
Madagascar	Malagasy ariary	NSO	2017	2000	SNA 1968		NSO	2018
Malawi	Malawian kwacha	NSO	2011	2010	SNA 2008		NSO	2018
Malaysia	Malaysian ringgit	NSO	2018	2015	SNA 2008		NSO	2018
Maldives	Maldivian rufiyaa	MoF and NSO	2018	2014	SNA 1993		CB	2018
Mali	CFA franc	NSO	2018	1999	SNA 1993		NSO	2018
Malta	Euro	NSO	2018	2010	ESA 2010	From 2000	NSO	2018
Marshall Islands	US dollar	NSO	2016/17	2003/04	SNA 1993		NSO	2016/17
Mauritania	New Mauritanian ouguiya	NSO	2014	2004	SNA 1993		NSO	2017
Mauritius	Mauritian rupee	NSO	2018	2006	SNA 1993	From 1999	NSO	2018
Mexico	Mexican peso	NSO	2018	2013	SNA 2008		NSO	2018
Micronesia	US dollar	NSO	2017/18	2003/04	SNA 1993		NSO	2017/18
Moldova	Moldovan leu	NSO	2018	1995	SNA 2008		NSO	2018
Mongolia	Mongolian tögrög	NSO	2016	2010	SNA 1993		NSO	2016/17
Montenegro	Euro	NSO	2018	2006	ESA 2010		NSO	2018
Morocco	Moroccan dirham	NSO	2018	2007	SNA 1993	From 1998	NSO	2018
Mozambique	Mozambican metical	NSO	2018	2009	SNA 1993/2008		NSO	2018
Myanmar	Myanmar kyat	MEP	2017/18	2010/11	. . .		NSO	2017/18
Namibia	Namibian dollar	NSO	2018	2000	SNA 1993		NSO	2018
Nauru	Australian dollar	. . .	2017/18	2006/07	SNA 1993		NSO	2016/17
Nepal	Nepalese rupee	NSO	2018/19	2000/01	SNA 1993		CB	2017/18
Netherlands	Euro	NSO	2018	2015	ESA 2010	From 1980	NSO	2018
New Zealand	New Zealand dollar	NSO	2018	2009/10	SNA 2008	From 1987	NSO	2018
Nicaragua	Nicaraguan córdoba	CB	2018	2006	SNA 1993	From 1994	CB	2018
Niger	CFA franc	NSO	2018	2000	SNA 1993		NSO	2018
Nigeria	Nigerian naira	NSO	2018	2010	SNA 2008		NSO	2018
North Macedonia	Macedonian denar	NSO	2018	2005	ESA 2010		NSO	2018
Norway	Norwegian krone	NSO	2018	2017	ESA 2010	From 1980	NSO	2018

Table G. Key Data Documentation *(continued)*

	Government Finance					Balance of Payments		
Country	Historical Data Source[1]	Latest Actual Annual Data	Statistics Manual in Use at Source	Subsectors Coverage[4]	Accounting Practice[5]	Historical Data Source[1]	Latest Actual Annual Data	Statistics Manual in Use at Source
Japan	GAD	2017	2014	CG,LG,SS	A	MoF	2018	BPM 6
Jordan	MoF	2018	2001	CG,NFPC	C	CB	2018	BPM 6
Kazakhstan	NSO	2018	2001	CG,LG	A	CB	2018	BPM 6
Kenya	MoF	2018	2001	CG	C	CB	2018	BPM 6
Kiribati	MoF	2017	1986	CG	C	NSO	2017	BPM 6
Korea	MoF	2017	2001	CG,SS	C	CB	2018	BPM 6
Kosovo	MoF	2018	. . .	CG,LG	C	CB	2018	BPM 6
Kuwait	MoF	2017	1986	CG	Mixed	CB	2017	BPM 6
Kyrgyz Republic	MoF	2018	. . .	CG,LG,SS	C	CB	2018	BPM 5
Lao P.D.R.	MoF	2017	2001	CG	C	CB	2017	BPM 5
Latvia	MoF	2018	ESA 2010	CG,LG,SS	C	CB	2018	BPM 6
Lebanon	MoF	2017	2001	CG	Mixed	CB and IMF staff	2017	BPM 5
Lesotho	MoF	2017/18	2001	CG,LG	C	CB	2017/18	BPM 5
Liberia	MoF	2018	2001	CG	A	CB	2018	BPM 5
Libya	MoF	2018	1986	CG,SG,LG	C	CB	2017	BPM 5
Lithuania	MoF	2018	2014	CG,LG,SS	A	CB	2018	BPM 6
Luxembourg	MoF	2018	2001	CG,LG,SS	A	NSO	2018	BPM 6
Macao SAR	MoF	2017	2014	CG,SS	C	NSO	2017	BPM 6
Madagascar	MoF	2018	1986	CG,LG	C	CB	2018	BPM 5
Malawi	MoF	2017/18	1986	CG	C	NSO and GAD	2017	BPM 6
Malaysia	MoF	2018	2001	CG,SG,LG	C	NSO	2018	BPM 6
Maldives	MoF	2018	1986	CG	C	CB	2018	BPM 6
Mali	MoF	2018	2001	CG	Mixed	CB	2018	BPM 6
Malta	NSO	2018	2001	CG,SS	A	NSO	2018	BPM 6
Marshall Islands	MoF	2016/17	2001	CG,LG,SS	A	NSO	2016/17	BPM 6
Mauritania	MoF	2017	1986	CG	C	CB	2016	BPM 5
Mauritius	MoF	2017/18	2001	CG,LG,NFPC	C	CB	2018	BPM 6
Mexico	MoF	2018	2014	CG,SS,NMPC,NFPC	C	CB	2018	BPM 6
Micronesia	MoF	2017/18	2001	CG,SG,LG,SS	. . .	NSO	2017/18	BPM 5
Moldova	MoF	2018	1986	CG,LG	C	CB	2018	BPM 6
Mongolia	MoF	2017/18	2001	CG,SG,LG,SS	C	CB	2016	BPM 6
Montenegro	MoF	2018	1986/2001	CG,LG,SS	C	CB	2018	BPM 6
Morocco	MEP	2018	2001	CG	A	GAD	2018	BPM 6
Mozambique	MoF	2018	2001	CG,SG	Mixed	CB	2018	BPM 6
Myanmar	MoF	2017/18	2014	CG,NFPC	C	IMF staff	2017/18	BPM 6
Namibia	MoF	2018/19	2001	CG	C	CB	2018	BPM 6
Nauru	MoF	2016/17	2001	CG	Mixed	IMF staff	2016/17	BPM 6
Nepal	MoF	2017/18	2001	CG	C	CB	2017/18	BPM 5
Netherlands	MoF	2018	2001	CG,LG,SS	A	CB	2018	BPM 6
New Zealand	MoF	2017/18	2001	CG, LG	A	NSO	2018	BPM 6
Nicaragua	MoF	2018	1986	CG,LG,SS	C	IMF staff	2018	BPM 6
Niger	MoF	2017	1986	CG	A	CB	2018	BPM 6
Nigeria	MoF	2018	2001	CG,SG,LG	C	CB	2018	BPM 6
North Macedonia	MoF	2018	1986	CG,SG,SS	C	CB	2018	BPM 6
Norway	NSO and MoF	2018	2014	CG,LG,SS	A	NSO	2017	BPM 6

Table G. Key Data Documentation *(continued)*

		National Accounts					Prices (CPI)	
Country	Currency	Historical Data Source[1]	Latest Actual Annual Data	Base Year[2]	System of National Accounts	Use of Chain-Weighted Methodology[3]	Historical Data Source[1]	Latest Actual Annual Data
Oman	Omani rial	NSO	2018	2010	SNA 1993		NSO	2018
Pakistan	Pakistan rupee	NSO	2017/18	2005/06[6]	. . .		NSO	2017/18
Palau	US dollar	MoF	2017/18	2014/15	SNA 1993		MoF	2017/18
Panama	US dollar	NSO	2018	2007	SNA 1993	From 2007	NSO	2018
Papua New Guinea	Papua New Guinea kina	NSO and MoF	2015	2013	SNA 1993		NSO	2015
Paraguay	Paraguayan guaraní	CB	2018	2014	SNA 2008		CB	2018
Peru	Peruvian nuevo sol	CB	2018	2007	SNA 1993		CB	2018
Philippines	Philippine peso	NSO	2018	2000	SNA 2008		NSO	2018
Poland	Polish zloty	NSO	2018	2010	ESA 2010	From 1995	NSO	2018
Portugal	Euro	NSO	2018	2016	ESA 2010	From 1980	NSO	2018
Puerto Rico	US dollar	NSO	2017/18	1954	SNA 1968		NSO	2017/18
Qatar	Qatari riyal	NSO and MEP	2018	2013	SNA 1993		NSO and MEP	2018
Romania	Romanian leu	NSO	2018	2010	ESA 2010	From 2000	NSO	2018
Russia	Russian ruble	NSO	2018	2016	SNA 2008	From 1995	NSO	2018
Rwanda	Rwandan franc	NSO	2018	2014	SNA 2008		NSO	2018
Samoa	Samoan tala	NSO	2017/18	2009/10	SNA 1993		NSO	2017/18
San Marino	Euro	NSO	2017	2007	. . .		NSO	2017
São Tomé and Príncipe	São Tomé and Príncipe dobra	NSO	2017	2008	SNA 1993		NSO	2017
Saudi Arabia	Saudi riyal	NSO	2018	2010	SNA 1993		NSO	2018
Senegal	CFA franc	NSO	2018	2014	SNA 1993		NSO	2018
Serbia	Serbian dinar	NSO	2018	2010	ESA 2010	From 2010	NSO	2018
Seychelles	Seychelles rupee	NSO	2017	2006	SNA 1993		NSO	2018
Sierra Leone	Sierra Leonean leone	NSO	2017	2006	SNA 1993	From 2010	NSO	2017
Singapore	Singapore dollar	NSO	2018	2015	SNA 2008	From 2015	NSO	2018
Slovak Republic	Euro	NSO	2018	2010	ESA 2010	From 1997	NSO	2018
Slovenia	Euro	NSO	2018	2010	ESA 2010	From 2000	NSO	2018
Solomon Islands	Solomon Islands dollar	CB	2018	2004	SNA 1993		NSO	2018
Somalia	US dollar	CB	2018	2013	SNA 1993		CB	2018
South Africa	South African rand	NSO	2018	2010	SNA 2008		NSO	2018
South Sudan	South Sudanese pound	NSO	2017	2010	SNA 1993		NSO	2018
Spain	Euro	NSO	2018	2010	ESA 2010	From 1995	NSO	2018
Sri Lanka	Sri Lankan rupee	NSO	2018	2010	SNA 1993		NSO	2018
St. Kitts and Nevis	Eastern Caribbean dollar	NSO	2018	2006	SNA 1993		NSO	2018
St. Lucia	Eastern Caribbean dollar	NSO	2018	2006	SNA 1993		NSO	2018
St. Vincent and the Grenadines	Eastern Caribbean dollar	NSO	2018	2006[6]	SNA 1993		NSO	2018
Sudan	Sudanese pound	NSO	2016	1982	SNA 1968		NSO	2018
Suriname	Surinamese dollar	NSO	2017	2007	SNA 1993		NSO	2018

Table G. Key Data Documentation *(continued)*

	Government Finance					Balance of Payments		
Country	Historical Data Source[1]	Latest Actual Annual Data	Statistics Manual in Use at Source	Subsectors Coverage[4]	Accounting Practice[5]	Historical Data Source[1]	Latest Actual Annual Data	Statistics Manual in Use at Source
Oman	MoF	2018	2001	CG	C	CB	2018	BPM 5
Pakistan	MoF	2017/18	1986	CG,SG,LG	C	CB	2017/18	BPM 6
Palau	MoF	2017/18	2001	CG	. . .	MoF	2017/18	BPM 6
Panama	MoF	2018	1986	CG,SG,LG,SS,NFPC	C	NSO	2018	BPM 6
Papua New Guinea	MoF	2015	1986	CG	C	CB	2015	BPM 5
Paraguay	MoF	2018	2001	CG,SG,LG,SS,MPC, NFPC	C	CB	2018	BPM 6
Peru	CB and MoF	2018	2001	CG,SG,LG,SS	Mixed	CB	2018	BPM 5
Philippines	MoF	2018	2001	CG,LG,SS	C	CB	2018	BPM 6
Poland	MoF and NSO	2018	ESA 2010	CG,LG,SS	A	CB	2018	BPM 6
Portugal	NSO	2018	2001	CG,LG,SS	A	CB	2018	BPM 6
Puerto Rico	MEP	2015/16	2001	. . .	A	. . .	. . .	. . .
Qatar	MoF	2018	1986	CG	C	CB and IMF staff	2018	BPM 5
Romania	MoF	2018	2001	CG,LG,SS	C	CB	2018	BPM 6
Russia	MoF	2018	2001	CG,SG,SS	Mixed	CB	2018	BPM 6
Rwanda	MoF	2018	1986	CG,LG	Mixed	CB	2018	BPM 6
Samoa	MoF	2017/18	2001	CG	A	CB	2017/18	BPM 6
San Marino	MoF	2017	. . .	CG	. . .	Other	2017	. . .
São Tomé and Príncipe	MoF and Customs	2018	2001	CG	C	CB	2017	BPM 6
Saudi Arabia	MoF	2018	2014	CG	C	CB	2018	BPM 6
Senegal	MoF	2018	2001	CG	C	CB and IMF staff	2018	BPM 6
Serbia	MoF	2018	1986/2001	CG,SG,LG,SS,other	C	CB	2018	BPM 6
Seychelles	MoF	2018	1986	CG,SS	C	CB	2016	BPM 6
Sierra Leone	MoF	2018	1986	CG	C	CB	2017	BPM 5
Singapore	MoF and NSO	2018/19	2014	CG	C	NSO	2018	BPM 6
Slovak Republic	NSO	2018	2001	CG,LG,SS	A	CB	2018	BPM 6
Slovenia	MoF	2018	1986	CG,SG,LG,SS	C	NSO	2018	BPM 6
Solomon Islands	MoF	2017	1986	CG	C	CB	2018	BPM 6
Somalia	MoF	2018	2001	CG	C	CB	2018	BPM 5
South Africa	MoF	2018	2001	CG,SG,SS	C	CB	2018	BPM 6
South Sudan	MoF and MEP	2018	. . .	CG	C	MoF, NSO, and MEP	2018	BPM 6
Spain	MoF and NSO	2018	ESA 2010	CG,SG,LG,SS	A	CB	2018	BPM 6
Sri Lanka	MoF	2018	2001	CG	C	CB	2018	BPM 6
St. Kitts and Nevis	MoF	2018	1986	CG, SG	C	CB	2018	BPM 6
St. Lucia	MoF	2017/18	1986	CG	C	CB	2018	BPM 6
St. Vincent and the Grenadines	MoF	2018	1986	CG	C	CB	2017	BPM 6
Sudan	MoF	2018	2001	CG	Mixed	CB	2018	BPM 6
Suriname	MoF	2017	1986	CG	Mixed	CB	2017	BPM 5

Table G. Key Data Documentation *(continued)*

		National Accounts					Prices (CPI)	
Country	Currency	Historical Data Source[1]	Latest Actual Annual Data	Base Year[2]	System of National Accounts	Use of Chain-Weighted Methodology[3]	Historical Data Source[1]	Latest Actual Annual Data
Sweden	Swedish krona	NSO	2018	2018	ESA 2010	From 1993	NSO	2018
Switzerland	Swiss franc	NSO	2017	2010	ESA 2010	From 1980	NSO	2018
Syria	Syrian pound	NSO	2010	2000	SNA 1993		NSO	2011
Taiwan Province of China	New Taiwan dollar	NSO	2018	2011	SNA 2008		NSO	2018
Tajikistan	Tajik somoni	NSO	2017	1995	SNA 1993		NSO	2017
Tanzania	Tanzanian shilling	NSO	2018	2015	SNA 2008		NSO	2018
Thailand	Thai baht	MEP	2018	2002	SNA 1993	From 1993	MEP	2018
Timor-Leste	US dollar	MoF	2017	2015[6]	SNA 2008		NSO	2018
Togo	CFA franc	NSO	2016	2007	SNA 1993		NSO	2018
Tonga	Tongan pa'anga	CB	2018	2010	SNA 1993		CB	2018
Trinidad and Tobago	Trinidad and Tobago dollar	NSO	2017	2012	SNA 1993		NSO	2018
Tunisia	Tunisian dinar	NSO	2017	2010	SNA 1993	From 2009	NSO	2016
Turkey	Turkish lira	NSO	2018	2009	ESA 2010	From 2009	NSO	2018
Turkmenistan	New Turkmen manat	NSO	2017	2008	SNA 1993	From 2000	NSO	2017
Tuvalu	Australian dollar	PFTAC advisors	2015	2005	SNA 1993		NSO	2018
Uganda	Ugandan shilling	NSO	2018	2010	SNA 1993		CB	2018/19
Ukraine	Ukrainian hryvnia	NSO	2018	2010	SNA 2008	From 2005	NSO	2018
United Arab Emirates	U.A.E. dirham	NSO	2017	2010	SNA 2008		NSO	2018
United Kingdom	British pound	NSO	2018	2016	ESA 2010	From 1980	NSO	2018
United States	US dollar	NSO	2018	2012	SNA 2008	From 1980	NSO	2018
Uruguay	Uruguayan peso	CB	2018	2005	SNA 1993		NSO	2018
Uzbekistan	Uzbek sum	NSO	2018	2015	SNA 1993		NSO and IMF staff	2018
Vanuatu	Vanuatu vatu	NSO	2017	2006	SNA 1993		NSO	2017
Venezuela	Venezuelan bolívar soberano	CB	2018	1997	SNA 2008		CB	2018
Vietnam	Vietnamese dong	NSO	2018	2010	SNA 1993		NSO	2018
Yemen	Yemeni rial	IMF staff	2017	1990	SNA 1993		NSO,CB, and IMF staff	2017
Zambia	Zambian kwacha	NSO	2017	2010	SNA 2008		NSO	2018
Zimbabwe	RTGS dollar	NSO	2015	2012	. . .		NSO	2018

Table G. Key Data Documentation *(continued)*

Country	Government Finance					Balance of Payments		
	Historical Data Source[1]	Latest Actual Annual Data	Statistics Manual in Use at Source	Subsectors Coverage[4]	Accounting Practice[5]	Historical Data Source[1]	Latest Actual Annual Data	Statistics Manual in Use at Source
Sweden	MoF	2018	2001	CG,LG,SS	A	NSO	2018	BPM 6
Switzerland	MoF	2017	2001	CG,SG,LG,SS	A	CB	2018	BPM 6
Syria	MoF	2009	1986	CG	C	CB	2009	BPM 5
Taiwan Province of China	MoF	2018	2001	CG,LG,SS	C	CB	2018	BPM 6
Tajikistan	MoF	2017	1986	CG,LG,SS	C	CB	2016	BPM 6
Tanzania	MoF	2018	1986	CG,LG	C	CB	2018	BPM 5
Thailand	MoF	2017/18	2001	CG,BCG,LG,SS	A	CB	2018	BPM 6
Timor-Leste	MoF	2017	2001	CG	C	CB	2017	BPM 6
Togo	MoF	2018	2001	CG	C	CB	2017	BPM 6
Tonga	MoF	2017	2014	CG	C	CB and NSO	2018	BPM 6
Trinidad and Tobago	MoF	2017/18	1986	CG	C	CB	2018	BPM 6
Tunisia	MoF	2016	1986	CG	C	CB	2018	BPM 5
Turkey	MoF	2018	2001	CG,LG,SS,other	A	CB	2018	BPM 6
Turkmenistan	MoF	2017	1986	CG,LG	C	NSO and IMF staff	2015	BPM 6
Tuvalu	MoF	2018	. . .	CG	Mixed	IMF staff	2012	BPM 6
Uganda	MoF	2018	2001	CG	C	CB	2018	BPM 6
Ukraine	MoF	2018	2001	CG,LG,SS	C	CB	2018	BPM 6
United Arab Emirates	MoF	2017	2001	CG,BCG,SG,SS	C	CB	2017	BPM 5
United Kingdom	NSO	2018	2001	CG,LG	A	NSO	2018	BPM 6
United States	MEP	2018	2014	CG,SG,LG	A	NSO	2018	BPM 6
Uruguay	MoF	2018	1986	CG,LG,SS,NFPC, NMPC	C	CB	2018	BPM 6
Uzbekistan	MoF	2018	2014	CG,SG,LG,SS	C	MEP	2018	BPM 6
Vanuatu	MoF	2017	2001	CG	C	CB	2017	BPM 6
Venezuela	MoF	2017	2001	BCG,NFPC	C	CB	2018	BPM 5
Vietnam	MoF	2017	2001	CG,SG,LG	C	CB	2018	BPM 5
Yemen	MoF	2017	2001	CG,LG	C	IMF staff	2017	BPM 5
Zambia	MoF	2017	1986	CG	C	CB	2017	BPM 6
Zimbabwe	MoF	2017	1986	CG	C	CB and MoF	2017	BPM 6

Note: BPM = *Balance of Payments Manual*; CPI = consumer price index; ESA = European System of National Accounts; SNA = System of National Accounts.
[1]CB = central bank; Customs = Customs Authority; GAD = General Administration Department; IEO = international economic organization; MEP = Ministry of Economy, Planning, Commerce, and/or Development; MoF = Ministry of Finance and/or Treasury; NSO = National Statistics Office; PFTAC = Pacific Financial Technical Assistance Centre.
[2]National accounts base year is the period with which other periods are compared and the period for which prices appear in the denominators of the price relationships used to calculate the index.
[3]Use of chain-weighted methodology allows countries to measure GDP growth more accurately by reducing or eliminating the downward biases in volume series built on index numbers that average volume components using weights from a year in the moderately distant past.
[4]BCG = budgetary central government; CG = central government; EUA = extrabudgetary units/accounts; LG = local government; MPC = monetary public corporation, including central bank; NFPC = nonfinancial public corporation; NMPC = nonmonetary financial public corporation; SG = state government; SS = social security fund; TG = territorial governments.
[5]Accounting standard: A = accrual accounting; C = cash accounting; CB = commitments basis accounting; Mixed = combination of accrual and cash accounting.
[6]Base year is not equal to 100 because the nominal GDP is not measured in the same way as real GDP or the data are seasonally adjusted.

Box A1. Economic Policy Assumptions Underlying the Projections for Selected Economies

Fiscal Policy Assumptions

The short-term fiscal policy assumptions used in the *World Economic Outlook* (WEO) are normally based on officially announced budgets, adjusted for differences between the national authorities and the IMF staff regarding macroeconomic assumptions and projected fiscal outturns. When no official budget has been announced, projections incorporate policy measures that are judged likely to be implemented. The medium-term fiscal projections are similarly based on a judgment about the most likely path of policies. For cases in which the IMF staff has insufficient information to assess the authorities' budget intentions and prospects for policy implementation, an unchanged structural primary balance is assumed unless indicated otherwise. Specific assumptions used in regard to some of the advanced economies follow. (See also Tables B5 to B9 in the online section of the Statistical Appendix for data on fiscal net lending/borrowing and structural balances.)[1]

Argentina: Fiscal projections are based on the available information regarding budget outturn and budget plans for the federal and provincial governments, fiscal measures announced by the authorities, and the IMF staff's macroeconomic projections.

Australia: Fiscal projections are based on data from the Australian Bureau of Statistics, the fiscal year 2019/20 budgets of the commonwealth and states, and the IMF staff's estimates and projections.

Austria: Fiscal projections are based on data from Statistics Austria, the authorities' projections, and the IMF staff's estimates and projections.

Belgium: Projections are based on the 2019–22 Stability Programme and other available information on the authorities' fiscal plans, with adjustments for the IMF staff's assumptions.

Brazil: Fiscal projections for 2019 take into account the deficit target approved in the budget law.

Canada: Projections use the baseline forecasts in the 2019 federal budget and the latest provincial budget updates as available. The IMF staff makes some adjustments to these forecasts, including for differences in macroeconomic projections. The IMF staff's forecast also incorporates the most recent data releases from Statistics Canada's Canadian System of National Economic Accounts, including federal, provincial, and territorial budgetary outturns through the first quarter of 2019.

Chile: Projections are based on the authorities' budget projections, adjusted to reflect the IMF staff's projections for GDP and copper prices.

China: Fiscal expansion is expected for 2019 due to a series of tax reforms and expenditure measures in response to the economic slowdown.

Denmark: Estimates for 2018 are aligned with the latest official budget numbers, adjusted where appropriate for the IMF staff's macroeconomic assumptions. For 2019, the projections incorporate key features of the medium-term fiscal plan as embodied in the authorities' Convergence Programme 2019 submitted to the European Union.

France: Projections for 2019 and beyond are based on the measures of the 2018 budget law, the multiyear law for 2018–22, and the 2019 budget law, adjusted for differences in assumptions on macroeconomic and financial variables, and revenue projections. Historical fiscal data reflect the May 2019 revisions and update of the historical fiscal accounts, debt data, and national accounts.

Germany: The IMF staff's projections for 2019 and beyond are based on the 2019 Stability Program and data updates from the national statistical agency, adjusted for the differences in the IMF staff's macroeconomic framework and assumptions concerning revenue elasticities. The estimate of gross debt includes portfolios of impaired assets and noncore business transferred to institutions that are winding up, as well as other financial sector and EU support operations.

Greece: Greece's general government primary balance estimate for 2018 is based on the April 2019 Excessive Deficit Procedure release by Eurostat. Historical data since 2010 reflect adjustments in line with the primary balance definition under the enhanced surveillance framework for Greece.

[1] The output gap is actual minus potential output, as a percentage of potential output. Structural balances are expressed as a percentage of potential output. The structural balance is the actual net lending/borrowing minus the effects of cyclical output from potential output, corrected for one-time and other factors, such as asset and commodity prices and output composition effects. Changes in the structural balance consequently include effects of temporary fiscal measures, the impact of fluctuations in interest rates and debt-service costs, and other noncyclical fluctuations in net lending/borrowing. The computations of structural balances are based on the IMF staff's estimates of potential GDP and revenue and expenditure elasticities. (See Annex I of the October 1993 WEO.) Net debt is calculated as gross debt minus financial assets corresponding to debt instruments. Estimates of the output gap and of the structural balance are subject to significant margins of uncertainty.

Box A1 *(continued)*

Hong Kong Special Administrative Region: Projections are based on the authorities' medium-term fiscal projections on expenditures.

Hungary: Fiscal projections include the IMF staff's projections of the macroeconomic framework and of the impact of recent legislative measures, as well as fiscal policy plans announced in the 2018 budget.

India: Historical data are based on budgetary execution data. Projections are based on available information on the authorities' fiscal plans, with adjustments for the IMF staff's assumptions. Subnational data are incorporated with a lag of up to one year; general government data are thus finalized well after central government data. IMF and Indian presentations differ, particularly regarding disinvestment and license-auction proceeds, net versus gross recording of revenues in certain minor categories, and some public-sector lending.

Indonesia: IMF projections are based on moderate tax policy and administration reforms and a gradual increase in social and capital spending over the medium term in line with fiscal space.

Ireland: Fiscal projections are based on the country's Budget 2019.

Israel: Historical data are based on government finance statistics data prepared by the Central Bureau of Statistics. The medium-term fiscal projections are not in line with medium-term fiscal targets, consistent with long experience of revisions to those targets.

Italy: The IMF staff's estimates and projections are informed by the fiscal plans included in the government's 2019 budget and April 2019 Economic and Financial Document. The IMF staff assumes that the automatic value-added tax hikes for future years will be canceled.

Japan: The projections reflect the consumption tax rate increase in October 2019, the mitigating measures included in the FY2019 budget and tax reform, and other fiscal measures already announced by the government.

Korea: The medium-term forecast incorporates the medium-term path for public spending announced by the government.

Mexico: Fiscal projections for 2019 are broadly in line with the approved budget; projections for 2020 onward assume compliance with rules established in the Fiscal Responsibility Law.

Netherlands: Fiscal projections for 2019–24 are based on the authorities' Bureau for Economic Policy Analysis budget projections, after differences in macroeconomic assumptions are adjusted for. Historical data were revised following the June 2014 Central Bureau of Statistics release of revised macro data because of the adoption of the European System of National and Regional Accounts (ESA 2010) and the revisions of data sources.

New Zealand: Fiscal projections are based on the fiscal year 2019/20 budget and the IMF staff's estimates.

Portugal: The projections for the current year are based on the authorities' approved budget, adjusted to reflect the IMF staff's macroeconomic forecast. Projections thereafter are based on the assumption of unchanged policies.

Puerto Rico: Fiscal projections are based on the Puerto Rico Fiscal and Economic Growth Plans (FEGPs), which were prepared in October 2018, and are certified by the Oversight Board. In line with this plan's assumptions, IMF projections assume federal aid for rebuilding after Hurricane Maria, which devastated the island in September 2017. The projections also assume revenue losses from the following: elimination of federal funding for the Affordable Care Act starting in 2020 for Puerto Rico; elimination of federal tax incentives starting in 2018 that had neutralized the effects of Puerto Rico's Act 154 on foreign firms; and the effects of the Tax Cuts and Jobs Act, which reduce the tax advantage of US firms producing in Puerto Rico. Given sizable policy uncertainty, some FEGP and IMF assumptions may differ, in particular those relating to the effects of the corporate tax reform, tax compliance, and tax adjustments (fees and rates); reduction of subsidies and expenses, freezing of payroll operational costs, and improvement of mobility; reduction of expenses; and increased health care efficiency. On the expenditure side, measures include extension of Act 66, which freezes much government spending, through 2020; reduction of operating costs; decreases in government subsidies; and spending cuts in education. Although IMF policy assumptions are similar to those in the FEGP scenario with full measures, the IMF's projections of fiscal revenues, expenditures, and balance are different from the FEGPs'. This stems from two main differences in methodologies: first, while IMF projections are on an accrual basis, the FEGPs' are on a cash basis. Second, the IMF and FEGPs make very different macroeconomic assumptions.

Russia: Projections for 2019–24 are based on the new oil price rule, with adjustments by the IMF staff.

Box A1 *(continued)*

Saudi Arabia: The IMF staff baseline projections of total government revenues, except exported oil revenues, are based on IMF staff understanding of government policies as announced in the 2019 Budget and Fiscal Balance Program 2019 Update. Exported oil revenues are based on WEO baseline oil prices and the assumption that Saudi Arabia will overperform the Organization of Petroleum Exporting Countries+ agreement. Expenditure projections take the 2019 budget and the Fiscal Balance Program 2019 Update as a starting point and reflect IMF staff estimates of the latest changes in policies and economic developments.

Singapore: For fiscal year 2019, projections are based on budget numbers. For the rest of the projection period, the IMF staff assumes unchanged policies.

South Africa: Fiscal assumptions are based on the 2019 Budget Review and the special appropriation of July 2019 for Eskom. Nontax revenue excludes transactions in financial assets and liabilities, as they involve primarily revenues associated with realized exchange rate valuation gains from the holding of foreign currency deposits, sale of assets, and conceptually similar items.

Spain: For 2019, projections assume expenditures under the 2018 budget extension scenario and already legislated measures, including pension and public wage increases, and the IMF staff's projection of revenues. For 2020 and beyond, fiscal projections are IMF staff projections, which assume an unchanged structural primary balance.

Sweden: Fiscal projections take into account the authorities' projections based on the 2019 Spring Budget. The impact of cyclical developments on the fiscal accounts is calculated using the 2014 Organisation for Economic Co-operation and Development's elasticity to take into account output and employment gaps.

Switzerland: The projections assume that fiscal policy is adjusted as necessary to keep fiscal balances in line with the requirements of Switzerland's fiscal rules.

Turkey: The fiscal projections assume a more negative primary and overall balance than envisaged in the authorities' New Economic Program 2019–21, based partly on recent weak growth and fiscal outturns and partly on definitional differences: the basis for the projections in the WEO and *Fiscal Monitor* is the IMF-defined fiscal balance, which excludes some revenue and expenditure items that are included in the authorities' headline balance.

United Kingdom: Fiscal projections are based on the UK's Spring Statement 2019, with expenditure projections based on the budgeted nominal values, but adjusted to account for the Spending Round 2019, and with revenue projections adjusted for differences between the IMF staff's forecasts of macroeconomic variables (such as GDP growth and inflation) and the forecasts of these variables assumed in the authorities' fiscal projections. The IMF staff's data exclude public sector banks and the effect of transferring assets from the Royal Mail Pension Plan to the public sector in April 2012. Real government consumption and investment are part of the real GDP path, which, according to the IMF staff, may or may not be the same as projected by the UK Office for Budget Responsibility. Fiscal year GDP is different from current year GDP. The fiscal accounts are presented in terms of fiscal year. Projections do not take into account revisions to the accounting (including on student loans) implemented on September 24, 2019.

United States: Fiscal projections are based on the August 2019 Congressional Budget Office baseline, adjusted for the IMF staff's policy and macroeconomic assumptions. Projections incorporate the effects of tax reform (the Tax Cuts and Jobs Act, signed into law at the end of 2017), the Bipartisan Budget Act of 2018 passed in February 2018, and the Bipartisan Budget Act of 2019 passed in July 2019. Finally, fiscal projections are adjusted to reflect the IMF staff's forecasts for key macroeconomic and financial variables and different accounting treatment of financial sector support and of defined-benefit pension plans and are converted to a general government basis. Data is compiled using SNA 2008; when translated into government finance statistics, this is in accordance with the *Government Finance Statistics Manual 2014*. Because of data limitations, most series begin in 2001.

Monetary Policy Assumptions

Monetary policy assumptions are based on the established policy framework in each country. In most cases, this implies a nonaccommodative stance over the business cycle: official interest rates will increase when economic indicators suggest that inflation will rise above its acceptable rate or range; they will decrease when indicators suggest inflation will not exceed the acceptable rate or range, that output growth is below its potential rate, and that the margin of slack in the economy is significant. On this basis, the London interbank offered rate on six-month US

Box A1 *(continued)*

dollar deposits is assumed to average 2.3 percent in 2019 and 2.0 percent in 2020 (see Table 1.1). The rate on three-month euro deposits is assumed to average –0.4 percent in 2019 and –0.6 percent in 2020. The interest rate on six-month Japanese yen deposits is assumed to average 0.0 percent in 2019 and –0.1 percent in 2020.

Argentina: Monetary policy assumptions are consistent with the current monetary policy framework, which targets zero base money growth in seasonally adjusted terms.

Australia: Monetary policy assumptions are in line with market expectations.

Brazil: Monetary policy assumptions are consistent with gradual convergence of inflation toward the middle of the target range.

Canada: Monetary policy assumptions are based on the IMF staff's analysis.

China: Monetary policy is expected to remain on hold.

Denmark: Monetary policy is to maintain the peg to the euro.

Euro area: Monetary policy assumptions for euro area member countries are in line with market expectations.

Hong Kong Special Administrative Region: The IMF staff assumes that the currency board system will remain intact.

India: Monetary policy projections are consistent with achieving the Reserve Bank of India's inflation target over the medium term.

Indonesia: Monetary policy assumptions are in line with the maintenance of inflation within the central bank's targeted band.

Japan: Monetary policy assumptions are in line with market expectations.

Korea: The projections assume no change in the policy rate in 2019–20.

Mexico: Monetary policy assumptions are consistent with attaining the inflation target.

Russia: Monetary projections assume that the Central Bank of Russia is moving toward a neutral monetary policy stance.

Saudi Arabia: Monetary policy projections are based on the continuation of the exchange rate peg to the US dollar.

Singapore: Broad money is projected to grow in line with the projected growth in nominal GDP.

South Africa: Monetary policy will be moderately accommodative.

Sweden: Monetary projections are in line with Riksbank projections.

Switzerland: The projections assume no change in the policy rate in 2019–20.

Turkey: The outlook for monetary and financial conditions assumes further monetary policy easing in 2019.

United Kingdom: The short-term interest rate path is based on market interest rate expectations.

United States: The IMF staff expects the Federal Open Market Committee to continue to adjust the federal funds target rate in line with the broader macroeconomic outlook.

List of Tables

Output

Inflation

Financial Policies

Foreign Trade

Current Account Transactions

Balance of Payments and External Financing

Flow of Funds

Medium-Term Baseline Scenario

Table A1. Summary of World Output[1]

(Annual percent change)

	Average									Projections		
	2001–10	2011	2012	2013	2014	2015	2016	2017	2018	2019	2020	2024
World	**3.9**	**4.3**	**3.5**	**3.5**	**3.6**	**3.5**	**3.4**	**3.8**	**3.6**	**3.0**	**3.4**	**3.6**
Advanced Economies	**1.7**	**1.7**	**1.2**	**1.4**	**2.1**	**2.3**	**1.7**	**2.5**	**2.3**	**1.7**	**1.7**	**1.6**
United States	1.7	1.6	2.2	1.8	2.5	2.9	1.6	2.4	2.9	2.4	2.1	1.6
Euro Area	1.2	1.6	–0.9	–0.3	1.4	2.1	1.9	2.5	1.9	1.2	1.4	1.3
Japan	0.6	–0.1	1.5	2.0	0.4	1.2	0.6	1.9	0.8	0.9	0.5	0.5
Other Advanced Economies[2]	2.8	3.0	2.0	2.4	2.9	2.1	2.1	2.7	2.2	1.5	1.8	2.1
Emerging Market and Developing Economies	**6.2**	**6.4**	**5.4**	**5.1**	**4.7**	**4.3**	**4.6**	**4.8**	**4.5**	**3.9**	**4.6**	**4.8**
Regional Groups												
Emerging and Developing Asia	8.5	7.9	7.0	6.9	6.8	6.8	6.7	6.6	6.4	5.9	6.0	6.0
Emerging and Developing Europe	4.4	5.8	3.0	3.1	1.9	0.8	1.8	3.9	3.1	1.8	2.5	2.5
Latin America and the Caribbean	3.2	4.6	2.9	2.9	1.3	0.3	–0.6	1.2	1.0	0.2	1.8	2.7
Middle East and Central Asia	5.3	4.6	4.9	3.0	3.1	2.6	5.0	2.3	1.9	0.9	2.9	3.3
Sub-Saharan Africa	5.9	5.3	4.7	5.2	5.1	3.1	1.4	3.0	3.2	3.2	3.6	4.2
Analytical Groups												
By Source of Export Earnings												
Fuel	5.5	5.2	5.0	2.6	2.2	0.3	2.2	0.9	0.8	–0.3	2.0	2.1
Nonfuel	6.4	6.7	5.4	5.7	5.3	5.2	5.1	5.6	5.3	4.7	5.0	5.3
Of Which, Primary Products	4.2	4.9	2.5	4.1	2.2	2.9	1.7	2.8	1.8	1.2	2.4	3.5
By External Financing Source												
Net Debtor Economies	5.1	5.3	4.4	4.7	4.5	4.1	4.1	4.8	4.6	4.0	4.6	5.1
Net Debtor Economies by Debt-Servicing Experience												
Economies with Arrears and/or Rescheduling during 2014–18	5.0	2.5	1.9	3.0	2.0	0.4	2.3	2.8	3.4	3.4	4.0	4.8
Other Groups												
European Union	1.6	1.8	–0.4	0.3	1.9	2.5	2.1	2.8	2.2	1.5	1.6	1.5
Low-Income Developing Countries	6.5	5.3	4.7	6.0	6.0	4.5	3.6	4.7	5.0	5.0	5.1	5.5
Middle East and North Africa	5.0	4.4	4.9	2.4	2.7	2.4	5.4	1.8	1.1	0.1	2.7	2.9
Memorandum												
Median Growth Rate												
Advanced Economies	2.2	1.9	1.0	1.4	2.5	2.2	2.4	3.0	2.7	1.8	1.8	1.7
Emerging Market and Developing Economies	4.6	4.7	4.2	4.1	3.8	3.3	3.2	3.5	3.5	3.2	3.5	3.5
Low-Income Developing Countries	5.3	6.0	5.1	5.2	5.4	3.9	4.2	4.5	4.0	5.0	5.0	4.8
Output per Capita[3]												
Advanced Economies	1.1	1.2	0.7	0.9	1.6	1.8	1.2	2.0	1.8	1.3	1.3	1.2
Emerging Market and Developing Economies	4.6	4.8	3.6	3.6	3.2	2.8	3.1	3.3	3.2	2.5	3.3	3.5
Low-Income Developing Countries	3.8	3.6	1.7	3.6	3.7	1.9	1.2	2.4	2.8	2.7	2.9	3.2
World Growth Rate Based on Market Exchange Rates	**2.6**	**3.1**	**2.5**	**2.6**	**2.8**	**2.8**	**2.6**	**3.2**	**3.1**	**2.5**	**2.7**	**2.9**
Value of World Output (billions of US dollars)												
At Market Exchange Rates	49,881	73,312	74,690	76,842	78,944	74,779	75,824	80,262	84,930	86,599	90,520	111,569
At Purchasing Power Parities	70,721	95,143	100,020	105,216	110,903	115,799	120,832	127,703	135,436	141,860	149,534	186,156

[1]Real GDP.

[2]Excludes the United States, euro area countries, and Japan.

[3]Output per capita is in international currency at purchasing power parity.

Table A2. Advanced Economies: Real GDP and Total Domestic Demand[1]

(Annual percent change)

													Fourth Quarter[2]		
	Average									Projections				Projections	
	2001–10	2011	2012	2013	2014	2015	2016	2017	2018	2019	2020	2024	2018:Q4	2019:Q4	2020:Q4
Real GDP															
Advanced Economies	**1.7**	**1.7**	**1.2**	**1.4**	**2.1**	**2.3**	**1.7**	**2.5**	**2.3**	**1.7**	**1.7**	**1.6**	**1.8**	**1.6**	**1.8**
United States	1.7	1.6	2.2	1.8	2.5	2.9	1.6	2.4	2.9	2.4	2.1	1.6	2.5	2.4	2.0
Euro Area	1.2	1.6	–0.9	–0.3	1.4	2.1	1.9	2.5	1.9	1.2	1.4	1.3	1.2	1.0	1.8
Germany	0.9	3.9	0.4	0.4	2.2	1.7	2.2	2.5	1.5	0.5	1.2	1.2	0.6	0.4	1.3
France	1.3	2.2	0.3	0.6	1.0	1.1	1.1	2.3	1.7	1.2	1.3	1.4	1.2	1.0	1.3
Italy	0.3	0.6	–2.8	–1.7	0.1	0.9	1.1	1.7	0.9	0.0	0.5	0.6	0.0	0.2	1.0
Spain	2.2	–1.0	–2.9	–1.7	1.4	3.6	3.2	3.0	2.6	2.2	1.8	1.6	2.3	2.0	1.8
Netherlands	1.4	1.5	–1.0	–0.1	1.4	2.0	2.2	2.9	2.6	1.8	1.6	1.5	2.1	1.7	1.8
Belgium	1.6	1.8	0.2	0.2	1.3	1.7	1.5	1.7	1.4	1.2	1.3	1.4	1.2	1.2	1.4
Austria	1.5	2.9	0.7	0.0	0.7	1.1	2.0	2.6	2.7	1.6	1.7	1.6	2.2	1.3	2.0
Ireland	2.8	0.3	0.2	1.4	8.5	25.1	3.7	8.1	8.3	4.3	3.5	2.7	3.7	3.4	4.4
Portugal	0.7	–1.7	–4.1	–0.9	0.8	1.8	2.0	3.5	2.4	1.9	1.6	1.5	2.0	1.8	1.7
Greece	1.8	–9.1	–7.3	–3.2	0.7	–0.4	–0.2	1.5	1.9	2.0	2.2	0.9	1.5	3.0	1.4
Finland	1.7	2.6	–1.4	–0.8	–0.6	0.5	2.8	3.0	1.7	1.2	1.5	1.3	0.8	1.7	1.4
Slovak Republic	4.9	2.8	1.7	1.5	2.8	4.2	3.1	3.2	4.1	2.6	2.7	2.5	3.7	2.2	2.7
Lithuania	4.3	6.0	3.8	3.5	3.5	2.0	2.4	4.1	3.5	3.4	2.7	2.3	3.7	2.3	1.6
Slovenia	2.7	0.9	–2.6	–1.0	2.8	2.2	3.1	4.8	4.1	2.9	2.9	2.1	3.0	3.1	2.8
Luxembourg	2.7	2.5	–0.4	3.7	4.3	3.9	2.4	1.5	2.6	2.6	2.8	2.6	1.7	3.3	2.1
Latvia	3.8	6.4	4.0	2.4	1.9	3.0	2.1	4.6	4.8	2.8	2.8	3.0	5.3	3.3	2.4
Estonia	3.4	7.4	3.1	1.3	3.0	1.8	2.6	5.7	4.8	3.2	2.9	2.8	5.0	2.1	3.4
Cyprus	3.3	0.4	–2.9	–5.8	–1.3	2.0	4.8	4.5	3.9	3.1	2.9	2.5	3.8	3.8	1.4
Malta	2.0	1.3	2.8	4.6	8.7	10.8	5.7	6.7	6.8	5.1	4.3	3.2	7.1	6.9	1.8
Japan	0.6	–0.1	1.5	2.0	0.4	1.2	0.6	1.9	0.8	0.9	0.5	0.5	0.3	0.3	1.2
United Kingdom	1.6	1.6	1.4	2.0	2.9	2.3	1.8	1.8	1.4	1.2	1.4	1.5	1.4	1.0	1.6
Korea	4.7	3.7	2.4	3.2	3.2	2.8	2.9	3.2	2.7	2.0	2.2	2.9	3.0	1.9	1.9
Canada	1.9	3.1	1.8	2.3	2.9	0.7	1.1	3.0	1.9	1.5	1.8	1.7	1.6	1.8	1.7
Australia	3.1	2.8	3.9	2.1	2.6	2.5	2.8	2.4	2.7	1.7	2.3	2.6	2.2	2.0	2.4
Taiwan Province of China	4.2	3.8	2.1	2.2	4.0	0.8	1.5	3.1	2.6	2.0	1.9	2.0	1.8	2.0	1.7
Singapore	5.8	6.3	4.4	4.8	3.9	2.9	3.0	3.7	3.1	0.5	1.0	2.5	1.4	0.8	1.2
Switzerland	1.8	1.8	1.0	1.9	2.5	1.3	1.7	1.9	2.8	0.8	1.3	1.6	1.5	1.1	1.6
Sweden	2.2	3.1	–0.6	1.1	2.7	4.4	2.4	2.4	2.3	0.9	1.5	2.0	2.3	0.0	2.4
Hong Kong SAR	4.1	4.8	1.7	3.1	2.8	2.4	2.2	3.8	3.0	0.3	1.5	2.9	1.2	0.5	2.8
Czech Republic	3.2	1.8	–0.8	–0.5	2.7	5.3	2.5	4.4	3.0	2.5	2.6	2.5	2.7	2.2	3.0
Norway	1.6	1.0	2.7	1.0	2.0	2.0	1.1	2.3	1.3	1.9	2.4	1.7	1.6	3.2	0.9
Israel	3.2	5.1	2.4	4.3	3.8	2.3	4.0	3.6	3.4	3.1	3.1	3.0	2.9	3.0	3.4
Denmark	0.8	1.3	0.2	0.9	1.6	2.3	2.4	2.3	1.5	1.7	1.9	1.5	2.6	1.5	1.9
New Zealand	2.7	1.9	2.5	2.2	3.1	4.0	4.2	2.6	2.8	2.5	2.7	2.5	2.5	2.1	3.4
Puerto Rico	0.7	–0.4	0.0	–0.3	–1.2	–1.0	–1.3	–2.7	–4.9	–1.1	–0.7	–0.8	. . .	. . .	. . .
Macao SAR	. . .	21.7	9.2	11.2	–1.2	–21.6	–0.9	9.7	4.7	–1.3	–1.1	0.3	. . .	. . .	. . .
Iceland	2.6	1.9	1.3	4.1	2.1	4.7	6.6	4.4	4.8	0.8	1.6	1.9	3.1	2.2	1.5
San Marino	. . .	–8.3	–7.0	–0.8	–0.7	2.5	2.5	0.6	1.1	0.8	0.7	0.5	. . .	. . .	. . .
Memorandum															
Major Advanced Economies	1.3	1.6	1.4	1.4	2.0	2.2	1.5	2.3	2.1	1.6	1.6	1.4	1.6	1.5	1.7
Real Total Domestic Demand															
Advanced Economies	**1.6**	**1.5**	**0.8**	**1.1**	**2.1**	**2.6**	**2.0**	**2.5**	**2.2**	**1.8**	**1.8**	**1.6**	**2.1**	**1.7**	**1.8**
United States	1.7	1.5	2.2	1.6	2.7	3.6	1.9	2.6	3.1	2.6	2.2	1.5	2.9	2.4	2.0
Euro Area	1.1	0.8	–2.4	–0.5	1.4	2.4	2.4	2.1	1.5	1.3	1.5	1.4	1.8	1.4	1.4
Germany	0.3	3.3	–0.9	1.1	1.7	1.6	3.0	2.4	2.1	1.3	1.7	1.3	2.1	0.8	1.4
France	1.5	2.1	–0.4	0.7	1.5	1.5	1.5	2.3	1.0	1.3	1.3	1.5	0.6	1.6	1.4
Italy	0.5	–0.6	–5.6	–2.6	0.2	1.5	1.5	1.5	1.0	–0.3	0.4	0.8	0.1	0.6	–0.3
Spain	2.3	–3.1	–5.1	–3.2	2.0	4.0	2.4	3.0	3.0	1.8	1.7	1.4	2.6	1.8	1.5
Japan	0.2	0.7	2.3	2.4	0.4	0.8	0.0	1.4	0.5	1.2	0.8	0.4	0.8	–0.1	1.7
United Kingdom	1.7	–0.2	1.8	2.1	3.2	2.3	2.4	1.4	1.6	1.1	1.6	1.5	2.0	–0.5	3.2
Canada	2.9	3.4	2.0	2.2	1.7	–0.1	0.7	3.9	1.8	0.8	1.3	1.9	0.3	1.1	1.7
Other Advanced Economies[3]	3.0	3.3	1.9	1.6	2.8	2.4	2.8	3.5	2.4	1.5	1.9	2.5	1.8	2.2	1.7
Memorandum															
Major Advanced Economies	1.3	1.4	1.1	1.4	2.0	2.4	1.7	2.3	2.2	1.8	1.7	1.3	2.0	1.5	1.8

[1]In this and other tables, when countries are not listed alphabetically, they are ordered on the basis of economic size.
[2]From the fourth quarter of the preceding year.
[3]Excludes the Group of Seven (Canada, France, Germany, Italy, Japan, United Kingdom, United States) and euro area countries.

Table A3. Advanced Economies: Components of Real GDP

(Annual percent change)

	Averages										Projections	
	2001–10	2011–20	2011	2012	2013	2014	2015	2016	2017	2018	2019	2020
Private Consumer Expenditure												
Advanced Economies	**1.8**	**1.8**	**1.2**	**0.9**	**1.1**	**1.9**	**2.5**	**2.2**	**2.2**	**2.1**	**1.8**	**1.7**
United States	2.1	2.5	1.9	1.5	1.5	3.0	3.7	2.7	2.6	3.0	2.5	2.2
Euro Area	1.1	0.8	0.1	–1.2	–0.7	0.9	1.9	2.0	1.6	1.4	1.2	1.3
Germany	0.4	1.4	1.9	1.5	0.4	1.1	1.9	2.3	1.3	1.3	1.4	1.3
France	1.8	0.9	0.6	–0.4	0.5	0.8	1.5	1.8	1.4	0.9	1.1	1.3
Italy	0.5	0.0	0.0	–4.0	–2.4	0.2	1.9	1.3	1.5	0.6	0.3	0.4
Spain	2.0	0.6	–2.4	–3.5	–3.1	1.5	3.0	2.9	2.5	2.3	1.5	1.5
Japan	0.9	0.5	–0.4	2.0	2.4	–0.9	–0.2	–0.1	1.1	0.3	0.6	0.2
United Kingdom	1.8	1.7	–0.7	1.5	1.8	2.0	2.6	3.1	2.1	1.7	1.6	1.4
Canada	3.1	2.3	2.3	1.9	2.6	2.6	2.3	2.2	3.5	2.1	1.6	1.6
Other Advanced Economies[1]	3.0	2.5	3.0	2.1	2.2	2.5	2.8	2.5	2.8	2.6	1.9	2.3
Memorandum												
Major Advanced Economies	1.6	1.7	1.2	1.1	1.2	1.8	2.5	2.1	2.1	2.0	1.8	1.6
Public Consumption												
Advanced Economies	**2.2**	**1.1**	**–0.6**	**0.0**	**–0.1**	**0.6**	**1.8**	**1.9**	**1.2**	**1.7**	**2.1**	**2.1**
United States	2.1	0.3	–3.0	–1.5	–1.9	–0.8	1.8	1.8	0.6	1.7	2.2	2.2
Euro Area	1.9	0.9	–0.1	–0.3	0.4	0.8	1.3	1.8	1.5	1.1	1.2	1.3
Germany	1.4	2.0	1.0	1.3	1.4	1.7	2.8	4.1	2.4	1.4	2.0	1.8
France	1.6	1.2	1.1	1.6	1.5	1.3	1.0	1.4	1.5	0.8	0.8	0.6
Italy	1.0	–0.5	–1.8	–1.4	–0.3	–0.7	–0.6	0.1	0.3	0.2	–0.9	0.4
Spain	4.7	0.2	–0.3	–4.7	–2.1	–0.3	2.0	1.0	1.9	2.1	1.6	1.1
Japan	1.5	1.3	1.9	1.7	1.5	0.5	1.5	1.4	0.3	0.8	1.7	1.8
United Kingdom	2.6	1.2	0.1	1.2	–0.2	2.2	1.4	0.8	–0.2	0.4	2.8	3.9
Canada	2.5	1.2	1.3	0.7	–0.8	0.6	1.4	1.8	2.1	2.9	0.7	1.1
Other Advanced Economies[1]	3.1	2.9	1.8	2.4	2.8	2.7	2.8	3.1	3.1	3.5	3.8	3.1
Memorandum												
Major Advanced Economies	1.9	0.8	–1.1	–0.2	–0.5	0.1	1.6	1.8	0.8	1.3	1.8	2.0
Gross Fixed Capital Formation												
Advanced Economies	**0.5**	**2.7**	**3.2**	**2.6**	**1.7**	**3.5**	**3.2**	**2.2**	**4.0**	**2.6**	**1.8**	**2.2**
United States	0.0	3.8	4.6	6.9	3.6	5.1	3.2	1.9	3.7	4.1	2.5	2.7
Euro Area	0.4	1.7	1.5	–3.3	–2.4	1.5	5.0	4.0	3.5	2.3	3.1	2.6
Germany	–0.3	2.6	7.4	–0.2	–1.3	3.2	1.8	3.8	2.5	3.5	3.1	2.5
France	1.2	1.7	2.0	0.2	–0.8	0.0	1.0	2.7	4.7	2.8	2.3	2.2
Italy	0.1	–0.3	–1.9	–9.3	–6.6	–2.3	2.1	3.5	4.3	3.4	2.8	2.2
Spain	1.2	1.0	–6.9	–8.6	–3.4	4.7	6.7	2.9	4.8	5.3	2.9	2.7
Japan	–2.2	2.1	1.7	3.5	4.9	3.1	1.6	–0.3	3.0	1.2	1.3	0.9
United Kingdom	0.3	2.4	2.6	2.1	3.4	7.2	3.4	2.3	3.5	0.2	–0.6	0.6
Canada	3.8	0.7	4.6	4.9	1.4	2.3	–5.2	–4.3	3.0	1.2	–1.4	1.2
Other Advanced Economies[1]	2.8	2.4	4.3	3.0	2.4	2.4	2.1	2.9	5.7	0.7	–0.7	1.5
Memorandum												
Major Advanced Economies	0.0	2.8	3.7	3.7	2.2	3.8	2.3	1.7	3.5	3.1	2.0	2.1

Table A3. Advanced Economies: Components of Real GDP *(continued)*

(Annual percent change)

	Averages										Projections	
	2001–10	2011–20	2011	2012	2013	2014	2015	2016	2017	2018	2019	2020
Final Domestic Demand												
Advanced Economies	**1.6**	**1.8**	**1.3**	**1.1**	**1.1**	**2.0**	**2.6**	**2.2**	**2.4**	**2.1**	**1.8**	**1.9**
United States	1.7	2.4	1.6	2.0	1.3	2.8	3.3	2.4	2.5	3.0	2.5	2.3
Euro Area	1.1	1.1	0.4	–1.4	–0.8	1.0	2.4	2.4	2.0	1.5	1.6	1.6
Germany	0.4	1.8	2.8	1.1	0.2	1.7	2.1	3.0	1.8	1.8	1.9	1.7
France	1.6	1.2	1.0	0.2	0.5	0.8	1.3	1.9	2.1	1.3	1.3	1.4
Italy	0.5	–0.2	–0.8	–4.5	–2.8	–0.4	1.4	1.4	1.8	1.0	0.5	0.8
Spain	2.3	0.6	–3.0	–4.8	–3.0	1.8	3.6	2.5	2.9	2.9	1.8	1.7
Japan	0.2	1.0	0.5	2.3	2.8	0.2	0.6	0.1	1.4	0.6	1.1	0.8
United Kingdom	1.7	1.7	0.0	1.6	1.7	2.9	2.5	2.5	1.9	1.2	1.4	1.7
Canada	3.1	1.7	2.6	2.4	1.6	2.1	0.3	0.6	3.1	2.1	0.7	1.5
Other Advanced Economies[1]	2.9	2.5	3.1	2.4	2.4	2.5	2.6	2.8	3.3	2.2	1.5	2.2
Memorandum												
Major Advanced Economies	1.3	1.8	1.3	1.4	1.1	2.0	2.3	2.0	2.2	2.1	1.9	1.8
Stock Building[2]												
Advanced Economies	**0.0**	**0.0**	**0.2**	**–0.3**	**0.0**	**0.1**	**0.1**	**–0.2**	**0.1**	**0.1**	**0.0**	**–0.1**
United States	0.0	0.0	–0.1	0.2	0.2	–0.1	0.3	–0.6	0.0	0.1	0.1	–0.2
Euro Area	0.0	0.0	0.4	–1.0	0.3	0.4	0.0	0.0	0.1	0.0	–0.3	–0.1
Germany	–0.1	–0.1	0.4	–1.8	0.8	0.0	–0.4	0.1	0.5	0.3	–0.5	0.0
France	–0.1	0.1	1.1	–0.6	0.2	0.7	0.3	–0.4	0.2	–0.3	0.0	0.0
Italy	0.0	–0.1	0.2	–1.1	0.2	0.6	0.1	0.1	–0.3	–0.1	–0.8	–0.3
Spain	0.0	0.0	–0.1	–0.2	–0.3	0.2	0.5	–0.1	0.1	0.1	0.0	0.0
Japan	0.0	0.0	0.2	0.0	–0.4	0.1	0.3	–0.1	0.0	0.1	0.0	0.0
United Kingdom	0.0	0.0	–0.2	0.2	0.2	0.7	–0.2	–0.1	–0.6	0.4	–0.3	–0.1
Canada	–0.1	0.1	0.7	–0.3	0.5	–0.4	–0.4	0.0	0.8	–0.2	0.1	–0.1
Other Advanced Economies[1]	0.0	–0.1	0.2	–0.4	–0.7	0.2	–0.1	0.0	0.2	0.2	0.1	–0.3
Memorandum												
Major Advanced Economies	0.0	0.0	0.2	–0.2	0.2	0.1	0.1	–0.3	0.1	0.1	–0.1	–0.1
Foreign Balance[2]												
Advanced Economies	**0.1**	**0.0**	**0.3**	**0.4**	**0.2**	**0.0**	**–0.3**	**–0.2**	**0.0**	**0.0**	**–0.1**	**–0.1**
United States	0.0	–0.2	0.0	0.0	0.2	–0.3	–0.8	–0.3	–0.3	–0.3	–0.3	–0.1
Euro Area	0.1	0.3	0.9	1.5	0.3	0.1	–0.2	–0.4	0.5	0.5	–0.1	–0.1
Germany	0.5	0.1	0.8	1.2	–0.5	0.7	0.3	–0.6	0.2	–0.5	–0.7	–0.3
France	–0.2	0.0	0.1	0.7	–0.1	–0.5	–0.4	–0.4	–0.1	0.7	0.0	–0.2
Italy	–0.2	0.4	1.2	2.8	0.8	–0.1	–0.5	–0.4	0.2	–0.1	0.3	0.1
Spain	–0.2	0.6	2.1	2.2	1.5	–0.5	–0.3	0.8	0.1	–0.3	0.4	0.2
Japan	0.3	–0.1	–0.9	–0.8	–0.4	0.0	0.3	0.6	0.5	0.0	–0.1	–0.2
United Kingdom	–0.1	–0.1	1.5	–0.4	–0.5	–0.4	–0.3	–0.7	0.5	–0.2	0.0	–0.2
Canada	–1.1	0.2	–0.3	–0.4	0.1	1.2	0.9	0.4	–1.1	0.0	0.7	0.4
Other Advanced Economies[1]	0.6	0.2	0.6	0.5	0.7	0.4	0.0	–0.1	–0.5	0.3	0.3	0.1
Memorandum												
Major Advanced Economies	0.0	–0.1	0.1	0.2	0.0	–0.1	–0.4	–0.2	0.0	–0.2	–0.2	–0.1

[1]Excludes the Group of Seven (Canada, France, Germany, Italy, Japan, United Kingdom, United States) and euro area countries.
[2]Changes expressed as percent of GDP in the preceding period.

Table A4. Emerging Market and Developing Economies: Real GDP

(Annual percent change)

	Average 2001–10	2011	2012	2013	2014	2015	2016	2017	2018	Projections 2019	2020	2024
Emerging and Developing Asia	**8.5**	**7.9**	**7.0**	**6.9**	**6.8**	**6.8**	**6.7**	**6.6**	**6.4**	**5.9**	**6.0**	**6.0**
Bangladesh	5.8	6.5	6.3	6.0	6.3	6.8	7.2	7.6	7.9	7.8	7.4	7.3
Bhutan	8.4	9.7	6.4	3.6	4.0	6.2	7.4	6.3	4.6	5.5	7.2	6.4
Brunei Darussalam	1.4	3.7	0.9	–2.1	–2.5	–0.4	–2.5	1.3	0.1	1.8	4.7	2.1
Cambodia	8.0	7.1	7.3	7.4	7.1	7.0	6.9	7.0	7.5	7.0	6.8	6.5
China	10.5	9.5	7.9	7.8	7.3	6.9	6.7	6.8	6.6	6.1	5.8	5.5
Fiji	1.3	2.7	1.4	4.7	5.6	4.7	2.5	5.4	3.5	2.7	3.0	3.2
India[1]	7.5	6.6	5.5	6.4	7.4	8.0	8.2	7.2	6.8	6.1	7.0	7.3
Indonesia	5.4	6.2	6.0	5.6	5.0	4.9	5.0	5.1	5.2	5.0	5.1	5.3
Kiribati	0.7	1.6	4.7	4.2	–0.7	10.4	5.1	0.3	2.3	2.3	2.3	1.8
Lao P.D.R.	7.2	8.0	7.8	8.0	7.6	7.3	7.0	6.8	6.3	6.4	6.5	6.8
Malaysia	4.6	5.3	5.5	4.7	6.0	5.0	4.4	5.7	4.7	4.5	4.4	4.9
Maldives	6.5	8.4	2.4	7.3	7.3	2.9	7.3	6.9	7.5	6.5	6.0	5.5
Marshall Islands	2.0	1.1	3.2	2.8	–0.7	–0.6	1.8	4.5	2.6	2.4	2.3	1.2
Micronesia	0.2	3.3	–2.0	–3.9	–2.2	5.0	0.7	2.4	1.2	1.4	0.8	0.6
Mongolia	6.3	17.3	12.3	11.6	7.9	2.4	1.2	5.3	6.9	6.5	5.4	5.0
Myanmar	10.7	5.5	6.5	7.9	8.2	7.5	5.2	6.3	6.8	6.2	6.3	6.4
Nauru	. . .	10.8	10.4	31.0	27.2	3.4	3.0	–5.5	–1.5	1.5	0.7	2.0
Nepal	4.0	3.4	4.8	4.1	6.0	3.3	0.6	8.2	6.7	7.1	6.3	5.0
Palau	0.3	4.9	1.8	–1.4	4.4	10.1	0.8	–3.5	1.7	0.3	1.8	2.0
Papua New Guinea	3.7	1.1	4.7	3.8	13.5	9.5	4.1	2.7	–1.1	5.0	2.6	3.5
Philippines	4.8	3.7	6.7	7.1	6.1	6.1	6.9	6.7	6.2	5.7	6.2	6.5
Samoa	2.5	5.6	0.4	–1.9	1.2	1.7	7.2	2.7	0.9	3.4	4.4	2.2
Solomon Islands	3.4	13.2	4.6	3.0	2.3	2.5	3.2	3.7	3.9	2.7	2.9	2.9
Sri Lanka	5.1	8.4	9.1	3.4	5.0	5.0	4.5	3.4	3.2	2.7	3.5	4.8
Thailand	4.6	0.8	7.2	2.7	1.0	3.1	3.4	4.0	4.1	2.9	3.0	3.6
Timor-Leste[2]	4.3	6.7	5.7	2.4	4.7	3.5	5.1	–3.5	–0.2	4.5	5.0	4.8
Tonga	1.2	2.0	–1.1	–0.6	2.7	3.6	4.7	2.7	1.5	3.5	3.7	2.0
Tuvalu	0.9	7.9	–3.8	4.6	1.3	9.1	3.0	3.2	4.3	4.1	4.4	2.7
Vanuatu	2.9	1.2	1.8	2.0	2.3	0.2	3.5	4.4	3.2	3.8	3.1	2.9
Vietnam	6.8	6.2	5.2	5.4	6.0	6.7	6.2	6.8	7.1	6.5	6.5	6.5
Emerging and Developing Europe	**4.4**	**5.8**	**3.0**	**3.1**	**1.9**	**0.8**	**1.8**	**3.9**	**3.1**	**1.8**	**2.5**	**2.5**
Albania	5.6	2.5	1.4	1.0	1.8	2.2	3.3	3.8	4.1	3.0	4.0	4.0
Belarus	7.4	5.5	1.7	1.0	1.7	–3.8	–2.5	2.5	3.0	1.5	0.3	–0.4
Bosnia and Herzegovina	3.9	0.9	–0.7	2.4	1.1	3.1	3.2	3.1	3.6	2.8	2.6	3.0
Bulgaria	4.6	1.9	0.0	0.5	1.8	3.5	3.9	3.8	3.1	3.7	3.2	2.8
Croatia	2.5	–0.3	–2.3	–0.5	–0.1	2.4	3.5	2.9	2.6	3.0	2.7	2.0
Hungary	2.0	1.7	–1.6	2.1	4.2	3.5	2.3	4.1	4.9	4.6	3.3	2.2
Kosovo	4.6	4.4	2.8	3.4	1.2	4.1	4.1	4.2	3.8	4.2	4.0	4.0
Moldova	5.1	5.8	–0.6	9.0	5.0	–0.3	4.4	4.7	4.0	3.5	3.8	3.8
Montenegro	3.3	3.2	–2.7	3.5	1.8	3.4	2.9	4.7	4.9	3.0	2.5	2.9
North Macedonia	3.0	2.3	–0.5	2.9	3.6	3.9	2.8	0.2	2.7	3.2	3.4	3.5
Poland	3.9	5.0	1.6	1.4	3.3	3.8	3.1	4.9	5.1	4.0	3.1	2.5
Romania	4.2	2.0	2.1	3.5	3.4	3.9	4.8	7.0	4.1	4.0	3.5	3.0
Russia	4.8	5.1	3.7	1.8	0.7	–2.3	0.3	1.6	2.3	1.1	1.9	1.8
Serbia	5.0	2.0	–0.7	2.9	–1.6	1.8	3.3	2.0	4.3	3.5	4.0	4.0
Turkey	4.0	11.1	4.8	8.5	5.2	6.1	3.2	7.5	2.8	0.2	3.0	3.5
Ukraine[1]	3.9	5.5	0.2	0.0	–6.6	–9.8	2.4	2.5	3.3	3.0	3.0	3.3
Latin America and the Caribbean	**3.2**	**4.6**	**2.9**	**2.9**	**1.3**	**0.3**	**–0.6**	**1.2**	**1.0**	**0.2**	**1.8**	**2.7**
Antigua and Barbuda	1.4	–2.0	3.4	–0.6	3.8	3.8	5.5	3.1	7.4	4.0	3.3	2.0
Argentina	3.4	6.0	–1.0	2.4	–2.5	2.7	–2.1	2.7	–2.5	–3.1	–1.3	3.2
Aruba	–0.8	3.5	–1.4	4.2	0.9	–0.4	0.5	2.3	1.2	0.7	1.0	1.1
The Bahamas	0.7	0.6	3.1	–3.0	0.7	0.6	0.4	0.1	1.6	0.9	–0.6	1.6
Barbados	0.7	–0.7	–0.4	–1.4	–0.1	2.4	2.5	0.5	–0.6	–0.1	0.6	1.8
Belize	3.9	2.2	2.9	0.9	3.7	3.4	–0.6	1.4	3.0	2.7	2.1	1.7
Bolivia	3.8	5.2	5.1	6.8	5.5	4.9	4.3	4.2	4.2	3.9	3.8	3.7
Brazil	3.7	4.0	1.9	3.0	0.5	–3.6	–3.3	1.1	1.1	0.9	2.0	2.3
Chile	4.2	6.1	5.3	4.0	1.8	2.3	1.7	1.3	4.0	2.5	3.0	3.2
Colombia	4.0	7.4	3.9	4.6	4.7	3.0	2.1	1.4	2.6	3.4	3.6	3.7

Table A4. Emerging Market and Developing Economies: Real GDP *(continued)*

(Annual percent change)

	Average 2001–10	2011	2012	2013	2014	2015	2016	2017	2018	Projections 2019	2020	2024
Latin America and the Caribbean (continued)	**3.2**	**4.6**	**2.9**	**2.9**	**1.3**	**0.3**	**–0.6**	**1.2**	**1.0**	**0.2**	**1.8**	**2.7**
Costa Rica	4.3	4.3	4.8	2.3	3.5	3.6	4.2	3.4	2.6	2.0	2.5	3.5
Dominica	2.4	–0.2	–1.1	–0.6	4.4	–2.6	2.5	–9.5	0.5	9.4	4.9	1.5
Dominican Republic	4.6	3.1	2.7	4.9	7.1	6.9	6.7	4.7	7.0	5.0	5.2	5.0
Ecuador	4.1	7.9	5.6	4.9	3.8	0.1	–1.2	2.4	1.4	–0.5	0.5	2.5
El Salvador	1.6	3.8	2.8	2.2	1.7	2.4	2.5	2.3	2.5	2.5	2.3	2.2
Grenada	1.8	0.8	–1.2	2.4	7.3	6.4	3.7	4.4	4.2	3.1	2.7	3.0
Guatemala	3.3	4.2	3.0	3.7	4.2	4.1	3.1	2.8	3.1	3.4	3.5	3.5
Guyana	2.4	5.4	5.0	5.0	3.9	3.1	3.4	2.1	4.1	4.4	85.6	3.2
Haiti	0.1	5.5	2.9	4.2	2.8	1.2	1.5	1.2	1.5	0.1	1.2	1.5
Honduras	4.1	3.8	4.1	2.8	3.1	3.8	3.8	4.9	3.7	3.4	3.5	3.9
Jamaica	0.6	1.4	–0.5	0.2	0.6	0.9	1.5	0.7	1.6	1.1	1.0	2.2
Mexico	1.5	3.7	3.6	1.4	2.8	3.3	2.9	2.1	2.0	0.4	1.3	2.4
Nicaragua	2.9	6.3	6.5	4.9	4.8	4.8	4.6	4.7	–3.8	–5.0	–0.8	1.5
Panama	5.9	11.3	9.8	6.9	5.1	5.7	5.0	5.3	3.7	4.3	5.5	5.5
Paraguay	3.7	4.2	–0.5	8.4	4.9	3.1	4.3	5.0	3.7	1.0	4.0	3.9
Peru	5.6	6.5	6.0	5.8	2.4	3.3	4.0	2.5	4.0	2.6	3.6	3.8
St. Kitts and Nevis	2.2	3.2	–4.4	6.4	7.2	1.6	1.8	0.9	4.6	3.5	3.5	2.7
St. Lucia	2.0	4.1	–0.4	–2.0	1.3	0.2	3.2	2.6	0.9	1.5	3.2	1.5
St. Vincent and the Grenadines	2.6	0.2	1.3	2.5	0.2	0.8	0.8	0.7	2.0	2.3	2.3	2.3
Suriname	5.0	5.8	2.7	2.9	0.3	–3.4	–5.6	1.7	2.0	2.2	2.5	2.6
Trinidad and Tobago[1]	5.7	–0.2	–0.7	2.0	–1.0	1.8	–6.5	–1.9	0.3	0.0	1.5	1.7
Uruguay	3.2	5.2	3.5	4.6	3.2	0.4	1.7	2.6	1.6	0.4	2.3	2.4
Venezuela	3.1	4.2	5.6	1.3	–3.9	–6.2	–17.0	–15.7	–18.0	–35.0	–10.0	. . .
Middle East and Central Asia	**5.3**	**4.6**	**4.9**	**3.0**	**3.1**	**2.6**	**5.0**	**2.3**	**1.9**	**0.9**	**2.9**	**3.3**
Afghanistan	. . .	6.5	14.0	5.7	2.7	1.0	2.2	2.7	2.7	3.0	3.5	5.5
Algeria	3.9	2.8	3.4	2.8	3.8	3.7	3.2	1.3	1.4	2.6	2.4	0.8
Armenia	8.1	4.7	7.1	3.3	3.6	3.3	0.2	7.5	5.2	6.0	4.8	4.5
Azerbaijan	14.4	–1.6	2.2	5.8	2.8	1.0	–3.1	0.2	1.0	2.7	2.1	2.4
Bahrain	5.4	2.0	3.7	5.4	4.4	2.9	3.5	3.8	1.8	2.0	2.1	3.0
Djibouti	3.5	7.3	4.8	5.0	7.1	7.7	6.9	5.1	5.5	6.0	6.0	6.0
Egypt	4.9	1.8	2.2	3.3	2.9	4.4	4.3	4.1	5.3	5.5	5.9	6.0
Georgia	6.3	7.2	6.4	3.4	4.6	2.9	2.8	4.8	4.7	4.6	4.8	5.2
Iran	4.7	3.1	–7.7	–0.3	3.2	–1.6	12.5	3.7	–4.8	–9.5	0.0	1.1
Iraq	12.1	7.5	13.9	7.6	0.7	2.5	15.2	–2.5	–0.6	3.4	4.7	2.1
Jordan	6.0	2.6	2.7	2.8	3.1	2.4	2.0	2.1	1.9	2.2	2.4	3.0
Kazakhstan	8.3	7.4	4.8	6.0	4.2	1.2	1.1	4.1	4.1	3.8	3.9	3.5
Kuwait	4.6	9.6	6.6	1.2	0.5	0.6	2.9	–3.5	1.2	0.6	3.1	2.9
Kyrgyz Republic	4.0	6.0	–0.1	10.9	4.0	3.9	4.3	4.7	3.5	3.8	3.4	3.4
Lebanon	5.7	0.9	2.7	2.6	1.9	0.4	1.6	0.6	0.2	0.2	0.9	2.7
Libya[1]	1.8	–66.7	124.7	–36.8	–53.0	–13.0	–7.4	64.0	17.9	–19.1	0.0	0.0
Mauritania	4.9	4.7	5.8	6.1	5.6	0.4	1.8	3.1	3.6	6.6	5.9	5.8
Morocco	4.9	5.2	3.0	4.5	2.7	4.5	1.1	4.2	3.0	2.7	3.7	4.5
Oman	3.0	2.6	9.1	5.1	1.4	4.7	4.9	0.3	1.8	0.0	3.7	1.6
Pakistan	4.5	3.6	3.8	3.7	4.1	4.1	4.6	5.2	5.5	3.3	2.4	5.0
Qatar	13.1	13.4	4.7	4.4	4.0	3.7	2.1	1.6	1.5	2.0	2.8	2.8
Saudi Arabia	3.4	10.0	5.4	2.7	3.7	4.1	1.7	–0.7	2.4	0.2	2.2	2.5
Somalia	. . .	. . .	1.2	1.9	2.4	3.5	2.9	1.4	2.8	2.9	3.2	3.5
Sudan[3]	5.1	–2.8	–17.0	2.0	4.7	1.9	2.9	1.7	–2.2	–2.6	–1.5	1.4
Syria[4]	4.5	. . .	. . .	. . .	. . .	. . .	. . .	. . .	. . .	. . .	. . .	. . .
Tajikistan	8.0	7.4	7.5	7.4	6.7	6.0	6.9	7.1	7.3	5.0	4.5	4.0
Tunisia	4.2	–1.9	4.0	2.9	3.0	1.2	1.3	1.8	2.5	1.5	2.4	4.4
Turkmenistan	13.2	14.7	11.1	10.2	10.3	6.5	6.2	6.5	6.2	6.3	6.0	5.8
United Arab Emirates	3.9	6.9	4.5	5.1	4.4	5.1	3.0	0.5	1.7	1.6	2.5	2.5
Uzbekistan	6.9	8.3	8.2	8.0	7.2	7.4	6.1	4.5	5.1	5.5	6.0	6.0
Yemen	4.3	–12.7	2.4	4.8	–0.2	–28.0	–9.4	–5.1	0.8	2.1	2.0	3.6

Table A4. Emerging Market and Developing Economies: Real GDP *(continued)*

(Annual percent change)

	Average 2001–10	2011	2012	2013	2014	2015	2016	2017	2018	Projections 2019	2020	2024
Sub-Saharan Africa	**5.9**	**5.3**	**4.7**	**5.2**	**5.1**	**3.1**	**1.4**	**3.0**	**3.2**	**3.2**	**3.6**	**4.2**
Angola	8.8	3.5	8.5	5.0	4.8	0.9	–2.6	–0.2	–1.2	–0.3	1.2	3.8
Benin	3.9	3.0	4.8	7.2	6.4	1.8	3.3	5.7	6.7	6.6	6.7	6.7
Botswana	4.1	6.0	4.5	11.3	4.1	–1.7	4.3	2.9	4.5	3.5	4.3	3.9
Burkina Faso	5.9	6.6	6.5	5.8	4.3	3.9	5.9	6.3	6.8	6.0	6.0	6.0
Burundi	3.7	4.0	4.4	5.9	4.5	–4.0	–1.0	0.0	0.1	0.4	0.5	0.5
Cabo Verde	5.4	4.0	1.1	0.8	0.6	1.0	4.7	3.7	5.1	5.0	5.0	5.0
Cameroon	3.9	4.1	4.5	5.4	5.9	5.7	4.6	3.5	4.1	4.0	4.2	5.4
Central African Republic	2.4	4.2	5.1	–36.4	0.1	4.3	4.7	4.5	3.8	4.5	5.0	5.0
Chad	9.8	0.1	8.8	5.8	6.9	1.8	–5.6	–2.4	2.4	2.3	5.4	3.7
Comoros	3.1	4.1	3.2	4.5	2.1	1.1	2.6	3.0	3.0	1.3	4.2	3.5
Democratic Republic of the Congo	4.7	6.9	7.1	8.5	9.5	6.9	2.4	3.7	5.8	4.3	3.9	4.6
Republic of Congo	4.7	3.4	3.8	3.3	6.8	2.6	–2.8	–1.8	1.6	4.0	2.8	2.3
Côte d'Ivoire	1.1	–4.9	10.9	9.3	8.8	8.8	8.0	7.7	7.4	7.5	7.3	6.4
Equatorial Guinea	15.2	6.5	8.3	–4.1	0.4	–9.1	–8.8	–4.7	–5.7	–4.6	–5.0	–2.8
Eritrea	1.3	25.7	1.9	–10.5	30.9	–20.6	7.4	–9.6	12.2	3.1	3.9	4.8
Eswatini	3.5	2.2	5.4	3.9	0.9	2.3	1.3	2.0	2.4	1.3	0.5	0.5
Ethiopia	8.5	11.4	8.7	9.9	10.3	10.4	8.0	10.1	7.7	7.4	7.2	6.5
Gabon	1.4	7.1	5.3	5.5	4.4	3.9	2.1	0.5	0.8	2.9	3.4	4.5
The Gambia	3.5	–8.1	5.2	2.9	–1.4	4.1	1.9	4.8	6.5	6.5	6.4	4.8
Ghana	5.8	17.4	9.0	7.9	2.9	2.2	3.4	8.1	6.3	7.5	5.6	5.1
Guinea	3.1	5.6	5.9	3.9	3.7	3.8	10.8	10.0	5.8	5.9	6.0	5.0
Guinea-Bissau	2.5	8.1	–1.7	3.3	1.0	6.1	6.3	5.9	3.8	4.6	4.9	5.3
Kenya	4.2	6.1	4.6	5.9	5.4	5.7	5.9	4.9	6.3	5.6	6.0	5.9
Lesotho	3.9	6.7	4.9	2.2	2.7	2.1	2.7	0.5	2.8	2.8	–0.2	1.3
Liberia	2.0	7.7	8.4	8.8	0.7	0.0	–1.6	2.5	1.2	0.4	1.6	3.7
Madagascar	2.6	1.4	3.0	2.2	3.3	3.1	4.2	4.3	5.2	5.2	5.3	4.8
Malawi	4.9	4.9	1.9	5.2	5.7	2.9	2.3	4.0	3.2	4.5	5.1	6.5
Mali	5.8	3.2	–0.8	2.3	7.1	6.2	5.8	5.4	4.7	5.0	5.0	4.8
Mauritius	4.0	4.1	3.5	3.4	3.7	3.6	3.8	3.8	3.8	3.7	3.8	4.0
Mozambique	8.2	7.1	7.2	7.1	7.4	6.6	3.8	3.7	3.3	1.8	6.0	11.5
Namibia	4.0	5.1	5.1	5.6	6.4	6.1	1.1	–0.9	–0.1	–0.2	1.6	3.0
Niger	5.4	2.2	11.8	5.3	7.5	4.3	4.9	4.9	6.5	6.3	6.0	6.8
Nigeria	8.9	4.9	4.3	5.4	6.3	2.7	–1.6	0.8	1.9	2.3	2.5	2.6
Rwanda	8.2	8.0	8.6	4.7	6.2	8.9	6.0	6.1	8.6	7.8	8.1	7.5
São Tomé and Príncipe	5.2	4.4	3.1	4.8	6.5	3.8	4.2	3.9	2.7	2.7	3.5	4.5
Senegal	4.0	1.5	5.1	2.8	6.6	6.4	6.4	7.1	6.7	6.0	6.8	8.0
Seychelles	2.0	5.4	3.7	6.0	4.5	4.9	4.5	4.3	4.1	3.5	3.3	3.6
Sierra Leone	8.9	6.3	15.2	20.7	4.6	–20.5	6.4	3.8	3.5	5.0	4.7	4.7
South Africa	3.5	3.3	2.2	2.5	1.8	1.2	0.4	1.4	0.8	0.7	1.1	1.8
South Sudan	. . .	. . .	–52.4	29.3	2.9	–0.2	–16.7	–5.5	–1.1	7.9	8.2	4.7
Tanzania	6.6	7.9	5.1	6.8	6.7	6.2	6.9	6.8	7.0	5.2	5.7	6.5
Togo	2.2	6.4	6.5	6.1	5.9	5.7	5.6	4.4	4.9	5.1	5.3	5.4
Uganda	7.9	6.8	2.2	4.7	4.6	5.7	2.3	5.0	6.1	6.2	6.2	10.1
Zambia	7.4	5.6	7.6	5.1	4.7	2.9	3.8	3.5	3.7	2.0	1.7	1.5
Zimbabwe[5]	–3.9	14.2	16.7	2.0	2.4	1.8	0.7	4.7	3.5	–7.1	2.7	2.2

[1]See country-specific notes for India, Libya, Trinidad and Tobago, and Ukraine in the "Country Notes" section of the Statistical Appendix.
[2]In this table only, the data for Timor-Leste are based on non-oil GDP.
[3]Data for 2011 exclude South Sudan after July 9. Data for 2012 and onward pertain to the current Sudan.
[4]Data for Syria are excluded for 2011 onward owing to the uncertain political situation.
[5]The Zimbabwe dollar ceased circulating in early 2009. Data are based on IMF staff estimates of price and exchange rate developments in US dollars. IMF staff estimates of US dollar values may differ from authorities' estimates. Real GDP is in constant 2009 prices.

Table A5. Summary of Inflation

(Percent)

	Average 2001–10	2011	2012	2013	2014	2015	2016	2017	2018	Projections 2019	Projections 2020	Projections 2024
GDP Deflators												
Advanced Economies	**1.7**	**1.4**	**1.3**	**1.3**	**1.5**	**1.2**	**1.0**	**1.4**	**1.6**	**1.5**	**1.6**	**1.8**
United States	2.1	2.1	1.9	1.8	1.9	1.0	1.0	1.9	2.4	1.8	2.0	2.0
Euro Area	1.9	1.1	1.3	1.2	0.9	1.3	0.8	0.9	1.3	1.5	1.6	1.9
Japan	–1.1	–1.7	–0.8	–0.3	1.7	2.1	0.3	–0.2	–0.1	0.7	1.0	0.9
Other Advanced Economies[1]	2.1	1.9	1.2	1.5	1.3	1.1	1.3	2.0	1.5	1.4	1.2	1.9
Consumer Prices												
Advanced Economies	**2.0**	**2.7**	**2.0**	**1.4**	**1.4**	**0.3**	**0.8**	**1.7**	**2.0**	**1.5**	**1.8**	**2.0**
United States	2.4	3.1	2.1	1.5	1.6	0.1	1.3	2.1	2.4	1.8	2.3	2.3
Euro Area[2]	2.1	2.7	2.5	1.3	0.4	0.2	0.2	1.5	1.8	1.2	1.4	1.8
Japan	–0.3	–0.3	–0.1	0.3	2.8	0.8	–0.1	0.5	1.0	1.0	1.3	1.3
Other Advanced Economies[1]	2.1	3.3	2.1	1.7	1.5	0.5	0.9	1.8	1.9	1.4	1.6	2.0
Emerging Market and Developing Economies[3]	**6.6**	**7.1**	**5.8**	**5.5**	**4.7**	**4.7**	**4.3**	**4.3**	**4.8**	**4.7**	**4.8**	**4.3**
Regional Groups												
Emerging and Developing Asia	4.3	6.5	4.6	4.6	3.4	2.7	2.8	2.4	2.6	2.7	3.0	3.3
Emerging and Developing Europe	11.5	7.9	6.2	5.6	6.5	10.5	5.5	5.4	6.2	6.8	5.6	5.3
Latin America and the Caribbean	5.8	5.2	4.6	4.6	4.9	5.5	5.6	6.0	6.2	7.2	6.7	4.3
Middle East and Central Asia	7.2	9.2	9.4	8.8	6.6	5.5	5.5	6.7	9.9	8.2	9.1	7.1
Sub-Saharan Africa	9.9	9.3	9.2	6.5	6.4	6.9	10.8	10.9	8.5	8.4	8.0	6.6
Analytical Groups												
By Source of Export Earnings												
Fuel	9.7	8.6	8.0	8.1	6.4	8.6	7.1	5.4	7.0	6.5	6.8	6.2
Nonfuel	5.7	6.7	5.3	4.9	4.3	3.8	3.7	4.0	4.3	4.4	4.4	3.9
Of Which, Primary Products[4]	6.5	6.9	6.9	6.5	7.0	5.2	6.1	11.1	13.4	16.5	15.6	8.8
By External Financing Source												
Net Debtor Economies	7.4	7.6	6.9	6.2	5.6	5.4	5.1	5.5	5.4	5.1	5.1	4.5
Net Debtor Economies by Debt-Servicing Experience												
Economies with Arrears and/or Rescheduling during 2014–18	10.0	10.3	8.0	6.8	10.1	14.3	11.2	18.4	17.5	14.0	11.7	8.3
Other Groups												
European Union	2.4	3.1	2.6	1.5	0.5	0.1	0.2	1.7	1.9	1.5	1.7	2.0
Low-Income Developing Countries	9.7	11.9	9.7	8.0	7.2	6.9	9.1	9.7	9.1	8.8	8.8	7.3
Middle East and North Africa	6.9	8.7	9.7	9.4	6.5	5.6	5.2	6.7	11.0	8.4	8.9	7.8
Memorandum												
Median Inflation Rate												
Advanced Economies	2.2	3.2	2.6	1.4	0.7	0.1	0.6	1.6	1.7	1.5	1.6	2.0
Emerging Market and Developing Economies[3]	5.2	5.5	4.6	3.8	3.1	2.7	2.7	3.3	3.0	2.9	3.2	3.0

[1]Excludes the United States, euro area countries, and Japan.
[2]Based on Eurostat's harmonized index of consumer prices.
[3]Excludes Venezuela but includes Argentina from 2017 onward. See country-specific notes for Venezuela and Argentina in the "Country Notes" section of the Statistical Appendix.
[4]Includes Argentina from 2017 onward. See country-specific note for Argentina in the "Country Notes" section of the Statistical Appendix.

Table A6. Advanced Economies: Consumer Prices[1]

(Annual percent change)

	Average									Projections			End of Period[2]	Projections	
	2001–10	2011	2012	2013	2014	2015	2016	2017	2018	2019	2020	2024	2018	2019	2020
Advanced Economies	**2.0**	**2.7**	**2.0**	**1.4**	**1.4**	**0.3**	**0.8**	**1.7**	**2.0**	**1.5**	**1.8**	**2.0**	**1.6**	**1.7**	**1.7**
United States	2.4	3.1	2.1	1.5	1.6	0.1	1.3	2.1	2.4	1.8	2.3	2.3	1.9	2.2	2.4
Euro Area[3]	2.1	2.7	2.5	1.3	0.4	0.2	0.2	1.5	1.8	1.2	1.4	1.8	1.5	1.3	1.3
Germany	1.6	2.5	2.2	1.6	0.8	0.7	0.4	1.7	1.9	1.5	1.7	2.1	1.8	1.8	1.7
France	1.9	2.3	2.2	1.0	0.6	0.1	0.3	1.2	2.1	1.2	1.3	1.7	2.0	1.0	1.4
Italy	2.2	2.9	3.3	1.2	0.2	0.1	–0.1	1.3	1.2	0.7	1.0	1.5	1.2	0.7	1.0
Spain	2.8	3.2	2.4	1.4	–0.2	–0.5	–0.2	2.0	1.7	0.7	1.0	1.8	1.2	0.7	1.1
Netherlands	2.1	2.5	2.8	2.6	0.3	0.2	0.1	1.3	1.6	2.5	1.6	2.0	1.8	2.1	1.7
Belgium	2.1	3.4	2.6	1.2	0.5	0.6	1.8	2.2	2.3	1.5	1.3	1.8	2.2	1.1	1.3
Austria	1.9	3.5	2.6	2.1	1.5	0.8	1.0	2.2	2.1	1.5	1.9	2.0	1.7	1.6	1.9
Ireland	2.2	1.2	1.9	0.5	0.3	0.0	–0.2	0.3	0.7	1.2	1.5	2.0	0.8	1.4	1.5
Portugal	2.5	3.6	2.8	0.4	–0.2	0.5	0.6	1.6	1.2	0.9	1.2	1.7	0.6	4.3	–3.1
Greece	3.4	3.1	1.0	–0.9	–1.4	–1.1	0.0	1.1	0.8	0.6	0.9	1.8	0.6	0.9	0.9
Finland	1.7	3.3	3.2	2.2	1.2	–0.2	0.4	0.8	1.2	1.2	1.3	1.8	1.3	1.1	1.3
Slovak Republic	4.1	4.1	3.7	1.5	–0.1	–0.3	–0.5	1.4	2.5	2.6	2.1	2.0	1.9	2.4	2.0
Lithuania	3.0	4.1	3.2	1.2	0.2	–0.7	0.7	3.7	2.5	2.3	2.2	2.2	1.8	2.4	2.2
Slovenia	4.2	1.8	2.6	1.8	0.2	–0.5	–0.1	1.4	1.7	1.8	1.9	2.0	1.4	2.2	1.9
Luxembourg	2.6	3.7	2.9	1.7	0.7	0.1	0.0	2.1	2.0	1.7	1.7	1.9	1.9	2.0	1.6
Latvia	5.4	4.2	2.3	0.0	0.7	0.2	0.1	2.9	2.6	3.0	2.6	2.2	2.5	2.1	2.3
Estonia	4.2	5.1	4.2	3.2	0.5	0.1	0.8	3.7	3.4	2.5	2.4	2.1	3.3	2.5	2.4
Cyprus	2.4	3.5	3.1	0.4	–0.3	–1.5	–1.2	0.7	0.8	0.7	1.6	2.0	1.1	1.2	1.3
Malta	2.4	2.5	3.2	1.0	0.8	1.2	0.9	1.3	1.7	1.7	1.8	2.0	1.2	2.0	1.9
Japan	–0.3	–0.3	–0.1	0.3	2.8	0.8	–0.1	0.5	1.0	1.0	1.3	1.3	0.8	1.6	0.2
United Kingdom	2.1	4.5	2.8	2.6	1.5	0.0	0.7	2.7	2.5	1.8	1.9	2.0	2.3	1.6	2.1
Korea	3.2	4.0	2.2	1.3	1.3	0.7	1.0	1.9	1.5	0.5	0.9	2.0	1.3	0.7	0.9
Canada	2.0	2.9	1.5	0.9	1.9	1.1	1.4	1.6	2.2	2.0	2.0	2.0	2.1	2.2	1.9
Australia	3.0	3.4	1.7	2.5	2.5	1.5	1.3	2.0	2.0	1.6	1.8	2.5	1.8	1.8	1.7
Taiwan Province of China	0.9	1.4	1.6	1.0	1.3	–0.6	1.0	1.1	1.5	0.8	1.1	1.4	–0.1	0.8	1.1
Singapore	1.6	5.2	4.6	2.4	1.0	–0.5	–0.5	0.6	0.4	0.7	1.0	1.5	0.5	0.7	1.1
Switzerland	0.9	0.2	–0.7	–0.2	0.0	–1.1	–0.4	0.5	0.9	0.6	0.6	1.0	0.7	0.3	0.9
Sweden	1.9	1.4	0.9	0.4	0.2	0.7	1.1	1.9	2.0	1.7	1.5	1.9	2.2	1.6	1.4
Hong Kong SAR	0.4	5.3	4.1	4.3	4.4	3.0	2.4	1.5	2.4	3.0	2.6	2.5	2.4	3.0	2.6
Czech Republic	2.5	1.9	3.3	1.4	0.4	0.3	0.7	2.5	2.2	2.6	2.3	2.0	2.0	2.3	2.0
Norway	2.0	1.3	0.7	2.1	2.0	2.2	3.6	1.9	2.8	2.3	1.9	2.0	3.5	1.9	1.9
Israel	2.1	3.5	1.7	1.5	0.5	–0.6	–0.5	0.2	0.8	1.0	1.3	2.0	0.8	1.1	1.8
Denmark	2.0	2.7	2.4	0.5	0.4	0.2	0.0	1.1	0.7	1.3	1.5	2.0	0.7	1.2	1.4
New Zealand	2.6	4.1	1.0	1.1	1.2	0.3	0.6	1.9	1.6	1.4	1.9	2.0	1.9	1.5	2.0
Puerto Rico	2.7	2.9	1.3	1.1	0.6	–0.8	–0.3	1.8	1.3	–0.1	1.0	1.2	0.6	–0.1	1.0
Macao SAR	. . .	5.8	6.1	5.5	6.0	4.6	2.4	1.2	3.0	2.4	2.7	3.0	2.9	2.4	2.7
Iceland	6.2	4.0	5.2	3.9	2.0	1.6	1.7	1.8	2.7	2.8	2.5	2.5	3.7	2.6	2.6
San Marino	. . .	2.0	2.8	1.6	1.1	0.1	0.6	1.0	1.5	1.3	1.5	1.7	1.5	1.3	1.5
Memorandum															
Major Advanced Economies	1.8	2.6	1.9	1.3	1.5	0.3	0.8	1.8	2.1	1.6	1.9	2.0	1.7	1.8	1.8

[1]Movements in consumer prices are shown as annual averages.
[2]Monthly year-over-year changes and, for several countries, on a quarterly basis.
[3]Based on Eurostat's harmonized index of consumer prices.

Table A7. Emerging Market and Developing Economies: Consumer Prices[1]

(Annual percent change)

	Average									Projections			End of Period[2]	Projections	
	2001–10	2011	2012	2013	2014	2015	2016	2017	2018	2019	2020	2024	2018	2019	2020
Emerging and Developing Asia	**4.3**	**6.5**	**4.6**	**4.6**	**3.4**	**2.7**	**2.8**	**2.4**	**2.6**	**2.7**	**3.0**	**3.3**	**2.3**	**2.8**	**3.0**
Bangladesh	6.3	11.5	6.2	7.5	7.0	6.2	5.7	5.6	5.6	5.5	5.5	5.5	5.5	5.5	5.5
Bhutan	4.6	7.3	9.3	11.3	9.5	7.6	7.6	5.5	3.5	3.6	4.2	4.5	3.2	3.1	3.9
Brunei Darussalam	0.5	0.1	0.1	0.4	–0.2	–0.4	–0.7	–0.2	0.1	0.1	0.2	0.2	0.0	0.1	0.2
Cambodia	5.1	5.5	2.9	3.0	3.9	1.2	3.0	2.9	2.4	2.2	2.5	3.0	1.6	2.3	2.5
China	2.1	5.4	2.6	2.6	2.0	1.4	2.0	1.6	2.1	2.3	2.4	3.0	1.9	2.2	2.4
Fiji	3.7	7.3	3.4	2.9	0.5	1.4	3.9	3.4	4.1	3.5	3.0	3.0	4.9	3.5	3.0
India	6.5	9.5	10.0	9.4	5.8	4.9	4.5	3.6	3.4	3.4	4.1	4.0	2.5	3.9	4.1
Indonesia	8.6	5.3	4.0	6.4	6.4	6.4	3.5	3.8	3.2	3.2	3.3	3.0	3.1	3.4	3.1
Kiribati	3.1	1.5	–3.0	–1.5	2.1	0.6	1.9	0.4	1.9	1.7	2.4	2.6	1.4	1.7	2.2
Lao P.D.R.	7.6	7.6	4.3	6.4	4.1	1.3	1.8	0.7	2.0	3.1	3.3	3.1	1.5	2.9	3.1
Malaysia	2.2	3.2	1.7	2.1	3.1	2.1	2.1	3.8	1.0	1.0	2.1	2.3	0.2	1.9	2.1
Maldives	4.0	11.3	10.9	3.8	2.1	1.9	0.8	2.3	1.4	1.5	2.3	2.0	0.5	2.1	2.4
Marshall Islands	. . .	5.4	4.3	1.9	1.1	–2.2	–1.5	0.0	0.8	0.6	1.8	2.1	0.8	0.6	1.8
Micronesia	3.2	4.1	6.3	2.3	0.7	0.0	–0.9	0.1	1.5	1.8	2.0	2.0	1.5	1.8	2.0
Mongolia	8.8	7.7	15.0	8.6	12.9	5.9	0.5	4.6	7.6	9.0	8.3	7.1	9.7	8.4	8.1
Myanmar	19.5	6.8	0.4	5.8	5.1	7.3	9.1	4.6	5.9	7.8	6.7	5.5	8.6	7.2	6.8
Nauru	. . .	–3.4	0.3	–1.1	0.3	9.8	8.2	5.1	0.5	2.5	2.3	2.0	3.4	1.5	2.2
Nepal	6.1	9.6	8.3	9.9	9.0	7.2	9.9	4.5	4.2	4.5	6.1	5.3	4.6	6.2	6.0
Palau	2.6	2.6	5.4	2.8	4.0	2.2	–1.3	0.9	1.6	2.2	2.0	2.0	1.4	2.2	2.0
Papua New Guinea	6.5	4.4	4.5	5.0	5.2	6.0	6.7	4.9	5.2	3.9	4.4	4.8	4.8	3.5	4.8
Philippines	5.2	4.8	3.0	2.6	3.6	0.7	1.3	2.9	5.2	2.5	2.3	3.0	5.1	1.6	3.0
Samoa	5.7	2.9	6.2	–0.2	–1.2	1.9	0.1	1.3	3.7	2.9	2.7	2.8	5.8	4.0	2.9
Solomon Islands	8.5	7.4	5.9	5.4	5.2	–0.6	0.5	0.5	2.7	0.4	2.2	4.3	3.2	3.2	3.5
Sri Lanka	9.7	6.7	7.5	6.9	2.8	2.2	4.0	6.6	4.3	4.1	4.5	5.0	2.8	4.2	4.6
Thailand	2.6	3.8	3.0	2.2	1.9	–0.9	0.2	0.7	1.1	0.9	0.9	2.0	0.4	1.3	1.2
Timor-Leste	4.5	13.2	10.9	9.5	0.8	0.6	–1.5	0.5	2.3	2.5	3.1	4.0	2.1	2.8	3.5
Tonga	7.7	6.3	1.1	2.1	1.2	–1.1	2.6	7.4	2.9	3.8	3.9	2.5	4.8	2.8	4.9
Tuvalu	2.9	0.5	1.4	2.0	1.1	3.1	3.5	4.1	2.1	2.1	3.2	2.0	2.3	2.1	3.2
Vanuatu	2.9	0.9	1.3	1.5	0.8	2.5	0.8	3.1	2.9	2.0	2.2	2.6	2.6	2.6	2.2
Vietnam	7.7	18.7	9.1	6.6	4.1	0.6	2.7	3.5	3.5	3.6	3.7	4.0	3.0	3.7	3.8
Emerging and Developing Europe	**11.5**	**7.9**	**6.2**	**5.6**	**6.5**	**10.5**	**5.5**	**5.4**	**6.2**	**6.8**	**5.6**	**5.3**	**7.4**	**6.0**	**5.5**
Albania	3.0	3.4	2.0	1.9	1.6	1.9	1.3	2.0	2.0	1.8	2.0	3.0	1.8	1.8	2.2
Belarus	20.1	53.2	59.2	18.3	18.1	13.5	11.8	6.0	4.9	5.4	4.8	4.0	5.6	5.0	4.5
Bosnia and Herzegovina	2.8	4.0	2.1	–0.1	–0.9	–1.0	–1.6	0.8	1.4	1.1	1.4	1.9	1.6	1.2	1.4
Bulgaria[3]	6.0	3.4	2.4	0.4	–1.6	–1.1	–1.3	1.2	2.6	2.5	2.3	2.2	2.3	2.5	2.2
Croatia	2.8	2.3	3.4	2.2	–0.2	–0.5	–1.1	1.1	1.5	1.0	1.2	1.5	0.9	1.2	1.3
Hungary	5.6	3.9	5.7	1.7	–0.2	–0.1	0.4	2.4	2.8	3.4	3.4	3.0	2.7	3.2	3.4
Kosovo	2.8	7.3	2.5	1.8	0.4	–0.5	0.3	1.5	1.1	2.8	1.5	2.0	2.9	1.6	1.7
Moldova	9.5	7.6	4.6	4.6	5.1	9.6	6.4	6.6	3.1	4.9	5.7	5.0	0.9	7.5	5.0
Montenegro	7.3	3.5	4.1	2.2	–0.7	1.5	–0.3	2.4	2.6	1.1	1.9	1.9	1.7	2.3	1.6
North Macedonia	2.1	3.9	3.3	2.8	–0.3	–0.3	–0.2	1.4	1.5	1.3	1.7	2.2	0.8	1.4	1.8
Poland	2.8	4.3	3.7	0.9	0.0	–0.9	–0.6	2.0	1.6	2.4	3.5	2.8	1.1	3.3	3.5
Romania	12.1	5.8	3.3	4.0	1.1	–0.6	–1.6	1.3	4.6	4.2	3.3	2.5	3.3	4.5	3.5
Serbia	12.5	8.4	5.1	6.8	7.8	15.5	7.0	3.7	2.9	4.7	3.5	4.0	4.3	3.8	3.7
Russia	14.7	11.1	7.3	7.7	2.1	1.4	1.1	3.1	2.0	2.2	1.9	3.0	2.0	2.0	2.2
Turkey	17.5	6.5	8.9	7.5	8.9	7.7	7.8	11.1	16.3	15.7	12.6	11.0	20.3	13.5	12.0
Ukraine[4]	11.1	8.0	0.6	–0.3	12.1	48.7	13.9	14.4	10.9	8.7	5.9	5.0	9.8	7.0	5.6
Latin America and the Caribbean[5]	**5.8**	**5.2**	**4.6**	**4.6**	**4.9**	**5.5**	**5.6**	**6.0**	**6.2**	**7.2**	**6.7**	**4.3**	**7.1**	**7.3**	**6.0**
Antigua and Barbuda	2.2	3.5	3.4	1.1	1.1	1.0	–0.5	2.4	1.2	1.6	2.0	2.0	1.7	2.0	2.0
Argentina[4]	9.5	9.8	10.0	10.6	. . .	. . .	. . .	25.7	34.3	54.4	51.0	17.0	47.6	57.3	39.2
Aruba	3.3	4.4	0.6	–2.4	0.4	0.5	–0.9	–0.5	3.6	3.0	2.0	2.2	4.6	1.8	2.7
The Bahamas	2.3	3.1	1.9	0.4	1.2	1.9	–0.3	1.6	2.2	1.8	2.6	2.2	2.0	2.8	2.4
Barbados	4.1	9.4	4.5	1.8	1.8	–1.1	1.5	4.4	3.7	1.9	1.8	2.3	0.6	1.4	2.3
Belize	2.5	1.7	1.2	0.5	1.2	–0.9	0.7	1.1	0.3	1.2	1.6	2.0	–0.1	2.4	0.8
Bolivia	4.6	9.9	4.5	5.7	5.8	4.1	3.6	2.8	2.3	1.7	3.1	5.0	1.5	2.3	4.0
Brazil	6.6	6.6	5.4	6.2	6.3	9.0	8.7	3.4	3.7	3.8	3.5	3.5	3.7	3.6	3.9
Chile	3.2	3.3	3.0	1.8	4.7	4.3	3.8	2.2	2.3	2.2	2.8	3.0	2.1	2.6	2.9
Colombia	5.6	3.4	3.2	2.0	2.9	5.0	7.5	4.3	3.2	3.6	3.7	3.0	3.2	3.9	3.1

Table A7. Emerging Market and Developing Economies: Consumer Prices[1] *(continued)*

(Annual percent change)

	Average									Projections			End of Period[2]	Projections	
	2001–10	2011	2012	2013	2014	2015	2016	2017	2018	2019	2020	2024	2018	2019	2020
Latin America and the Caribbean (continued)[5]	**5.8**	**5.2**	**4.6**	**4.6**	**4.9**	**5.5**	**5.6**	**6.0**	**6.2**	**7.2**	**6.7**	**4.3**	**7.1**	**7.3**	**6.0**
Costa Rica	10.3	4.9	4.5	5.2	4.5	0.8	0.0	1.6	2.2	2.7	3.1	3.0	2.0	3.2	3.0
Dominica	2.2	1.1	1.4	0.0	0.8	–0.9	0.0	0.6	1.4	1.6	1.8	2.0	1.4	1.8	1.8
Dominican Republic	12.1	8.5	3.7	4.8	3.0	0.8	1.6	3.3	3.6	1.8	4.1	4.0	1.2	3.0	4.0
Ecuador	8.1	4.5	5.1	2.7	3.6	4.0	1.7	0.4	–0.2	0.4	1.2	1.1	0.3	0.5	1.1
El Salvador	3.4	5.1	1.7	0.8	1.1	–0.7	0.6	1.0	1.1	0.9	1.1	1.0	0.4	1.4	1.2
Grenada	3.0	3.0	2.4	0.0	–1.0	–0.6	1.7	0.9	0.8	1.0	1.6	1.9	1.4	1.0	1.9
Guatemala	6.8	6.2	3.8	4.3	3.4	2.4	4.4	4.4	3.8	4.2	4.2	4.3	2.3	3.8	3.9
Guyana	5.9	4.4	2.4	1.9	0.7	–0.9	0.8	1.9	1.3	2.1	3.3	2.8	1.6	2.7	3.5
Haiti	14.0	7.4	6.8	6.8	3.9	7.5	13.4	14.7	12.9	17.6	17.1	5.9	13.3	19.7	15.0
Honduras	7.6	6.8	5.2	5.2	6.1	3.2	2.7	3.9	4.3	4.4	4.2	4.0	4.2	4.4	4.2
Jamaica	11.8	7.5	6.9	9.4	8.3	3.7	2.3	4.4	3.7	3.6	4.6	5.0	2.4	4.7	4.5
Mexico	4.7	3.4	4.1	3.8	4.0	2.7	2.8	6.0	4.9	3.8	3.1	3.0	4.8	3.2	3.0
Nicaragua	8.3	8.1	7.2	7.1	6.0	4.0	3.5	3.9	5.0	5.6	4.2	5.0	3.9	7.0	4.2
Panama	2.6	5.9	5.7	4.0	2.6	0.1	0.7	0.9	0.8	0.0	1.5	2.0	0.2	0.8	1.8
Paraguay	7.8	8.3	3.7	2.7	5.0	3.1	4.1	3.6	4.0	3.5	3.7	3.7	3.2	3.7	3.7
Peru	2.4	3.4	3.7	2.8	3.2	3.5	3.6	2.8	1.3	2.2	1.9	2.0	2.2	1.9	2.0
St. Kitts and Nevis	3.3	5.8	0.8	1.1	0.2	–2.3	–0.3	0.0	–0.2	0.6	2.0	2.0	–0.7	2.0	2.0
St. Lucia	2.6	2.8	4.2	1.5	3.5	–1.0	–3.1	0.1	2.0	2.1	2.3	2.0	2.2	2.1	2.2
St. Vincent and the Grenadines	2.9	3.2	2.6	0.8	0.2	–1.7	–0.2	2.2	2.3	1.4	2.0	2.0	1.4	2.0	2.0
Suriname	13.1	17.7	5.0	1.9	3.4	6.9	55.5	22.0	6.9	5.5	5.8	4.8	5.4	7.1	4.8
Trinidad and Tobago	7.0	5.1	9.3	5.2	5.7	4.7	3.1	1.9	1.0	0.9	1.5	2.6	1.0	0.9	1.5
Uruguay	8.7	8.1	8.1	8.6	8.9	8.7	9.6	6.2	7.6	7.6	7.2	7.0	8.0	7.5	7.0
Venezuela[4]	22.0	26.1	21.1	40.6	62.2	121.7	254.9	438.1	65,374.1	200,000	500,000	. . .	130,060.2	200,000	500,000
Middle East and Central Asia	**7.2**	**9.2**	**9.4**	**8.8**	**6.6**	**5.5**	**5.5**	**6.7**	**9.9**	**8.2**	**9.1**	**7.1**	**11.1**	**7.9**	**8.9**
Afghanistan	. . .	11.8	6.4	7.4	4.7	–0.7	4.4	5.0	0.6	2.6	4.5	5.0	0.8	4.5	4.5
Algeria	3.6	4.5	8.9	3.3	2.9	4.8	6.4	5.6	4.3	2.0	4.1	8.7	2.7	3.9	3.2
Armenia	4.4	7.7	2.5	5.8	3.0	3.7	–1.4	1.0	2.5	1.7	2.5	4.1	1.9	1.5	3.3
Azerbaijan	7.4	7.8	1.0	2.4	1.4	4.0	12.4	12.8	2.3	2.8	3.0	3.5	2.3	2.8	3.0
Bahrain	1.8	–0.4	2.8	3.3	2.7	1.8	2.8	1.4	2.1	1.4	2.8	2.2	1.9	2.0	2.8
Djibouti	3.7	5.2	4.2	1.1	1.3	–0.8	2.7	0.6	0.1	2.2	2.0	2.0	2.0	2.0	2.0
Egypt	7.9	11.1	8.6	6.9	10.1	11.0	10.2	23.5	20.9	13.9	10.0	7.1	14.4	9.4	8.7
Georgia	6.6	8.5	–0.9	–0.5	3.1	4.0	2.1	6.0	2.6	4.2	3.8	3.0	1.5	5.4	3.0
Iran	14.7	21.5	30.6	34.7	15.6	11.9	9.1	9.6	30.5	35.7	31.0	25.0	47.5	31.1	30.0
Iraq	. . .	5.6	6.1	1.9	2.2	1.4	0.5	0.1	0.4	–0.3	1.0	2.0	–0.1	0.3	1.2
Jordan	4.0	4.2	4.5	4.8	2.9	–0.9	–0.8	3.3	4.5	2.0	2.5	2.5	3.6	2.5	2.5
Kazakhstan	8.6	8.4	5.1	5.8	6.7	6.7	14.6	7.4	6.0	5.3	5.2	4.0	5.3	5.7	4.7
Kuwait	3.2	4.9	3.2	2.7	3.1	3.7	3.5	1.5	0.6	1.5	2.2	2.5	0.4	1.8	3.0
Kyrgyz Republic	7.4	16.6	2.8	6.6	7.5	6.5	0.4	3.2	1.5	1.3	5.0	5.0	0.5	4.0	5.1
Lebanon	2.6	5.0	6.6	4.8	1.8	–3.7	–0.8	4.5	6.1	3.1	2.6	2.4	4.0	3.4	2.4
Libya[4]	0.4	15.9	6.1	2.6	2.4	9.8	25.9	28.5	9.3	4.2	8.9	6.5	–4.5	12.0	6.5
Mauritania	6.5	5.7	4.9	4.1	3.8	0.5	1.5	2.3	3.1	3.0	3.4	4.0	3.2	2.8	4.0
Morocco	1.8	0.9	1.3	1.9	0.4	1.5	1.6	0.8	1.9	0.6	1.1	2.0	0.1	0.6	1.1
Oman	2.9	4.0	2.9	1.2	1.0	0.1	1.1	1.6	0.9	0.8	1.8	2.5	0.9	0.8	1.8
Pakistan	8.1	13.7	11.0	7.4	8.6	4.5	2.9	4.1	3.9	7.3	13.0	5.0	5.2	8.9	11.8
Qatar	5.1	2.0	1.8	3.2	3.4	1.8	2.7	0.4	0.2	–0.4	2.2	2.0	. . .	. . .	. . .
Saudi Arabia	2.1	3.8	2.9	3.5	2.2	1.3	2.0	–0.9	2.5	–1.1	2.2	2.1	2.3	–1.1	2.2
Somalia	. . .	. . .	. . .	. . .	. . .	. . .	. . .	. . .	. . .	. . .	. . .	. . .	3.2	4.0	3.0
Sudan[6]	10.8	18.1	35.6	36.5	36.9	16.9	17.8	32.4	63.3	50.4	62.1	74.7	72.9	56.9	66.9
Syria[7]	5.7	. . .	. . .	. . .	. . .	. . .	. . .	. . .	. . .	. . .	. . .	. . .	. . .	. . .	. . .
Tajikistan	13.5	12.4	5.8	5.0	6.1	5.8	5.9	7.3	3.8	7.4	7.1	6.5	5.4	7.0	6.8
Tunisia	3.3	3.2	4.6	5.3	4.6	4.4	3.6	5.3	7.3	6.6	5.4	4.0	7.5	5.9	5.5
Turkmenistan	7.2	5.3	5.3	6.8	6.0	7.4	3.6	8.0	13.2	13.4	13.0	6.0	7.2	9.0	8.0
United Arab Emirates	5.5	0.9	0.7	1.1	2.3	4.1	1.6	2.0	3.1	–1.5	1.2	2.1	3.1	–1.5	1.2
Uzbekistan	14.5	12.4	11.9	11.7	9.1	8.5	8.8	13.9	17.5	14.7	14.1	7.6	14.3	15.6	12.4
Yemen	10.9	19.5	9.9	11.0	8.2	22.0	21.3	30.4	27.6	14.7	35.5	5.0	14.3	15.0	36.3

Table A7. Emerging Market and Developing Economies: Consumer Prices[1] *(continued)*

(Annual percent change)

	Average									Projections			End of Period[2]	Projections	
	2001–10	2011	2012	2013	2014	2015	2016	2017	2018	2019	2020	2024	2018	2019	2020
Sub-Saharan Africa	**9.9**	**9.3**	**9.2**	**6.5**	**6.4**	**6.9**	**10.8**	**10.9**	**8.5**	**8.4**	**8.0**	**6.6**	**7.9**	**9.0**	**7.4**
Angola	42.4	13.5	10.3	8.8	7.3	9.2	30.7	29.8	19.6	17.2	15.0	6.0	18.6	17.0	12.0
Benin	3.1	2.7	6.7	1.0	–1.1	0.2	–0.8	1.8	0.8	–0.3	1.0	2.0	–0.1	0.5	1.1
Botswana	8.6	8.5	7.5	5.9	4.4	3.1	2.8	3.3	3.2	3.0	3.5	4.0	3.5	2.7	3.5
Burkina Faso	2.8	2.8	3.8	0.5	–0.3	0.9	–0.2	0.4	2.0	1.1	1.4	2.0	0.3	2.0	2.0
Burundi	8.9	9.6	18.2	7.9	4.4	5.6	5.5	16.6	1.2	7.3	9.0	9.0	5.3	9.0	9.0
Cabo Verde	2.4	4.5	2.5	1.5	–0.2	0.1	–1.4	0.8	1.3	1.2	1.6	1.8	1.0	1.0	1.6
Cameroon	2.6	2.9	2.4	2.1	1.9	2.7	0.9	0.6	1.1	2.1	2.2	2.0	2.0	2.3	2.2
Central African Republic	3.3	1.2	5.9	6.6	11.6	4.5	4.6	4.5	1.6	3.0	2.6	2.5	4.6	3.0	2.5
Chad	3.2	2.0	7.5	0.2	1.7	4.8	–1.6	–0.9	4.0	3.0	3.0	4.2	4.4	9.1	–6.4
Comoros	4.2	2.2	5.9	0.4	0.0	0.9	0.8	0.1	1.7	3.2	1.4	1.9	0.9	4.8	0.6
Democratic Republic of the Congo	36.8	14.9	0.9	0.9	1.2	0.7	3.2	35.8	29.3	5.5	5.0	5.0	7.2	5.5	5.0
Republic of Congo	2.9	1.8	5.0	4.6	0.9	3.2	3.2	0.4	1.2	1.5	1.8	3.0	0.9	1.9	2.5
Côte d'Ivoire	2.9	4.9	1.3	2.6	0.4	1.2	0.7	0.7	0.4	1.0	2.0	2.0	1.1	1.0	2.0
Equatorial Guinea	5.6	4.8	3.4	3.2	4.3	1.7	1.4	0.7	1.3	0.9	1.7	2.0	2.6	1.6	1.7
Eritrea	18.0	5.9	4.8	5.9	10.0	28.5	–5.6	–13.3	–14.4	–27.6	0.0	2.0	–29.3	–0.1	0.0
Eswatini	7.1	6.1	8.9	5.6	5.7	5.0	7.8	6.2	4.8	2.8	4.0	7.0	5.3	2.3	4.4
Ethiopia	11.1	33.2	24.1	8.1	7.4	9.6	6.6	10.7	13.8	14.6	12.7	8.0	10.6	14.5	10.0
Gabon	1.2	1.3	2.7	0.5	4.5	–0.1	2.1	2.7	4.8	3.0	3.0	2.5	6.3	3.0	3.0
The Gambia	7.0	4.8	4.6	5.2	6.3	6.8	7.2	8.0	6.5	6.9	6.5	5.0	6.4	7.0	6.0
Ghana	15.9	7.7	7.1	11.7	15.5	17.2	17.5	12.4	9.8	9.3	9.2	8.0	9.4	9.3	9.0
Guinea	16.0	21.4	15.2	11.9	9.7	8.2	8.2	8.9	9.8	8.9	8.3	7.8	9.9	8.6	8.1
Guinea-Bissau	2.3	5.1	2.1	0.8	–1.0	1.5	1.5	1.1	1.4	–2.6	1.3	2.5	5.9	1.5	–1.4
Kenya	7.0	14.0	9.4	5.7	6.9	6.6	6.3	8.0	4.7	5.6	5.3	5.0	5.7	6.2	6.2
Lesotho	7.0	6.0	5.5	5.0	4.6	4.3	6.2	4.5	4.7	5.9	5.7	5.5	5.2	6.0	5.3
Liberia	10.0	8.5	6.8	7.6	9.9	7.7	8.8	12.4	23.5	22.2	20.5	13.5	28.5	20.6	19.0
Madagascar	10.2	9.5	5.7	5.8	6.1	7.4	6.7	8.3	7.3	6.7	6.3	5.0	6.1	6.4	6.0
Malawi	8.1	7.6	21.3	28.3	23.8	21.9	21.7	11.5	9.2	8.8	8.4	5.0	9.9	8.6	7.8
Mali	2.7	3.1	5.3	–2.4	2.7	1.4	–1.8	1.8	1.7	0.2	1.3	1.9	1.0	1.0	1.5
Mauritius	5.7	6.5	3.9	3.5	3.2	1.3	1.0	3.7	3.2	0.9	2.3	3.3	1.8	2.0	2.7
Mozambique	11.0	11.2	2.6	4.3	2.6	3.6	19.9	15.1	3.9	5.6	7.6	5.5	3.5	8.5	6.5
Namibia	7.1	5.0	6.7	5.6	5.3	3.4	6.7	6.1	4.3	4.8	5.5	5.5	5.1	4.8	5.5
Niger	2.5	2.9	0.5	2.3	–0.9	1.0	0.2	0.2	2.7	–1.3	2.2	2.0	1.6	0.4	2.0
Nigeria	12.9	10.8	12.2	8.5	8.0	9.0	15.7	16.5	12.1	11.3	11.7	11.0	11.4	11.7	11.7
Rwanda	7.9	5.7	6.3	4.2	1.8	2.5	5.7	4.8	1.4	3.5	5.0	5.0	1.1	5.0	5.0
São Tomé and Príncipe	16.2	14.3	10.6	8.1	7.0	5.2	5.4	5.7	7.9	8.8	8.9	3.0	9.0	7.8	10.0
Senegal	2.1	3.4	1.4	0.7	–1.1	0.1	0.8	1.3	0.5	1.0	1.5	1.5	1.3	2.0	1.5
Seychelles	7.6	2.6	7.1	4.3	1.4	4.0	–1.0	2.9	3.7	2.0	1.8	3.0	3.4	2.3	1.9
Sierra Leone	8.3	6.8	6.6	5.5	4.6	6.7	10.9	18.2	16.9	15.7	13.0	8.3	17.5	14.0	12.0
South Africa	5.9	5.0	5.6	5.8	6.1	4.6	6.3	5.3	4.6	4.4	5.2	5.3	4.9	4.7	5.3
South Sudan	. . .	. . .	45.1	0.0	1.7	52.8	379.8	187.9	83.5	24.5	16.9	8.0	40.1	35.9	10.8
Tanzania	6.6	12.7	16.0	7.9	6.1	5.6	5.2	5.3	3.5	3.6	4.2	5.0	3.3	4.1	4.3
Togo	2.6	3.6	2.6	1.8	0.2	1.8	0.9	–0.2	0.9	1.4	2.0	2.0	2.0	1.7	2.2
Uganda	6.4	15.0	12.7	4.9	3.1	5.4	5.5	5.6	2.6	3.2	3.8	5.0	2.2	3.5	3.9
Zambia	15.4	8.7	6.6	7.0	7.8	10.1	17.9	6.6	7.0	9.9	10.0	8.0	7.9	12.0	8.0
Zimbabwe[8]	–5.6	3.5	3.7	1.6	–0.2	–2.4	–1.6	0.9	10.6	161.8	49.7	3.0	42.1	182.9	9.4

[1]Movements in consumer prices are shown as annual averages.
[2]Monthly year-over-year changes and, for several countries, on a quarterly basis.
[3]Based on Eurostat's harmonized index of consumer prices.
[4]See country-specific notes for Argentina, Libya, Ukraine, and Venezuela in the "Country Notes" section of the Statistical Appendix.
[5]Excludes Venezuela but includes Argentina from 2017 onward. See country-specific notes for Venezuela and Argentina in the "Country Notes" section of the Statistical Appendix.
[6]Data for 2011 exclude South Sudan after July 9. Data for 2012 and onward pertain to the current Sudan.
[7]Data for Syria are excluded for 2011 onward owing to the uncertain political situation.
[8]The Zimbabwe dollar ceased circulating in early 2009. Data are based on IMF staff estimates of price and exchange rate developments in US dollars. IMF staff estimates of US dollar values may differ from authorities' estimates.

Table A8. Major Advanced Economies: General Government Fiscal Balances and Debt[1]

(Percent of GDP unless noted otherwise)

	Average							Projections		
	2001–10	2013	2014	2015	2016	2017	2018	2019	2020	2024
Major Advanced Economies										
Net Lending/Borrowing	–4.6	–4.3	–3.6	–3.0	–3.2	–3.1	–3.6	–3.8	–3.6	–3.3
Output Gap[2]	–0.4	–1.8	–1.2	–0.6	–0.5	0.2	0.8	0.8	0.9	0.8
Structural Balance[2]	–4.3	–3.8	–3.2	–2.9	–3.2	–3.3	–3.8	–4.1	–4.0	–3.6
United States										
Net Lending/Borrowing[3]	–5.2	–4.6	–4.0	–3.6	–4.3	–4.5	–5.7	–5.6	–5.5	–5.1
Output Gap[2]	–0.4	–1.9	–1.1	0.0	0.0	0.6	1.5	1.8	2.0	1.5
Structural Balance[2]	–4.7	–4.5	–3.8	–3.6	–4.4	–4.8	–6.0	–6.3	–6.3	–5.7
Net Debt	47.8	80.8	80.4	80.3	81.6	81.6	80.0	80.9	83.9	94.4
Gross Debt	68.3	104.8	104.4	104.7	106.8	106.0	104.3	106.2	108.0	115.8
Euro Area										
Net Lending/Borrowing	–3.0	–3.1	–2.5	–2.0	–1.6	–1.0	–0.5	–0.9	–0.9	–0.8
Output Gap[2]	0.4	–2.9	–2.5	–2.0	–1.3	–0.3	0.3	0.1	0.0	0.0
Structural Balance[2]	–3.2	–1.2	–0.9	–0.8	–0.7	–0.7	–0.6	–0.7	–0.9	–0.8
Net Debt	56.5	75.1	75.4	74.2	73.8	71.8	70.0	68.9	67.6	62.7
Gross Debt	70.6	91.9	92.1	90.2	89.5	87.3	85.4	83.9	82.3	76.1
Germany										
Net Lending/Borrowing	–2.6	0.0	0.6	0.9	1.2	1.2	1.9	1.1	1.0	1.0
Output Gap[2]	–0.2	–0.8	–0.3	–0.3	0.1	0.9	1.1	0.4	0.1	0.0
Structural Balance[2]	–2.2	0.6	1.2	1.2	1.3	1.1	1.4	0.9	1.0	1.0
Net Debt	54.3	58.6	55.0	52.1	49.3	45.6	42.7	40.1	37.8	29.9
Gross Debt	66.5	78.6	75.6	72.0	69.1	65.2	61.7	58.6	55.7	45.6
France										
Net Lending/Borrowing	–3.8	–4.1	–3.9	–3.6	–3.5	–2.8	–2.5	–3.3	–2.4	–2.6
Output Gap[2]	–0.1	–1.1	–1.0	–0.9	–1.0	–0.1	0.3	0.2	0.1	0.0
Structural Balance[2]	–3.8	–3.4	–3.3	–3.0	–2.8	–2.6	–2.5	–2.4	–2.5	–2.6
Net Debt	59.1	83.0	85.5	86.4	89.2	89.5	89.5	90.4	90.4	88.9
Gross Debt	68.3	93.4	94.9	95.6	98.0	98.4	98.4	99.3	99.2	97.8
Italy										
Net Lending/Borrowing	–3.4	–2.9	–3.0	–2.6	–2.5	–2.4	–2.1	–2.0	–2.5	–2.6
Output Gap[2]	0.0	–4.1	–4.1	–3.4	–2.7	–1.4	–0.9	–1.0	–0.8	–0.1
Structural Balance[2]	–4.0	–0.6	–1.1	–0.7	–1.4	–1.7	–1.8	–1.5	–2.1	–2.6
Net Debt	95.7	116.5	118.7	119.4	119.0	119.2	120.2	121.3	122.0	123.2
Gross Debt	104.2	129.0	131.8	131.6	131.4	131.4	132.2	133.2	133.7	134.0
Japan										
Net Lending/Borrowing	–6.4	–7.9	–5.6	–3.8	–3.7	–3.2	–3.2	–3.0	–2.2	–2.0
Output Gap[2]	–1.6	–1.7	–2.0	–1.5	–1.7	–0.5	–0.5	–0.2	–0.2	0.1
Structural Balance[2]	–6.0	–7.5	–5.5	–4.3	–4.1	–3.4	–3.1	–2.9	–2.1	–2.0
Net Debt	99.9	146.4	148.5	147.8	152.6	151.1	153.2	153.8	153.7	153.6
Gross Debt[4]	175.9	232.5	236.1	231.6	236.3	235.0	237.1	237.7	237.6	237.6
United Kingdom										
Net Lending/Borrowing	–4.1	–5.3	–5.3	–4.2	–2.9	–1.8	–1.4	–1.4	–1.5	–1.0
Output Gap[2]	0.6	–1.7	–0.5	0.0	0.1	0.3	0.1	–0.1	–0.1	0.0
Structural Balance[2]	–4.5	–4.0	–4.7	–4.1	–2.9	–2.0	–1.5	–1.3	–1.4	–1.1
Net Debt	40.4	76.8	78.8	79.3	78.8	77.5	77.5	76.1	75.4	73.9
Gross Debt	45.4	85.2	87.0	87.9	87.9	87.1	86.8	85.6	84.8	83.3
Canada										
Net Lending/Borrowing	–0.2	–1.5	0.2	–0.1	–0.4	–0.3	–0.4	–0.7	–0.7	–0.4
Output Gap[2]	–0.3	–0.8	–0.3	–1.7	–2.1	–0.6	–0.4	–0.6	0.1	0.1
Structural Balance[2]	–0.1	–1.1	0.1	0.8	0.7	0.0	–0.2	–0.5	–0.8	–0.4
Net Debt[5]	29.7	29.8	28.6	28.5	28.8	27.6	26.8	26.4	25.7	22.1
Gross Debt	74.5	86.2	85.7	91.3	91.8	90.1	89.9	87.5	85.0	74.6

Note: The methodology and specific assumptions for each country are discussed in Box A1. The country group composites for fiscal data are calculated as the sum of the US dollar values for the relevant individual countries.

[1]Debt data refer to the end of the year and are not always comparable across countries. Gross and net debt levels reported by national statistical agencies for countries that have adopted the System of National Accounts 2008 (Australia, Canada, Hong Kong SAR, United States) are adjusted to exclude unfunded pension liabilities of government employees' defined-benefit pension plans. Fiscal data for the aggregated major advanced economies and the United States start in 2001, and the average for the aggregate and the United States is therefore for the period 2001–07.

[2]Percent of potential GDP.

[3]Figures reported by the national statistical agency are adjusted to exclude items related to the accrual-basis accounting of government employees' defined-benefit pension plans.

[4]Nonconsolidated basis.

[5]Includes equity shares.

Table A9. Summary of World Trade Volumes and Prices

(Annual percent change)

	Averages										Projections	
	2001–10	2011–20	2011	2012	2013	2014	2015	2016	2017	2018	2019	2020
Trade in Goods and Services												
World Trade[1]												
Volume	5.0	3.6	7.0	3.1	3.6	3.9	2.8	2.3	5.7	3.6	1.1	3.2
Price Deflator												
In US Dollars	3.9	–0.5	11.1	–1.8	–0.7	–1.8	–13.2	–4.1	4.2	5.5	–1.6	–0.3
In SDRs	2.4	0.6	7.3	1.2	0.1	–1.7	–5.8	–3.4	4.4	3.3	0.8	0.1
Volume of Trade												
Exports												
Advanced Economies	3.9	3.3	6.2	2.9	3.2	4.0	3.8	1.8	4.7	3.1	0.9	2.5
Emerging Market and Developing Economies	8.2	4.1	7.9	3.5	4.7	3.3	1.4	3.0	7.3	3.9	1.9	4.1
Imports												
Advanced Economies	3.5	3.3	5.4	1.7	2.6	3.9	4.8	2.6	4.7	3.0	1.2	2.7
Emerging Market and Developing Economies	9.2	4.4	10.6	5.4	5.1	4.3	–0.9	1.8	7.5	5.1	0.7	4.3
Terms of Trade												
Advanced Economies	–0.1	0.1	–1.5	–0.7	1.0	0.3	1.8	1.2	–0.2	–0.7	0.0	–0.1
Emerging Market and Developing Economies	1.0	–0.3	3.6	0.7	–0.6	–0.6	–4.2	–1.6	0.8	1.5	–1.3	–1.1
Trade in Goods												
World Trade[1]												
Volume	5.0	3.5	7.5	2.9	3.3	3.0	2.2	2.1	5.8	3.7	0.9	3.3
Price Deflator												
In US Dollars	3.9	–0.7	12.2	–1.9	–1.3	–2.4	–14.4	–4.8	4.8	5.9	–1.8	–0.7
In SDRs	2.3	0.3	8.4	1.1	–0.5	–2.3	–7.1	–4.2	5.0	3.7	0.6	–0.3
World Trade Prices in US Dollars[2]												
Manufactures	1.9	–0.2	4.3	2.3	–2.8	–0.4	–3.1	–5.1	–0.3	1.9	1.4	–0.2
Oil	10.8	–3.1	31.7	0.9	–0.9	–7.5	–47.2	–15.7	23.3	29.4	–9.6	–6.2
Nonfuel Primary Commodities	8.9	–1.0	20.0	–7.8	–5.4	–5.4	–17.1	–1.0	6.4	1.6	0.9	1.7
Food	5.6	–0.3	18.8	–3.8	0.7	–1.4	–16.8	0.0	3.9	–0.6	–3.4	2.8
Beverages	8.4	–1.8	24.1	–18.1	–13.7	20.1	–7.2	–3.1	–4.7	–8.2	–5.1	6.2
Agricultural Raw Materials	5.9	–2.6	24.3	–20.5	–4.4	–7.5	–11.5	0.0	5.2	1.9	–5.7	–1.9
Metal	14.5	–3.7	12.7	–17.8	–3.9	–12.2	–27.3	–5.3	22.2	6.6	4.3	–6.2
World Trade Prices in SDRs[2]												
Manufactures	0.4	0.8	0.8	5.4	–2.0	–0.4	5.2	–4.5	–0.1	–0.2	3.9	0.2
Oil	9.2	–2.1	27.2	4.0	–0.1	–7.5	–42.7	–15.1	23.6	26.7	–7.4	–5.9
Nonfuel Primary Commodities	7.4	0.0	15.9	–4.9	–4.7	–5.4	–10.0	–0.4	6.7	–0.5	3.3	2.1
Food	4.0	0.7	14.8	–0.8	1.5	–1.3	–9.7	0.7	4.2	–2.6	–1.1	3.2
Beverages	6.8	–0.8	20.0	–15.6	–13.0	20.1	0.7	–2.5	–4.5	–10.1	–2.8	6.6
Agricultural Raw Materials	4.3	–1.6	20.1	–18.1	–3.7	–7.5	–4.0	0.6	5.5	–0.2	–3.5	–1.6
Metal	12.9	–2.7	8.9	–15.3	–3.1	–12.1	–21.1	–4.7	22.5	4.4	6.8	–5.9
World Trade Prices in Euros[2]												
Manufactures	–1.7	1.5	–0.6	10.8	–5.9	–0.5	16.1	–4.9	–2.3	–2.6	6.7	0.0
Oil	6.9	–1.4	25.5	9.2	–4.1	–7.6	–36.8	–15.4	20.8	23.7	–4.9	–6.0
Nonfuel Primary Commodities	5.1	0.7	14.4	–0.2	–8.5	–5.5	–0.7	–0.8	4.3	–2.8	6.1	2.0
Food	1.8	1.4	13.2	4.2	–2.6	–1.4	–0.4	0.3	1.8	–4.9	1.6	3.1
Beverages	4.5	–0.1	18.4	–11.4	–16.4	20.0	11.1	–2.8	–6.6	–12.2	–0.1	6.5
Agricultural Raw Materials	2.1	–1.0	18.5	–14.0	–7.5	–7.6	5.9	0.3	3.1	–2.6	–0.8	–1.7
Metal	10.4	–2.1	7.4	–11.0	–7.0	–12.2	–12.9	–5.0	19.7	1.9	9.7	–6.0

Table A9. Summary of World Trade Volumes and Prices *(continued)*

(Annual percent change)

	Averages										Projections	
	2001–10	2011–20	2011	2012	2013	2014	2015	2016	2017	2018	2019	2020
Trade in Goods												
Volume of Trade												
Exports												
Advanced Economies	3.8	3.1	6.4	2.7	2.6	3.2	3.2	1.5	4.7	3.1	0.6	2.6
Emerging Market and Developing Economies	8.0	3.9	8.0	3.9	4.7	2.7	1.1	2.9	7.0	3.8	1.5	3.9
Fuel Exporters	4.8	1.7	5.9	2.7	2.1	–0.4	3.1	1.2	1.4	0.3	–2.6	3.0
Nonfuel Exporters	9.3	4.6	8.8	4.4	5.8	3.9	0.4	3.3	8.4	4.7	2.7	4.2
Imports												
Advanced Economies	3.5	3.1	6.0	1.1	2.3	3.4	3.8	2.2	5.0	3.5	1.0	2.8
Emerging Market and Developing Economies	9.3	4.3	11.4	5.2	4.7	2.7	–0.7	2.2	7.8	5.0	0.4	4.7
Fuel Exporters	11.0	1.7	11.9	8.5	3.6	1.0	–7.1	–5.5	5.0	–1.7	0.2	3.2
Nonfuel Exporters	8.9	4.8	11.3	4.4	5.0	3.0	0.7	3.8	8.4	6.2	0.4	4.9
Price Deflators in SDRs												
Exports												
Advanced Economies	1.7	0.2	6.1	–0.5	0.4	–1.9	–6.5	–2.1	4.3	2.9	0.0	–0.3
Emerging Market and Developing Economies	4.3	0.5	13.1	3.0	–1.3	–3.1	–8.9	–7.2	6.6	4.9	0.8	–1.0
Fuel Exporters	7.7	–1.0	25.4	4.3	–2.6	–6.9	–30.0	–12.7	17.0	15.7	–3.2	–5.1
Nonfuel Exporters	3.0	0.9	8.2	2.5	–0.7	–1.5	–0.8	–5.7	4.0	2.1	1.9	0.0
Imports												
Advanced Economies	1.7	0.2	8.1	0.6	–0.6	–2.0	–8.0	–3.5	4.4	3.7	0.0	–0.1
Emerging Market and Developing Economies	3.1	0.7	8.2	2.4	–0.8	–2.7	–4.7	–5.6	5.5	3.7	2.3	–0.1
Fuel Exporters	3.7	0.9	6.2	2.9	0.2	–2.4	–3.4	–3.3	3.6	1.5	3.1	0.5
Nonfuel Exporters	3.0	0.7	8.6	2.3	–1.0	–2.7	–4.9	–6.1	5.9	4.1	2.1	–0.2
Terms of Trade												
Advanced Economies	–0.1	0.0	–1.8	–1.0	1.0	0.1	1.7	1.4	–0.1	–0.8	0.0	–0.2
Emerging Market and Developing Economies	1.2	–0.2	4.5	0.6	–0.5	–0.4	–4.4	–1.7	1.0	1.2	–1.5	–0.9
Regional Groups												
Emerging and Developing Asia	–1.3	0.5	–2.7	1.5	1.1	2.4	8.5	0.0	–3.4	–2.2	0.1	0.3
Emerging and Developing Europe	2.1	–0.6	11.3	1.5	–3.1	–0.6	–10.9	–6.0	2.9	4.5	–2.7	–1.0
Middle East and Central Asia	2.3	–0.9	5.1	–1.8	–1.1	–2.5	–8.8	0.8	3.5	–0.5	–1.4	–1.3
Latin America and the Caribbean	3.2	–1.6	12.8	0.2	–0.1	–4.4	–24.8	–5.5	10.4	10.5	–4.6	–4.6
Sub-Saharan Africa	3.9	–0.7	12.8	–1.3	–2.4	–2.8	–14.6	–0.3	6.6	4.0	–4.3	–2.0
Analytical Groups												
By Source of Export Earnings												
Fuel	3.9	–1.9	18.1	1.4	–2.7	–4.6	–27.5	–9.7	12.9	14.0	–6.1	–5.6
Nonfuel	0.0	0.2	–0.4	0.2	0.3	1.3	4.3	0.4	–1.8	–1.9	–0.2	0.2
Memorandum												
World Exports in Billions of US Dollars												
Goods and Services	13,477	23,161	22,315	22,608	23,319	23,752	21,096	20,713	22,801	24,882	24,739	25,381
Goods	10,661	17,992	17,928	18,129	18,542	18,632	16,197	15,737	17,439	19,106	18,898	19,312
Average Oil Price[3]	10.8	–3.1	31.7	0.9	–0.9	–7.5	–47.2	–15.7	23.3	29.4	–9.6	–6.2
In US Dollars a Barrel	54.25	74.39	104.05	105.01	104.07	96.25	50.79	42.84	52.81	68.33	61.78	57.94
Export Unit Value of Manufactures[4]	1.9	–0.2	4.3	2.3	–2.8	–0.4	–3.1	–5.1	–0.3	1.9	1.4	–0.2

[1]Average of annual percent change for world exports and imports.

[2]As represented, respectively, by the export unit value index for manufactures of the advanced economies and accounting for 83 percent of the advanced economies' trade (export of goods) weights; the average of UK Brent, Dubai Fateh, and West Texas Intermediate crude oil prices; and the average of world market prices for nonfuel primary commodities weighted by their 2014–16 shares in world commodity imports.

[3]Percent change of average of UK Brent, Dubai Fateh, and West Texas Intermediate crude oil prices.

[4]Percent change for manufactures exported by the advanced economies.

Table A10. Summary of Current Account Balances
(Billions of US dollars)

	2011	2012	2013	2014	2015	2016	2017	2018	Projections 2019	2020	2024
Advanced Economies	**–38.7**	**25.3**	**203.9**	**225.4**	**269.7**	**337.7**	**411.5**	**362.3**	**304.9**	**252.2**	**261.4**
United States	–445.7	–426.8	–348.8	–365.2	–407.8	–428.3	–439.6	–491.0	–539.5	–569.1	–586.5
Euro Area	–12.4	173.5	300.7	340.4	313.1	370.3	409.7	396.6	376.6	368.9	344.1
Germany	232.9	251.6	244.7	280.0	288.4	293.8	295.8	289.5	269.1	261.0	270.3
France	–24.6	–25.9	–14.3	–27.3	–9.0	–11.5	–18.7	–16.2	–13.7	–13.7	–14.2
Italy	–68.3	–7.0	21.0	41.1	24.6	47.5	50.7	52.0	57.0	58.8	46.4
Spain	–47.4	–3.1	20.7	14.9	13.9	27.9	24.3	13.2	12.8	15.0	17.6
Japan	129.8	59.7	45.9	36.8	136.4	197.9	202.0	175.3	172.1	180.5	228.6
United Kingdom	–51.6	–100.9	–141.9	–149.6	–142.4	–139.3	–88.1	–109.1	–94.7	–99.6	–115.4
Canada	–49.6	–65.7	–59.3	–43.2	–55.2	–48.9	–46.3	–45.2	–32.5	–30.2	–36.4
Other Advanced Economies[1]	264.6	274.1	342.1	357.2	359.8	343.1	328.5	359.2	349.6	326.4	339.2
Emerging Market and Developing Economies	**376.6**	**343.2**	**170.1**	**173.0**	**–60.3**	**–81.3**	**12.6**	**1.9**	**–14.4**	**–134.8**	**–383.2**
Regional Groups											
Emerging and Developing Asia	98.0	120.6	98.8	229.3	309.4	226.9	175.2	–20.1	82.6	47.6	–70.2
Emerging and Developing Europe	–38.7	–27.7	–63.3	–12.7	30.9	–14.4	–23.7	63.7	60.4	23.2	–7.4
Latin America and the Caribbean	–110.2	–146.5	–169.4	–183.2	–170.5	–97.7	–78.8	–99.2	–80.9	–81.9	–122.6
Middle East and Central Asia	436.1	423.3	340.4	202.5	–137.3	–139.9	–23.9	101.4	–14.9	–54.7	–107.8
Sub-Saharan Africa	–8.6	–26.6	–36.4	–62.9	–92.7	–56.3	–36.2	–43.8	–61.6	–69.0	–75.2
Analytical Groups											
By Source of Export Earnings											
Fuel	619.8	596.2	465.1	311.2	–76.3	–73.7	84.9	297.9	145.5	68.7	16.5
Nonfuel	–243.1	–253.0	–295.0	–138.2	16.0	–7.6	–72.3	–296.0	–159.9	–203.5	–399.7
Of Which, Primary Products	–28.1	–61.3	–83.2	–53.8	–66.1	–41.4	–57.4	–72.7	–51.4	–49.9	–65.2
By External Financing Source											
Net Debtor Economies	–327.8	–407.3	–381.9	–349.9	–318.7	–226.1	–241.9	–291.8	–292.4	–332.2	–463.1
Net Debtor Economies by Debt-Servicing Experience											
Economies with Arrears and/or Rescheduling during 2014–18	–18.3	–34.7	–39.4	–33.4	–52.2	–49.4	–35.4	–24.1	–33.9	–40.3	–41.9
Memorandum											
World	**338.0**	**368.5**	**374.0**	**398.4**	**209.4**	**256.3**	**424.1**	**364.2**	**290.5**	**117.4**	**–121.9**
European Union	75.2	206.3	277.2	288.7	282.8	323.2	412.6	383.9	372.6	358.4	319.2
Low-Income Developing Countries	–21.8	–31.1	–37.1	–41.5	–74.6	–37.4	–33.2	–52.9	–66.6	–74.9	–81.1
Middle East and North Africa	405.2	413.0	333.5	193.7	–120.3	–116.9	–4.4	118.3	2.8	–41.2	–88.6

Table A10. Summary of Current Account Balances *(continued)*
(Percent of GDP)

									Projections		
	2011	2012	2013	2014	2015	2016	2017	2018	2019	2020	2024
Advanced Economies	**–0.1**	**0.1**	**0.4**	**0.5**	**0.6**	**0.7**	**0.9**	**0.7**	**0.6**	**0.5**	**0.4**
United States	–2.9	–2.6	–2.1	–2.1	–2.2	–2.3	–2.3	–2.4	–2.5	–2.5	–2.3
Euro Area	–0.1	1.4	2.3	2.5	2.7	3.1	3.2	2.9	2.8	2.7	2.2
Germany	6.2	7.1	6.6	7.2	8.6	8.5	8.1	7.3	7.0	6.6	5.8
France	–0.9	–1.0	–0.5	–1.0	–0.4	–0.5	–0.7	–0.6	–0.5	–0.5	–0.4
Italy	–3.0	–0.3	1.0	1.9	1.3	2.5	2.6	2.5	2.9	2.9	2.1
Spain	–3.2	–0.2	1.5	1.1	1.2	2.3	1.8	0.9	0.9	1.0	1.0
Japan	2.1	1.0	0.9	0.8	3.1	4.0	4.2	3.5	3.3	3.3	3.7
United Kingdom	–2.0	–3.8	–5.1	–4.9	–4.9	–5.2	–3.3	–3.9	–3.5	–3.7	–3.7
Canada	–2.8	–3.6	–3.2	–2.4	–3.5	–3.2	–2.8	–2.6	–1.9	–1.7	–1.6
Other Advanced Economies[1]	4.0	4.1	5.0	5.1	5.6	5.2	4.7	4.9	4.8	4.4	3.8
Emerging Market and Developing Economies	**1.4**	**1.2**	**0.6**	**0.6**	**–0.2**	**–0.3**	**0.0**	**0.0**	**0.0**	**–0.4**	**–0.8**
Regional Groups											
Emerging and Developing Asia	0.8	0.9	0.7	1.5	2.0	1.4	1.0	–0.1	0.4	0.2	–0.2
Emerging and Developing Europe	–0.9	–0.6	–1.4	–0.3	0.9	–0.4	–0.6	1.7	1.6	0.6	–0.1
Latin America and the Caribbean	–1.9	–2.5	–2.8	–3.1	–3.2	–1.9	–1.4	–1.9	–1.6	–1.5	–1.9
Middle East and Central Asia	12.1	11.4	8.8	5.2	–3.9	–4.1	–0.7	2.7	–0.4	–1.4	–2.2
Sub-Saharan Africa	–0.6	–1.7	–2.2	–3.6	–6.0	–3.9	–2.3	–2.7	–3.6	–3.8	–3.1
Analytical Groups											
By Source of Export Earnings											
Fuel	10.5	9.7	7.4	5.1	–1.5	–1.6	1.7	5.6	2.8	1.3	0.3
Nonfuel	–1.2	–1.1	–1.2	–0.6	0.1	0.0	–0.3	–1.0	–0.5	–0.6	–0.9
Of Which, Primary Products	–1.6	–3.3	–4.3	–2.8	–3.5	–2.3	–2.9	–3.8	–2.8	–2.6	–2.7
By External Financing Source											
Net Debtor Economies	–2.5	–3.0	–2.7	–2.4	–2.4	–1.7	–1.7	–2.0	–1.9	–2.0	–2.1
Net Debtor Economies by Debt-Servicing Experience											
Economies with Arrears and/or Rescheduling during 2014–18	–2.2	–3.9	–4.2	–3.5	–5.9	–5.7	–4.4	–2.9	–3.9	–4.3	–3.5
Memorandum											
World	**0.5**	**0.5**	**0.5**	**0.5**	**0.3**	**0.3**	**0.5**	**0.4**	**0.3**	**0.1**	**–0.1**
European Union	0.4	1.2	1.5	1.5	1.7	2.0	2.4	2.0	2.0	1.9	1.4
Low-Income Developing Countries	–1.5	–1.9	–2.1	–2.1	–4.0	–2.1	–1.8	–2.6	–3.1	–3.2	–2.5
Middle East and North Africa	13.5	13.5	10.6	6.0	–4.3	–4.2	–0.2	3.8	0.1	–1.3	–2.3

Table A10. Summary of Current Account Balances *(continued)*

(Percent of exports of goods and services)

									Projections		
	2011	2012	2013	2014	2015	2016	2017	2018	2019	2020	2024
Advanced Economies	**–0.3**	**0.2**	**1.4**	**1.5**	**2.0**	**2.5**	**2.8**	**2.3**	**2.0**	**1.6**	**1.4**
United States	–21.0	–19.2	–15.2	–15.4	–18.0	–19.3	–18.7	–19.6	–21.5	–22.0	–19.1
Euro Area	–0.4	5.4	8.8	9.5	9.6	11.4	11.6	10.3	. . .	. . .	. . .
Germany	13.8	15.4	14.4	15.8	18.3	18.4	17.0	15.5	14.7	13.9	11.9
France	–3.0	–3.2	–1.7	–3.1	–1.2	–1.5	–2.3	–1.8	–1.5	–1.4	–1.2
Italy	–11.1	–1.2	3.4	6.5	4.5	8.6	8.3	7.9	8.9	8.8	5.8
Spain	–11.0	–0.8	4.7	3.3	3.5	6.8	5.4	2.7	2.7	3.0	2.9
Japan	13.9	6.5	5.5	4.3	17.4	24.4	23.1	18.9	19.0	19.8	22.0
United Kingdom	–6.4	–12.6	–17.3	–17.5	–17.9	–18.5	–11.1	–12.9	–11.6	–12.6	–13.1
Canada	–9.1	–11.9	–10.7	–7.6	–11.2	–10.3	–9.1	–8.3	–5.9	–5.3	–5.5
Other Advanced Economies[1]	6.8	6.8	8.2	8.6	9.7	9.4	8.3	8.4	8.4	7.7	6.7
Emerging Market and Developing Economies	**4.5**	**3.7**	**1.9**	**2.2**	**–0.7**	**–1.0**	**0.1**	**0.0**	**–0.2**	**–1.4**	**–3.2**
Regional Groups											
Emerging and Developing Asia	2.8	3.3	2.6	5.7	8.2	6.2	4.3	–0.5	1.8	1.0	–1.2
Emerging and Developing Europe	–2.8	–1.9	–4.3	–0.9	2.6	–1.3	–1.8	4.2	3.9	1.5	–0.4
Latin America and the Caribbean	–8.9	–11.5	–13.4	–14.7	–15.8	–9.3	–6.7	–7.8	–6.4	–6.3	–7.7
Middle East and Central Asia	25.6	22.5	19.2	12.9	–10.2	–11.5	–2.0	6.6	–1.0	–3.5	–6.5
Sub-Saharan Africa	–1.8	–5.6	–7.6	–13.8	–26.9	–17.8	–9.9	–10.4	–15.1	–16.4	–14.2
Analytical Groups											
By Source of Export Earnings											
Fuel	25.4	22.6	18.5	13.8	–4.1	–4.7	4.8	14.6	7.7	3.9	1.0
Nonfuel	–4.2	–4.2	–4.6	–2.1	0.3	–0.1	–1.1	–4.1	–2.2	–2.7	–4.1
Of Which, Primary Products	–5.7	–12.5	–17.2	–11.4	–16.4	–10.4	–12.9	–15.2	–10.8	–10.1	–10.7
By External Financing Source											
Net Debtor Economies	–8.3	–10.1	–9.2	–8.4	–8.7	–6.2	–5.8	–6.4	–6.2	–6.8	–7.2
Net Debtor Economies by Debt-Servicing Experience											
Economies with Arrears and/or Rescheduling during 2014–18	–5.9	–11.2	–12.8	–11.8	–24.0	–25.5	–15.8	–9.3	–12.7	–14.3	–11.7
Memorandum											
World	**1.5**	**1.5**	**1.6**	**1.8**	**1.0**	**1.3**	**1.8**	**1.5**	**1.2**	**0.5**	**–0.4**
European Union	1.0	2.8	3.6	3.6	3.9	4.4	5.2	4.4	4.3	4.0	3.0
Low-Income Developing Countries	–4.6	–6.5	–7.2	–7.8	–15.5	–7.8	–5.9	–8.2	–9.9	–10.2	–7.5
Middle East and North Africa	27.1	24.9	21.3	14.1	–9.9	–10.7	–0.6	8.6	0.2	–2.9	–6.0

[1]Excludes the Group of Seven (Canada, France, Germany, Italy, Japan, United Kingdom, United States) and euro area countries.

Table A11. Advanced Economies: Balance on Current Account

(Percent of GDP)

									Projections		
	2011	2012	2013	2014	2015	2016	2017	2018	2019	2020	2024
Advanced Economies	**–0.1**	**0.1**	**0.4**	**0.5**	**0.6**	**0.7**	**0.9**	**0.7**	**0.6**	**0.5**	**0.4**
United States	–2.9	–2.6	–2.1	–2.1	–2.2	–2.3	–2.3	–2.4	–2.5	–2.5	–2.3
Euro Area[1]	–0.1	1.4	2.3	2.5	2.7	3.1	3.2	2.9	2.8	2.7	2.2
Germany	6.2	7.1	6.6	7.2	8.6	8.5	8.1	7.3	7.0	6.6	5.8
France	–0.9	–1.0	–0.5	–1.0	–0.4	–0.5	–0.7	–0.6	–0.5	–0.5	–0.4
Italy	–3.0	–0.3	1.0	1.9	1.3	2.5	2.6	2.5	2.9	2.9	2.1
Spain	–3.2	–0.2	1.5	1.1	1.2	2.3	1.8	0.9	0.9	1.0	1.0
Netherlands	8.5	10.2	9.8	8.2	6.3	8.1	10.8	10.9	9.8	9.5	8.5
Belgium	–1.1	–0.1	–0.3	–0.9	–1.0	–0.6	0.7	–1.3	–1.1	–0.8	–1.3
Austria	1.6	1.5	1.9	2.5	1.7	2.5	2.0	2.3	1.6	1.8	1.9
Ireland	–1.6	–3.4	1.6	1.1	4.4	–4.2	0.5	10.6	10.8	9.6	5.7
Portugal	–6.0	–1.8	1.6	0.1	0.1	0.6	0.4	–0.6	–0.6	–0.7	–1.5
Greece	–10.0	–2.4	–2.6	–2.3	–1.5	–2.3	–2.4	–3.5	–3.0	–3.3	–4.5
Finland	–1.7	–2.3	–1.9	–1.5	–0.7	–0.7	–0.7	–1.6	–0.7	–0.5	0.4
Slovak Republic	–5.0	0.9	1.9	1.1	–1.7	–2.2	–2.0	–2.5	–2.5	–1.7	0.1
Lithuania	–4.6	–1.4	0.8	3.2	–2.8	–0.8	0.9	1.6	1.1	1.1	–0.8
Slovenia	–0.8	1.3	3.3	5.1	3.8	4.8	6.1	5.7	4.2	4.1	1.4
Luxembourg	6.0	5.6	5.4	5.2	5.1	5.1	5.0	4.7	4.5	4.5	4.4
Latvia	–3.2	–3.6	–2.7	–1.7	–0.5	1.6	0.7	–1.0	–1.8	–2.1	–3.4
Estonia	1.3	–1.9	0.5	0.8	1.8	2.0	3.2	1.7	0.7	0.3	–0.8
Cyprus	–4.1	–6.0	–4.9	–4.3	–1.5	–5.1	–8.4	–7.0	–7.8	–7.5	–5.0
Malta	–0.2	1.7	2.7	8.7	2.8	3.8	10.5	9.8	7.6	6.2	6.1
Japan	2.1	1.0	0.9	0.8	3.1	4.0	4.2	3.5	3.3	3.3	3.7
United Kingdom	–2.0	–3.8	–5.1	–4.9	–4.9	–5.2	–3.3	–3.9	–3.5	–3.7	–3.7
Korea	1.3	3.8	5.6	5.6	7.2	6.5	4.6	4.4	3.2	2.9	2.9
Canada	–2.8	–3.6	–3.2	–2.4	–3.5	–3.2	–2.8	–2.6	–1.9	–1.7	–1.6
Australia	–3.1	–4.3	–3.4	–3.1	–4.6	–3.3	–2.6	–2.1	–0.3	–1.7	–1.9
Taiwan Province of China	7.8	8.7	9.7	11.4	13.9	13.5	14.5	12.2	11.4	10.8	8.0
Singapore	22.2	17.6	15.7	18.0	17.2	17.5	16.4	17.9	16.5	16.6	15.0
Switzerland	7.8	10.7	11.6	8.5	11.2	9.4	6.7	10.2	9.6	9.8	9.8
Sweden	5.5	5.5	5.2	4.5	4.1	3.8	2.8	1.7	2.9	2.7	2.4
Hong Kong SAR	5.6	1.6	1.5	1.4	3.3	4.0	4.6	4.3	5.5	5.1	4.0
Czech Republic	–2.1	–1.6	–0.5	0.2	0.2	1.6	1.7	0.3	–0.1	–0.2	–0.7
Norway	12.4	12.5	10.3	10.5	7.9	4.0	5.7	8.1	6.9	7.2	5.9
Israel	2.1	0.5	2.9	4.4	5.0	3.6	2.7	2.7	2.4	2.5	2.5
Denmark	6.6	6.3	7.8	8.9	8.2	7.9	8.0	5.7	5.5	5.2	4.6
New Zealand	–2.8	–3.9	–3.2	–3.1	–3.0	–2.2	–2.9	–3.8	–4.1	–4.3	–4.3
Puerto Rico	...	...	...	...	...	...	...	...	...	...	...
Macao SAR	40.9	39.3	40.2	34.2	25.3	27.2	33.1	35.2	35.7	35.3	29.8
Iceland	–5.1	–3.8	5.8	3.9	5.1	7.6	3.8	2.8	3.1	1.6	0.3
San Marino	...	...	...	...	...	...	–0.5	0.4	0.4	0.2	0.2
Memorandum											
Major Advanced Economies	–0.8	–0.9	–0.7	–0.6	–0.5	–0.2	–0.1	–0.4	–0.5	–0.5	–0.4
Euro Area[2]	0.8	2.3	2.8	2.9	3.2	3.5	3.6	3.5	3.4	3.2	2.7

[1]Data corrected for reporting discrepancies in intra-area transactions.
[2]Data calculated as the sum of the balances of individual euro area countries.

Table A12. Emerging Market and Developing Economies: Balance on Current Account

(Percent of GDP)

									Projections	
	2011	2012	2013	2014	2015	2016	2017	2018	2019	2020	2024
Emerging and Developing Asia	**0.8**	**0.9**	**0.7**	**1.5**	**2.0**	**1.4**	**1.0**	**–0.1**	**0.4**	**0.2**	**–0.2**
Bangladesh	–1.0	0.7	1.2	1.3	1.9	0.6	–2.1	–2.7	–2.0	–2.1	–2.0
Bhutan	–29.8	–21.4	–25.4	–26.8	–27.2	–30.8	–23.0	–18.4	–12.5	–9.6	6.4
Brunei Darussalam	34.7	29.8	20.9	31.9	16.7	12.9	16.4	7.9	8.5	12.0	19.8
Cambodia	–7.9	–8.5	–8.4	–8.5	–8.7	–8.4	–7.9	–11.3	–12.5	–12.3	–8.8
China	1.8	2.5	1.5	2.2	2.7	1.8	1.6	0.4	1.0	0.9	0.4
Fiji	–4.7	–1.3	–8.9	–6.1	–3.8	–3.9	–7.0	–8.9	–7.3	–6.2	–5.2
India	–4.3	–4.8	–1.7	–1.3	–1.0	–0.6	–1.8	–2.1	–2.0	–2.3	–2.5
Indonesia	0.2	–2.7	–3.2	–3.1	–2.0	–1.8	–1.6	–3.0	–2.9	–2.7	–2.5
Kiribati	–9.5	1.9	–5.5	31.1	32.8	10.8	38.0	36.2	13.2	2.4	–4.2
Lao P.D.R.	–15.3	–21.3	–26.5	–23.3	–22.4	–11.0	–10.6	–12.0	–12.1	–12.0	–10.9
Malaysia	10.7	5.1	3.4	4.3	3.0	2.4	2.8	2.1	3.1	1.9	0.9
Maldives	–14.8	–6.6	–4.3	–3.7	–7.5	–23.2	–21.9	–25.3	–20.4	–15.7	–8.7
Marshall Islands	–2.2	–6.3	–10.7	–1.7	14.4	9.7	4.8	5.1	4.1	3.2	–0.2
Micronesia	–20.0	–14.6	–11.6	–0.9	1.6	3.9	7.5	24.5	15.7	2.6	–4.2
Mongolia	–26.5	–27.4	–25.4	–11.3	–4.0	–6.3	–10.1	–17.0	–14.4	–12.4	–8.8
Myanmar	–1.7	–1.7	–0.6	–4.2	–3.1	–4.0	–6.5	–4.2	–4.8	–4.9	–4.6
Nauru	28.7	35.7	49.5	25.2	–21.3	2.0	12.7	1.9	3.6	–4.3	–3.6
Nepal	–1.0	4.8	3.3	4.5	5.0	6.3	–0.4	–8.1	–8.3	–10.0	–5.0
Palau	–12.7	–15.3	–14.2	–17.9	–8.7	–13.6	–19.1	–16.6	–25.4	–24.8	–19.9
Papua New Guinea	–24.0	–36.1	–30.8	12.3	17.5	34.6	28.7	27.4	23.0	24.8	22.2
Philippines	2.5	2.8	4.2	3.8	2.5	–0.4	–0.7	–2.6	–2.0	–2.3	–1.9
Samoa	–6.9	–9.0	–1.7	–8.1	–3.1	–4.7	–1.8	2.3	–0.6	–0.3	–1.2
Solomon Islands	–8.2	1.5	–3.4	–4.3	–3.0	–4.0	–4.8	–5.2	–7.1	–8.2	–6.8
Sri Lanka	–7.1	–5.8	–3.4	–2.5	–2.3	–2.1	–2.6	–3.2	–2.6	–2.8	–2.1
Thailand	2.5	–1.2	–2.1	2.9	6.9	10.5	9.7	6.4	6.0	5.4	3.7
Timor-Leste	39.1	39.7	42.4	27.1	6.6	–21.7	–11.4	–7.0	1.1	–2.9	–9.1
Tonga	–16.9	–12.3	–8.0	–10.0	–10.7	–6.6	–6.2	–7.7	–11.0	–13.2	–12.2
Tuvalu	–37.1	18.2	–6.6	2.9	–52.8	23.2	30.9	7.1	29.9	–7.5	1.1
Vanuatu	–7.8	–6.5	–3.3	6.2	–1.6	0.8	–6.4	3.4	6.1	–5.6	–3.7
Vietnam	0.2	6.0	4.5	4.9	–0.1	2.9	2.1	2.4	2.2	1.9	1.0
Emerging and Developing Europe	**–0.9**	**–0.6**	**–1.4**	**–0.3**	**0.9**	**–0.4**	**–0.6**	**1.7**	**1.6**	**0.6**	**–0.1**
Albania	–13.2	–10.1	–9.3	–10.8	–8.6	–7.6	–7.5	–6.8	–6.6	–6.4	–6.2
Belarus	–8.2	–2.8	–10.0	–6.6	–3.3	–3.4	–1.7	–0.4	–0.9	–3.4	–2.8
Bosnia and Herzegovina	–9.5	–8.7	–5.3	–7.4	–5.3	–4.7	–4.7	–4.1	–4.8	–4.9	–4.8
Bulgaria	0.3	–0.9	1.3	1.2	0.0	2.6	3.1	4.6	3.2	2.5	0.3
Croatia	–0.7	–0.1	0.9	2.0	4.6	2.5	3.5	2.5	1.7	1.0	0.0
Hungary	0.4	1.5	3.6	1.3	2.4	4.6	2.3	–0.5	–0.9	–0.6	0.0
Kosovo	–12.7	–5.8	–3.4	–6.9	–8.6	–7.9	–6.4	–8.0	–6.5	–6.6	–7.2
Moldova	–10.1	–7.4	–5.2	–6.0	–6.0	–3.5	–5.8	–10.5	–9.1	–8.9	–6.8
Montenegro	–14.8	–15.3	–11.4	–12.4	–11.0	–16.2	–16.1	–17.2	–17.1	–14.9	–9.5
North Macedonia	–2.5	–3.2	–1.6	–0.5	–2.1	–3.1	–1.3	–0.3	–0.7	–1.2	–2.0
Poland	–5.2	–3.7	–1.3	–2.1	–0.6	–0.5	0.1	–0.6	–0.9	–1.1	–2.1
Romania	–5.0	–4.8	–1.1	–0.7	–1.2	–2.1	–3.2	–4.5	–5.5	–5.2	–4.4
Russia	4.8	3.3	1.5	2.8	5.0	1.9	2.1	6.8	5.7	3.9	3.2
Serbia	–8.1	–10.8	–5.7	–5.6	–3.5	–2.9	–5.2	–5.2	–5.8	–5.1	–4.1
Turkey	–8.9	–5.5	–6.7	–4.7	–3.7	–3.8	–5.6	–3.5	–0.6	–0.9	–1.9
Ukraine[1]	–6.3	–8.1	–9.2	–3.9	1.7	–1.5	–2.2	–3.4	–2.8	–3.5	–3.3
Latin America and the Caribbean	**–1.9**	**–2.5**	**–2.8**	**–3.1**	**–3.2**	**–1.9**	**–1.4**	**–1.9**	**–1.6**	**–1.5**	**–1.9**
Antigua and Barbuda	. . .	. . .	. . .	0.3	2.2	–2.4	–8.8	–7.0	–6.1	–5.5	–4.7
Argentina	–1.0	–0.4	–2.1	–1.6	–2.7	–2.7	–4.9	–5.3	–1.2	0.3	–1.6
Aruba	–10.5	3.5	–12.9	–5.1	4.2	5.0	1.0	0.2	–1.8	–1.1	0.7
The Bahamas	–11.8	–14.0	–14.1	–17.4	–12.0	–6.0	–12.4	–12.1	–7.4	–12.8	–5.5
Barbados	–11.8	–8.5	–8.4	–9.2	–6.1	–4.3	–3.8	–3.7	–3.9	–3.5	–2.5
Belize	–1.1	–1.2	–4.5	–7.9	–9.8	–9.0	–7.0	–8.1	–7.0	–6.4	–4.7
Bolivia	2.2	7.2	3.4	1.7	–5.8	–5.6	–5.0	–4.9	–5.0	–4.1	–3.0
Brazil	–2.9	–3.4	–3.2	–4.1	–3.0	–1.3	–0.4	–0.8	–1.2	–1.0	–1.6
Chile	–1.7	–3.9	–4.1	–1.7	–2.3	–1.6	–2.1	–3.1	–3.5	–2.9	–1.7
Colombia	–2.9	–3.1	–3.3	–5.2	–6.3	–4.3	–3.3	–4.0	–4.2	–4.0	–3.7

Table A12. Emerging Market and Developing Economies: Balance on Current Account *(continued)*

(Percent of GDP)

	2011	2012	2013	2014	2015	2016	2017	2018	Projections 2019	2020	2024
Latin America and the Caribbean (continued)	**–1.9**	**–2.5**	**–2.8**	**–3.1**	**–3.2**	**–1.9**	**–1.4**	**–1.9**	**–1.6**	**–1.5**	**–1.9**
Costa Rica	–5.3	–5.1	–4.8	–4.8	–3.5	–2.2	–2.9	–3.1	–2.4	–2.5	–3.3
Dominica	. . .	. . .	. . .	–6.9	–7.6	–8.9	–12.7	–43.4	–33.6	–25.8	–9.5
Dominican Republic	–7.5	–6.5	–4.1	–3.2	–1.8	–1.1	–0.2	–1.4	–1.3	–1.1	–2.5
Ecuador	–0.5	–0.2	–1.0	–0.7	–2.2	1.3	–0.5	–1.4	0.1	0.7	1.7
El Salvador	–5.5	–5.8	–6.9	–5.4	–3.2	–2.3	–1.9	–4.8	–4.9	–5.0	–5.3
Grenada	. . .	. . .	. . .	–11.6	–12.2	–11.0	–12.0	–11.2	–11.3	–9.9	–8.9
Guatemala	–3.4	–2.6	–2.5	–2.1	–0.2	1.5	1.6	0.8	0.6	0.3	–1.0
Guyana	–12.2	–11.3	–13.3	–9.5	–5.1	0.4	–6.8	–17.5	–22.7	–18.4	1.7
Haiti	–4.3	–5.7	–6.6	–8.5	–3.0	–0.9	–1.0	–3.7	–3.3	–3.2	–2.6
Honduras	–8.0	–8.5	–9.5	–6.9	–4.7	–2.6	–1.8	–4.2	–4.2	–4.3	–3.9
Jamaica	–12.2	–11.1	–9.2	–7.5	–3.1	–1.4	–2.6	–2.4	–2.5	–2.2	–3.1
Mexico	–1.0	–1.5	–2.5	–1.9	–2.6	–2.2	–1.7	–1.8	–1.2	–1.6	–2.0
Nicaragua	–11.9	–10.7	–10.9	–7.1	–9.0	–6.6	–4.9	0.6	2.3	1.8	–1.0
Panama	–13.0	–9.2	–9.0	–13.4	–9.0	–8.0	–7.9	–7.8	–6.1	–5.3	–5.5
Paraguay	0.6	–0.9	1.6	–0.1	–0.4	3.5	3.1	0.5	–0.1	1.3	1.8
Peru	–2.0	–3.2	–5.1	–4.5	–5.0	–2.6	–1.2	–1.6	–1.9	–2.0	–1.8
St. Kitts and Nevis	. . .	. . .	. . .	0.1	–9.4	–13.8	–11.7	–7.4	–6.3	–15.8	–13.1
St. Lucia	. . .	. . .	. . .	–0.3	2.3	–4.6	1.5	3.0	2.5	1.7	0.8
St. Vincent and the Grenadines	. . .	. . .	. . .	–26.3	–15.3	–13.0	–12.0	–12.2	–11.6	–10.7	–9.0
Suriname	9.8	3.3	–3.8	–7.9	–16.4	–5.4	–0.1	–5.5	–5.7	–5.8	–2.6
Trinidad and Tobago	16.9	12.9	20.0	14.6	7.4	–4.0	5.0	7.1	2.4	1.7	2.4
Uruguay	. . .	–4.0	–3.6	–3.2	–0.9	0.6	0.8	–0.6	–1.7	–3.0	–1.8
Venezuela	4.9	0.8	2.0	2.3	–5.0	–1.4	6.1	6.4	7.0	1.5	. . .
Middle East and Central Asia	**12.1**	**11.4**	**8.8**	**5.2**	**–3.9**	**–4.1**	**–0.7**	**2.7**	**–0.4**	**–1.4**	**–2.2**
Afghanistan	26.6	10.9	0.3	5.8	2.9	8.4	4.7	9.1	2.0	0.2	–1.6
Algeria	9.9	5.9	0.4	–4.4	–16.4	–16.5	–13.2	–9.6	–12.6	–11.9	–6.9
Armenia	–10.4	–10.0	–7.3	–7.6	–2.6	–2.3	–2.4	–9.4	–7.4	–7.4	–5.9
Azerbaijan	26.0	21.4	16.6	13.9	–0.4	–3.6	4.1	12.9	9.7	10.0	7.6
Bahrain	8.8	8.4	7.4	4.6	–2.4	–4.6	–4.5	–5.9	–4.3	–4.4	–4.1
Djibouti	–1.8	–23.4	–29.7	23.1	27.7	–1.0	–3.6	15.1	–0.3	0.6	2.6
Egypt	–2.5	–3.6	–2.2	–0.9	–3.7	–6.0	–6.1	–2.4	–3.1	–2.8	–2.5
Georgia	–12.8	–11.9	–5.9	–10.8	–12.6	–13.1	–8.8	–7.7	–5.9	–5.8	–5.3
Iran	10.4	6.0	6.7	3.2	0.3	4.0	3.8	4.1	–2.7	–3.4	–3.6
Iraq	10.9	5.1	1.1	2.6	–6.5	–8.3	1.8	6.9	–3.5	–3.7	–7.3
Jordan	–10.2	–15.0	–10.3	–7.2	–9.0	–9.4	–10.6	–7.0	–7.0	–6.2	–6.0
Kazakhstan	5.3	1.1	0.8	2.8	–3.3	–5.9	–3.1	0.0	–1.2	–1.5	–0.9
Kuwait	42.9	45.5	40.3	33.4	3.5	–4.6	8.0	14.4	8.2	6.8	3.2
Kyrgyz Republic	–7.7	–15.5	–13.9	–17.0	–15.9	–11.6	–6.2	–8.7	–10.0	–8.3	–9.4
Lebanon	–15.7	–25.2	–27.4	–28.2	–19.3	–23.1	–25.9	–25.6	–26.4	–26.3	–23.1
Libya[1]	9.9	29.9	0.0	–78.4	–54.4	–24.7	7.9	2.2	–0.3	–11.6	–7.6
Mauritania	–5.0	–24.2	–22.0	–27.3	–19.8	–15.1	–14.4	–18.4	–13.7	–20.1	–7.1
Morocco	–7.6	–9.3	–7.6	–5.9	–2.1	–4.0	–3.4	–5.4	–4.5	–3.8	–2.8
Oman	13.0	10.2	6.6	5.2	–15.9	–19.1	–15.6	–5.5	–7.2	–8.0	–9.1
Pakistan	0.1	–2.1	–1.1	–1.3	–1.0	–1.7	–4.1	–6.3	–4.6	–2.6	–1.8
Qatar	31.1	33.2	30.4	24.0	8.5	–5.5	3.8	8.7	6.0	4.1	3.3
Saudi Arabia	23.6	22.4	18.1	9.8	–8.7	–3.7	1.5	9.2	4.4	1.5	–1.8
Somalia	. . .	. . .	–2.9	–7.0	–6.0	–9.4	–9.0	–8.3	–8.0	–7.7	–9.7
Sudan[2]	–4.0	–12.8	–11.0	–5.8	–8.4	–7.6	–10.0	–13.6	–7.4	–12.5	–10.9
Syria[3]	. . .	. . .	. . .	. . .	. . .	. . .	. . .	. . .	. . .	. . .	. . .
Tajikistan	–6.3	–9.0	–10.4	–3.4	–6.1	–4.2	2.2	–5.0	–5.8	–5.8	–5.5
Tunisia	–8.4	–9.1	–9.7	–9.8	–9.7	–9.3	–10.2	–11.1	–10.4	–9.4	–5.7
Turkmenistan	–0.8	–0.9	–7.3	–6.1	–15.6	–20.2	–10.3	5.7	–0.6	–3.0	–7.4
United Arab Emirates	12.6	19.7	19.0	13.5	4.9	3.7	7.3	9.1	9.0	7.1	5.2
Uzbekistan	4.8	1.0	2.4	1.4	0.6	0.4	2.5	–7.1	–6.5	–5.6	–4.2
Yemen	–3.0	–1.7	–3.1	–0.7	–7.1	–3.2	–0.2	–1.8	–4.0	1.3	–0.8

Table A12. Emerging Market and Developing Economies: Balance on Current Account *(continued)*

(Percent of GDP)

									Projections		
	2011	2012	2013	2014	2015	2016	2017	2018	2019	2020	2024
Sub-Saharan Africa	**–0.6**	**–1.7**	**–2.2**	**–3.6**	**–6.0**	**–3.9**	**–2.3**	**–2.7**	**–3.6**	**–3.8**	**–3.1**
Angola	11.7	10.8	6.1	–2.6	–8.8	–4.8	–0.5	6.1	0.9	–0.7	–0.9
Benin	–5.3	–5.4	–6.1	–7.2	–7.3	–6.8	–7.3	–6.0	–6.1	–5.8	–5.0
Botswana	3.1	0.3	8.9	15.4	7.8	7.8	5.3	1.9	–3.0	–1.0	3.0
Burkina Faso	–1.5	–1.5	–11.3	–8.1	–8.6	–7.2	–7.3	–5.8	–5.7	–4.0	–3.7
Burundi	–14.4	–18.6	–19.3	–18.5	–17.7	–13.1	–12.3	–13.4	–12.6	–11.9	–8.8
Cabo Verde	–16.3	–12.6	–4.9	–9.1	–3.2	–3.9	–6.6	–4.5	–4.4	–4.2	–3.6
Cameroon	–2.5	–3.3	–3.5	–4.0	–3.8	–3.2	–2.7	–3.7	–3.7	–3.5	–3.2
Central African Republic	–6.8	–5.6	–2.9	–13.3	–9.1	–5.3	–7.8	–8.0	–4.1	–4.9	–5.0
Chad	–5.8	–7.8	–9.1	–8.9	–13.6	–10.2	–6.6	–3.4	–6.4	–6.1	–5.9
Comoros	–3.6	–3.2	–4.1	–3.8	–0.3	–4.3	–2.2	–3.8	–8.0	–7.4	–4.4
Democratic Republic of the Congo	–5.0	–4.3	–5.0	–4.7	–3.8	–4.1	–3.2	–4.6	–3.4	–4.2	–4.5
Republic of Congo	13.9	17.7	13.8	1.3	–54.2	–63.5	–5.9	6.7	6.8	5.3	–2.1
Côte d'Ivoire	10.4	–1.2	–1.4	1.4	–0.6	–1.2	–2.7	–4.7	–3.8	–3.8	–3.1
Equatorial Guinea	–5.7	–1.1	–2.4	–4.3	–16.4	–13.0	–5.8	–5.4	–5.9	–6.2	–5.6
Eritrea	13.4	12.9	2.3	17.3	20.8	15.3	23.8	16.6	11.3	13.2	2.9
Eswatini	–5.8	5.0	10.8	11.6	12.9	7.8	7.0	2.0	2.5	5.0	4.2
Ethiopia	–2.5	–7.1	–6.1	–6.6	–11.7	–9.4	–8.6	–6.5	–6.0	–5.3	–3.9
Gabon	24.0	17.9	7.3	7.6	–5.6	–9.9	–4.4	–2.4	0.1	0.9	4.0
The Gambia	–7.4	–4.5	–6.7	–7.3	–9.9	–9.2	–7.4	–9.7	–9.4	–13.1	–11.4
Ghana	–6.6	–8.7	–9.0	–7.0	–5.8	–5.2	–3.4	–3.1	–3.6	–3.8	–2.0
Guinea	–18.4	–19.9	–12.5	–12.9	–12.9	–31.9	–7.1	–18.4	–20.7	–17.7	–10.3
Guinea-Bissau	–1.3	–8.4	–4.6	0.5	1.9	1.3	0.3	–4.5	–4.2	–3.7	–2.2
Kenya	–9.2	–8.4	–8.8	–10.4	–6.7	–4.9	–6.2	–5.0	–4.7	–4.6	–4.7
Lesotho	–13.4	–8.4	–5.1	–4.9	–4.0	–8.4	–4.7	–8.6	–14.6	–4.9	–5.6
Liberia	–17.6	–17.3	–21.7	–26.4	–26.7	–18.6	–23.4	–23.4	–21.2	–21.0	–14.7
Madagascar	–7.7	–8.9	–6.3	–0.3	–1.9	0.6	–0.5	0.8	–1.6	–2.7	–4.1
Malawi	–8.6	–9.2	–8.4	–8.2	–17.2	–18.5	–25.6	–15.3	–14.3	–14.2	–10.2
Mali	–5.1	–2.2	–2.9	–4.7	–5.3	–7.2	–7.3	–3.8	–5.5	–5.5	–6.6
Mauritius	–13.5	–7.1	–6.2	–5.4	–3.6	–4.0	–4.6	–5.8	–7.2	–6.5	–5.0
Mozambique	–25.3	–44.7	–42.9	–38.2	–40.3	–39.0	–20.0	–30.4	–58.0	–66.7	–39.3
Namibia	–3.0	–5.7	–4.0	–10.8	–12.4	–15.4	–5.0	–2.1	–4.1	–2.3	–4.5
Niger	–22.3	–14.7	–15.0	–15.8	–20.5	–15.5	–15.7	–18.1	–20.0	–22.7	–12.1
Nigeria	2.6	3.8	3.7	0.2	–3.2	0.7	2.8	1.3	–0.2	–0.1	–0.2
Rwanda	–7.3	–9.9	–8.7	–11.8	–13.3	–14.3	–6.8	–7.8	–9.2	–8.7	–8.0
São Tomé and Príncipe	–27.9	–21.8	–14.5	–21.7	–12.2	–6.6	–13.2	–10.9	–11.5	–9.0	–6.5
Senegal	–6.5	–8.7	–8.2	–7.0	–5.6	–4.0	–7.3	–8.8	–8.5	–11.1	–3.3
Seychelles	–23.0	–21.1	–11.9	–23.1	–18.6	–20.6	–20.4	–17.0	–16.7	–17.0	–16.8
Sierra Leone	–65.0	–31.8	–17.5	–9.3	–15.5	–4.4	–14.4	–13.8	–12.3	–10.5	–8.0
South Africa	–2.2	–5.1	–5.8	–5.1	–4.6	–2.9	–2.5	–3.5	–3.1	–3.6	–4.7
South Sudan	18.2	–15.9	–3.9	–1.5	–2.5	4.9	–3.4	–6.5	2.3	–4.2	–10.0
Tanzania	–11.0	–12.0	–10.7	–10.0	–7.9	–4.3	–3.0	–3.7	–4.1	–3.6	–2.6
Togo	–7.8	–7.6	–13.2	–10.0	–11.0	–9.8	–2.0	–4.9	–6.3	–5.5	–4.4
Uganda	–9.9	–6.7	–7.2	–8.1	–7.3	–3.4	–5.0	–8.9	–11.5	–10.5	–1.6
Zambia	4.7	5.4	–0.6	2.1	–3.9	–4.5	–3.9	–2.6	–3.6	–3.4	–2.0
Zimbabwe[4]	–17.2	–10.7	–13.2	–11.6	–7.6	–3.6	–1.3	–4.9	–0.5	–2.5	–2.8

[1]See country-specific notes for Libya and Ukraine in the "Country Notes" section of the Statistical Appendix.
[2]Data for 2011 exclude South Sudan after July 9. Data for 2012 and onward pertain to the current Sudan.
[3]Data for Syria are excluded for 2011 onward owing to the uncertain political situation.
[4]The Zimbabwe dollar ceased circulating in early 2009. Data are based on IMF staff estimates of price and exchange rate developments in US dollars. IMF staff estimates of US dollar values may differ from authorities' estimates.

Table A13. Summary of Financial Account Balances
(Billions of US dollars)

	2011	2012	2013	2014	2015	2016	2017	2018	Projections 2019	2020
Advanced Economies										
Financial Account Balance	–237.6	–153.5	230.0	314.6	324.8	436.4	394.7	323.0	386.0	255.7
Direct Investment, Net	358.3	116.8	155.0	210.4	–39.1	–260.0	322.1	–148.2	14.9	42.2
Portfolio Investment, Net	–1,110.4	–248.8	–553.0	74.1	252.3	558.2	5.7	353.5	417.1	471.9
Financial Derivatives, Net	–4.8	–97.7	74.7	–2.7	–88.7	20.3	13.6	57.9	–15.4	–18.7
Other Investment, Net	169.6	–198.2	399.0	–102.5	–25.4	–60.8	–191.1	–69.6	–92.5	–296.5
Change in Reserves	349.9	273.2	153.1	134.9	226.8	178.6	244.3	129.3	60.9	56.7
United States										
Financial Account Balance	–526.0	–448.2	–400.3	–297.3	–325.9	–382.0	–357.6	–445.5	–442.0	–560.9
Direct Investment, Net	173.1	126.9	104.7	135.7	–202.0	–176.1	29.9	–336.8	–164.0	–159.1
Portfolio Investment, Net	–226.3	–498.3	–30.7	–114.9	–53.5	–195.1	–223.1	18.4	–248.9	–157.9
Financial Derivatives, Net	–35.0	7.1	2.2	–54.3	–27.0	7.8	24.0	–20.7	–20.0	–4.5
Other Investment, Net	–453.7	–88.4	–473.4	–260.1	–37.1	–20.8	–186.7	–111.3	–9.3	–239.4
Change in Reserves	15.9	4.5	–3.1	–3.6	–6.3	2.1	–1.7	5.0	0.2	0.0
Euro Area										
Financial Account Balance	–40.9	182.6	439.0	337.6	297.9	372.6	424.8	330.1	. . .	. . .
Direct Investment, Net	124.9	58.9	13.5	69.1	178.5	206.8	88.7	42.3	. . .	. . .
Portfolio Investment, Net	–383.4	–177.0	–168.5	75.4	191.2	509.8	335.4	255.6	. . .	. . .
Financial Derivatives, Net	5.5	38.9	41.8	65.8	95.6	16.9	27.1	114.5	. . .	. . .
Other Investment, Net	197.7	242.8	544.2	123.0	–179.2	–378.0	–24.8	–111.9	. . .	. . .
Change in Reserves	14.3	19.0	8.0	4.4	11.8	17.1	–1.6	29.5	. . .	. . .
Germany										
Financial Account Balance	167.7	194.3	300.0	317.8	259.4	286.8	319.9	270.4	269.1	261.0
Direct Investment, Net	10.3	33.6	26.0	87.8	68.4	46.5	54.0	51.4	53.0	55.0
Portfolio Investment, Net	–51.4	66.8	209.6	177.7	209.9	220.3	224.5	133.6	178.3	163.4
Financial Derivatives, Net	39.8	30.9	31.8	50.8	33.8	32.1	13.2	27.5	22.3	19.0
Other Investment, Net	165.1	61.1	31.4	4.8	–50.3	–14.0	29.7	57.4	15.5	23.5
Change in Reserves	3.9	1.7	1.2	–3.3	–2.4	1.9	–1.5	0.5	0.0	0.0
France										
Financial Account Balance	–78.6	–48.0	–19.2	–10.3	–0.8	–18.6	–35.0	–32.3	–11.4	–11.4
Direct Investment, Net	19.8	19.4	–13.9	47.2	7.9	41.8	11.5	65.2	45.6	48.1
Portfolio Investment, Net	–335.2	–50.6	–79.3	–23.8	43.2	0.2	26.6	–5.9	50.0	60.0
Financial Derivatives, Net	–19.4	–18.4	–22.3	–31.8	14.5	–17.6	–1.4	–30.5	–39.8	–52.5
Other Investment, Net	263.9	–3.6	98.2	–2.9	–74.2	–45.4	–68.3	–73.3	–69.7	–69.5
Change in Reserves	–7.7	5.2	–1.9	1.0	8.0	2.5	–3.4	12.3	2.4	2.5
Italy										
Financial Account Balance	–79.9	–4.1	29.0	68.5	39.1	66.3	58.1	35.4	58.7	60.5
Direct Investment, Net	17.2	6.8	0.9	3.1	2.7	–10.7	3.7	–3.7	–3.0	–2.5
Portfolio Investment, Net	25.6	–22.4	–5.4	5.5	108.2	176.5	98.8	143.8	10.5	33.5
Financial Derivatives, Net	–10.1	7.5	4.0	–4.8	2.6	–3.3	–8.2	–3.3	–1.3	–0.4
Other Investment, Net	–113.9	2.1	27.5	65.9	–75.0	–95.0	–39.2	–104.5	52.5	30.0
Change in Reserves	1.3	1.9	2.0	–1.3	0.6	–1.3	3.0	3.1	0.0	0.0

Table A13. Summary of Financial Account Balances *(continued)*

(Billions of US dollars)

									Projections	
	2011	2012	2013	2014	2015	2016	2017	2018	2019	2020
Spain										
Financial Account Balance	–41.4	2.4	44.2	16.1	24.3	27.4	24.4	26.2	20.1	22.5
Direct Investment, Net	12.8	–27.2	–24.6	8.6	28.4	16.0	19.1	–11.0	–3.7	–3.7
Portfolio Investment, Net	43.1	53.7	–83.6	–12.1	11.8	56.1	28.6	10.1	48.4	49.5
Financial Derivatives, Net	2.9	–10.7	1.4	1.7	–1.3	–3.3	–2.5	1.5	0.0	0.0
Other Investment, Net	–114.2	–16.3	150.3	12.8	–20.1	–50.5	–24.8	23.1	–24.7	–23.4
Change in Reserves	13.9	2.8	0.7	5.1	5.6	9.1	4.0	2.5	0.0	0.0
Japan										
Financial Account Balance	158.4	53.9	–4.3	58.9	180.9	266.8	166.8	182.7	169.1	176.8
Direct Investment, Net	117.8	117.5	144.7	118.6	133.3	137.5	153.4	132.9	145.1	156.4
Portfolio Investment, Net	–162.9	28.8	–280.6	–42.2	131.5	276.5	–50.6	91.5	72.8	64.9
Financial Derivatives, Net	–17.1	6.7	58.1	34.0	17.7	–16.1	30.4	0.8	0.9	0.9
Other Investment, Net	43.4	–61.1	34.8	–60.1	–106.7	–125.4	10.0	–66.6	–60.8	–56.9
Change in Reserves	177.3	–37.9	38.7	8.5	5.1	–5.7	23.6	24.0	11.0	11.5
United Kingdom										
Financial Account Balance	–43.3	–92.6	–132.5	–154.2	–142.6	–145.8	–115.8	–85.8	–97.2	–102.0
Direct Investment, Net	53.4	–34.8	–11.2	–176.1	–106.0	–219.5	16.3	–14.6	–0.8	–11.7
Portfolio Investment, Net	–215.5	275.0	–284.2	16.4	–201.8	–195.4	–134.9	–361.7	0.0	0.0
Financial Derivatives, Net	7.4	–65.8	63.4	31.2	–128.6	29.3	13.3	17.7	–5.0	–10.3
Other Investment, Net	103.4	–279.1	91.8	–37.5	261.6	231.0	–19.2	248.1	–106.4	–95.6
Change in Reserves	7.9	12.1	7.8	11.7	32.2	8.8	8.8	24.8	15.1	15.6
Canada										
Financial Account Balance	–49.4	–62.7	–56.9	–42.3	–56.2	–49.5	–40.4	–36.4	–32.5	–30.2
Direct Investment, Net	12.5	12.8	–12.0	1.3	23.6	33.9	55.0	7.4	–8.0	5.3
Portfolio Investment, Net	–104.4	–63.8	–27.1	–32.9	–48.1	–118.6	–80.5	–8.2	–30.0	–27.8
Financial Derivatives, Net	...	...	...	...	...	...	...	...	...	...
Other Investment, Net	34.3	–13.4	–22.5	–16.0	–40.2	29.5	–15.6	–34.0	5.5	–7.7
Change in Reserves	8.1	1.7	4.7	5.3	8.6	5.6	0.8	–1.5	0.0	0.0
Other Advanced Economies[1]										
Financial Account Balance	286.0	253.4	376.1	343.1	291.0	332.1	306.7	324.7	338.2	325.9
Direct Investment, Net	–6.2	–33.7	30.8	–6.3	–101.2	–71.9	–73.8	–71.2	–55.3	–47.6
Portfolio Investment, Net	47.2	150.0	139.6	181.5	335.5	264.0	179.3	361.1	314.2	273.7
Financial Derivatives, Net	31.1	–28.8	–33.5	–23.5	–12.9	4.1	–4.2	27.6	9.0	9.2
Other Investment, Net	88.8	–110.0	136.7	84.7	–105.5	–14.4	–7.7	–44.4	41.7	68.3
Change in Reserves	125.1	274.7	101.3	106.3	175.9	150.2	213.1	51.6	27.6	22.3

Table A13. Summary of Financial Account Balances *(continued)*
(Billions of US dollars)

									Projections	
	2011	2012	2013	2014	2015	2016	2017	2018	2019	2020
Emerging Market and Developing Economies										
Financial Account Balance	232.9	106.9	26.5	28.8	–272.8	–395.9	–239.1	–160.6	21.5	–100.4
Direct Investment, Net	–531.6	–494.2	–482.8	–430.1	–344.8	–259.4	–302.9	–383.2	–384.9	–408.6
Portfolio Investment, Net	–134.3	–244.5	–150.2	–89.7	123.3	–54.6	–210.6	–116.1	–20.9	–8.1
Financial Derivatives, Net	. . .	. . .	. . .	. . .	. . .	. . .	. . .	. . .	. . .	. . .
Other Investment, Net	152.7	415.2	75.6	408.5	468.8	396.7	110.8	232.7	312.3	238.9
Change in Reserves	742.0	432.4	583.7	126.4	–527.1	–471.0	161.3	102.8	115.8	77.1
Regional Groups										
Emerging and Developing Asia										
Financial Account Balance	61.9	13.4	37.2	152.8	75.4	–24.5	–63.8	–204.0	93.0	52.4
Direct Investment, Net	–276.7	–220.0	–271.3	–201.3	–139.5	–25.7	–103.3	–182.9	–178.6	–191.8
Portfolio Investment, Net	–57.9	–115.6	–64.8	–124.4	81.6	31.0	–69.7	–101.3	5.2	35.8
Financial Derivatives, Net	–0.3	1.5	–2.0	0.7	0.7	–4.6	2.3	4.7	–1.3	–0.9
Other Investment, Net	–29.8	209.5	–72.9	281.9	461.5	356.8	–88.3	53.0	191.2	139.5
Change in Reserves	428.6	140.3	444.9	193.3	–330.0	–382.2	197.1	23.6	77.3	71.0
Emerging and Developing Europe										
Financial Account Balance	–32.6	–25.9	–64.6	–30.2	63.2	2.7	–18.0	104.7	71.1	33.9
Direct Investment, Net	–39.5	–37.7	–15.6	0.5	–25.9	–45.1	–28.0	–20.6	–12.8	–6.2
Portfolio Investment, Net	–40.7	–92.9	–37.8	23.5	54.1	–7.3	–35.1	13.9	–15.7	–12.3
Financial Derivatives, Net	3.6	–1.7	–1.1	5.5	5.4	0.2	–2.3	–3.0	0.7	0.9
Other Investment, Net	16.8	54.8	–2.5	62.1	31.4	20.0	30.9	67.0	41.6	12.6
Change in Reserves	27.2	51.6	–7.7	–121.8	–1.8	35.0	16.5	47.4	57.3	38.9
Latin America and the Caribbean										
Financial Account Balance	–126.6	–155.9	–196.8	–196.7	–186.8	–97.1	–89.2	–113.9	–80.6	–81.1
Direct Investment, Net	–146.8	–158.5	–149.8	–138.4	–131.9	–125.4	–122.0	–145.5	–139.9	–137.3
Portfolio Investment, Net	–104.4	–80.9	–100.4	–109.4	–50.8	–49.4	–41.9	–4.9	9.2	–13.0
Financial Derivatives, Net	5.5	2.5	1.8	7.0	1.2	–2.9	3.9	3.9	3.4	3.6
Other Investment, Net	11.0	22.1	39.8	4.8	23.6	59.5	53.4	18.9	50.5	55.3
Change in Reserves	108.1	58.9	11.8	39.3	–28.8	21.1	17.2	13.8	–3.7	10.5
Middle East and Central Asia										
Financial Account Balance	343.8	299.9	305.8	179.6	–152.5	–218.8	–31.1	95.9	–8.9	–46.1
Direct Investment, Net	–36.0	–43.2	–22.7	–42.6	–10.3	–29.1	–12.6	–4.6	–9.7	–23.2
Portfolio Investment, Net	88.0	73.0	75.2	129.9	61.8	–12.2	–41.5	–3.9	–9.7	–6.3
Financial Derivatives, Net	. . .	. . .	. . .	. . .	. . .	. . .	. . .	. . .	. . .	. . .
Other Investment, Net	135.0	108.5	121.3	68.6	–51.7	–42.3	105.5	90.5	23.9	29.9
Change in Reserves	157.5	161.7	132.0	23.7	–151.8	–135.0	–82.3	14.1	–12.8	–45.8
Sub-Saharan Africa										
Financial Account Balance	–13.6	–24.5	–55.0	–76.6	–72.1	–58.2	–36.9	–43.3	–53.1	–59.5
Direct Investment, Net	–32.6	–34.6	–23.5	–48.3	–37.3	–34.1	–37.0	–29.5	–43.9	–50.2
Portfolio Investment, Net	–19.2	–28.2	–22.3	–9.3	–23.4	–16.7	–22.4	–19.9	–9.8	–12.4
Financial Derivatives, Net	–1.7	–1.7	–0.8	–1.5	–0.4	0.9	0.3	–0.5	–0.5	–0.5
Other Investment, Net	19.7	20.4	–10.2	–8.9	4.0	2.7	9.3	3.2	5.1	1.7
Change in Reserves	20.6	20.0	2.6	–8.0	–14.7	–10.0	12.8	3.7	–2.3	2.6

Table A13. Summary of Financial Account Balances *(continued)*

(Billions of US dollars)

	2011	2012	2013	2014	2015	2016	2017	2018	Projections 2019	Projections 2020
Analytical Groups										
By Source of Export Earnings										
Fuel										
Financial Account Balance	512.1	447.1	375.3	226.9	–82.8	–156.2	66.3	278.2	152.1	78.2
Direct Investment, Net	–23.1	–28.2	14.8	6.6	6.3	–27.7	22.4	38.3	23.5	18.8
Portfolio Investment, Net	98.1	41.4	87.5	177.4	93.2	–12.3	–42.1	–4.7	–11.7	–4.9
Financial Derivatives, Net	...	...	...	...	...	...	...	...	...	...
Other Investment, Net	243.7	198.9	174.4	145.0	–1.7	30.1	140.7	181.0	113.2	86.0
Change in Reserves	192.7	233.6	98.1	–107.6	–187.5	–146.4	–55.3	64.3	27.4	–21.4
Nonfuel										
Financial Account Balance	–279.2	–340.2	–348.7	–198.2	–190.0	–239.7	–305.4	–438.9	–130.6	–178.5
Direct Investment, Net	–508.5	–466.0	–497.5	–436.7	–351.1	–231.8	–325.3	–421.5	–408.4	–427.5
Portfolio Investment, Net	–232.4	–285.9	–237.7	–267.1	30.1	–42.3	–168.5	–111.4	–9.2	–3.2
Financial Derivatives, Net	5.8	–0.9	–2.4	6.5	–0.2	–6.4	3.7	5.8	2.4	3.2
Other Investment, Net	–90.9	216.3	–98.8	263.5	470.5	366.6	–29.9	51.7	199.1	153.0
Change in Reserves	549.2	198.8	485.6	234.0	–339.6	–324.7	216.6	38.4	88.4	98.5
By External Financing Source										
Net Debtor Economies										
Financial Account Balance	–355.5	–409.9	–403.0	–357.5	–293.8	–229.4	–267.2	–279.7	–262.0	–307.6
Direct Investment, Net	–275.8	–278.8	–270.0	–279.8	–289.3	–288.5	–265.8	–305.4	–307.6	–324.2
Portfolio Investment, Net	–186.3	–221.5	–178.3	–188.4	–30.7	–54.2	–119.1	–21.7	–72.0	–77.4
Financial Derivatives, Net	...	...	...	...	...	...	...	...	...	...
Other Investment, Net	–67.9	–27.0	–29.5	–2.5	38.5	39.3	13.5	37.1	35.9	30.7
Change in Reserves	171.9	121.8	74.2	103.4	–10.6	88.1	102.4	11.9	81.6	61.9
Net Debtor Economies by Debt-Servicing Experience										
Economies with Arrears and/or Rescheduling during 2014–18										
Financial Account Balance	–14.6	–38.1	–36.5	–28.9	–47.0	–53.3	–34.8	–22.1	–27.9	–35.3
Direct Investment, Net	–14.6	–16.6	–10.1	–16.6	–34.4	–23.7	–13.9	–17.7	–23.5	–28.2
Portfolio Investment, Net	1.0	–1.3	–11.8	–1.7	–1.2	–2.3	–24.8	–18.9	–9.4	–10.5
Financial Derivatives, Net	...	...	...	...	...	...	...	...	...	...
Other Investment, Net	4.4	0.5	–18.2	1.8	–15.8	–21.0	10.1	10.1	1.7	1.0
Change in Reserves	–5.5	–20.8	3.8	–12.1	4.7	–6.0	–5.9	4.8	3.8	3.0
Memorandum										
World										
Financial Account Balance	–4.7	–46.6	256.6	343.4	52.1	40.5	155.6	162.3	407.4	155.3

Note: The estimates in this table are based on individual countries' national accounts and balance-of-payments statistics. Country group composites are calculated as the sum of the US dollar values for the relevant individual countries. Some group aggregates for the financial derivatives are not shown because of incomplete data. Projections for the euro area are not available because of data constraints.

[1]Excludes the Group of Seven (Canada, France, Germany, Italy, Japan, United Kingdom, United States) and euro area countries.

Table A14. Summary of Net Lending and Borrowing
(Percent of GDP)

	Averages								Projections		
	2001–10	2005–12	2013	2014	2015	2016	2017	2018	2019	2020	Average 2021–24
Advanced Economies											
Net Lending and Borrowing	–0.7	–0.6	0.5	0.5	0.6	0.7	0.8	0.6	0.6	0.5	0.4
Current Account Balance	–0.7	–0.6	0.4	0.5	0.6	0.7	0.9	0.7	0.6	0.5	0.4
Savings	21.7	21.5	21.9	22.6	22.8	22.3	22.7	22.6	22.5	22.4	22.6
Investment	22.4	22.1	21.2	21.5	21.6	21.4	21.8	22.0	22.0	22.0	22.2
Capital Account Balance	0.0	0.0	0.0	0.0	0.0	0.0	0.0	–0.1	0.0	0.0	0.0
United States											
Net Lending and Borrowing	–4.4	–4.0	–2.1	–2.1	–2.2	–2.3	–2.2	–2.4	–2.5	–2.5	–2.3
Current Account Balance	–4.4	–4.0	–2.1	–2.1	–2.2	–2.3	–2.3	–2.4	–2.5	–2.5	–2.4
Savings	17.3	16.8	19.2	20.3	20.2	18.6	18.6	18.4	18.5	18.5	18.9
Investment	21.5	20.8	20.4	20.8	21.1	20.4	20.6	21.0	21.1	21.1	21.3
Capital Account Balance	0.0	0.0	0.0	0.0	0.0	0.0	0.1	0.0	0.0	0.0	0.0
Euro Area											
Net Lending and Borrowing	0.1	0.1	2.5	2.6	2.9	3.1	3.1	2.6	. . .	. . .	. . .
Current Account Balance	0.0	0.0	2.3	2.5	2.7	3.1	3.2	2.9	2.8	2.7	2.3
Savings	22.9	22.8	22.5	23.0	23.8	24.3	24.9	25.1	25.0	25.1	25.1
Investment	22.5	22.2	19.8	20.1	20.6	20.9	21.3	21.6	21.7	21.8	22.2
Capital Account Balance	0.1	0.1	0.2	0.1	0.2	0.0	–0.2	–0.3	. . .	. . .	. . .
Germany											
Net Lending and Borrowing	4.2	6.0	6.5	7.3	8.6	8.5	8.0	7.4	7.0	6.6	6.0
Current Account Balance	4.2	6.0	6.6	7.2	8.6	8.5	8.1	7.3	7.0	6.6	6.0
Savings	24.8	26.3	26.6	27.6	28.6	28.7	28.8	29.1	28.8	28.7	28.9
Investment	20.6	20.4	20.1	20.4	20.0	20.2	20.7	21.8	21.8	22.1	23.0
Capital Account Balance	0.0	0.0	0.0	0.1	0.0	0.1	–0.1	0.1	0.0	0.0	0.0
France											
Net Lending and Borrowing	0.7	–0.3	–0.5	–1.0	–0.4	–0.4	–0.7	–0.5	–0.4	–0.4	–0.3
Current Account Balance	0.7	–0.3	–0.5	–1.0	–0.4	–0.5	–0.7	–0.6	–0.5	–0.5	–0.4
Savings	23.0	22.5	21.8	21.8	22.3	22.1	22.6	22.9	22.8	22.8	22.6
Investment	22.4	22.9	22.3	22.7	22.7	22.6	23.4	23.5	23.3	23.3	23.0
Capital Account Balance	0.0	0.0	0.0	–0.1	0.0	0.1	0.0	0.1	0.1	0.1	0.1
Italy											
Net Lending and Borrowing	–1.2	–1.8	0.9	2.1	1.7	2.4	2.6	2.5	2.9	3.0	2.5
Current Account Balance	–1.3	–1.9	1.0	1.9	1.3	2.5	2.6	2.5	2.9	2.9	2.4
Savings	19.9	18.7	17.9	18.9	18.6	20.1	20.2	20.5	20.4	20.4	20.2
Investment	21.1	20.7	17.0	17.0	17.3	17.6	17.6	18.0	17.6	17.5	17.8
Capital Account Balance	0.1	0.1	0.0	0.2	0.4	–0.2	0.0	0.0	0.1	0.1	0.1
Spain											
Net Lending and Borrowing	–5.5	–5.4	2.2	1.6	1.8	2.5	2.1	1.4	1.4	1.6	1.6
Current Account Balance	–6.1	–5.9	1.5	1.1	1.2	2.3	1.8	0.9	0.9	1.0	1.1
Savings	21.9	20.7	20.2	20.5	21.6	22.7	22.9	22.8	23.1	23.3	23.6
Investment	28.0	26.5	18.7	19.5	20.4	20.4	21.1	21.9	22.2	22.3	22.6
Capital Account Balance	0.6	0.5	0.6	0.5	0.7	0.2	0.2	0.5	0.5	0.5	0.5
Japan											
Net Lending and Borrowing	3.2	3.0	0.7	0.7	3.1	3.9	4.1	3.5	3.3	3.3	3.4
Current Account Balance	3.3	3.1	0.9	0.8	3.1	4.0	4.2	3.5	3.3	3.3	3.5
Savings	27.4	26.3	24.1	24.7	27.1	27.4	28.1	28.0	27.9	28.0	28.1
Investment	24.1	23.2	23.2	23.9	24.0	23.4	23.9	24.4	24.6	24.7	24.6
Capital Account Balance	–0.1	–0.1	–0.1	0.0	–0.1	–0.1	–0.1	0.0	–0.1	–0.1	–0.1
United Kingdom											
Net Lending and Borrowing	–2.9	–3.2	–5.2	–5.0	–5.0	–5.3	–3.4	–4.0	–3.5	–3.8	–3.8
Current Account Balance	–2.9	–3.2	–5.1	–4.9	–4.9	–5.2	–3.3	–3.9	–3.5	–3.7	–3.7
Savings	14.3	13.4	11.1	12.3	12.3	12.0	13.9	13.3	13.0	12.6	13.0
Investment	17.2	16.6	16.2	17.3	17.2	17.3	17.2	17.2	16.4	16.2	16.7
Capital Account Balance	0.0	0.0	–0.1	–0.1	–0.1	–0.1	–0.1	–0.1	–0.1	–0.1	–0.1

Table A14. Summary of Net Lending and Borrowing *(continued)*
(Percent of GDP)

	Averages								Projections		
	2001–10	2005–12	2013	2014	2015	2016	2017	2018	2019	2020	Average 2021–24
Canada											
Net Lending and Borrowing	0.4	–1.1	–3.2	–2.4	–3.5	–3.2	–2.8	–2.6	–1.9	–1.7	–1.6
Current Account Balance	0.5	–1.1	–3.2	–2.4	–3.5	–3.2	–2.8	–2.6	–1.9	–1.7	–1.6
Savings	22.6	22.5	21.7	22.5	20.3	19.7	20.7	20.4	20.7	20.8	21.0
Investment	22.1	23.6	24.9	24.9	23.8	22.9	23.5	23.0	22.6	22.5	22.6
Capital Account Balance	0.0	0.0	0.0	0.0	0.0	0.0	0.0	0.0	0.0	0.0	0.0
Other Advanced Economies[1]											
Net Lending and Borrowing	4.0	4.0	5.0	5.0	5.2	5.3	4.5	4.8	4.7	4.3	4.0
Current Account Balance	4.0	4.0	5.0	5.1	5.6	5.2	4.7	4.9	4.8	4.4	4.0
Savings	30.0	30.5	30.4	30.6	30.8	30.3	30.4	30.3	29.9	29.4	29.0
Investment	25.7	26.2	25.3	25.3	24.9	25.0	25.5	25.5	25.0	24.9	24.8
Capital Account Balance	0.0	0.0	0.1	–0.1	–0.4	0.1	–0.2	–0.1	–0.1	–0.1	–0.1
Emerging Market and Developing Economies											
Net Lending and Borrowing	2.5	2.7	0.7	0.6	–0.1	–0.2	0.1	0.1	0.0	–0.3	–0.6
Current Account Balance	2.5	2.6	0.6	0.6	–0.2	–0.3	0.0	0.0	0.0	–0.4	–0.7
Savings	30.3	32.6	32.9	32.9	32.3	31.7	32.3	32.9	32.6	32.2	31.8
Investment	28.1	30.3	32.5	32.5	32.7	31.9	32.5	33.0	32.7	32.7	32.6
Capital Account Balance	0.1	0.2	0.2	0.0	0.1	0.1	0.1	0.1	0.1	0.1	0.1
Regional Groups											
Emerging and Developing Asia											
Net Lending and Borrowing	3.7	3.7	0.8	1.6	2.0	1.4	1.0	–0.1	0.4	0.2	–0.1
Current Account Balance	3.6	3.6	0.7	1.5	2.0	1.4	1.0	–0.1	0.4	0.2	–0.1
Savings	39.8	43.1	43.1	43.6	42.5	41.0	41.0	40.4	39.9	39.2	38.1
Investment	36.4	39.6	42.3	42.1	40.5	39.6	40.1	40.6	39.5	39.0	38.2
Capital Account Balance	0.1	0.1	0.1	0.0	0.0	0.0	0.0	0.0	0.0	0.0	0.0
Emerging and Developing Europe											
Net Lending and Borrowing	0.1	–0.5	–0.9	–0.7	1.6	–0.1	–0.3	2.2	1.9	0.9	0.2
Current Account Balance	0.2	–0.6	–1.4	–0.3	0.9	–0.4	–0.6	1.7	1.6	0.6	0.0
Savings	22.9	23.5	22.8	23.4	24.6	23.5	24.2	25.8	25.2	24.4	24.1
Investment	22.6	24.0	24.2	23.7	23.6	23.8	24.8	24.0	23.5	23.8	24.1
Capital Account Balance	–0.2	0.1	0.5	–0.4	0.7	0.3	0.3	0.5	0.4	0.3	0.2
Latin America and the Caribbean											
Net Lending and Borrowing	–0.1	–0.5	–2.8	–3.0	–3.2	–1.9	–1.4	–1.9	–1.5	–1.5	–1.7
Current Account Balance	–0.2	–0.6	–2.8	–3.1	–3.2	–1.9	–1.4	–1.9	–1.6	–1.5	–1.7
Savings	20.4	21.1	19.1	17.8	16.4	16.9	16.7	17.7	17.8	18.0	18.1
Investment	20.6	21.6	22.2	21.5	21.1	18.5	18.5	19.6	19.4	19.5	19.8
Capital Account Balance	0.1	0.1	0.1	0.0	0.0	0.0	0.0	0.0	0.0	0.0	0.0
Middle East and Central Asia											
Net Lending and Borrowing	7.3	9.5	9.0	5.8	–3.6	–3.9	–0.7	2.8	–0.3	–1.2	–2.0
Current Account Balance	7.7	9.9	8.8	5.2	–3.9	–4.1	–0.7	2.7	–0.4	–1.4	–2.2
Savings	34.3	37.1	35.1	31.4	23.7	23.2	27.6	29.7	27.3	27.3	27.1
Investment	27.6	28.0	25.9	25.6	27.2	26.5	28.6	27.1	27.7	28.7	29.4
Capital Account Balance	0.1	0.1	0.0	0.2	0.0	0.1	0.1	0.1	0.1	0.1	0.1
Sub-Saharan Africa											
Net Lending and Borrowing	1.8	1.9	–1.8	–3.2	–5.6	–3.5	–1.9	–2.3	–3.2	–3.4	–3.0
Current Account Balance	0.5	0.5	–2.2	–3.6	–6.0	–3.9	–2.3	–2.7	–3.6	–3.8	–3.4
Savings	20.8	21.7	19.5	19.3	17.3	18.0	19.0	18.0	17.6	17.6	18.7
Investment	20.9	21.6	21.7	22.6	22.8	21.5	21.2	20.6	21.2	21.4	21.6
Capital Account Balance	1.3	1.4	0.4	0.4	0.4	0.4	0.4	0.4	0.4	0.4	0.4

Table A14. Summary of Net Lending and Borrowing *(continued)*
(Percent of GDP)

	Averages								Projections		
	2001–10	2005–12	2013	2014	2015	2016	2017	2018	2019	2020	Average 2021–24
Analytical Groups											
By Source of Export Earnings											
Fuel											
Net Lending and Borrowing	8.7	10.0	7.4	4.7	–1.5	–1.5	1.7	5.6	2.8	1.4	0.4
Current Account Balance	9.2	10.4	7.4	5.1	–1.5	–1.6	1.7	5.6	2.8	1.3	0.4
Savings	33.6	35.3	32.2	29.7	24.2	24.2	27.8	30.8	28.6	28.0	27.6
Investment	25.0	25.3	25.1	24.7	26.7	24.5	26.4	25.0	25.6	26.5	27.1
Capital Account Balance	–0.2	0.0	0.0	–0.7	–0.1	0.0	0.0	0.0	0.0	0.0	0.0
Nonfuel											
Net Lending and Borrowing	0.9	0.6	–1.0	–0.4	0.2	0.1	–0.2	–0.9	–0.4	–0.5	–0.8
Current Account Balance	0.6	0.4	–1.2	–0.6	0.1	0.0	–0.3	–1.0	–0.5	–0.6	–0.8
Savings	29.4	31.9	33.0	33.7	33.9	33.1	33.2	33.3	33.2	32.9	32.5
Investment	29.0	31.6	34.3	34.3	33.8	33.2	33.5	34.4	33.8	33.6	33.3
Capital Account Balance	0.2	0.2	0.2	0.2	0.2	0.1	0.1	0.1	0.1	0.1	0.1
By External Financing Source											
Net Debtor Economies											
Net Lending and Borrowing	–0.7	–1.3	–2.4	–2.1	–2.1	–1.5	–1.5	–1.7	–1.7	–1.8	–2.0
Current Account Balance	–1.0	–1.6	–2.7	–2.4	–2.4	–1.7	–1.7	–2.0	–1.9	–2.0	–2.1
Savings	22.9	23.8	22.8	22.8	22.4	22.4	22.7	22.8	22.9	23.1	23.8
Investment	24.1	25.6	25.4	25.1	24.8	24.1	24.4	24.8	24.8	25.2	25.8
Capital Account Balance	0.3	0.3	0.3	0.3	0.3	0.2	0.2	0.2	0.2	0.2	0.1
Net Debtor Economies by Debt-Servicing Experience											
Economies with Arrears and/or Rescheduling during 2014–18											
Net Lending and Borrowing	0.0	–1.2	–4.0	–3.2	–5.6	–5.7	–4.2	–2.7	–3.6	–4.0	–3.6
Current Account Balance	–0.4	–1.7	–4.2	–3.5	–5.9	–5.7	–4.4	–2.9	–3.9	–4.3	–3.9
Savings	22.1	21.7	16.3	17.2	14.5	13.9	15.5	17.0	16.6	17.0	17.9
Investment	23.2	23.6	20.5	20.1	20.5	19.9	20.4	20.0	20.7	21.5	21.9
Capital Account Balance	0.5	0.5	0.2	0.3	0.2	0.1	0.2	0.2	0.2	0.2	0.2
Memorandum											
World											
Net Lending and Borrowing	0.1	0.4	0.6	0.5	0.3	0.4	0.5	0.4	0.4	0.2	0.0
Current Account Balance	0.1	0.3	0.5	0.5	0.3	0.3	0.5	0.4	0.3	0.1	0.0
Savings	24.1	25.0	26.2	26.7	26.5	26.0	26.5	26.7	26.5	26.5	26.6
Investment	24.0	24.7	25.5	25.8	26.0	25.4	26.0	26.3	26.2	26.3	26.6
Capital Account Balance	0.1	0.1	0.1	0.0	0.0	0.0	0.0	0.0	0.0	0.0	0.0

Note: The estimates in this table are based on individual countries' national accounts and balance-of-payments statistics. Country group composites are calculated as the sum of the US dollar values for the relevant individual countries. This differs from the calculations in the April 2005 and earlier issues of the *World Economic Outlook,* in which the composites were weighted by GDP valued at purchasing power parities as a share of total world GDP. The estimates of gross national savings and investment (or gross capital formation) are from individual countries' national accounts statistics. The estimates of the current account balance, the capital account balance, and the financial account balance (or net lending/net borrowing) are from the balance-of-payments statistics. The link between domestic transactions and transactions with the rest of the world can be expressed as accounting identities. Savings (S) minus investment (I) is equal to the current account balance (CAB) ($S - I = CAB$). Also, net lending/net borrowing (NLB) is the sum of the current account balance and the capital account balance (KAB) ($NLB = CAB + KAB$). In practice, these identities do not hold exactly; imbalances result from imperfections in source data and compilation as well as from asymmetries in group composition due to data availability.

[1]Excludes the Group of Seven (Canada, France, Germany, Italy, Japan, United Kingdom, United States) and euro area countries.

Table A15. Summary of World Medium-Term Baseline Scenario

	Averages				Projections			
							Averages	
	2001–10	2011–20	2017	2018	2019	2020	2017–20	2021–24
				Annual Percent Change				
World Real GDP	**3.9**	**3.6**	**3.8**	**3.6**	**3.0**	**3.4**	**3.5**	**3.6**
Advanced Economies	1.7	1.9	2.5	2.3	1.7	1.7	2.0	1.6
Emerging Market and Developing Economies	6.2	4.8	4.8	4.5	3.9	4.6	4.4	4.8
Memorandum								
Potential Output								
Major Advanced Economies	1.8	1.4	1.5	1.6	1.5	1.5	1.5	1.4
World Trade, Volume[1]	**5.0**	**3.6**	**5.7**	**3.6**	**1.1**	**3.2**	**3.4**	**3.8**
Imports								
Advanced Economies	3.5	3.3	4.7	3.0	1.2	2.7	2.9	3.1
Emerging Market and Developing Economies	9.2	4.4	7.5	5.1	0.7	4.3	4.4	5.1
Exports								
Advanced Economies	3.9	3.3	4.7	3.1	0.9	2.5	2.8	3.1
Emerging Market and Developing Economies	8.2	4.1	7.3	3.9	1.9	4.1	4.3	4.6
Terms of Trade								
Advanced Economies	–0.1	0.1	–0.2	–0.7	0.0	–0.1	–0.2	0.1
Emerging Market and Developing Economies	1.0	–0.3	0.8	1.5	–1.3	–1.1	0.0	–0.1
World Prices in US Dollars								
Manufactures	1.9	–0.2	–0.3	1.9	1.4	–0.2	0.7	0.8
Oil	10.8	–3.1	23.3	29.4	–9.6	–6.2	7.8	–1.2
Nonfuel Primary Commodities	8.9	–1.0	6.4	1.6	0.9	1.7	2.6	0.7
Consumer Prices								
Advanced Economies	2.0	1.5	1.7	2.0	1.5	1.8	1.7	1.9
Emerging Market and Developing Economies	6.6	5.1	4.3	4.8	4.7	4.8	4.6	4.4
Interest Rates				*Percent*				
Real Six-Month LIBOR[2]	0.7	–0.6	–0.4	0.1	0.5	0.0	0.1	0.2
World Real Long-Term Interest Rate[3]	1.9	0.2	–0.2	–0.1	–0.3	–0.8	–0.4	–0.2
Current Account Balances				*Percent of GDP*				
Advanced Economies	–0.7	0.5	0.9	0.7	0.6	0.5	0.7	0.4
Emerging Market and Developing Economies	2.5	0.3	0.0	0.0	0.0	–0.4	–0.1	–0.7
Total External Debt								
Emerging Market and Developing Economies	30.4	29.9	30.7	31.6	31.0	30.2	30.9	28.4
Debt Service								
Emerging Market and Developing Economies	9.0	10.7	9.9	11.0	10.9	10.6	10.6	10.1

[1]Data refer to trade in goods and services.
[2]London interbank offered rate on US dollar deposits minus percent change in US GDP deflator.
[3]GDP-weighted average of 10-year (or nearest-maturity) government bond rates for Canada, France, Germany, Italy, Japan, the United Kingdom, and the United States.

WORLD ECONOMIC OUTLOOK SELECTED TOPICS

World Economic Outlook Archives

World Economic Outlook: Financial Systems and Economic Cycles	September 2006
World Economic Outlook: Spillovers and Cycles in the Global Economy	April 2007
World Economic Outlook: Globalization and Inequality	October 2007
World Economic Outlook: Housing and the Business Cycle	April 2008
World Economic Outlook: Financial Stress, Downturns, and Recoveries	October 2008
World Economic Outlook: Crisis and Recovery	April 2009
World Economic Outlook: Sustaining the Recovery	October 2009
World Economic Outlook: Rebalancing Growth	April 2010
World Economic Outlook: Recovery, Risk, and Rebalancing	October 2010
World Economic Outlook: Tensions from the Two-Speed Recovery—Unemployment, Commodities, and Capital Flows	April 2011
World Economic Outlook: Slowing Growth, Rising Risks	September 2011
World Economic Outlook: Growth Resuming, Dangers Remain	April 2012
World Economic Outlook: Coping with High Debt and Sluggish Growth	October 2012
World Economic Outlook: Hopes, Realities, Risks	April 2013
World Economic Outlook: Transitions and Tensions	October 2013
World Economic Outlook: Recovery Strengthens, Remains Uneven	April 2014
World Economic Outlook: Legacies, Clouds, Uncertainties	October 2014
World Economic Outlook: Uneven Growth—Short- and Long-Term Factors	April 2015
World Economic Outlook: Adjusting to Lower Commodity Prices	October 2015
World Economic Outlook: Too Slow for Too Long	April 2016
World Economic Outlook: Subdued Demand—Symptoms and Remedies	October 2016
World Economic Outlook: Gaining Momentum?	April 2017
World Economic Outlook: Seeking Sustainable Growth: Short-Term Recovery, Long-Term Challenges	October 2017
World Economic Outlook: Cyclical Upswing, Structural Change	April 2018
World Economic Outlook: Challenges to Steady Growth	October 2018
World Economic Outlook: Growth Slowdown, Precarious Recovery	April 2019
World Economic Outlook: Global Manufacturing Downturn, Rising Trade Barriers	October 2019

I. Methodology—Aggregation, Modeling, and Forecasting

Measuring Inequality: Conceptual, Methodological, and Measurement Issues	October 2007, Box 4.1
New Business Cycle Indices for Latin America: A Historical Reconstruction	October 2007, Box 5.3
Implications of New PPP Estimates for Measuring Global Growth	April 2008, Appendix 1.1
Measuring Output Gaps	October 2008, Box 1.3
Assessing and Communicating Risks to the Global Outlook	October 2008, Appendix 1.1
Fan Chart for Global Growth	April 2009, Appendix 1.2
Indicators for Tracking Growth	October 2010, Appendix 1.2
Inferring Potential Output from Noisy Data: The Global Projection Model View	October 2010, Box 1.3
Uncoordinated Rebalancing	October 2010, Box 1.4

II. Historical Surveys

III. Economic Growth—Sources and Patterns

IV. Inflation and Deflation and Commodity Markets

Is Inflation Back? Commodity Prices and Inflation	October 2008, Chapter 3
Does Financial Investment Affect Commodity Price Behavior?	October 2008, Box 3.1
Fiscal Responses to Recent Commodity Price Increases: An Assessment	October 2008, Box 3.2
Monetary Policy Regimes and Commodity Prices	October 2008, Box 3.3
Assessing Deflation Risks in the G3 Economies	April 2009, Box 1.3
Will Commodity Prices Rise Again When the Global Economy Recovers?	April 2009, Box 1.5
Commodity Market Developments and Prospects	April 2009, Appendix 1.1
Commodity Market Developments and Prospects	October 2009, Appendix 1.1
What Do Options Markets Tell Us about Commodity Price Prospects?	October 2009, Box 1.6
What Explains the Rise in Food Price Volatility?	October 2009, Box 1.7
How Unusual Is the Current Commodity Price Recovery?	April 2010, Box 1.2
Commodity Futures Price Curves and Cyclical Market Adjustment	April 2010, Box 1.3
Commodity Market Developments and Prospects	October 2010, Appendix 1.1
Dismal Prospects for the Real Estate Sector	October 2010, Box 1.2
Have Metals Become More Scarce and What Does Scarcity Mean for Prices?	October 2010, Box 1.5
Commodity Market Developments and Prospects	April 2011, Appendix 1.2
Oil Scarcity, Growth, and Global Imbalances	April 2011, Chapter 3
Life Cycle Constraints on Global Oil Production	April 2011, Box 3.1
Unconventional Natural Gas: A Game Changer?	April 2011, Box 3.2
Short-Term Effects of Oil Shocks on Economic Activity	April 2011, Box 3.3
Low-Frequency Filtering for Extracting Business Cycle Trends	April 2011, Appendix 3.1
The Energy and Oil Empirical Models	April 2011, Appendix 3.2
Commodity Market Developments and Prospects	September 2011, Appendix 1.1
Financial Investment, Speculation, and Commodity Prices	September 2011, Box 1.4
Target What You Can Hit: Commodity Price Swings and Monetary Policy	September 2011, Chapter 3
Commodity Market Review	April 2012, Chapter 1, Special Feature
Commodity Price Swings and Commodity Exporters	April 2012, Chapter 4
Macroeconomic Effects of Commodity Price Shocks on Low-Income Countries	April 2012, Box 4.1
Volatile Commodity Prices and the Development Challenge in Low-Income Countries	April 2012, Box 4.2
Commodity Market Review	October 2012, Chapter 1, Special Feature
Unconventional Energy in the United States	October 2012, Box 1.4
Food Supply Crunch: Who Is Most Vulnerable?	October 2012, Box 1.5
Commodity Market Review	April 2013, Chapter 1, Special Feature
The Dog That Didn't Bark: Has Inflation Been Muzzled or Was It Just Sleeping?	April 2013, Chapter 3
Does Inflation Targeting Still Make Sense with a Flatter Phillips Curve?	April 2013, Box 3.1
Commodity Market Review	October 2013, Chapter 1, Special Feature
Energy Booms and the Current Account: Cross-Country Experience	October 2013, Box 1.SF.1
Oil Price Drivers and the Narrowing WTI-Brent Spread	October 2013, Box 1.SF.2
Anchoring Inflation Expectations When Inflation Is Undershooting	April 2014, Box 1.3
Commodity Prices and Forecasts	April 2014, Chapter 1, Special Feature
Commodity Market Developments and Forecasts, with a Focus on Natural Gas in the World Economy	October 2014, Chapter 1, Special Feature
Commodity Market Developments and Forecasts, with a Focus on Investment in an Era of Low Oil Prices	April 2015, Chapter 1, Special Feature
The Oil Price Collapse: Demand or Supply?	April 2015, Box 1.1

V. Fiscal Policy

VI. Monetary Policy, Financial Markets, and Flow of Funds

Will the Revival in Capital Flows to Emerging Markets Be Sustained?	October 2017, Box 1.2
The Role of Financial Sector Repair in the Speed of the Recovery	October 2018, Box 2.3
Clarity of Central Bank Communications and the Extent of Anchoring of Inflation Expectations	October 2018, Box 3.2

VII. Labor Markets, Poverty, and Inequality

The Globalization of Labor	April 2007, Chapter 5
Emigration and Trade: How Do They Affect Developing Countries?	April 2007, Box 5.1
Labor Market Reforms in the Euro Area and the Wage-Unemployment Trade-Off	October 2007, Box 2.2
Globalization and Inequality	October 2007, Chapter 4
The Dualism between Temporary and Permanent Contracts: Measures, Effects, and Policy Issues	April 2010, Box 3.1
Short-Time Work Programs	April 2010, Box 3.2
Slow Recovery to Nowhere? A Sectoral View of Labor Markets in Advanced Economies	September 2011, Box 1.1
The Labor Share in Europe and the United States during and after the Great Recession	April 2012, Box 1.1
Jobs and Growth: Can't Have One without the Other?	October 2012, Box 4.1
Reforming Collective-Bargaining Systems to Achieve High and Stable Employment	April 2016, Box 3.2
Understanding the Downward Trend in Labor Shares	April 2017, Chapter 3
Labor Force Participation Rates in Advanced Economies	October 2017, Box 1.1
Recent Wage Dynamics in Advanced Economies: Drivers and Implications	October 2017, Chapter 2
Labor Market Dynamics by Skill Level	October 2017, Box 2.1
Worker Contracts and Nominal Wage Rigidities in Europe: Firm-Level Evidence	October 2017, Box 2.2
Wage and Employment Adjustment after the Global Financial Crisis: Firm-Level Evidence	October 2017, Box 2.3
Labor Force Participation in Advanced Economies: Drivers and Prospects	April 2018, Chapter 2
Youth Labor Force Participation in Emerging Market and Developing Economies versus Advanced Economies	April 2018, Box 2.1
Storm Clouds Ahead? Migration and Labor Force Participation Rates	April 2018, Box 2.4
Are Manufacturing Jobs Better Paid? Worker-Level Evidence from Brazil	April 2018, Box 3.3
The Global Financial Crisis, Migration, and Fertility	October 2018, Box 2.1
The Employment Impact of Automation Following the Global Financial Crisis: the Case of Industrial Robots	October 2018, Box 2.2
Labor Market Dynamics in Select Advanced Economies	April 2019, Box 1.1
Worlds Apart? Within-Country Regional Disparities	April 2019, Box 1.3
Closer Together or Further Apart? Within-Country Regional Disparities and Adjustment in Advanced Economies	October 2019, Chapter 2
Climate Change and Subnational Regional Disparities	October 2019, Box 2.2

VIII. Exchange Rate Issues

How Emerging Market Countries May Be Affected by External Shocks	September 2006, Box 1.3
Exchange Rates and the Adjustment of External Imbalances	April 2007, Chapter 3
Exchange Rate Pass-Through to Trade Prices and External Adjustment	April 2007, Box 3.3
Depreciation of the U.S. Dollar: Causes and Consequences	April 2008, Box 1.2
Lessons from the Crisis: On the Choice of Exchange Rate Regime	April 2010, Box 1.1
Exchange Rate Regimes and Crisis Susceptibility in Emerging Markets	April 2014, Box 1.4
Exchange Rates and Trade Flows: Disconnected?	October 2015, Chapter 3
The Relationship between Exchange Rates and Global-Value-Chain-Related Trade	October 2015, Box 3.1
Measuring Real Effective Exchange Rates and Competitiveness: The Role of Global Value Chains	October 2015, Box 3.2
Labor Force Participation Rates in Advanced Economies	October 2017, Box 1.1
Recent Wage Dynamics in Advanced Economies: Drivers and Implications	October 2017, Chapter 2

IX. External Payments, Trade, Capital Movements, and Foreign Debt

X. Regional Issues

XI. Country-Specific Analyses

XII. Special Topics

IMF EXECUTIVE BOARD DISCUSSION OF THE OUTLOOK, OCTOBER 2019

The following remarks were made by the Chair at the conclusion of the Executive Board's discussion of the Fiscal Monitor, Global Financial Stability Report, *and* World Economic Outlook *on October 3, 2019.*

Executive Directors broadly shared the assessment of global economic prospects and risks. They observed that global growth in 2019 is expected to slow to its lowest level since the global financial crisis, reflecting a broad-based weakening of industrial output and business confidence amid rising trade tensions. While growth is expected to pick up modestly in 2020, the outlook is precariously hinged on a turnaround in a small number of countries that are currently underperforming or under stress. Meanwhile, overall growth in low-income developing countries continues to be relatively resilient, although prospects for convergence toward advanced economy income levels remain challenging.

Directors noted with concern that the global economy faces increased downside risks. Most notable in the near term are intensifying trade, technology, and geopolitical tensions with associated increases in policy uncertainty. Directors also pointed to the risk of an abrupt tightening of financial conditions that could be triggered by a range of events. They noted that downside risks remain elevated in the medium term, reflecting increased trade barriers, a further accumulation of financial vulnerabilities, and the consequences of unmitigated climate change.

Given these risks, Directors stressed the need to enhance multilateral cooperation, with most considering it a priority to de-escalate trade tensions, roll back the recent tariff increases, and resolve trade disagreements cooperatively. Directors also urged policymakers to limit greenhouse gas emissions and reduce global imbalances. Closer multilateral cooperation on international taxation and global financial regulatory reforms would help address vulnerabilities and broaden the gains from economic integration.

Directors underscored the urgency of deploying policies proactively to secure growth and enhance resilience. They supported the more accommodative monetary policy stance in many economies while emphasizing the continued importance of remaining data-dependent and clearly communicating policy decisions. Directors noted that the very low interest rates have expanded fiscal resources in many countries. They broadly agreed that, where fiscal space exists and debt is sustainable, high-quality fiscal policy should be used to support aggregate demand where needed. Ensuring debt sustainability requires rebuilding buffers in countries with relatively weaker fiscal positions, although the pace could be calibrated as market conditions permit to avoid prolonged economic weakness and disinflationary dynamics. If downside risks materialize, policymakers should stand ready to implement a contingent, and possibly coordinated, response.

Directors emphasized the importance of growth-enhancing structural reforms in all economies. The priority is to raise medium-term growth, improve inclusiveness, and strengthen resilience. Structural policies can help ease adjustment to shocks and boost output over the medium term, narrow within-country income differences, and encourage faster convergence across countries. Many countries should continue to strengthen institutions, governance, and policy frameworks to bolster resilience and growth prospects.

Directors noted that the prolonged low interest rate environment in advanced economies has encouraged risk-taking, including among institutional investors, and led to a continued build-up in financial vulnerabilities. These include rising risks in non-bank financial institutions, mounting corporate debt burdens, and a growing reliance on external borrowing by emerging and frontier market economies. Directors highlighted the urgent need to safeguard financial stability through stronger and broader macroprudential policies, and address corporate vulnerabilities with stricter supervision and oversight. They also supported the call for strengthened oversight and disclosures of institutional investors and prudent sovereign debt management practices and frameworks, as well as a closer monitoring of U.S. dollar funding fragility. Directors reiterated their call for the full implementation of the global regulatory reform agenda.

Directors noted that emerging market and developing economies need to implement an appropriate mix of fiscal, monetary, exchange rate, and macroprudential policies. Ensuring financial resilience is a priority in emerging and frontier markets that are vulnerable to abrupt reversals of capital flows.

Directors urged low-income developing economies to adopt policies aimed at lifting potential growth, improving inclusiveness, and combating challenges that hinder progress toward the 2030 Sustainable Development Goals. Priorities include strengthening monetary and macroprudential policy frameworks and tackling debt vulnerabilities. Directors emphasized the need for fiscal policy to be in line with debt sustainability and progress toward development goals, importantly through building tax capacity while protecting the vulnerable. Complementarity between domestic revenues, official assistance, and private financing is essential for success, while investing in disaster readiness and climate-smart infrastructure will also be important. Countries need to improve education quality, narrow infrastructure gaps, enhance financial inclusion, and boost private investment. Commodity exporters should continue diversifying their economies.

Directors broadly welcomed the focus of the *Fiscal Monitor* on climate change. Most Directors concurred that carbon taxation, or similar pricing approaches such as emissions trading systems, is an effective tool for reducing emissions. Depending on country circumstances and preferences, other approaches, such as feebates and regulations, are also worth considering. Directors noted that, for climate change mitigation policies to be widely acceptable, they should be part of a comprehensive strategy that includes productive and equitable use of revenues, a social safety net for vulnerable groups, and supportive measures for clean technology investment. While many Directors noted that an international carbon price floor could help scale up mitigation efforts, further work and greater collaboration at the global level would be necessary to reach a broad-based agreement on a fair burden-sharing basis. Many Directors took the opportunity to welcome the Fund's work on analyzing mitigation policy options and integrating such analysis into its surveillance activity, leveraging the expertise within its mandate. Most Directors welcomed the attention paid to sustainable finance that embraces environmental, social, and governance considerations in investment decisions, and emphasized the importance of continued cooperation with other international organizations.

Highlights from IMF Publications

$30. English. Paperback
ISBN 978-1-48432-594-0
imfbk.st/24708

$25. English. Paperback
ISBN 978-1-51355-890-5
imfbk.st/23550

$29 annual subscription fee.
Free to developing countries.
English ISSN 978-1-49831-651-4
imfbk.st/26081

$30. English. Paperback
ISBN 978-1-48433-974-9
imfbk.st/24306

$25. English. Paperback
ISBN 978-1-48435-384-4
imfbk.st/25145

$40. English. Paperback
ISBN 978-1-48437-2-142
imfbk.st/25402

Bookstore.IMF.org